Hermann Levi

From Brahms to Wagner

Frithjof Haas

Translated by Cynthia Klohr

THE SCARECROW PRESS, INC.
Lanham • Toronto • Plymouth, UK
2012

Published by Scarecrow Press, Inc.
A wholly owned subsidiary of The Rowman & Littlefield Publishing Group, Inc.
4501 Forbes Boulevard, Suite 200, Lanham, Maryland 20706
www.rowman.com

10 Thornbury Road, Plymouth PL6 7PP, United Kingdom

Copyright © 2012 by Frithjof Haas
Translation copyright © 2012 by Cynthia Klohr

All rights reserved. No part of this book may be reproduced in any form or by any electronic or mechanical means, including information storage and retrieval systems, without written permission from the publisher, except by a reviewer who may quote passages in a review.

British Library Cataloguing in Publication Information Available

Library of Congress Cataloging-in-Publication Data

Haas, Frithjof.
 [Zwischen Brahms und Wagner. English]
 Hermann Levi : from Brahms to Wagner / Frithjof Haas ; translated by Cynthia Klohr.
   p. cm.
 Includes bibliographical references and index.
 ISBN 978-0-8108-8418-2 (cloth : alk. paper) — ISBN 978-0-8108-8419-9 (ebook)
 1. Levi, Hermann. 2. Conductors (Music)—Germany—Biography. 3. Music—Germany—19th century—History and criticism. I. Title.
 ML422.L66H3313 2012
 782.1092—dc23
 [B]   2012007830

∞™ The paper used in this publication meets the minimum requirements of American National Standard for Information Sciences—Permanence of Paper for Printed Library Materials, ANSI/NISO Z39.48-1992.

Printed in the United States of America

For Eve

Contents

Preface to the English Edition	vii
Artwork Permissions	xi
Introduction	xiii
Abbreviations	xv

1 Family, Studies, and First Positions — 1

    From Giessen to Mannheim — 1
    Studies in Leipzig and Paris — 10
    Years in Saarbrücken, Mannheim, and Rotterdam — 26

First Intermezzo: The Composer Hermann Levi — 43

2 Karlsruhe and Brahms — 51

    Chief Conductor at the Court Theater in Karlsruhe — 51
    Friendship with Johannes Brahms — 60
    From *A German Requiem* to *The Mastersingers of Nuremberg* — 75
    Farewell to Karlsruhe, *Triumphlied* — 94

Second Intermezzo: The Conductor Hermann Levi — 113

3 Bavarian Court Conductor Levi — 119

    An End to Friendship with Brahms — 136
    Society around Paul Heyse and Franz von Lenbach — 147
    The Spell of the Grail — 158

Third Intermezzo: Editor Hermann Levi — 185

4 The Struggle over the Bayreuth Legacy   193

    From Perfall to Possart—And the Advent of Anton Bruckner   200
    Cosima Wagner and Her "Major"   220
    Literary Ambition: Mozart and Goethe   236

Epilogue: Levi's Religion   253

Appendix: Works by Hermann Levi   257

Bibliography   265

Index   267

About the Author   279

Preface to the English Edition

This new edition of my biography of Hermann Levi (1839–1900) makes me very happy. Now readers of English, too, can meet Hermann Levi, a friend to both Johannes Brahms *and* Richard Wagner, two composers that represent some of the greatest European music of the latter half of the nineteenth century. Contemporary conductors will note not only Levi's broad education in music and the humanities, but also his exceptional modesty, lacking the slightest air of stardom. Levi taught his musicians and his audience what it really means to lead an orchestra: not only to shape the interplay of all instruments, but to grasp and convey the essence and the intelligence of a work of music.

Hermann Levi's own compositions are virtually unknown because few were published. Overwhelmed by Brahms's and Wagner's capacities, he stopped composing and destroyed pages of his own notes. A few poetic melodies written for songs did survive, and these even bear comparison with Brahms's own. After orchestral parts were discovered in Zurich, conductor Martin Wettges from Munich reconstructed the full score for Levi's piano concerto op. 1 and has meanwhile had it performed several times.

When in 1894 prominent conductors were invited to succeed Hans von Bülow as director of Berlin's Philharmonic Orchestra, Hermann Levi was among them, presenting a symphony. He became the orchestra's first choice, but the distinguished offer came too late. Levi had already decided to give up conducting for reasons of health.

Yet behind Levi's decision to withdraw from the limelight in his mid-fifties stood more than a medical condition. In the 1890s anti-Jewish sentiments spread throughout Central Europe. Hermann Levi was one of the first prominent German artists to suffer from it. Particularly in Bayreuth he sensed disloyalty and resentment as a Jew conducting *Parsifal*. He faced it with candor, remaining friends with some of the most stalwart proponents of anti-Semitism, such as

Hermann Levi in 1864. Stadtarchiv Karlsruhe, sign. 8/PBS III 927.

Houston Stewart Chamberlain from Bayreuth and Adolf Stoecker, court chaplain to Kaiser Wilhelm II in Berlin. And yet the ailment that ultimately led to Levi's withdrawal from public appearances had psychological causes as well. He identified so thoroughly with German culture, with its music and intellectual world, that to be rejected for reasons of religion, or—as it later came to be seen—for reasons of race, was incomprehensible to him.

In his last years, Levi became preoccupied with Mozart and Goethe, as we see in chapter 4. Unfortunately today the outcomes of those studies—Levi's editions of short novels and tales by Goethe and a calendar for the year 1900 adorned with quotes from Goethe—can only be found with luck at antiquarian bookshops. The original editions of Mozart's *Da Ponte* operas in Levi's fine translation into German are now rarely used because today those operas are almost always performed in Italian. But it is worth noting that it was Levi's rendition that triggered a Mozart renaissance in the early twentieth century.

Finally, I would like especially to thank Rowman & Littlefield and Scarecrow Press, and Senior Editor Bennett Graff, for taking interest in my work on Hermann Levi. I would like to thank the entire editorial staff for enabling this publication in English with its many pictures that illustrate a musical life of the times. I would also like to thank all of the libraries, archives, and private owners that granted permission to reproduce these images in this publication by Scarecrow Press, and to thank Cynthia Klohr for the translation.

Frithjof Haas

Artwork Permissions

The following people and institutions have granted written permission to reproduce images of photographs, etchings, paintings, sculpture, and printed matter in this book:

Badisches Generallandesarchiv Karlsruhe, Karlsruhe
Bayerische Staatsbibliothek München, Musikabteilung, Munich
Bayerische Staatsbibliothek München, Nachlass-Abteilung, Munich
Bayerische Staatsgemäldesammlungen, Fotoarchiv, Munich
Brahms-Institut der Musikhochschule Lübeck, Lübeck
Frithjof Haas, Karlsruhe
Hachette Publishing Company, New York
Josef-Rheinberger Archiv, Liechtensteinisches Landesarchiv, Vaduz
Morgan Library & Museum, New York
Münchener Stadtmuseum, Munich
Nationalarchiv der Richard-Wagner-Stiftung, Bayreuth
Regina Heilmann-Thon, Baldham
Reiss Museum Mannheim, Mannheim
Staatsbibliothek zu Berlin—Preußischer Kulturbesitz, Berlin
Stadtarchiv Gießen, Gießen
Stadtarchiv Karlsruhe, Karlsruhe
Stadtarchiv Saarbrücken, Saarbrücken
Stadtarchiv Überlingen, Überlingen am Bodensee
Stadtmuseum und Stadtarchiv Baden-Baden, Baden-Baden
Wilhelm-Busch-Gesellschaft, Hanover
Wissenschaftliche Stadtbibliothek Mainz, Mainz

Introduction

As conductor at the Badisches Staatstheater in Karlsruhe, I often came across traces of Hermann Levi, conductor for the grand ducal court of Baden in the mid-nineteenth century. I prepared rehearsals using his translations of *Le nozze di Figaro*, *Don Giovanni*, and *Così fan tutte* and often found skilled notes by his hand in old scores for Gluck's *Armida*, Cherubini's *Medea*, and Schumann's *Genoveva*. In chamber music concerts I presented Levi's almost forgotten songs along with lieder by Felix Mottl, Levi's successor in Karlsruhe and Munich.

Among older residents of Karlsruhe I discovered people from Anna Ettlinger's circle of friends who could still recall what they had heard in their youth about Hermann Levi's work at the Badisches Staatstheater. At my mentor Walter Braunfels's home, I often heard of Levi's time in Munich, his unique Mozart and Berlioz renditions, and of the time he and his wife visited sculptor Adolf von Hildebrand in Florence.

The more I learned about the composer and conductor Hermann Levi, the more fascinated I was by his sophistication and sparkle, his challenging intellect, subtle musicality, and unerring integrity. As a young conductor and assistant at Bayreuth, Felix von Weingartner compared Hermann Levi to Hans von Bülow, Felix Mottl, and Hans Richter. Years later he wrote: "Enlightened by the spirit of art itself and combining in his person the virtues of all three colleagues, Hermann Levi surpassed them all."

Hermann Levi exemplified the conductor of nineteenth-century German courts. Though skilled at composing, he preferred to render the works by composers recognized as the greatest of their time. As a young man he was close to Brahms. Later he strove to become part of Bayreuth's inner circle around Richard and Cosima Wagner. He conducted acclaimed premieres of works by Wagner, Brahms, Verdi, Bruckner, Tchaikovsky, Cornelius, Humperdinck, and Richard Strauss. As we know from his correspondence, he communicated personally with most of these composers. Among his friends were writers Ivan Turgenev, Paul Heyse, and Wilhelm Busch, and artists Anselm Feuerbach, Adolf von Hildebrand, Franz von Lenbach, and Hans Thoma, and philosopher Conrad Fiedler.

Levi's letters to prominent contemporaries, some of which have been published in various places, reveal both his learning and his talent for writing. Had he written his memoirs, they would give us a fascinating chronicle of the times. A large number of documents that have survived disclose the difficult story of Levi's life and shed light on an eventful epoch in the history of music, too. Levi's victories and defeats clearly reflect those times, both their glorious peaks and shameful pain.

Levi went from a childhood in a traditional rabbinical family to a successful career in conducting and ultimately to directing the first production of Wagner's *Parsifal* in Bayreuth. He then became ill and resigned in the prime of manhood: his is a story of the rise, triumph, and tragedy of a Jewish conductor in an age of emancipation, liberation from ghetto life, secularization, and assimilation under the banner of national self-awareness, burdened by setbacks from anti-Semitism that rose in a country amassing power.

In early 1933 fortunate circumstances enabled the Bavarian National Library to acquire Hermann Levi's complete estate from his heirs. There it survived the chaos of war intact and unscathed by political mischief. The library's large collection of documents called the "Leviana" is an invaluable source of information on both the musician and the man Hermann Levi and impressively documents trends in the arts of the late nineteenth century.

Hermann Levi managed his correspondence meticulously. He copied by hand all important letters, saving some of them in books set aside just for that purpose, and carefully filed significant replies. The Leviana Collection in Munich thus contains a vast exchange with Cosima Wagner, Max Bruch, Engelbert Humperdinck, Felix von Weingartner, Richard Strauss, Paul Heyse, and Franz von Lenbach, as well as Levi's own private notes on editions, translations, and literary studies.

I owe much to the Bavarian National Library's manuscript department for kindly supporting my work over a period of several years. I thank the many librarians and archivists that helped me with the papers and script and I am particularly grateful for generous support from the Badische Landesbibliothek (Baden State Library) and the Badisches Generallandesarchiv (Baden General State Archive) in Karlsruhe.

Working on Hermann Levi's biography woke from their slumber some of his most personal thoughts and brought them to the light of day. These, too, help us to understand an extraordinary life and an epoch in music marked by its two greatest antipodes: Johannes Brahms and Richard Wagner.

Abbreviations

AMZ	*Allgemeine Musikalische Zeitung*, Leipzig.
Brahms	*Johannes Brahms Briefwechsel.* Johannes Brahms's correspondence in sixteen volumes (in German), reprint Tutzing, 1974.
Cosima	*Cosima Wagner: Die Tagebücher.* Cosima Wagner's diaries in two volumes, edited and provided with a commentary (in German) by Martin Gregor-Dellin and Dietrich Mack, Munich/Zurich, 1976–1977.
Devrient	*Eduard Devrient: Aus seinen Tagebüchern.* Eduard Devrient's diaries in two volumes (in German), edited by Rolf Kabel, Weimar, 1964.
DLA	Deutsches Literaturarchiv Marbach (German Archive for Literature in Marbach).
GLA	Generallandesarchiv Karlsruhe (State Archive at Karlsruhe).
Hildebrand	*Adolf von Hildebrand und seine Welt: Briefe und Erinnerungen* (Adolf von Hildebrand and His World: Letters and Memories) (in German), arranged by Bernhard Sattler, Munich, 1962.
Kalbeck	*Johannes Brahms*, by Max Kalbeck. Four volumes (in German), reprint Tutzing, 1976.
Lachner-Levi	*Briefe Vincenz Lachners an Hermann Levi* (Vincenz Lachner's Letters to Hermann Levi), by Friedrich Walter, Mannheim, 1931.

Leviana	Bayerische Staatsbibliothek Handschriften-Abt. Leviana (Manuscript department at the Bavarian State Library, Hermann Levi Collection called "Leviana").
Litzmann	*Clara Schumann: Ein Künstlerleben nach Tagebüchern und Briefen* (Clara Schumann: An Artist's Life in Diaries and Letters), by Berthold Litzmann, Leipzig, 1910.
Mack	*Cosima Wagner: Das zweite Leben; Briefe und Aufzeichnungen 1883–1903* (Cosima Wagner's Second Life: Letters and Notes from 1883 to 1930), edited by Dietrich Mack, Munich/Zurich, 1980.
MGG	*Musik in Geschichte und Gegenwart* (Musik of the Past and Present), Kassel, 1949–1979 (series).
National Archiv Bayreuth	National Archive of the Richard Wagner Foundation, Bayreuth, Villa Wahnfried.
NZfM	*Neue Zeitschrift für Musik*, Leipzig.
Orel	*Johannes Brahms und Julius Allgeyer*, by Alfred Orel, Tutzing, 1964.
Sietz	*Beiträge zu eine Biographie Ferdinand Hillers* (Contributions for a Biography of Ferdinand Hiller), by Rheinhold Sietz, in *Ferdinand Hillers Briefwechsel* (Ferdinand Hiller's Correspondence), Cologne, 1961.
Stabi	Bayerische Staatsbibliothek (Bavarian National Library), Munich.

Chapter One

Family, Studies, and First Positions

FROM GIESSEN TO MANNHEIM

> We Jews are not immigrants, we are indigenous, and because we are, we have no claim to homeland anywhere else. We are either Germans or homeless.
>
> —Gabriel Riesser

When Hermann Levi was born on 7 November 1839 in Giessen to the family of rural Hessian rabbi Dr. Benedict Levi, the little university town of the grand duchy of Hesse-Darmstadt had already seen six hundred years of eventful history. Here where the river Wieseck flows into the river Lahn, in the year 1150 Count von Gleiberg had built a castle, called it *Zu den Giezzen*, and surrounded it with a moat. One hundred years later, the town of Giessen is mentioned for the first time as property of the Palatine count of Tübingen, who soon sold it to the landgrave of Hesse. The little settlement with its chiefly agricultural population and its rampart constituted the southernmost corner post of the landgraviate Hesse. After the Reformation, Landgrave Philip the Magnanimous had a fortification built to protect the town's 250 homes.

Due to disputes among Hessian landgraves, after Philip's death Giessen was handed over to Hesse-Marburg. But following the Hessian War, the Peace of Westphalia assigned the town to Hesse-Darmstadt. During the Seven Years' War, it was occupied for four years by the French; during the revolutionary wars, it was attacked by the Austrian army. In the early nineteenth century, the city's ramparts were leveled and sentries set up on the incoming roads for the collection of duties.

In 1821 administration reforms for the grand duchy of Hesse-Darmstadt made Giessen the seat of the provincial government for Upper Hesse; ten years

Kreuz Square in Giessen, around 1880. Stadtarchiv Giessen.

later it was one of the major cities of the district. A new church was provided for Protestants and the small Catholic community was allowed to build its own place of worship.

In the fourteenth century, Jews, too, had begun settling in Giessen. Many Jewish families moved to the city from surrounding rural communities around the year 1600. They bought expensive letters of safe conduct from the officials for the privilege of residing within city walls. With the support of his Protestant court pastor Haberkorn, at the end of the Thirty Years' War Hessian Landgrave George II had the church organize so-called convents to give Jews an opportunity to convert. The mindless attempts failed and drove the Jewish population away. But as the decades passed, many returned and their number grew, particularly after the *Leibzoll* tax on Jewish residents was abolished in 1805.

By 1810 the Jewish community in Giessen had around 200 members and was in need of a rabbi. Services were held in a makeshift prayer room at a private home on the marketplace. In 1829 twenty-three-year-old Dr. Benedict Samuel Levi was appointed as a liberal rabbi for Giessen.[1]

Hermann Levi's father, with his Christian-sounding first name, "Benedict,"[2] had been born in Worms in 1806 as the son of Rabbi Samuel Wolf Levi. According to tradition, this family of rabbis descended from the tribe of Levi.[3] Hermann Levi often said that his paternal ancestors had been rabbis for fourteen generations. The fact is documented for ten generations, going back to the mid-sixteenth century. From 1764 to 1792, Hermann Levi's great-grandfather, Benjamin Wolf Spiro Segal, son of a rabbi from Prague, was a rabbi for Swabia.[4]

Samuel Wolf Levi (1715–1813), Rabbi in Worms and Mainz. Stadtarchiv Worms.

Benjamin's son Samuel Wolf Levi seems to have been trained by his own father. He attended school in Augsburg and became a rabbi in Worms.

Samuel Wolf Levi, Hermann Levi's grandfather, was well educated. When Worms was occupied by the French in 1797, the city's German-speaking mayor and council met regularly at his home in order that Samuel Levi, who spoke fluent French, might translate for them the regulations imposed by the occupying French forces. Samuel Levi was a member of the Sanhedrin and of the Assembly of Notables that met at Napoleon's initiative in Paris in the spring of 1807.[5] Although the resolutions formed by the Assembly under the chairmanship of Strasbourg's Rabbi David Sinzheim only pertained to regions under French administration, they also had a sustained effect on German Jewry and certainly influenced the religious bearings of the Levi family for the next two generations. The Assembly in Paris chose to separate the religious status of Jews from their political station, thus integrating them entirely within the national system of civic rights and duties.

Shortly after returning from Paris, Samuel Wolf Levi became grand rabbi for Mainz, and was given the lofty title of the Grand Rabbin du Consistoire du Département de Mont-Tonnere (Donnersberg). Not long before he died he was even granted the privilege of a private audience with Emperor Napoleon.

Awareness of the history of the long-standing Jewish communities in Worms and Mainz is important for understanding Hermann Levi's rabbinical family tradition. Jewish groups had lived in these two cities for centuries. Legend says that as early as 586 BC, after destruction of the first temple, Jews fleeing Jerusalem settled in the area around Worms in the belief that they had found New Jerusalem. In the Middle Ages, the Israelite communities of Speyer, Worms, and Mainz constituted an extended congregation.[6] Mainz's Rabbi Gershon Ben Jehuda, rector of the Talmud Academy around the year 1000, laid the foundation for biblical and Talmudic scholarship among German and French Jews.

It was within this momentous Jewish tradition that Hermann Levi's father Benedict was raised in Mainz, the capital city of the French Department of Mont-Tonnere. At the age of five, he began Talmud studies under Rabbi Eisek Schwalje, who, when Napoleon paraded through Mainz, put the boy on his shoulders to shout the blessing prescribed by Jewish doctrine in the presence of the Crown. At the age of ten, Benedict Levi entered the newly established secondary school under the direction of Michael Creizenach, a pioneer of reformed Judaism that had a lasting influence on him. After completing school, Benedict devoted five years to Talmud study under rabbis Gumpel Weissmann and Ephraim Kastel in Mainz. He then studied philosophy, history, art, and teaching at the university in Würzburg. In 1828 he attained a doctoral degree in philosophy from the University of Giessen. He then lived for one year with Rabbi Jakob Bamberger in Worms to learn the practical work of a rabbi. Benedict Levi then took state examinations in philosophy and theology in Giessen.

When shortly thereafter Rabbi Abraham Wolff from Giessen was called to Copenhagen, twenty-three-year-old Benedict Levi was appointed as his successor. During a visit by Hessian grand duke Ludwig II, the young rabbi presented himself so favorably that the latter made him rabbi for the other surrounding Jewish congregations in Upper Hesse as well. Three years later Benedict Levi married twenty-six-year-old Henriette Mayer from Mannheim. The Levis from Mainz and the Mayer family from Mannheim had known each other for generations.

These relatives of means in Mannheim played an important role in the lives of the Levis in Giessen, particularly when it came to Hermann's upbringing. In contrast to provincial Giessen, Mannheim meant high society. It was a city on the Rhine with a harbor, industry, and imposing financial institutions. And it was a city where the theater regularly performed plays and opera. Giessen, in contrast, was a modest, though confident place of 8000 inhabitants, proud of the university founded there in 1607 and proud, too, of its renowned professors, though less happy with the wayward life of its students. In his autobiographical *Dichtung und Wahrheit* (Poetry and Truth), Goethe boasts of Giessen's university by recounting the story of his visit with Johann Heinrich Merck and Charlotte Buff to famous jurist Friedrich Hoepfner.

Benedict Levi (1806–1899), Rabbi in Giessen and Hermann Levi's father. Portrait by Franz von Lenbach, 1886. Reiss Museum Mannheim.

What a change it must have been for Henriette Mayer in 1832 to move from urban Mannheim to provincial Giessen to run a young rabbi's modest household. It is said that she filled their home with esprit and musical talent and was admired as the most attractive woman in Giessen's society. Among her friends was Justus von Liebig, who taught at the University of Giessen after 1824, establishing there his later famous laboratory for chemistry.

Henriette's first child, Wilhelm, was born a year after the wedding. Three years later came daughter Emma and again three years later, Hermann. Henriette apparently played the piano well; she instructed her own children in music.

Few sources tell us of Hermann Levi's childhood in Giessen. He rarely spoke or wrote of it. His father Benedict's diary remained with descendants in Mannheim until 1940, but was then lost in the war.

Hermann Levi regretted having no clear memory of his mother. (He shared this sentiment with Richard Wagner, who also considered himself half-orphaned.) Henriette Levi died in 1842 when Hermann was just three years old. Two years later his father married Gitel Worms, the daughter of a merchant in Giessen. But she, too, died within a year, just some weeks after giving birth to daughter Auguste, nicknamed "Gustchen." Justus von Liebig's sister looked after the children, and thirty-nine-year-old rabbi Benedict Levi raised the four children on his own and remained a widower for the next fifty-four years of his life. Many of his letters suggest a preference for his younger son, whose interest in music perhaps reminded him of his first wife.

Hermann's musicality became apparent at a very young age. His hometown took him for a *Wunderkind* at the piano. At the age of six, he publicly performed a concerto by Hummel, accompanied by his brother Wilhelm at a second grand piano. A year later he performed a piano concerto by Mozart. Benedict soon began steering his sons toward careers in the arts. One wonders why he did not insist that one of his sons uphold the century-long family tradition and become a rabbi.

Until the time of Hermann's grandfather, Levi's ancestors had lived disadvantaged in isolated communities. As staunch members of the "chosen people," they resigned themselves to a lack of civic rights, always prepared to migrate. It was Hermann Levi's grandfather who, under Napoleon in the region west of the Rhine, attained a publicly acknowledged and legally secure position. When Hermann's father Benedict was appointed rabbi for Hesse, Jewish emancipation was barely known in German principalities. Progress in civil rights for Hessian Jews was slow: in the 1830s attempts were still made to tie the granting of civic equality to conversion to Christianity.

Benedict Levi joined a group of German rabbis that under the influence of French reforms tried to subordinate the Law of Moses to the duties of the German citizen. The reform-eager group endorsed the general nationalistic tendency of the times. One generation later that desire for emancipation culminated in self-denial. Gabriel Riesser, vice president and one of four Jewish members of the 1848 National Assembly at Frankfurt's Church of St. Paul, declared as early as 1830 that the Jews constituted one religious community within the German nation and were thus full-fledged members of the German state.

By supporting his sons' talents for careers in the arts, Benedict Levi perhaps hoped to spare them the humiliation of anti-Semitism. Surely, as an interpreter of Bach, Mozart, and Beethoven, one would be on equal footing with all German musicians. For him his son, the conductor at Bayreuth, was a worthy descendant of a rabbinical family. Benedict's late letters to his son, when Hermann was on the verge of a nervous breakdown, are touchingly naïve, ignoring the rise of anti-Semitism.

There were visible signs of assimilation; perhaps these made it difficult to imagine what would come. The Christian custom of German choral singing had

Mannheim's Kaufhaus and Parade Square, etching by Joh. Georg Wissger based on a sketch by Joseph A. Bertels, around 1770. Reiss Museum Mannheim.

been introduced into Sabbath worship services. Benedict Levi resolutely advocated the liberal innovation,[7] allowing his ten-year-old son to accompany the congregation at the organ. By the time the boy was twelve, his skill at music was so well developed that Benedict sent him to Mannheim for further instruction. Hermann then lived with his aunt, Rosalie Feidel (née Ladenburg), and entered the eighth grade at the secondary school in Mannheim.

Mannheim, situated where the river Neckar joins the Rhine, was an ambitious industrial city known for music. Elector Karl Theodor had built Mannheim's palace to be the largest of its kind in Europe and his opera house was considered the most beautiful of the time. Author Friedrich Heinrich Jacobi called Mannheim a "paradise for musicians." The city was so well known for the composers living there that "Mannheim" came to designate an epoch in the history of music. Mozart, on his way to Paris, had stayed in Mannheim for half a year, and a pretty girl almost caused him to settle there permanently.

When schoolboy Hermann Levi arrived at Mannheim almost one hundred years later, that great past was but a memory. Elector Karl Theodor had moved his household to Munich and left the theater built in 1778 as a gift to the citizens of Mannheim. It was to last for centuries, becoming the first German stage that was not dependent on a court. Known to this day as the *Mannheimer Nationaltheater*, it was "the people's theater."

Vincenz Lachner, court conductor in Mannheim from 1836 to 1872. Lithograph by Carl Lang, 1854. Reiss Museum Mannheim.

Plays dominated the stage for a long time, while opera played a lesser role. That changed in 1836 when Vincenz Lachner succeeded his brother Franz Lachner as conductor for the court. Vincenz, a competent, experienced opera conductor, was the youngest of the three musical Lachner brothers. He composed vocals, works for the orchestra and chamber orchestra, and was well versed in the many practices of music. During his career of more than thirty years in Mannheim, he built up a huge opera repertoire, guided by a conservative taste. Albert Lortzing, whom he invited to Mannheim to direct *Zar und Zimmermann*, was his friend. Vincenz Lachner disapproved of Richard Wagner and the so-called New-German trend, but nonetheless conducted *Der Fliegende Holländer* (The Flying Dutchman), *Tannhäuser, Lohengrin,* and even *Die Meistersinger von Nürnberg* (The Mastersingers of Nuremberg). He radically pruned these works, however, which once provoked their composer to exit the theater in protest. While rehearsing *Meistersinger*, Lachner wrote to his colleague Karl Reiss in Kassel that Wagner's operas drove him crazy.

The Ladenburg family's connections enabled them to introduce young Hermann to music director Lachner and get permission for him to study music alongside normal school attendance. His instruction in music covered learning an instrument (piano), music theory, composition, and repertoire studies. It meant comprehensive practical training modeled after that of the old masters. Instruction in theory was enhanced by practical examples from Lachner's real opera and concert rehearsals and the resulting performances. Ten years later, after Hermann Levi had become a conductor, Lachner's preference for Gluck, Cherubini, and Méhul, and for French opera in general, at first continued to inform his repertoire. This initially made it difficult for Levi to approach Richard Wagner. Ultimately, his love for Wagner was to put an end to his friendship with Lachner.

Half-orphan Hermann Levi enjoyed a familial sense of belonging among the Ladenburgs, his mother's numerous relatives that had lived as Jews in Mannheim under the protection of the court since the early eighteenth century.[8] His great-grandfather, Wolf Hajum Ladenburg, founder of the Ladenburg Bank, died just before Hermann took up the study of music in Mannheim. Through prudent marriage choices, Wolf Hajum's children had increased the family's affluence and repute. Their in-laws included the Gottschalk Mayer family (owners of a cigarette factory) and the Hohenemser family (owners of Mannheim's second largest bank).[9]

Hermann Levi was welcome at the homes of all of these relatives, coming and going with the numerous children and grandchildren. At the time, the Ladenburg Bank was directed by the brothers Hermann and Seligmann Ladenburg. Seligmann had economic vision and was engaged in the development of northern Baden's transportation systems and industry. He founded Mannheim's steamship company, supported the extension of the railway west of the Rhine, and financed the founding of BASF in Ludwigshafen. He was even a leading figure in planning the railroad from Mannheim to Karlsruhe (via Schwetzingen) that one day his great-nephew Hermann Levi in Karlsruhe would take to visit his many relatives in Mannheim.

Although their artistic nephew from Giessen was an exception in the chiefly money-oriented Ladenburg family, under the protection of his influential uncle the boy was allowed to train in music. For two years Vincenz Lachner instructed him in music on school-free afternoons. At the age of fourteen, Hermann finished the ninth grade and left school to devote his time exclusively to the study of music. His intellectual gift and thirst for knowledge compensated for a lack of formal education. He understood Italian, spoke fluent French, and had a profound knowledge of European literature that later enabled him to translate, and to write essays.

Through his studies with Lachner, Levi gained experience in practical matters in music. On the occasion of his twenty-fifth anniversary of working with the Mannheim Opera, Vincenz Lachner wrote up a list of his accomplishments that shows the broad repertoire to which he introduced his pupil. By that time Lachner had already directed 159 operas by 53 different composers, 33 of which were German, 16 French, and 7 Italian. Hermann was made familiar with all of these works through rehearsals and performances. It later helped him to master a comprehensive repertoire of great works when he worked for the opera houses of Karlsruhe and Munich.

Lachner had a close, even fatherly relationship to his pupil. He soon realized that one day this boy would surpass him. We know what he thought of the young man and his background from a letter of recommendation written a few years later for the Cecilia Association, a fraternity in Frankfurt:

> Although Jewish by birth, Hermann Levi has not one of the unpleasant traits that bias links to that extraction and that may often be true of other members of that heritage. Far from being forward or immodest, he is exactly the opposite and of a candid and honest nature seldom to be found. In short, and without exaggeration, I can say that one quickly discovers Levi's endearing, amiable character.
>
> He came to me as a boy of twelve (shortly before his thirteenth birthday) for instruction in composition. He was already excellent at the piano, brilliant at sight-reading, and had a deep sense of music paired with keen perceptual skills. After carefully instructing him for three years, I advised him to study at the Leipzig Conservatory, to continue by studying with Rietz and Hauptmann, and most of all to seek stimulation by competing with other young musicians, and also to become familiar with the new trend in music represented primarily in Leipzig.[10]

Thus in the summer of 1855, three weeks before his sixteenth birthday, Hermann Levi left his master Lachner and relatives in Mannheim and traveled to Leipzig alone to take entrance exams for the famous conservatory.

STUDIES IN LEIPZIG AND PARIS

> In light of today's for the most part positive technical and material progress it will be twice as important, but also twice as difficult to sustain and promote true appreciation for the arts.
>
> —Mendelssohn, writing to district director Von Falkenstein

At the time there was no better place in the German-speaking world to seriously study music than in Leipzig, the city that Goethe had once called "Little Paris."

Its economic importance lay in being a hub between the East and the West. The *Leipziger Messe*, an annual trade exposition, dated from an imperial privilege granted in 1497 and had become more important year after year. The residents of this busy place of trade were interested in culture, too. Among the students of the university, founded in 1409, had been Leibniz, Klopstock, Lessing, and Goethe. Church and city organizations offered a wide variety of musical events and opportunities to participate in making music. The city had also become a place of choice for publishing books and printing music.

Here both musical instruction and performance followed a centuries-old pattern that can be traced back to the year 1358 when the choir of St. Thomas sang for the first time at a Catholic mass. When four hundred years later Johann Sebastian Bach became director of music at St. Thomas, his job was not only to teach music in school, but also to supervise and organize church music for all four congregations (St. Thomas, St. Nikolai, St. Francis, and St. Peter) and to oversee the musical activity of the entire city as well.

That included citizen and student choirs and musical ensembles outside the church, too. At an initiative of Georg Philipp Telemann, these groups met in cafés to practice and give concerts. When their audiences became too large, they began performing at the tavern Three Swans and organizing subscription concerts. After 1781 their events were taken to the newly erected hall for the clothiers' trade, the *Gewandhaus*, and became known as "Gewandhaus Concerts."

Having acquired the position of Gewandhaus conductor in 1835, Felix Mendelssohn began planning a school for training in music, "in order to keep our

The old Gewandhaus in Leipzig. Etching by Benjamin Schwarze. Courtesy of Frithjof Haas.

young musicians from going to London or Paris, where they make money fast, but neglect to complete their education in music." Mendelssohn wrote a long exposé naming the reasons for his plan:

> Here in Leipzig one urgently senses the need for a school of music, where music might be taught seriously in a careful course of studies. Leipzig lends itself for many reasons. . . . Most other big German cities have numerous public amusements that are harmful and distracting to young people. But here, where leisure activity generally involves music, or making music, and where access to other pleasures is limited, this might support both our cause and our people all the more. Furthermore, few other cities have as many concerts and sacred musical events as Leipzig, a branch of music that for budding musicians always lays the foundation for studying music, mastering instruments, and composing. For 50 years the city has actively acknowledged the major works of the greatest masters (often being the first place in Germany to do so) and the care with which those works have been performed awards Leipzig a singular status among the musical cities of the nation.[11]

Mendelssohn's project benefited from the will of a resident (Heinrich Blümner) who had bequeathed 20,000 talers to the support of "a non-profit German institute of the arts or science."

Finally in early 1843 the king of Saxony gave his permission for

> the establishment of a school for the furtherance of music alongside Leipzig's already famous institutions for the arts and science, in honorable recognition of Mendelssohn's merits both overall and particularly in furthering Leipzig's musical culture.[12]

Having passed the entrance exam, Hermann Levi was enrolled at the Leipzig Conservatory on 2 October 1855 as student number 548 and given a copy of the school's statutes as laid out by Mendelssohn, who had died eight years before. The curriculum could still be used today:

Theory: 3 years in the theory of music and composition.

    a. Harmony (9 courses). First year: harmony and part-writing. Second year: continued harmony and counterpoint. Third year: continued harmony and double counterpoint, fugue.

    b. Lectures and exercises in form and composition (5 courses): vocal and instrumental composition, various forms and their development, analysis of classical works of music.

    c. Studying scores, knowledge of conducting (including practice experience).

    d. Italian.

Theoretical instruction also includes annual lectures on musical topics, such as the history of music, musical aesthetics, and so on. Practical instruction aims to train mechanical skill at one or more instruments, including solo work with accompaniment, playing in an ensemble, and public performance.

The old Conservatory for Music in Leipzig. Courtesy of Frithjof Haas.

Students will also find ample educational opportunities outside of the conservatory:
   a. 20 internationally renowned Gewandhaus concerts, including rehearsals;
   b. quartet performances, also given in the Gewandhaus hall;
   c. weekend performances of church music by the famous St. Thomas choir; and
   d. opera performances.

Besides these ways of studying music, the local university and other institutions of learning provide students with opportunities for further scientific training of every kind. Students that distinguish themselves as vocal or instrumental soloists will regularly be given opportunities at the conservatory to perform publicly under the supervision of their instructor.

The entire course of studies costs 80 talers annually, to be paid quarterly in advance to the conservatory's financial office in installments of 20 talers each.[13]

Mendelssohn had set up the conservatory with a five-member board of directors, including court councilor Keil, district director Von Falkenstein, lawyer Schleinitz, city councilor Seeburg, and music shop proprietor Kistner. Representatives of pertinent professions became substitutes and successors to the board. Precautions were taken to make certain that in the future the conservatory would be supervised and controlled by experienced persons from both the imperial administration and from society's middle class. Mendelssohn's far-reaching contacts and the degree of excellence expected of a school under his leadership enabled him to win the best musicians of the times for his staff. Early instructors were, among others, Robert and Clara Schumann and violinist Ferdinand David, joined later by Joseph Joachim, conductor Ferdinand Hiller, and composer Niels Wilhelm Gade.

Among the few surviving documents from Hermann Levi's years as a student in Leipzig we find a report on the young man's progress written on 18 February 1856 for his first semester of instruction in theory and composition, piano, violin, lectures, and song.[14] His most important teachers were Moritz Hauptmann for theory, Ignaz Moscheles for piano, and Julius Rietz for composition and conducting.

Moritz Hauptmann's competence in musical theory was renowned. He had been violinist for the Kassel court orchestra under the direction of Louis Spohr for two decades before at Mendelssohn's recommendation he was called to become the choir director at St. Thomas in Leipzig and the conservatory simultaneously took him on as an instructor for theory and composition. His broad education in music and his distinct sense of systematic and logical relationships made him an excellent teacher. Among his pupils we find names like Ferdinand David, Norbert Burgmüller, Joseph Joachim, Franz von Holstein, and Hans von Bülow. Beethoven was his musical role model, particularly the works from the middle period. Like most musicians of his time, he found Beethoven's late works unintelligible. One hundred years after Bach, Hauptmann was the first to reintroduce Bach's cantatas to the St. Thomas choir's repertory, although he

Family, Studies, and First Positions

Moritz Hauptmann, Levi's instructor in music theory. Courtesy of Frithjof Haas.

created idiosyncratic versions by adding instruments to the middle parts and letting clarinets and bassoons play the continuo bass. But his merits for the renaissance of Bach remain. As chairman of the Bach Society, he worked on the first publication of the complete edition of Bach's works, giving special attention to score authenticity.

Hauptmann enhanced his student's instruction in theory by providing practical examples at the church of St. Thomas on the weekends, where he sometimes performed his own works. The allure of his adept compositions, however, faded with time. Hauptmann was a prominent figure during an era of the rediscovery

Julius Rietz, Levi's instructor for composition and conducting. Courtesy of Frithjof Haas.

of the baroque masters and his views shaped young Hermann Levi. Ferdinand Hiller once described Hauptmann in a way that twenty-five years later could also have been used to describe Hermann Levi:

> It is difficult to find a person of such broad learning, mental maturity, fine taste, and keen and clear judgment. This serenity, this smiling seriousness of opinion and mild fairness in verdict! . . . Though lacking every pretense, and modest in judging his own work, he could not prevent that one always looked up to him.[15]

Pianist Ignaz Moscheles was entirely different. After a long, brilliant virtuoso career he had accepted a call to London as professor for the Royal Academy of Music and conductor for the Royal Philharmonic Society. Persuaded by his friend Mendelssohn, in 1846 Moscheles resigned from his positions in London to supervise the study of piano and piano composition at the conservatory in Leipzig. His technical editions of piano works by Haydn, Mozart, and Beethoven are proof of his dexterity at teaching. He had also written a piano score for *Fidelio* under the personal auspice of Beethoven. Moscheles was a specimen of the typical musical personality from a great past: early in the century he had kept company with Beethoven in Vienna and taken instruction in theory from Albrechtsberger and Salieri. Eduard Hanslick said that Moscheles stood for classical piano technique, but also marked the beginning of a new epoch in virtuosity.

Levi's most important instructor in terms of shaping his future as a conductor was Gewandhaus Kapellmeister Julius Rietz. Like Mendelssohn, Rietz had come to Leipzig from Berlin; they had been friends from youth. Julius Rietz's brother Eduard had been concertmaster in Mendelssohn's Berlin performance of the *Passion of Matthew*. Julius began his career as a cellist in the royal city theater orchestra in Berlin and then followed his friend Mendelssohn to Dusseldorf, where he first was Mendelssohn's assistant and later became the city's director of music. As of 1847 he was conductor for the City Theater in Leipzig; later he became the director of the Sing Academy and the Gewandhaus concerts. At the conservatory he taught composition. It had not yet become common to teach conducting; most conductors were appointed based on their reputations as soloists or composers. Julius Rietz, too, had been known as the composer of the opera *Der Korsar* (The Corsair), performed for the first time in Leipzig, and other pieces as well. Rietz's work as conductor of the Gewandhaus orchestra was to become pivotal for Levi's future. After enjoying a Gewandhaus concert in the spring of 1857, Peter Cornelius wrote to his sister:

> If you could just once hear an orchestra like this, you would know what music really is. Imagine 32 violins, 9 violas, 9 cellos, and 6 double basses. It's a wonderful army of instruments, and all the violins play as if they were one![16]

As a loyal follower of Mendelssohn, Julius Rietz pursued a conservative line of music. The example he set as an objective interpreter of classical and early romantic music shaped Levi's development. Programs for Gewandhaus concerts from the 1850s show the orchestral repertoire to which he introduced his students.

Works by Beethoven were what was performed most often. During Hermann Levi's three years of study at the conservatory, the orchestra publicly performed all of Beethoven's symphonies, including the ninth symphony twice or more, followed by Beethoven overtures, piano concertos, and the violin concerto. They performed Mozart's *Prague Symphony* and his last three symphonies and four of Haydn's London symphonies, but only excerpts from *The Creation* and *The Seasons*. The only Schubert work that the orchestra rehearsed was the so-called "great" symphony in C major that Schumann had "rediscovered."[17] On the other hand, they played lots of Mendelssohn: all of the symphonies, concertos, and overtures and the entire *Elias*. All four of Schumann's symphonies were performed several times; in January 1857 Clara Schumann played the piano concerto written by her husband, who had died five months earlier.

Young Levi had opportunities to indulge in music outside the conservatory and Gewandhaus, too. "Euterpe" was an association of musically enthusiastic citizens named after a mythological Muse that inspired poets, musicians, and artists. Twice a year the association organized ten subscription concerts directed by capable Hermann Langer. These events, highly praised by Schumann himself, had become a major supplement to the Gewandhaus concerts. With its large choir, Euterpe could present not only classical symphonic works, but oratorios as well. This is where Levi the student could hear Haydn's *Creation* and *Seasons*, and Handel's *Judas Maccabaeus*.

Over the years, performance at the city opera became less sophisticated because Rietz had resigned from the theater. The opera's colorful program included many works by French composers Auber, Méhul, Hérold, and Meyerbeer. This may have been when Levi developed a distaste for Meyerbeer; but it may also have been when he discovered his liking for Méhul's *Joseph* and Marschner's *Hans Heiling*.

Real competition for the St. Thomas choir came from the Riedel Association, founded in 1854. Directed by the excellent conductor Carl Riedel himself (who had studied under Hauptmann and Rietz), the choir cultivated *a cappella* music. With a purity of style that was to set the standard for the future, the choir performed vocal works by Vittoria, Palestrina, Praetorius, and Schütz.

If we count regular quartet evenings organized by Gewandhaus concertmaster Ferdinand David and the many special concerts given by notable visiting soloists such as Franz Liszt, Hans von Bülow, Clara Schumann, Joseph Joachim, Jenny Lind, and Pauline Viardot-García, we find that in Leipzig a student of music had almost daily a choice of outstanding musical events to select from, more so than in any other German city at the time.

And yet, among the most often performed contemporary composers (including Niels W. Gade, Ferdinand Hiller, Johann Nepomuk Hummel, Wilhelm Kalliwoda, Franz Lachner, Julius Rietz, and Louis Spohr), none was a master of the highest rank. Young Brahms had not yet written any works for the orchestra and conductor Julius Rietz shunned works by Wagner and Liszt. This may explain why later, as a conductor, Levi was thrilled to meet Brahms. As a student in Leipzig, he had joined a group of progressively minded young musicians that admired Schumann. They imagined themselves members of Schumann's fantasy music society called the *Davidsbündler* (League of David) in defiance of the artistic mediocrity that they sensed around them. Having first been published in 1833, twenty years later Schumann's poetic thoughts on artists and the arts continued to inspire students:

Finder! You have been chosen for the Good and the Great! You shall become a member of the League of David, you shall translate the secrets of the league for the world, the league that shall smite the Philistines, musical and otherwise. . . . It would be true fortune if the world of art were to produce a line of Bilfingers, who, as is well-known, had two pesky extra fingers; then we'd have ten less virtuosos and one more artist.[18]

Hermann Levi heard lectures on so-called "musical topics" given by Franz Brendel, who had followed Robert Schumann as editor of the *Neue Zeitschrift für Musik* (New Journal for Music). Music scholar Brendel thought highly of Wagner and the so-called New-German musicians. While his verdict on composer and conductor Julius Rietz was acerbic, Brendel wrote four pages in praise of Franz Liszt's performance as a conductor (with Hans von Bülow as the soloist at the piano), closing with the words: "The entire concert was epoch-making; it marks a turning point in the annals of musical life at Leipzig."[19]

Liszt's and Bülow's performances in February 1857 deeply impressed Levi and made him question whether he should continue his studies in Leipzig for a third year. This seems at least to be why his father wrote to Julius Rietz to learn of Hermann's progress. Rietz's reply shows that the teacher was disconcerted by certain "random and wild tendencies" to which the seventeen-year-old student appears to have been exposed:

> On the topic of our correspondence, I am in general happy to be able to report only good things about your son. He is a bright, receptive young man, and although he is not a world-storming genius, he is highly talented and promising. However, these days, young musicians struggle with dubious influences. The musical scene teems with so many uninhibited, rampant, wild, ugly, and un-artistic tendencies, and so much propaganda for their strange products and that entire tendency in music, that it takes a lot of proper good sense and much strength of will and character not to go along with it, not to fall for this mischief. . . . I believe that your son has not won that battle yet, it is not entirely clear to him where he wants to go. However, his work, that as a whole is sound and by no means shallow or frivolous, has good and lovely aspects, yet also contains so much gloom, crudity, and Weltschmerz, that the above mentioned influences cannot be denied. . . . It is a shame that though music has labored for a thousand years to achieve truth and beauty, your son is devoting his talent to a trend that will not only not survive, but has hardly even been born. Above all, I believe that he should be kept from every further distraction, things that would cause him to absorb more new impressions. Thus I must firmly reply in the negative, Esteemed Sir, to your inquiry as to whether your son should continue his studies elsewhere at some other institution. Leave your son with us and we will get the most satisfactory results. I have heard only good reports about his skill at the piano, and in general he is one of the most adroit, versatile pupils at our institute.[20]

Between the lines we find Rietz worried about losing this talented pupil and his influence on him.

A few weeks later, as part of a major exam, Levi performed publicly for the first time in a concert organized by the conservatory. One of the tasks was to sight-read and play, at the piano and from the score, the wind parts for an orchestra consisting otherwise only of string players. The *Neue Zeitschrift für Musik* reported that the concert lasted three and a quarter hours, mentioning particularly that as one of the institute's most adept students, Hermann Levi had proven himself to be "a musically well-trained score player."

A week later again, on the first of May, the conservatory held the second public examination and here Levi exhibited his talent at composition. Accompanying violinist Johann Naret-Koning, Levi presented his own three-movement violin sonata. The *New Journal for Music* called it the best part of the concert:

> Not only do the work's lovely and noble main and secondary motifs, flowing from a genuine musical soul, breathe efflorescent, fresh life, but its careful and skilled elaboration also testify most honorably to Hermann Levi's diligence and technical facility for composition. Clearly the piece emerged under a certain influence by Schumann; but this is no flaw, on the contrary, this reverence for Schumann appears to be a good sign of robust earnestness.[21]

Levi and his fellow student Naret-Koning became friends and remained so for years to come. In the spring of 1857, Naret-Koning left the conservatory to become concertmaster at Frankfurt's opera house. Levi stayed in Leipzig to study for another year. This he had no reason to regret, for besides his own significant performances, in early November 1857 famous soloists gave impressive guest performances within a very short period of time. First there were celebrations of Mendelssohn at the conservatory where Joseph Joachim performed the String Quartet in F Minor, op. 80, together with Jakob Grün, Ferdinand David, and Julius Rietz. The next day, at the Gewandhaus, Joachim played Mendelssohn's Violin Concerto, and Rietz conducted the *Hebrides Overture*, *Italian Symphony*, and the finale of act 1 from Mendelssohn's opera fragment *Loreley*. Just two days later, Clara Schumann and Joseph Joachim gave a duet-soirée, playing mostly works by Bach and Handel. And at a chamber concert another two days later, Anton Rubinstein played the piano part from a piano trio. A music critic remarked that Rubinstein's performance was chilled by romantic heroic idealist virility. In the following Gewandhaus concert, Rubinstein conducted the premier performance of his own first symphony, op. 40.

Besides all of these diversions that left Levi's teacher Rietz with mixed feelings, Levi found time to practice the piano and to write music. His own public performances became more frequent during his last semester in Leipzig. At a conservatory concert on 12 December 1857 "in honor of the birthday of His Majesty, King Johann of Saxe," Levi played the first movement of Robert

Schumann's Sonata, op. 11. At the end of March 1858, in public performances, he passed two final exams in piano and composition.

The first was a concert on March 21. Student Bertha Nuhr from Königsberg sang Levi's three songs *Das zerbrochene Ringlein* (The Little Broken Ring), *Verratene Liebe* (Betrayed Love), and *Der letzte Gruß* (The Last Farewell). The second and third song are among the few compositions that Levi later published at Rieter-Biedermann in Leipzig.

The second part of the public exam took place on March 24 in the presence of Crown Prince Albert of Saxe. Levi played Beethoven's Sonata in C Minor, op. 111. A critic from the *New Journal of Music* found Levi "one of the conservatory's most talented, versatile, and perhaps most mature students." Levi began the concert with one of his own compositions, demonstrating his skill at orchestra conducting. The journal wrote:

> Part One began with a three-movement symphony by H. Levi from Giessen. The question for such a large work by a young person is whether it reveals both talent and proper study; one does not expect the form to be permeated by intellectual content. But both were the case; the piece was impressive and was applauded. The third movement seems to be the most original, while the first reminds us very much of Schumann.[22]

Having thus completed his studies, Hermann Levi left Leipzig and returned to his father's home in Giessen.

During his time in Leipzig, Levi had kept in touch with Vincenz Lachner. He wrote regularly to inform his mentor of his progress.[23] Widening his own musical horizon, he tried to convince his former teacher of new ideas in music and sent him symphonies and overtures by Schumann that were entirely unknown in Mannheim. Lachner was skeptical:

> How unfortunate that this man's creative compositions are so poorly suited to become popular because he does not know how to achieve the right effect and the strength of his melodies remains hidden. It is one thing to popularize Schumann in Leipzig, where they have perhaps forty concerts a year, but here where we have only four. . . . I am glad you are coming and as promised I shall apply all of my experience to making a conductor out of you. Find yourself some nice operetta material that you can write music for while you are here. Perhaps you can even take the first step toward practical experience by rehearsing it and—I hope, conducting it yourself.[24]

Levi's own sense of judgment, however, had meanwhile matured and he chose not to write an operetta, but to increase his knowledge and experience in music by going to Paris. His Francophile family certainly encouraged the decision. His grandfather had been the privileged Grand Rabbi under Napoleon's rule, and since then in France the assimilation of Jews had made great progress. In 1840

Heinrich Heine wrote: "In France the Jews . . . have almost vanished entirely, that is, they have been completely absorbed by the French nationality."[25]

Paris was considered Europe's most beautiful city. To study there, or at least visit and take part in the city's arts and society, was the desire of every young person aspiring to finish his education with a bit of polish. During the middle of the century, the French metropolis had become even more outwardly attractive. Napoleon III executed a generous construction program: the grand boulevards were extended to create views of the city's squares, the Bois de Boulogne was transformed into a grand English park, a gigantic new building enhanced the Louvre. On April 5, Hermann Levi witnessed the ceremonious presentation of the new Boulevard Sebastopol: a vast tent opened to display the boulevard's broad panorama into which the emperor marched, followed by his staff of generals. Paris was undergoing a lavish architectural redesigning that was to shape its image for the next one hundred years.

When nineteen-year-old Hermann Levi arrived in the fall of 1858, not only did an urban appeal, but also an artistic life of dazzling diversity await him. The musical scene was powered by the opera attended by the city's prosperous residents that had little knowledge of music. Their primary interest was amusement, edification, and perhaps also the playing out of secret desires and fantasies. They loved feeling part of a grand heroic past.

At the time, Gioacchino Rossini, the old master of Italian opera buffa, lived in the suburb Passy and wrote music only occasionally but kept an apartment downtown and received guests from all over the world. He glossed the city's musical events with sarcastic *bon mots*, even the performances of his own works that had been disfigured by prima donna coloraturas. The most successful opera composer of the time was Giacomo Meyerbeer, whose opulent operas *Robert le Diable* and *Les Huguénots* thrilled Parisian audiences more than ever. Prussian king Friedrich Wilhelm IV had made Meyerbeer his General Superintendent for Music (a title that before then did not exist) but could not tie him permanently to Berlin. The next Parisian premiere of *Le Prophète* heightened the composer's fame. On 4 April 1859, Hermann Levi witnessed the first performance of Meyerbeer's second to last opera, *Le Pardon de Ploërmel*, at the Opéra Comique. This play opera with its folk songs and bagpipe tunes showed Paris's astonished opera goers an entirely different side of Meyerbeer that they greeted with equal enthusiasm. Except for Dinorah's virtuoso phantom aria, today we rarely hear any of this forgotten work. Emperor Napoleon III and his wife attended the premiere, summoning the composer during the break to their loge to flatter him.

Hermann Levi was perhaps familiar with Robert Schumann's opinion of Meyerbeer's operas as being "piles of monstrosities." At any rate, the performances Levi did attend in Paris could not convince him of Meyerbeer's talent, as his later derisive word on the success of *L'Africaine* (African Woman), when performed in Karlsruhe, shows. The fact that Meyerbeer, like Levi himself, came from a German-Jewish background made Levi twice as apprehensive of Meyerbeer's meteoric career.

A highly regarded premiere had taken place at the Opéra Lyrique just two weeks before the premiere of Meyerbeer's new work at the Opéra Comique. On 19 March 1859, Charles Gounod's *Faust* was performed for the first time. For months the event had aroused curiosity in the Parisian world of music. Could Goethe's *Faust* be made into a grand French opera? It seemed quite a venture for a hitherto unsung composer, known as an author of only two other works. But the premiere got much applause. Hector Berlioz attended the performance twice and found it promising.[26] Thirteen years earlier he himself had experienced a miserable failure with concert performances of his dramatic legend *La Damnation de Faust*.

In the spring of 1859, Hermann Levi, too, saw Gounod's *Faust* and liked it. But it strayed, he thought, too far from the German idea of the legend of *Faust*, as shaped by Goethe, to easily find its way onto German stages. He was wrong. Soon after its premiere in Paris, the piece (renamed *Margarethe*) conquered German stages, too, and has remained to this day the most successful opera version of Goethe's *Faust*.

Hector Berlioz, an admiring critic of Meyerbeer and Gounod, was the most important French composer living in Paris at the time, though in the French capital itself his fame had faded. His early work, the *Symphonie fantastique*, had been successful thirty years earlier, and now the composer, unwilling to yield to popular taste, remained an eccentric outsider in France. He had more followers in Germany. He wrote brilliant essays and music reviews, appearing only rarely in public to conduct his own works. On 23 April 1859, at the Opéra Comique in Paris, he directed a concert performance of his oratorio *L'Enfance du Christ*, a piece he had written five years earlier. At the time he was working on his stage piece *Les Troyens* (The Trojans) that failed to stir interest and no one wanted to perform.

It is unlikely that young Levi understood Berlioz's music or sought him out personally. At the time, Berlioz's music was too far removed from Levi's artistic ideas and the ideals after which he modeled his own compositions. He could not know that in the future, as a conductor in Munich, he would prepare the first performances of *Les Troyens* and *Benvenuto Cellini* and campaign for Berlioz in Germany.

It is safe to say that in the theaters of Paris Levi probably saw older, well-loved play operas by François-Adrien Boïeldieu, Ferdinand Hérold, Adolphe Adam, and Daniel-François Auber. The latter was the esteemed director of the conservatory. We don't know whether Levi also went to popular "Bouffes Parisiennes" on the Champs Elysées. For three years operettas and opera parodies by Jacques

Offenbach had been performed there with increasing success. The resourceful entrepreneur of this little theater (which began with three-actor pieces) was in reality Jakob Eberst, born in Cologne to Marianne Rindskopf and Isaak Juda Eberst from Offenbach. He had already launched twenty operettas. His greatest triumph was *Orpheus in the Underworld* in 1858. It was so sensationally successful that the performance was repeated 228 times.

Hermann Levi was mainly interested in concerts, but in early mid-century Paris pure concert performances were thought secondary and performed only in modest accommodations. Less elegant and representative than society's big events, these were the gatherings of the true musicians. Smaller ensembles performed in the rooms of piano manufacturers Erard and Pleyel. Orchestral concerts took place in the hall of the conservatory. When after 1851 the public developed a taste for music other than opera, concerts were moved to the Barthélemy Hall, which seated three thousand. Winter season subscription concerts by the Orchestre du Conservatoire (eighty-five musicians directed by Narcisse Girard) were mostly sold out. Mendelssohn said it was the best orchestra he had ever heard. Programs lasted three hours and consisted of six to eight pieces. The middle part of the program was always reserved for solo performers. Conservative works were favored; 43 percent of the pieces were by Beethoven, 11 percent by Haydn, 9 percent by Weber, and 6 percent by Mendelssohn and Mozart. Only 1 percent of the performances used music by living French composers.[27]

If, during his studies in Paris, Hermann Levi wanted to discover new music, he had to visit private musical salons. His brother Wilhelm was schooling his bass voice at the conservatory and introduced Hermann to private circles of musicians. Singer Julius Stockhausen, performing at the time at the Opéra Comique, directed in Paris a choir society made up of mostly Germans. There Levi met precocious Friedrich Gernsheim, who was his age and also came from an old Jewish family from Worms that in the past had known the Levi family. In the years to come, Levi's and Gernsheim's paths were to cross often. Stockhausen's choir also sang at the salon of Pauline Viardot-García, an opera star who in turn was a friend of Russian writer Ivan Turgenev. Many of the acquaintances that Levi made there later became important for him in Karlsruhe and Baden-Baden.

Forty-year-old composer Louis Theodor Gouvy from Lorraine also spent that winter season in Paris, presenting his newest works. Levi found Gouvy's delicate, transparent instrumental music fascinating and later, as a conductor in Saarbrücken, made a special effort to promote it.[28]

Another new acquaintance for Levi in Paris was twenty-four-year-old Camille Saint-Saëns, the organist at the Church of Madeleine, who sparked furor with the virtuoso performance of his own early piano works. Although neoclassical in bearing, Saint-Saëns counted as an early follower of Richard Wagner, whom he assisted in 1860 at concerts and in rehearsals for *Tannhäuser* in Paris. Later,

"Une soirée musicale"; Louis Girard, La Deuxiéme République et le Second Empire: 1848–1870 *(Paris: Hachette Publishing Co., 1981).*

Saint-Saëns became a frequent guest at Levi's academy concerts in Munich, playing his own piano works there.

Hermann Levi used his time in Paris to study and compose, too. He began working on a three-movement piano concerto that he later published at Rieter-Biedermann in Leipzig. He dedicated six songs, op. 2 (also published by Rieter-Biedermann) "in friendship" to pianist Wilhelmine Clauss-Szarvady. He had met this esteemed musician and her husband, writer Friedrich Szarvady, in Paris. Levi may have taken a few lessons with her to perfect his piano skills. At the time, he was still undecided as to whether to become a concert pianist or a conductor. Trusting Vincenz Lachner's advice, he returned to Mannheim.

The winter of 1858–1859 spent in Paris, acquiring a command of the French language and being preoccupied with French music and literature—all of this shaped Hermann Levi's frame of mind. The Francophile mind-set lasted his entire life and guided the selection of works for the concert programs that he planned. He also later translated novels by Anatole France and opera texts by Berlioz and Chabrier. His friendship with individuals from Paris lasted for decades, surviving even the war of 1870–1871. And his experience with the progressive assimilation of Jews in France instilled hope and gave Levi confidence for his own chances at a musical career at home.

YEARS IN SAARBRÜCKEN, MANNHEIM, AND ROTTERDAM

> I have always found the people of Saarbrücken very polite and accommodating to strangers.
>
> —Baron Von Knigge

While still in Paris, Levi asked his former teacher in Mannheim, Vincenz Lachner, for advice on where to go and how to best launch his career. Lachner suggested that Levi stay, if only temporarily, with his aunt, Rosalie Feidel, in Mannheim until an appropriate position could be found. He then placed an advertisement in the music press:

> To stages seeking a conductor or music director, a young man with excellent skills can be recommended by V. Lachner, to whom postage-paid inquiries may be addressed.[29]

In southern Germany, Lachner's word carried considerable weight. Right after his return from Paris in 1859, Levi became director of music for Saarbrücken.

The ambitious town of Saarbrücken on the border to France consisted at the time of two separate communities, Saarbrücken and St. Johann, and offered a young conductor favorable conditions for earning his first merits. Once the

Saarbrücken.

politically restless years were over, the town turned to cultural activity. In 1792, troops of French revolutionaries had ousted the prince regent of Nassau-Saarbrücken and set fire to the palace. Against the will of most of its inhabitants, Saarbrücken was annexed to the *Département de la Sarre* and became French. Bonaparte then bestowed economic privileges on Saarland to encourage ties to France and, in 1804, when asked to elect him emperor of France, the majority of the people in Saarbrücken did. But Saarbrücken did not remain French for long. On 8 January 1815, the Congress of Vienna allotted Saarland to Prussia and thereafter a Prussian administrator ran the mayor's office of Saarbrücken and the surrounding communities of St. Johann, Malstatt-Burbach, St. Arnual, and Brebach. St. Johann and Saarbrücken, communities that faced each other across the river and were linked by a narrow bridge, counted together about 12,000 inhabitants. Remnants of formerly illustrious regal times, spacious baroque buildings, designed by royal architect Friedrich Stengel, were everywhere to be found: the palace half in ruins, the grand Catholic church St. Johann and the Lutheran Ludwig's Church standing tall before modest residential homes. In 1852 a new railway connected Ludwigshafen, Saarbrücken, and Metz. In 1860, while Levi was active there, railways were added to link Saarbrücken to Trier and Bingen. This new transportation route increased coal export, thereby strengthening the region's economy.

As commerce thrived, the citizenry took greater interest in culture. In 1846, residents founded a male choir. A year later they organized an association for musical instruments, and three years later established the choral society, a mixed choir. The task of the local director of music was to organize orchestral and choir concerts with these various musical associations, which was not always easy and took considerable effort and skill at coordinating people. Levi's wide range of experience from Mannheim, Leipzig, and Paris helped.

It was the first time that a proficient conductor had come to the city. But if upon his arrival Levi had happened to glance through the newspaper *Saarzeitung*, he would have been amazed at the flurry of cultural activities that the town had to offer:

> String quartet and a sausage picnic at widow Eichacker's "Golden Barrel" / Grand Concert in the "Saar Pleasure Garden" by the Music Corps of the Fortieth Infantry Regiment directed by Kapellmeister Mahler, including good wine, suckling pig, pullet, etc., at reasonable prices / Evening Concert at the Garden Restaurant Reinhold by the Music Corps of the Rhine Ulan Regiment directed by Staff Trumpeter Wagner / National Concert of the Alps Choir Quartet in the yard of Mrs. Lina Lehman, wives and society welcome / Josef Trombetta presents mechanical pulley machines, a light show, caricatures, and color effects.

While the town's ambitious new director of music could not eradicate these popular summer diversions, within two years he was able to show the public that just as in the neighboring cities of Mannheim and Karlsruhe, here, too, one could have well-prepared sophisticated concerts and opera performances.

Levi's first task was to prepare a festive concert for the evening before the celebration of Friedrich Schiller's one hundredth birthday. The first half of the concert was an orchestra association performance of Rossini's overture for *Wilhelm Tell* and Mendelssohn's *Wedding March*, followed by the choir singing Franz Otto's *The German Heart* and Schiller's *Ode to Joy* by an unnamed composer. After intermission the choir joined the orchestra for "Bell Song" as arranged by Andreas Romberg. It was the new conductor's first appearance and the program was a spontaneous success: "Music Director Levy [*sic*] has proven himself to be not only a most versatile, but also a prudent conductor, on whose appointment we can congratulate ourselves."[30] Following the concert in the Wilhelm Hall at the Rothenhof Court, there was dinner and further entertainment in the casino salon.[31]

The following Wednesday, 10 November 1859, the whole town celebrated Schiller's one hundredth birthday like a national event. A huge parade marched through the streets, including a delegation from Marbach[32] carrying a laurel-wreathed bust of Schiller. The ceremony ended by planting a Schiller oak[33] behind the Ludwig Church. In the afternoon a troupe of hometown actors performed the closing acts of *Don Carlos* and *Wallenstein* and then everyone went to the taverns. The people at the German border found the Schiller festival an occasion to commemorate their heritage.

Levi's concerts in Saarbrücken were enhanced by his good connections to musicians from Mannheim. On November 24, six soloists from the National Theater in Mannheim (Sophie Wlzcek, Henriette Rohn, Josepf Schlösser, Carl Stepan, Leopold Rocke, and Carl Ditt) performed a selection of opera pieces for the benefit of the theater's pension fund. The newspaper stressed "Music Director Levy's masterly accompaniment at the piano."

During the winter Levi organized three new subscription concerts, combining performances of the instrument association, the men's choir, and the choral society. The first concert, on November 15, opened with Mozart's *Jupiter Symphony*, followed by Mendelssohn's violin concert, performed by Naret-Koning, Levi's friend from days at the conservatory in Leipzig, who meanwhile had become the concertmaster in Mannheim. Following intermission, the choral society sang excerpts from Schumann's oratorio *Das Paradies und die Peri*. At the second concert, on 15 February 1860, Levi conducted Beethoven's Symphony no. 5 and performed the *Moonlight Sonata* at the piano himself. In the third concert, the people of Saarbrücken were introduced to their music director's talent at composing. Accompanied by Levi at the piano, Mannheim's soprano Wilhelmine Wolff sang Levi's songs "Lotus Flower" and "The Last Farewell."[34] The concert opened with Haydn's Symphony in B Minor (probably Hoboken no. 102) and closed with Mendelssohn's opera fragment, the finale from act 1 of *Loreley*.

During the summer months of June and July 1860, Levi and the orchestra association staged a few operas. For the main roles they brought soloists from several other German opera houses to Saarbrücken for four weeks: soprano Michaelesi and tenor Meffert from Weimar, baritone Starke from Mainz, and bass Raberg from Hamburg. Volunteers from the men's choir and the choral society sang the choir parts and some even took on minor solo parts. They performed *Alessandro Stradella* and *Martha* by Flotow, *Der Freischütz* (The Marksman) by Weber, *La muette de Portici* (The Mute Girl of Portici) by Auber, and Donizetti's *La fille du regiment* (The Daughter of the Regiment).

Since the orchestra was made up mainly of amateurs, one can imagine what it must have meant for the conductor to rehearse five complex operas with them in just three weeks. Between performances they had merely a few days to prepare for the next work. And because many of the lay singers had other occupations, full rehearsals could only be held in the evening.

That first "Opera Season" organized by their ambitious young director of music must have been a sensation for the people of Saarbrücken. Considering the circumstances, Levi himself can hardly have been satisfied with the results, although the experience did give him valuable insight into how to manage an opera troupe. The selections he made for the programs had to take the limited repertories of the singers into account. He had to skip Mozart operas and Beethoven's *Fidelio*, which would have been more of a challenge. None of the operas were repeated and even the local press left them unmentioned.

During the winter season of 1860–1861, Levi once again organized subscription concerts, but now with more daring programs. In the first concert (November 27) the orchestra performed Gouvy's Symphony op. 12. Theodor Gouvy lived in nearby Gaffontaine and had remained in touch with Levi since Paris. At the time, Levi overestimated Gouvy's compositions. They were masterly, but clearly modeled on Mendelssohn, perhaps even resembling Levi's own pieces. Famous French music critic Léon Kreutzer wrote that "with just one-hundredth of Gouvy's talent one could write pieces for grand opera houses, become a member of the Legion of Honor, and earn 30,000 francs a year, but why the devil does Gouvy write symphonies?"[35] The Saarbrücken audience celebrated him as a local composer, but the newspaper ignored it, taking considerable notice instead of the concert that followed:

> Master Haydn himself would have been pleased by this ardent performance. All of the participants did an excellent job, most of all Music Director Levi, whose talented leadership, care, and truly artistic ambition is the cause of the triumphs celebrated recently by the local world of music.[36]

In the third concert Levi presented for the first time in Saarbrücken Robert Schumann's first symphony, followed by himself performing Beethoven's Sonata for Piano in E Minor, op. 90, and then closing the concert with excerpts from Mendelssohn's oratorio *St. Paul.*

In another charity concert given with singers from Mannheim in March 1861, Levi once more presented some of his own compositions: two song arrangements for a male quartet and two lieder for soprano. These works have not survived and like his violin sonata were perhaps among the pieces that Levi later destroyed.[37]

On his days off, Levi left for Mannheim to keep in touch with the musical scene there, realizing that his artistic development would be hedged by staying in Saarbrücken for another year. Vincenz Lachner encouraged him to continue composing and to perform more at the piano. He had introduced Levi as a concert pianist at an academy event in April 1860 in Mannheim and tried to quiet his qualms:

> Let your work go out into the world as it is. Since it appears as Opus 1, no reasonable person will say that it is not perfect in every way, but will instead discover so much excellence, so much novelty in this first work that he will admit to his surprise. Before the cognoscente can put a magnifying glass to it, the naked eye will admire it.[38]

The amiable audience in the city of Levi's relatives and friends confirmed Lachner's foresight and celebrated the young artist. A few weeks later, Levi presented his new sonata for violin and piano together with concertmaster Naret-Koning at a chamber music concert at the National Theater; four years earlier they had premiered the composition together in Leipzig.

It took some persuasion, but finally in May 1861 Vincenz Lachner came to Saarbrücken to conduct a special concert. Levi played his piano concerto, Lachner conducted a *Prize Overture* of his own, Naret-Koning played the solo part of a violin concerto by Antonio Bazzini[39] and then, together with Levi, one of Beethoven's violin sonatas. The people of Saarbrücken did not know that this was to be Levi's last concert there.

In June, at short notice, Levi was asked to substitute at Mannheim's opera for second conductor Hetsch who had taken ill. Lachner, not wanting to cancel his scheduled vacation, had diplomatically proposed approaching his former student for this task and, pointing out Levi's success in Saarbrücken, had dismissed doubts that Levi was too young. Levi left for Mannheim instantly and on June 19 directed Dittersdorf's *Das rothe Käppchen* (Red Riding Hood) at the National Theater.

Among the operas that Levi directed over the next three weeks were Bellini's *La sonnambula*, Lortzing's *Zar und Zimmermann*, Weber's *Freischütz*, and probably Spohr's *Jessonda*, Méhul's *Joseph*, and Mozart's *Le nozze di Figaro*, too. The billing made no mention of the name of the conductor. A letter from Lachner reveals that Levi's work was successful: "Perhaps your great modesty

Mannheim's National Theater in 1782, copper etching by the Klauber Bros. Reiss Museum Mannheim.

keeps you from writing to me. But I'd like to hear from you what everyone I've seen from Mannheim has been telling me, namely that you did an excellent job as a conductor."[40]

Kapellmeister Hetsch recovered by autumn and returned to his post and Levi's work at the theater was done. In gratitude, Lachner let Levi conduct an academy concert on October 31, where in the presence of Theodor Gouvy he once again had the orchestra perform that composer's symphony. Levi never returned to the post in Saarbrücken; after his success in Mannheim, it would have meant a step backward. In two years of hard work, he had shown what idealism could accomplish with the limited resources of Saarbrücken. Now he wanted to work on his own and wait for an adequate position to present itself. He recommended his friend Friedrich Gernsheim[41] as his successor in Saarbrücken. Writing on Gernsheim's first concert as Saarbrücken's new conductor, the newspaper *Saarbrücker Zeitung* praised the town's former director of music:

> We have every reason to believe that Gernsheim will uphold the standards of musicality of our former conductor, Levi. The musical circumstances in a small town, of course, cannot hold such a truly ingenious musician as Levi for long. Levi has accomplished more for the understanding of real and genuine music here than any that went before him.[42]

Throughout the winter of 1861–1862, Levi concentrated on piano study and composing, also keeping abreast of Mannheim's opera performances in order to enhance his knowledge of opera. He recommended himself as a concert pianist to Carl Reinecke, the new conductor at the Gewandhaus in Leipzig, not failing to mention that in Mannheim he had already directed ten different operas. He was promptly engaged to play his piano concerto at the Gewandhaus on 7 November 1861. On his twenty-second birthday it meant a triumphant return to Leipzig, the town he had left just three years earlier as a graduate of the conservatory. The performance, however, disappointed. The critical Leipzig public did not like Levi's piece:

> In the past we have had the opportunity to acquaint ourselves with this young musician, trained at the local conservatory. But his performance today did not confirm the aspirations set for him based on his former achievements or allow a favorable opinion of his facilities. His technique is accomplished and elegant, but exhibits no other particular features. Little praiseworthy can be said about the piece. He wrote for the orchestra with skill, proving study and talent, but that is about all we can say. The piece is endlessly reminiscent of Mendelssohn, Gade, etc., leaving an impression of being thrown together like potpourri, having no ideally organic cohesion. Overall it was dull, sometimes awkward; the audience seemed bored and unmoved. A rare unlucky star shone on the performance.[43]

Composers greater than Levi had survived scathing critiques from Leipzig. Brahms had gotten the same after presenting his first piano concerto there. Theodor Gouvy had recently sent Levi a report on the *Tannhäuser* fiasco in Paris. But that was about Wagner, already acknowledged then as one of the greatest living composers, while Levi had yet to make a name for himself. The failure in Leipzig was a bitter lesson and surely shaped Levi's later appraisal of his own creativity. Never again did he propose anywhere to perform his piano concerto. We shall later return to discuss Levi's compositions (see First Intermezzo).

In the course of the winter, at the piano Levi accompanied violinist Naret-Koning and cellist Kündinger at their performances. On 22 March 1862, Lachner had a double choir sing Levi's composition for Psalm 25 at a concert in the Musical Academy. The words of David met Levi's emotional needs:

> Unto thee, O Lord, do I lift up my soul.
> O my God, I trust in thee: let me not be ashamed,
> let not mine enemies triumph over me.
> Show me thy ways, O Lord, teach me thy paths.
> Remember not the sins of my youth, nor my transgressions.
> Let integrity and uprightness preserve me;
> for I put my trust in thee.[44]

At the recommendation of Vincenz Lachner, in February 1862 Hermann Levi applied to the German Opera in Rotterdam for the position of director that was currently open. The budding enterprise had been founded in 1860 at the initiative of Amsterdam's composer Willem Thooft with the support of many Germans that lived in Holland. The Rotterdam Opera Society was unusually democratic: the shareholders of the theater company were the concert subscribers themselves; they elected a committee of twenty-one, from which in turn a core committee of five ran the operation together with director Eduard de Fries and conductor Franz Škroup.[45] Meanwhile the widely known Czech conductor and composer had died, and Hermann Levi and Franz Dupont (born in Rotterdam and at the time director of music at Nuremberg's city theater) had the best chances of getting the job. Surprisingly, the committee favored Levi. Perhaps it was because at the age of twenty-three he was half a generation younger than the competition and would therefore demand less salary.

In March 1862 Levi went to Rotterdam to introduce himself and get a first impression. He was struck by the German opera troupe's capacity: they performed eight different operas within two weeks, in between which they had concerts featuring Italian prima donna Adelina Patti and Belgian violinist Henri Vieuxtemps playing his new fifth concerto for violin in A minor. During that visit Levi was able to convince the committee of five of his skills and make a favorable impression. They made him the first conductor for the coming season of 1862–1863. The press saw in him a very promising new musical director. The liberally minded Dutch made no fuss over Levi's religion.

In mid-August Levi moved to Rotterdam, stopping first in Giessen at his parents' home, and then in Cologne to visit his brother who sang there in the opera. Compared to Mannheim, Rotterdam was new musical territory for him; it had no tradition to uphold. It was true that two hundred years earlier in the neighboring metropolis of Amsterdam Jan Pietersz Sweelinck, the organist of the *Oude Kerk*, had attained European acclaim. And true, too, that paintings by Franz Hals, Gerard Terborch, and Jan Steen showed musicians playing their lutes and theorbos for the Dutch to admire. But for nineteenth-century Rotterdam, these were things of the far past. This formerly significant place of commerce had lost rank, it was further from the sea and its waterways were clogged with sand. Not until neighboring industrial areas on the rivers Rhine and Ruhr emerged did Rotterdam once again become known for importing and exporting ore, coal, and steel. In the latter half of the century, a waterway to Hoek van Holland, which had been in the planning for 150 years, was finally completed.

Little by little the people of Rotterdam found not only new business, but discovered cultural needs as well. As commerce increased with neighboring Germany, they began to observe the opera activity across the border. Rotterdam wanted a repertory theater like those of other cities.

The German opera of Rotterdam, established in 1860, was successful and had a good name. High salaries attracted famous German stage singers. Among the five female and seven male soloists, Deetz (soprano) and Ellinger (heroic tenor) were the public's favorites.[46] The playing season began in October. The agenda was eclectic, relying on some repertory from the previous season: Mozart's *Don Giovanni* and *Le nozze di Figaro*, Weber's *Freischütz*, Lortzing's *Zar und Zimmermann*, Kreutzer's *Nachtlager von Grenada* (Night Camp in Granada), Meyerbeer's *Huguénots*, Halévy's *La Juive*, Rossini's *Wilhelm Tell*, and Donizetti's *Lucia di Lammermoor*. Levi was familiar with these productions from Mannheim and had no trouble repeating the pieces rehearsed with the troupe's former director. His assistant, Eugen Drobisch, however, had little experience in conducting, thus Levi almost always conducted the performances, three times a week.

The new production he prepared for early November was Richard Wagner's *Lohengrin*, stage-directed by Carl Jencke from Wiesbaden. The problem for the orchestra was that Wagner asked for three sets of woodwinds, while in Rotterdam they had only two. With the enthusiasm of youth, Levi found it better to present the work with fewer instruments than not at all. Ten years later, as an experienced conductor of Wagner's music, he would have claimed otherwise. But for now he committed himself to the arduous task of rewriting the wind and brass parts for fewer players—of all things, for the score of *Lohengrin*, the prime example of music written for triple woodwinds. The trumpets that Wagner had let sound from the stage, Levi let sound from the orchestra pit instead. He bought a new bass clarinet for 88 guldens because they didn't have one.

The premiere was an unexpected great success for the orchestra and its young conductor. With Ellinger singing Lohengrin, Deetz as Elsa, and Kapp-Young as Ortrud, Levi had presented an ensemble "that many a German court theater would have been proud of."[47] They performed it six times in just three weeks. Following the last performance, the orchestra presented its conductor with a silver-plated baton, engraved with words of appreciation.

Levi seriously considered inviting Richard Wagner to guest conduct one of the performances. He contacted his former conservatory friend from his days in Leipzig, Wendelin Weissheimer,[48] about it. Weissheimer gave concerts all over to raise funds for Wagner who was constantly threatened by financial ruin. The master said he would be willing to conduct two evenings in Rotterdam for a compensation of 1000 guldens. In thanks he would recommend Weissheimer as Levi's successor in Rotterdam. But the committee turned down the proposal, even Levi's suggestion that Wagner conduct just one performance of *Lohengrin* for 500 to 600 guldens. It had been Levi's hope to meet the master. But in the end he was relieved that Wagner did not hear the *Lohengrin* arrangement he had written for an inadequate number of musicians.

On 26 January 1863, Levi presented Wagner's *Tannhäuser* and the audience was pleased. They had not appreciated the Italian operas *Lucia di Lammermoor*, *Troubadour*, and *Sonambula*. The day after the *Tannhäuser* performance, Levi signed a contract to conduct for a second year in Rotterdam, this time with more say in selecting pieces and soloists.

Ferdinand Hiller (1811–1885), conductor in Cologne. Courtesy of Frithjof Haas.

From Holland Levi corresponded often with Cologne's conductor Ferdinand Hiller. The latter was a friend of Levi's mentors Vincenz Lachner and Julius Rietz, and he had met him personally years before. While still in Saarbrücken, Levi had offered Hiller that he [Levi] come and play his own piano composition as a soloist. In July 1862 in Wiesbaden, Levi had heard a performance of Hiller's opera *Die Katakomben* (*The Catacombs*) and planned to bring it to Rotterdam. But because it was impossible to engage the right performers, the project was put off for a year.

At the end of April, the opera season closed in Rotterdam and Levi began traveling to German theaters to find good new singers for his stage. In early July he spent a week in Baden-Baden and met Hiller there. European artists and musicians gathered at this world-famous bath spa, and Levi, too, made valuable contacts. On recommendation from Vincenz Lachner he introduced himself to Karlsruhe's theater director Eduard Devrient and spoke with him about working there in the future. He was also invited to Clara Schumann's new home in Lichtental, where he met composers Anton Rubinstein and Theodor Kirchner. During those years Anton Rubinstein, whose physiognomy somewhat resembled that of Beethoven, was one of the leading figures on the European musical scene. A virtuoso and genius pianist at interpretation, he fascinated audiences around the world. He was also known as a composer of symphonies and operas, although after his death his compositions were soon forgotten.

Compared to Rubinstein's commanding personality, Theodor Kirchner, an organist by trade, was more humble. And yet today his compositions for the piano are valued as masterpieces of the lesser form. At Clara Schumann's home, Levi enjoyed the immense artistic scope of late musical romanticism. She introduced him to Brahms's works; he played Schubert's oratorio *Lazarus* for her.

During his second season in Rotterdam, Levi began rehearsing Mozart's *Entführung aus dem Serail* (Abduction from the Seraglio), while simultaneously preparing Hiller's *Catacombs*. When writing to Hiller to report on how the rehearsals were moving along, he also recommended his brother Wilhelm, asking Hiller whether Wilhelm might not also give courses in harmony or piano alongside his engagement as a singer at Cologne's opera. Hermann, the younger and more talented of the two, mentored his brother. Wilhelm (who married a Catholic woman and changed his surname to "Lindeck") did not become Hermann's financial adviser until 1868 when he gave up his singing career and started working for the Ladenburg Bank in Mannheim that had been established by their great-grandfather.

The premiere of *Catacombs* was postponed several times, forcing Levi to write Hiller letters of regret that provide interesting details on making music in Rotterdam. He writes, for example, of his adept first concertmaster Eduard Rappoldi,[49] whom he also instructed in composition on the side and whom he helped write a string quartet. Recommended by Levi, the next year Rappoldi took up the study of composition under Hiller in Cologne. In another case, Levi writes that for a concert in celebration of Beethoven's birthday he performed Goethe's *Egmont* using texts by Michael Bernays. This literary personality, later to become professor at the university in Munich, one day befriended Levi and introduced him to people around Wagner in Bayreuth.

Finally, as 1863 drew to a close, *Catacombs* got its premiere. Hiller arrived a few days early, stayed with the Van Hoop family, took part in the final rehearsals, and then directed the piece himself. Wanting to demonstrate his skills, Levi had prepared a full program for his guest. He conducted both *Fidelio* and a dress rehearsal for Handel's *Athalia*. On the morning of the premiere for *Catacombs*, Hiller also heard the Rappoldi Quartet practice in Levi's home to get an idea of what the first violinist had been composing.

Reviews indicate that on December 19 the premiere for *Catacombs* went well, although the audience was reserved: it called only once for the composer, which was unusual for such a performance. Certainly the operagoers noted the huge discrepancy between *Catacombs* and *Lohengrin*. Nonetheless, Hiller was content with the rendition and the evening; almost immediately he wrote to a friend that from now on he intended to write music exclusively for the theater. The day after the premiere, the Van Hoop family hosted a festive soirée in their home, bestowing honor upon honor on the composer. Levi and Hiller parted as good friends and later, as the director of Cologne's musical life, Hiller confidentially advised Levi in negotiations for engaging artists in Karlsruhe. He was thoroughly acquainted with the circumstances at Baden's royal theater. When on 14 November 1863 Hiller conducted the first performance of *Catacombs* in Karlsruhe, Eduard Devrient proposed that Hiller succeed Joseph Strauss as the conductor there. Hiller declined, despite fabulous contract conditions.

By his second season in Rotterdam, Levi had decided not to renew his contract. He saw no way to develop further there. And he was lonely. During the last year at the conservatory in Leipzig, he had shown interest in Lachner's daughter Rosine, but not in the least thought of making a commitment at such a young age. That did not stop Lachner from secretly thinking of him as a son-in-law. But tragically, in 1860 Rosine died at the age of twenty. In letters to Lachner, Levi found kind words for her, perhaps out of loneliness and in need of close ties:

> And then, as a human being, I miss a lot of things here; neither the language, the customs, nor (except for a few women) even people's faces are to my liking. Very rarely is one introduced to families; men all work until late at night, and like the young girls in France and the women in England, the young ladies here are not emancipated, they are stuck in formality.[50]

Thus the offer of a contract in Karlsruhe provided a welcome opportunity to return to familiar terrain. Levi's Rotterdam contract ended on 30 April 1864. Before leaving he produced Gluck's *Alceste*, a piece that he came to enjoy presenting all of his life. He recommended that his longtime friend Friedrich Gernsheim become his successor. Gernsheim had succeeded him in Saarbrücken and in the autumn of 1864 moved on to follow Levi as conductor of the Opera of Rotterdam.

Levi's work in Rotterdam completed, as it were, his years of apprenticeship. He had held three responsible positions, gained experience as a conductor of concerts and operas, and developed the confidence one needs to work with large and prominent orchestras. At just twenty-five, he was a polished conductor with clear ideas of his art. He felt well prepared to successfully direct the musical operations of a large court theater, and was eager to compete with the best of conductors.

NOTES

1. For a history of Jewish communities in Giessen, see Erwin Knauss, *Die jüdische Bevölkerung Giessens 1933–1945* (Wiesbaden, 1982). In 1829 Giessen also had another, an orthodox rabbi.

2. Benedict is the latinized form of the Jewish name Benet.

3. The Israelite tribe of Levi can be traced back to Levi, the third son of Jacob and Leah (Old Testament, Genesis 29:34). During the era of the kings (1020–587 BC), temple priests were exclusively Levites. Thereafter the Levites became temple servants, while the Aaronites (descendants of Aaron, also from the tribe of Levi) enjoyed the privilege of priesthood.

4. Among Hermann Levi's other ancestors we find the following well-known rabbis: Samuel Lichtenstadt-Wedeles Segal, school rabbi in Prague; Abraham Aaron Lichtenstadt, head rabbi of Bohemia from 1673 to 1693, died 1701 in Prague; Abraham Öttingen-Ries, died 1637, rabbi and spokesman for the Jewish community in Vienna; Elia Öttingen, rabbi in Frankfurt, distinguished as a Gaon, married to a daughter of wellknown Simon Günzburg (1505–1568). The Günzburgs had flown from Ulm and thus originally went by the name of Ulmo-Günzburg.

I thank Stefan Rohrbacher for this information on Hermann Levi's early ancestors.

5. The Sanhedrin, or Synedrion, was the Jewish council of elders that, in Jerusalem during the time of ancient Greece and Rome, exercised jurisdiction in common and religious matters. It goes back to the seventy elders from the time of Moses (Old Testament, Numbers 11:16). Modeled after the Sanhedrin, Napoleon called together the Jewish Notables, two-thirds of which were rabbis and one-third laymen, to meet in eight sessions in Paris, where they negotiated the rights and duties of Jewish citizens in France.

6. The congregation was called "Schum" after the first letters of the names of the cities, Ushpiro (Speyer), Uormatia (Worms), and Magenza (Mainz).

7. Benedict Levi, "Beweis der Zulässigkeit des deutschen Choralgesanges mit Orgelbegleitung beim sabbathlichen Gottesdienste der Juden" (Proof That German Choral Singing and Organ Accompaniment Is Permitted in Jewish Sabbath Worship Services), in *Archiv der Kirchenwissenschaft*, vol. 3 (Frankfurt, 1832).

8. In 1660 elector Karl Ludwig had invited Jewish families to settle in Mannheim and granted them twelve years of exemption from safe conduct taxes on the condition that each family build a two-story home.

9. Wolf Hajum Ladenburg's daughter Rebekka married Hajum Gottschalk Mayer, son of court manufacturer Gottschalk Mayer. Rebekka's brother Herrmann married Gottschalk Mayer's daughter Sara; their sister Regine married Joseph Hohenemser, owner of the bank H. L. Hohenemser & Söhne (established in 1792); in 1793 their cousin Joseph Hohenemser had married one of Hajum Ladenburg's sisters (Karl Otto Watzinger, *Geschichte der Juden in Mannheim* [History of the Jews in Mannheim] [Stuttgart, 1984]).

10. Friedrich Walter, "Von den Lachners und Hermann Levi," *Rheinische Thalia*, no. 33, Mannheim, April 1922.

11. Emil Kneschke, *Das Conservatorium der Musik in Leipzig* (Leipzig, 1868), 7ff.

12. Ibid., 9.

13. See Emil Kneschke, *Das Conservatorium der Musik in Leipzig* (Leipzig, 1868), 19ff for the program in its entirety.

Family, Studies, and First Positions 39

14. Bayerische Staatsbibliothek, Manuscripts, Leviana. Leipzig Conservatory report on attendance in instruction in theory and composition, piano, violin, and song.

15. Wolfgang Hanke, *Die Thomaner* (Berlin, 1985), 129.

16. Peter Cornelius, *Ausgewählte Briefe* (Selected Letters), 2 vols. (Leipzig, 1904), 1:258f.

17. This symphony written by Schubert in 1828 was not performed during his lifetime. While visiting Vienna in early 1839, Robert Schumann discovered the manuscript at the home of Schubert's brother Ferdinand. He gave the work to Felix Mendelssohn-Bartholdy who had it premiered at the Leipzig Gewandhaus on 21 March 1839.

18. Robert Schumann, *Die Davidsbündler*; taken from *Der junge Schumann: Dichtungen und Briefe* (Leipzig, 1904), 9 and 12.

19. *Neue Zeitschrift für Musik* 46, no. 10 (6 March 1857): 101 ff. Program for 26 February 1857 at the Gewandhaus:
Part I (conducted by Julius Rietz) Robert Schumann, Overture to *Hermann and Dorothea*, op. 136, Prayer for Genoveva (sung by Rosa von Milde); Henri Vieuxtemps: *Adagio* and Rondo for violin and orchestra (played by Jakob Grimm).
Part II (conducted by Franz Liszt) Franz Liszt, *Les Préludes*; Richard Wagner, Duet from *Der fliegende Holländer* (sung by Hans Feodor and Rosa Milde); Franz Liszt, Piano Concerto no. 1 in E-flat Major (played by Hans von Bülow).
A week later Liszt conducted *Tannhäuser* at Leipzig's theater.

20. Bayerische Staatsbibliothek, Manuscripts, Leviana. Letter from Julius Rietz to Benedict Levi dated 1 March 1857.

21. *Neue Zeitschrift für Musik* 46, no. 19 (8 May 1857): 205.

22. *Neue Zeitschrift für Musik* 48, no. 14 (2 April 1858): 154.

23. These letters have not survived. Their content can only be reconstructed based on passages taken from Friedrich Walter (see note 24 below).

24. Friedrich Walter: *Briefe Vincenz Lachners an Hermann Levi* (Lachner's Letters to Hermann Levi) (Mannheim, 1931). Letter dated January 1858.

25. Heinrich Heine, *Lutetia*, 27 May 1840 (Munich, 1969), 4:174. Complete works in four volumes.

26. Hector Berlioz, *Die Musiker und die Musik* (Leipzig: Literarische Werke, 1903), 9:201.

27. Jeffrey Cooper, *The Rise of Instrumental Music and Concert Series in Paris 1828–1871* (Ann Arbor, MI: UMI Research Press, 1983), 31.

28. Louis Theodore Gouvy, born 2 July 1819 in Gaffontaine near Saarbrücken, son of a Lorraine smelting works owner, died 21 April 1898 in Leipzig. He wrote three symphonies as well as chamber music. Gouvy spent most of his life in Paris, in touch with Berlioz and Halévy. Levi was introduced to him in Paris, probably at the home of pianist Wilhelmine Clauss-Szarvady.

29. Friedrich Walter, *Briefe Vincenz Lachners an Hermann Levi* (Mannheim, 1931), 7.

30. *Saarzeitung*, no. 171, 12 November 1859.

31. In 1828 the Casino Society, a literary-artistic association, purchased the "Salon of the Casino on Wilhelm Street" and the house of J. Karcher. In 1866 a new building was erected in the surrounding park.

32. Schiller's place of birth.

33. The tree toppled and fell in 1993.

34. The program's mention of Levi as the composer of "Lotus Flower" was possibly an error. We know of no composition of Levi's that goes by that name. It might have been *Lotus Flower*, op. 27, by Robert Schumann.

35. Friedrich Blume, ed., *Musik in Geschichte und Gegenwart* (= MGG; Music of the Past and Present) (Kassel, 1949 ff.), 6:606.

36. *Saarbrücker Zeitung*, no. 48, 26 February 1861.

37. See the appendix: Symphony in Three Movements and Two Quartets for Male Voices.

38. Friedrich Walter, *Briefe Vincenz Lachners an Hermann Levi* (Mannheim, 1931), letter from summer 1860.

39. Antonio Bazzini, born 11 March 1818 in Brescia, died 10 February 1897 in Milan, was a virtuoso violinist and composer. In 1873 he taught composition at Milan's conservatory, where he became director in 1892. He wrote an opera, *Turanda* (Milan, 1867). Giacomo Puccini was one of his students.

40. Friedrich Walter, *Briefe Vincenz Lachners an Hermann Levi* (Mannheim, 1931), letter dated 4 August 1861.

41. Friedrich Gernsheim, born 17 July 1839 in Worms, died 11 September 1916 in Berlin, studied piano and violin at the Leipzig Conservatory, became Director of Music in Saarbrücken in 1861, teacher for piano and composition at the Cologne Conservatory in 1865, Director of the German Opera in Rotterdam in 1874, teacher at the Stern Conservatory in Berlin in 1890, and in 1901 director of the master class for composition at the Academy of Arts in Berlin. He wrote chamber music and pieces for the orchestra, including four symphonies in a late romantic style. As the descendant of a distinguished Jewish family from Worms, and through his association with Brahms, Gernsheim had much contact with Levi.

42. *Saarbrücker Zeitung*, no. 234, 7 October 1861.

43. *Neue Zeitschrift für Musik* 25, no. 21 (15 November 1861): 185.

44. King James version of the Holy Bible, Psalms of David, 25.

45. Franz (František) Škroup, born 3 June 1801 in Osice (Bohemia), died 7 February 1862 in Rotterdam, came from a well-known Czech family of musicians. From 1827 to 1857, he was conductor of the Prague Opera; as of 1860 he conducted for the German Opera in Rotterdam. His opera *Drátenik* (The Wire Puller, Prague, 1826) is considered the first Czech national opera. Škroup's musical piece *Fidlovačka* (Prague, 1834) includes what was later to become the Czech national anthem.

46. On 20 October 1862, the newspaper *Rheinische Musikzeitung* wrote that Deetz's "soubrette parts are unsurpassable" and Ellinger, "the heroic tenor, has a beautiful voice with a middle range that no baritone would be ashamed of."

47. Reinhold Sietz, *Beiträge zu einer Biographie Ferdinand Hillers: Aus Ferdinand Hillers Briefwechsel* (Cologne, 1961), letter from Levi to Hiller dated 11 December 1862.

48. Conductor and composer Wendelin Weissheimer, born 26 February 1838 in Osthofen/Rhenish Hesse, died 10 June 1910 in Nuremberg, was a friend of both Wagner and Liszt as of 1858. He had become friends with Levi when they had both studied in Leipzig. See also Weissheimer's biography: Wendelin Weissheimer, *Erlebnisse mit Richard Wagner, Franz Liszt und vielen anderen Zeitgenossen* (Experiences with Richard Wagner, Franz Liszt, and Many Other Contemporaries) (Stuttgart/Leipzig, 1896).

49. Eduard Rappoldi, born 21 February 1839 in Vienna, died 16 May 1903 in Dresden, was a violinist with the Vienna Court Opera Orchestra from 1861 to 1866 and concertmaster in Rotterdam. He conducted for the operas of Lübeck, Stettin, and Prague. In 1871 he became instructor for violin at the Berlin College for Music and second violinist in the Joachim Quartet. In 1877 he became court conductor and professor for violin in Dresden.

50. Reinhold Sietz, *Beiträge zu einer Biographie Ferdinand Hillers: Aus Ferdinand Hillers Briefwechsel*, vol. 2 (Cologne, 1961), letter from Levi to Hiller dated 31 December 1863.

First Intermezzo

The Composer Hermann Levi

I imagined I'd amount to something and wrote piles of music.

—Hermann Levi to an unnamed pianist

In the mid-nineteenth century, when Hermann Levi began his career, it was customary for a conductor to also compose works of his own. Conductors before and after Levi in Karlsruhe—Franz Danzi, Joseph Strauss, Otto Dessoff, and even Felix Mottl—were all accomplished composers, as was his predecessor in Munich, Franz Lachner. Mastery of composition was considered an indispensable tool for a conductor. Conductor positions were often given to composers that convincingly presented works of their own. It was true of Felix Mottl, Richard Strauss, and Felix Weingartner. One waited to see in which of the two areas one would be more successful—at creating or reproducing music—and then made a career choice. Mottl and Weingartner were more inclined to conducting, while Richard Strauss limited his conducting to have more time to write music. Only Gustav Mahler tried with unparalleled focus to write music *and* stand out as a conductor.

When Hermann Levi took up his first post in Saarbrücken, he was unsure of whether he would become a composer or a conductor. He presented many of his own works at subscription concerts. But two years later, while still conductor at the opera in Rotterdam, he told Clara Schumann that the world would not be better off by his composing; and a year later he said that he had stopped composing altogether. This may have been prompted by talks with Johannes Brahms, once Brahms had become familiar with Levi's compositions. A remark in one of Levi's letters from November 1864 suggests that Brahms did know some of them: "Send me your symphony and next summer I will show you mine."[1] A few months later, Levi mentioned his symphony again, saying that he had reworked it. Apparently he was no longer satisfied with his own piece after—having seen Brahms's work—becoming aware of higher standards.

In the winter of 1865–1866, when Brahms lived in Karlsruhe for several months working on *Ein Deutsches Requiem* (A German Requiem), the two talked one afternoon about Levi's compositions. As usual, Brahms's critique was astute. In his next letter, Levi recalls their discussion:

> I am grateful for every bitter word you said that afternoon; they humble me; those few feathers that my old wings left on my back and that I thought would allow me to rise a few feet off the ground, I have now plucked out entirely and am as naked as a church mouse.[2]

To which Brahms replied: "Let your wings grow again. There are seven mansions in heaven, but yours will not be that of the composer."[3]

The well-meant word was disheartening. Correspondence between Levi and Brahms stopped for almost two years. While Levi himself had decided to stop composing, he had perhaps still hoped for a bit of encouragement from Brahms. The very lack of it provoked him to try his hand at composing once more. And thus, to surprise Clara Schumann on her birthday on 13 September 1868, he put

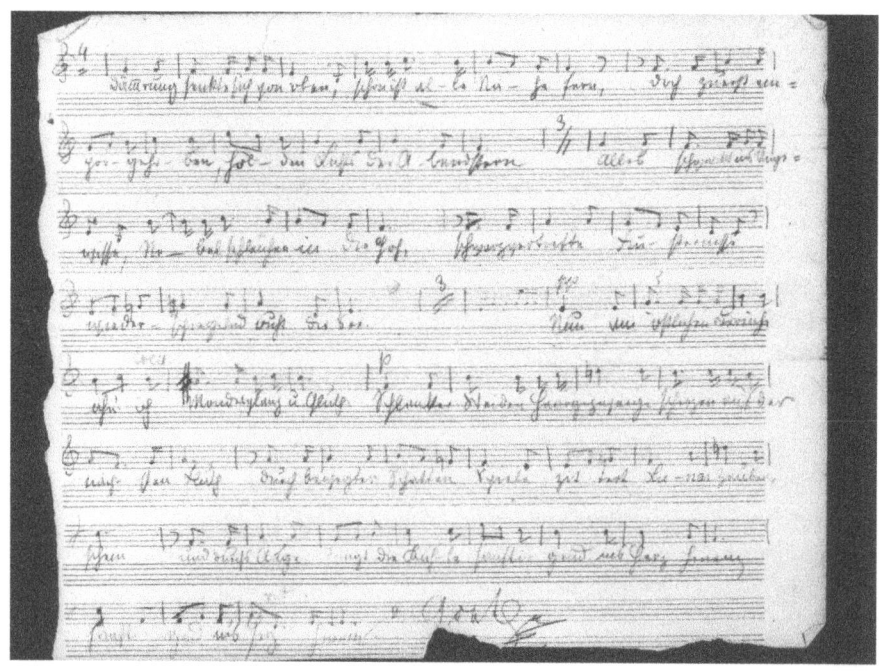

Hermann Levi's notes to the song Dämmrung senkte sich von oben. *Brahms silently slipped it into his pocket. Morgan Library and Museum, New York.*

notes to Goethe's poem *Dämmrung senkte sich von oben* (Twilight Settled from Above). This piece is the best surviving composition by Hermann Levi. It is worth noting how it came to be.

Levi wrote this piece of music in the first half of the year 1868. At the time he was preoccupied with how Brahms wrote music for poems and even owned some of Brahms's unpublished manuscripts, including *Von ewiger Liebe* (On Eternal Love), *Mainacht* (May Night), and *Herbstgefühl* (Autumn Feeling). Levi could not resist the temptation to write music for a song himself; he wanted to prove his own creative skill when compared to Brahms. He found a text by Goethe that he considered "already music in itself." Brahms heard that Levi had again tried to compose something and asked Allgeyer to give him the details. But Levi addressed Brahms directly, belittling his own short piece as a mere birthday gift that one need not take seriously, and suggested that Brahms, too, write music for the same poem.

Max Kalbeck, going by Levi's own description of events, tells us how Brahms familiarized himself with Levi's piece and then wrote his own music to the poem.[4] In 1869, namely, at a soirée hosted by the Von Poetz family in Karlsruhe, Brahms inquired as to what music Levi had written for the text. Levi sat down and wrote—by memory—the vocal part of his short composition. Johanna Schwarz, a singer performing that evening, sight-read and sang the song to Levi's accompaniment at the piano. Afterward, Brahms casually put the slip of paper in his pocket. Three days later he returned it to Levi with his own music suggestion for the same poem, noting in the margin of the manuscript: "An attempt to translate the attached palimpsest."[5]

Guided somewhat by Levi's arrangement, Brahms had written his own music for the piece but made no effort to look up Goethe's original text, thereby carrying over a mistake that Levi had made when writing it down from memory. Levi had written "through the eye, coolness penetrates and quiets the heart" (Goethe: "coolness steals into and quiets the heart"). Brahms did not catch the error until the piece went to the printer. As if nodding to a friend, in the vocal part Brahms used precisely the melody that Levi had given to the words "now in the eastern region." Notably, when Levi later re-edited his own composition, he altered the notes of just those measures, perhaps to prevent anyone from thinking that *he* had copied *Brahms*.

Levi's composition is the superior of the two. While Brahms's melody is more creative and his rhythmic structure richer, Levi more convincingly matched the atmospheric intention of the poem. An ostinato of sixteenth notes mirrors the mood of "Luna's magical glow shivers through quivering shadows."

Levi's sketch of the vocal part that Brahms simply took home has survived. Thus we can compare the first version from 1868 with a version printed thirty years later in a set of three songs based on poems by Goethe that Levi dedicated to his wife. The late version strays considerably from the original: Levi eliminated

First edition of Levi's piano concerto, op. 1, 1861, title page. Dedicated to Vincenz Lachner. Staatsbibliothek zu Berlin—Preußischer Kulturbesitz, Musikabteilung, sign. DMS 23 304.

the part that Brahms had adopted. And additional chromatic passages that fade into remote keys hint at influence by Wagner.

The lied from 1868 demonstrates the direction Hermann Levi might have taken as a composer, had not his confidence in his own creativity been shaken by Brahms's overwhelming genius. Faced with Brahms's keen judgment, in his own eyes Levi's pieces could not make the mark. He was more tolerant, however, of work by other music writers. He performed works by Hiller, the Lachner brothers, and Gernsheim, but deeply revered Berlioz, Wagner, and Bruckner.

Levi had expected his opus 1, the piano concerto, to set him on a path to success. In 1860 Vincenz Lachner had conducted the premiere performance of the concerto in Mannheim and encouraged him: "Get out onto the sea in public view as fast as you can! There are few concertos like yours floating around in the contemporary world of music."[6] The piece is characterized by the traditional style of the Leipzig School, modeled after Mendelssohn and Schumann. Levi's treatment of the concerto form is remarkable; he worked the themes in counterpoint, weaving the piano passages tightly with those of the orchestra instruments. The solo part is sophisticated, allowing a virtuoso pianist to shine with striking runs, arpeggios, and moves up and down the octaves. The first movement is the most important. It contains particularly dramatic symphonic moments in the interplay between the piano and the orchestra. The middle section of the slow movement is emotional; its sharp, rhythmic series of chords would seem to be influenced by Brahms, but we know with certainty that at the time Levi could not possibly have been familiar with Brahms's first piano concerto. (When Brahms presented his concerto in Leipzig, Levi was writing his concerto in Paris.) The idea for the closing movement is the weakest, dominated by mere pianist virtuosity.

In Mannheim Levi's solo debut playing his own piano concerto had been splendid. But the poor response at Leipzig's Gewandhaus was disappointing. His former composition instructor Julius Rietz wrote:

> The piece proves that my belief in your proficiency *was not misguided* but while your concerto is overall honest, able, and sound, the pure pleasure of it is spoiled by a few places where old Adam got his way. Continue to work, but remain very self-critical.[7]

Levi remained self-critical for the rest of his life. Many years later he wrote to a young pianist wanting to perform his piano concerto for him: "Dear Miss, . . . play me Bach's fugues or Beethoven's sonatas, but don't perform any concerto by Levi."[8]

More important than Levi's piano concerto are the six songs that he soon thereafter published as opus 2. They were based on texts by Böttger, Immermann, Heine, Eichendorff, and Chamisso and demonstrate Levi's profound grasp of romantic poetry. As with the Goethe poem mentioned above, Levi's extreme empathy for poetic texts enabled him to give them remarkable musical

Wanderers Nachtlied, *based on a poem by Goethe, composed by Hermann Levi prior to 1868, published by Otto Halbreiter, Munich, and dedicated to "Mary." Bayerische Staatsbibliothek, Musikabteilung, shelfmark 4 Mus. Pr 2587.*

designs. Each of the lieder has its own, very specific piano movement. Here we find free musical ideas; the composer has liberated himself from his role models. Lied no. 6, *Letzter Gruß* (The Last Farewell) is based on a text by Heinrich Heine. It reflects the romantic mood well and was once very popular and published a number of times. Levi himself often included it in his programs.

Now lost pieces were mostly vocals, but there was also some chamber music, a violin sonata that Levi often performed with Naret-Koning, and the symphony he had written during his studies in Leipzig. Had Levi then known the works of contemporaneous composers Rheinberger, Ries, and Volkmann, he would not have quit composing so soon.

It was Brahms who made Levi question his own inspiration, but the encounter with the intolerant Wagner confirmed his doubt altogether. He had read Wagner's prose "Judaism in Music" carefully and it was grist to the mill of his self-criticism. He did not want to be counted among the composers that Wagner claimed lacked personal creative productivity because they were Jewish.

With friends Levi often spoke of his deliberate decision to abstain from composing. In a letter to an unnamed pianist, he described his "auto-da-fé":

> The moment came suddenly when I looked at my immortal works through the eyes of a serene critic and realized that for me it would be better to open a shop for imports from the colonies than to write music. I drew a thick line and held my own auto-da-fé, letting songs and quartets and symphonies go up in idle smoke, wiped a tear from my eye and swore to forever spare the world of my creations.[9]

Between 1868 and 1870 Levi destroyed all of his scores. What survived were the three pieces already published, his piano concerto opus 1, the six songs that make up opus 2, and a few album pages. In 1899 he published music to *Three Poems by Goethe* that he had either kept all the while, or composed at a later time.

When, a year before he died, Levi scrapped his oath and dug up these three compositions, re-edited them, and had them published, they were not really meant for the general public but as a gesture of gratitude to his wife Mary, who, during the last years of his life, had been a great comfort to him. It was also a bow to Johann Wolfgang von Goethe, who had meant much to him throughout his life.

Was Hermann Levi a composer? He had the courage and insight to abstain from composing and put his entire creative talent into reproducing the works of others—ultimately enabling the creation of an impressive life's work. His editions and translations were fair accomplishments; his productions set standards for future performances.

NOTES

1. Brahms's correspondence in 16 volumes, *Johannes Brahms's Briefwechsel*, reprint Tutzing, 1974, vol. 7, letter dated 9 November 1864.

2. Ibid., letter dated 6 May 1866.
3. Ibid., letter from May 1866.
4. On 30 September 1899, Max Kalbeck wrote to Levi: "Thank you for all the manuscripts. You are such a good person" (Leviana).
5. Levi's sheet of music and Brahms's autograph of the lied can be found in the Pierpont Morgan Library in New York.
6. Friedrich Walter, *Briefe Vincenz Lachners an Hermann Levi* (Mannheim, 1931), letter from Lachner to Levi dated summer 1860.
7. Bayerische Staatsbibliothek, Manuscripts, Leviana; letter dated 21 April 1860.
8. Stadts- und Universitätsbibliothek Frankfurt/Main; letter dated 13 August 1871. Conductor Martin Wettges discovered the orchestra material for Hermann Levi's piano concerto, op. 1, in the library of the University of Zurich. He reconstructed the full score and on 1 June 2008 performed it for the first time, featuring pianist Katharina Khodos and the symphony orchestra of the German National Academic Foundation (Studienstiftung des deutschen Volkes).
9. Stadts- und Universitätsbibliothek Frankfurt/Main; letter dated 13 August 1871.

Chapter Two

Karlsruhe and Brahms

CHIEF CONDUCTOR AT
THE COURT THEATER IN KARLSRUHE

Censeo autem: Off to Karlsruhe!

—Vincenz Lachner to Hermann Levi

In the year 1860 the one-hundred-and-fifty-year-old city of Karlsruhe counted almost 27,000 inhabitants. Within its city gates, two- and three-story residential homes nestled around the grand ducal palace. Next to the formidable palace in a spacious park stood the new court theater, built in 1852 by Heinrich Hübsch. Court administration offices and dwellings for court officials lined a half-circle lane between the palace and the markets. Streets rayed outward from the palace like a fan, in all directions. To the south they led to the residential areas of the citizenry, to the north they led through the palace park to the ducal hunting grounds in the vast nearby Hardt Forest. The center spoke of the city's layout, intended by its master-builder Weinbrenner to be a *via triumphalis*, led to the market square and the tomb of city founder Margrave Karl Wilhelm, and then on toward Ettlingen Gate. From east to west, the city's main street cut straight through the market square and because it was long, it was simply called *Lange Strasse*. After the founding of the German empire it was renamed *Kaiser Strasse*. This street ran from Durlach Gate in the east to Mühlburg Gate in the west. From there it continued on down to the old settlement of Mühlburg and the lowlands along the Rhine River.

The city's well-proportioned symmetrical layout reflected the neat and orderly circumstances of this capitol of the grand duchy of Baden. People enjoyed living in this residence town built in the middle of the woods just a few generations

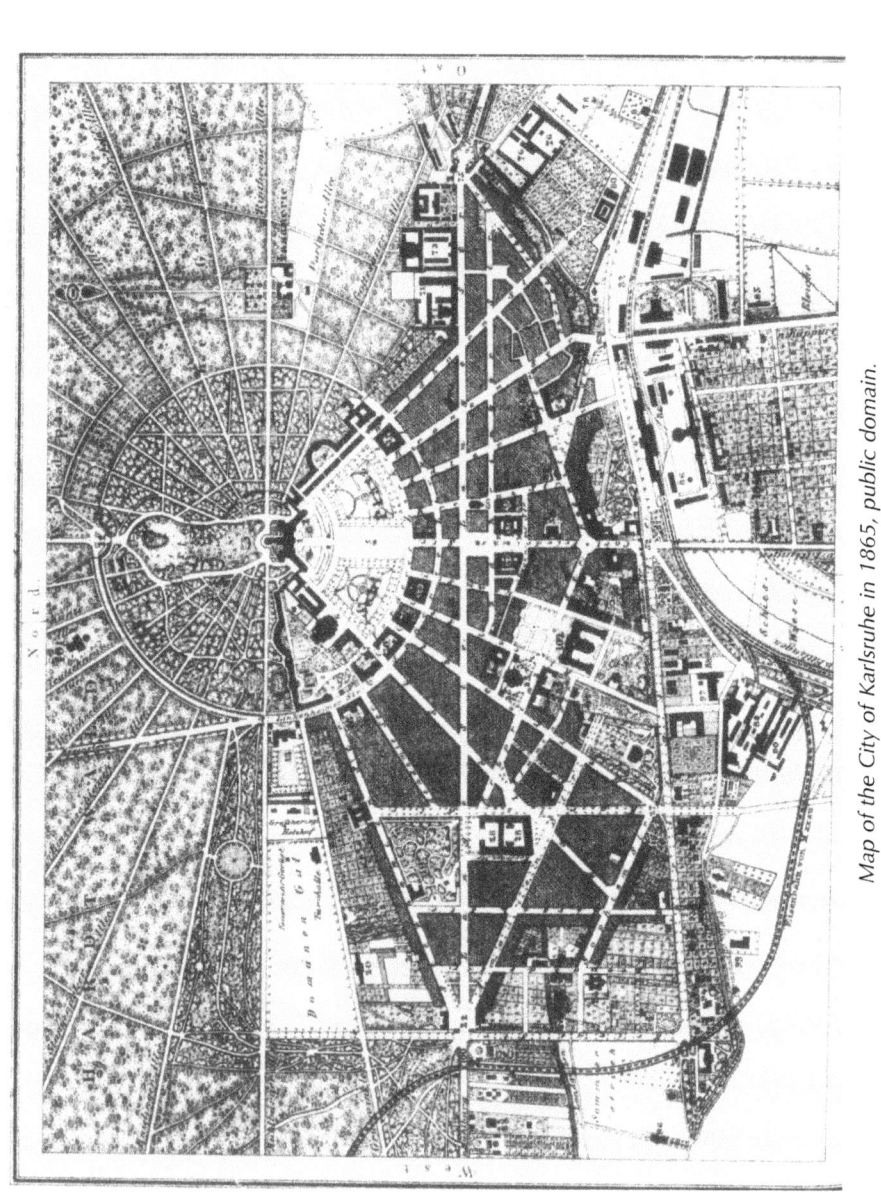

Map of the City of Karlsruhe in 1865, public domain.

earlier. In 1839 Karl Gutzkow described Karlsruhe as "friendly, bright, and spacious" and "where neighbors close ranks." In fact, active residents had founded all sorts of societies. The Philharmonic Society organized grand choir and orchestra concerts. The town had an instrument club for musical amateurs and six different glee clubs. Literati held reading meetings at the Museum Association, where Ivan Turgenev turned up from Baden-Baden from time to time. Artists and patrons had founded a fraternity of the arts, supervised by gallery director Carl Friedrich Lessing. A club called *Eintracht* (Concord) catered to general interest in the arts, organizing lecture evenings and chamber music concerts.

But the town's main artistic and social attraction was the Grand Ducal Court Theater. Since the new building had opened in May 1853, operations were managed by Eduard Devrient. In a stroke of luck for Karlsruhe's stage, upon taking office one of the first official acts of young Prince Regent Friedrich I was to summon this esteemed actor and influential director to Karlsruhe.

Eduard Devrient came from a widely branched family of people in the theater. His uncle Ludwig was a celebrated actor at Berlin's Royal Theater and had played Lear, Shylock, and Falstaff. Eduard's brothers were also well-known actors on other German stages; most famous was Emil, indisputably the star at Dresden's court. The oldest brother, Karl, also acted there. He was married to soprano Wilhelmine Schröder-Devrient, whom Richard Wagner adored. The

Baden's Grand Ducal Court Theater. Badisches Generallandesarchiv Karlsruhe, sign. J-B Karlsruhe no. 163.

Eduard Devrient, theater director in Karlsruhe. Stadtarchiv Karlsruhe, sign. 8/PBS III 1963.

middle of the three brothers, Eduard, who became Karlsruhe's theater director, as a young man had a pleasant baritone voice. At the age of nineteen, he debuted in *Don Giovanni*, singing the role of Masetto at the Opera House in Berlin. He stayed there for a decade, successfully performing *Don Giovanni* and *Faust* (Spohr's opera of the same name). Together with Carl Friedrich Zelter, his closest boyhood friend and fellow pupil under Felix Mendelssohn, Eduard Devrient organized the first reproduction of Bach's *Passion of Matthew*, singing the part of Jesus under the direction of Mendelssohn on 11 March 1829. It was a remarkable evening for Berlin's Sing-Academy. Eduard's singing career ended abruptly when four years later he took on the leading role in Heinrich Marschner's opera *Der Templer und die Jüdin* (The Templar and the Jewish

Woman), for which he had written the libretto himself. To rescue the performance, he sang despite illness and ruined his singing voice. He turned to acting and soon played heroes and character parts in German drama. And he began to write. In a series called "Letters from Paris," he launched trendsetting ideas for establishing theatrical schools that would systematically train young actors. In 1844 the king of Saxony made him the head theater director for Dresden, where he also acted. While there, he wrote his most important publication, *Geschichte der deutschen Schauspielkunst* (History of German Acting). When the first volumes became available, the ducal court in Baden took note of him.

Eduard Devrient was a theater expert. He had sung, acted, and directed, knew a repertoire of opera and plays, and from his own experience at large theaters had intimate knowledge of the challenges that plague stage artists. A picture of him shortly before taking up his work at Baden's court theater shows him as a resilient, youthful, beardless man, although he was fifty years old. His poise speaks of ceaseless, respect-commanding vitality, yet his clear eyes look kind.

Devrient gathered an excellent company of performers in Karlsruhe that for two decades heaved a huge repertoire in every category. He systematically built up a set of classical plays. After ten years his group could perform twenty different pieces by Shakespeare in one single season and the next year present a cycle of twenty-one Lessing, Schiller, and Goethe dramas. For the opera he preferred Gluck and Mozart; he translated their works himself and published new editions. His versions became style models for modernizing Mozart presentation at the turn of the twentieth century. He replaced the secco recitatives in *Così fan tutte* and *Le nozze di Figaro* with a string quartet, but this may have been catering to the taste of the times, or simply reflect the fact that he had no equally qualified music adviser at his side.

The ducal court's orchestra was conducted by Joseph Strauss. In 1824 he had been called to Karlsruhe as concertmaster and a year later he became the orchestra's conductor. He came from Vienna and had studied composition under Ignaz Seyfried, one of Mozart's pupils. As a violinist he had participated in premieres of Beethoven symphonies conducted by the composer himself. Joseph Strauss was an accomplished and spirited conductor, praised even by Richard Wagner.[1] With sound skill he wrote chamber music, concerts, play music, and operas for the stage in Karlsruhe. He tackled his many different theater obligations until he turned seventy. When word of his approaching retirement reached Mannheim, Vincenz Lachner contacted Karlsruhe to recommend Hermann Levi for the position.

In a letter to Levi in Rotterdam dated 29 April 1863,[2] Vincenz Lachner described the pleasant side of working in Baden's ducal town:

The advantages of Karlsruhe:
   1. Well-ordered, reliable conditions. The fact that much in the opera needs reforming will be conducive to your success.

2. The director there is more capable and knows and understands more about the stage than any other in Germany.

3. Our best theatrical institutions are the court theaters. . . . It is a great advantage to work at a court that makes no distinction between Christians and Jews. . . . The grand duchess loves to make music, although her taste is a bit Wagnerian. I doubt whether the grand duke really loves music, but he does pursue it and shows interest in it to an extent that leaves nothing to be desired. It's a good sign that he does not hinder Devrient in rigorously refusing to do bad Italian opera.

4. The connection between the theater in Karlsruhe and the town of Baden-Baden will benefit you in many ways. . . . First-class artists visit Baden-Baden during the summer months and being a place where people from all over the world meet, the town is like a trumpet that broadcasts all the events to the most remote corners of the earth. . . . You shouldn't stay in Karlsruhe forever. You must want to move on to Berlin, Vienna, Munich, Dresden, Hanover. . . . I'd say, work there for five years at the most. But not less than three! At any rate, you must return to Germany as soon as possible.

In another letter he says: "Karlsruhe is one of the few places where they make no difference between Christian and Jew."[3]

In fact, the grand duchy of Baden was progressive and liberal. In 1809 it had issued a "Jewish Edict" abolishing practices that restricted Jews in education and choice of occupation. On 4 October 1862, Grand Duke Friedrich I made Jews equal citizens, emancipating the 24,000 Jews in Baden ten years before it was done in any other German principality.

As a young prince, in May 1849 Grand Duke Friedrich I, who reigned as of 1852, had witnessed mutiny by Baden's regiments and had been forced to flee by night with the entire ducal family. Soon after the rebellion was crushed and the ducal family returned to its residence, the prince assumed the regency. His first directives were guided by a spirit of reconciliation and a desire for peace.

Friedrich I's reign was marked by tolerance and charity. The grand duke firmly believed that the arts significantly shape the moral attitudes of people. He asked painter Johann Ludwig Schirmer to found an art academy in Karlsruhe. He appointed Eduard Devrient and gave him the budget and authority to make Karlsruhe's court theater one of Germany's best stages. Devrient and the sovereign made the theater prosper after 1854. And in appointing Hermann Levi, they were of one accord.

In July 1863 Hermann Levi took a vacation trip to Giessen and Baden-Baden, stopping in Karlsruhe to meet theater director Devrient for the first time. They quickly agreed on main points and by the end of the year Levi got a contract offer from Karlsruhe. He hesitated to sign it, though, because he thought that his status with respect to the current conductor, Wilhelm Kalliwoda,[4] seemed somewhat obscure.

Wilhelm Kalliwoda, who had already been Karlsruhe's music director[5] for a decade, naturally hoped he would get the first position when conductor Strauss

Wilhelm Kalliwoda (1827–1893), conductor at Karlsruhe's court theater. Photograph by Albert Obermüller, around 1865. Courtesy of Frithjof Haas.

retired. He was apparently unaware that for some time Devrient had been dissatisfied with his work. Devrient complained of Kalliwoda's "inability to conduct an orchestra that dodders and scrapes along."[6] Kalliwoda, who in Leipzig had enjoyed instruction under Mendelssohn, was certainly a sensitive and intelligent musician. He was a skillful pianist, but he lacked the assertiveness required for conducting opera.

Not knowing Devrient's opinion of Kalliwoda, Levi was reluctant to sign a contract that formally put him on equal standing with the latter. He consulted Ferdinand Hiller in Cologne. Hiller, who had recommended Levi for the post in

Karlsruhe, dispelled his worries. And in late 1863, Levi announced his decision. To his "esteemed maestro" Ferdinand Hiller, he wrote: "Since I am certain that Kalliwoda will by no means be given the position of chief conductor, I hope within a year to overcome the obstacles (name, religion, youth, [lack of] nobility) still in my way."[7] In January 1864 Eduard Devrient informed the administration for the ducal court theater:

> Since in Germany at the present no conductor of great acclaim is available, circumstances at the Grand Ducal Court Theater suggest that we appoint a talented young musician, putting him temporarily on equal standing with Music Director Kalliwoda, and that we wait to see whether circumstances allow the one or the other to qualify for the higher position. From the many competent musicians considered for the post, Hermann Levi's strong recommendations and personal acquaintances make him appear to be the best candidate.[8]

Levi's contract made him a music director for one trial year for an annual salary of 1400 guldens. After nine months he was to be informed of whether he qualified for the position of the first conductor.

On 1 August 1864, twenty-four-year-old Hermann Levi moved into his first apartment in Karlsruhe at 48 *Herren Strasse*. From the railway station it was a ten-minute walk to his apartment near Karl's Gate; from there it took another ten minutes to reach the court theater next to the palace.

The Grand Ducal Palace in Karlsruhe in the mid-nineteenth century. Generallandesarchiv Karlsruhe, sign. J-B Karlsruhe no. 99.

The first of August also ended the theater's off-season and rehearsals for plays and operas began. That morning, Devrient held the first conference on repertoire. There was much to discuss, perhaps because it was the first time that both music directors, Kalliwoda and Levi, sat in one room. Deciding who would conduct which operas immediately sparked rivalry for *Fidelio*. The two directors were also told that they would take turns at monthly stints of administration work. Members of the court orchestra were informed by bulletin.

Levi presented himself to his audience in Karlsruhe for the first time with a production of *Lohengrin*.[9] Since the piece had been part of the theater's annual repertoire since 1856, he was given only five days to rehearse it. Dress rehearsal was the evening before the performance. Devrient noted in his diary that he found the orchestra setup confusing. He thought that Levi had handled the rehearsal well, but had stopped too often to correct players. Levi's strict insistence on correct musical performance was not customary for opera productions at the time.

Devrient and Kalliwoda sat in the loge for the premiere on August 7. The director found Levi's management of the orchestra "confident, free, energetic, and refined." An unknown gentleman expressed his pleasure at the performance by sending the director a diamond ring. Devrient returned it, saying that such a gift befits only a long relationship: the gentleman should first attend many operas and wait before expressing his appreciation. He, the theater's director, had only done his duty.

During Levi's first season with the theater in Karlsruhe, the company's repertoire included forty different operas. Most of these works had been performed in the same way for years. Every season the group worked on eight new operas and prepared around thirty other musical performances with little rehearsal. The court orchestra also provided music for the theater's plays; they played Beethoven for Goethe's play *Egmont*, Mendelssohn for Shakespeare's *A Midsummer Night's Dream*, and Weber for Pius Alexander Wolff's play *Preziosa*. For Shakespeare's *Tragedy of Coriolanus* they first played Beethoven's *Overture* and then music by Kalliwoda.

The large operas and six subscription concerts that took place between November and March in the hall of the Museum Society involved all forty-eight musicians of the court orchestra.[10] Wednesdays were reserved for performing plays and operas in Baden-Baden; once a week the entire troupe took a first-class chartered train to Baden-Baden, getting off—instruments, props, and all—right in the middle of town.

The enormous amount of work involved in the organization and production of all these events was managed by a surprisingly small number of people. The superintendent had only one clerk for finances, one librarian, one secretary, and one cashier. The workshop employed three painters, three lighting technicians, one machinist, a prop manager, eight people for costumes and cloakrooms, two hairdressers, one person in charge of boots, and one responsible for weapons. They had one concierge, one attendant, two ushers, and two people that handed out programs. The drama section had seven actresses and thirteen actors, three of which (one woman and two men) also sang in the opera. Not to forget the prompter. The choir consisted of twenty-two men and twenty-five women, some of whom also acted in the plays. Besides the ballet master, the ballet had one male and one female solo dancer and a group of eleven female dancers and one male dancer. The pianist for the ballet also played the viola in the orchestra.[11]

Altogether, a total of about 175 people ran theater operations on stage, behind stage, and in the administration. One hundred years later it took three times as many for a similarly situated theater to present such a sophisticated repertoire.

FRIENDSHIP WITH JOHANNES BRAHMS

My friends are the best part of me.

—Hermann Levi to Clara Schumann

In August, Kalliwoda directed the theater. That gave Hermann Levi time to settle and make friends.

The first guest to come and stay with Levi at 48 *Herren Strasse* was Johannes Brahms. Brahms had come from his summer residence in Lichtental near Baden-Baden to attend events in Karlsruhe organized by the German Association of Composers. After Hans von Bülow had turned down an offer to conduct it, for the Association's conference musicians from Stuttgart (Württemberg's court orchestra) were added to Karlsruhe's (i.e., Baden's) court orchestra and then conducted by court conductor Max Seifriz from Hohenzollern-Hechingen. Franz Liszt brought his daughter Cosima von Bülow along, who at the time was two months pregnant with Isolde, her first child by Richard Wagner. Brahms and Liszt had known one another since 1853, when Brahms had played his early piano compositions for Liszt at the Altenburg in Weimar. And yet it is unlikely that in 1864 in Karlsruhe Brahms and Levi spent time with Franz Liszt and Cosima. Neither Brahms nor Levi appreciated Liszt's work. And Levi had no way of knowing what Cosima would one day come to mean to him.

It is easily imaginable that Brahms and Levi even scoffed at the events of the German Association of Composers. Brahms wrote to Joseph Joachim:

> The worst rascals didn't even attend and there weren't enough others even for tam-tams. . . . It gave me a horrible headache. Except for a few quiet musicians that would have liked to have laughed or booed, most of the audience enjoyed the performances and for four long days kept calling the performers back on stage and demanding encores.[12]

Devrient, too, was appalled by the claque for members of the Association: "Together with Liszt," he said, "they raise furor and lavish applause on works from his school, the worst scraps of what could possibly be called music."[13]

During his years spent in Karlsruhe, Levi's personal friendship with Brahms shaped his musical bearings. This was Levi's first close encounter with a musical genius that he admired unconditionally and to whom he was truly devoted.

Levi had first met Brahms in the summer of 1862, when on his way to Rotterdam he visited the composer in Hamm near Hamburg.[14] One summer later he met Brahms again at Clara Schumann's home in Baden-Baden. When he left for vacation on the Dutch coast, Levi had Brahms's complete published works sent to him from Frankfurt, and to the horror of the other vacationers and the guest in the next room (conductor Louis Schindelmeisser from Darmstadt),[15] he played Brahms's music for two hours every morning, learning the *Handel Variations* by heart.

This intense preoccupation with Brahms coincided with Levi's fledgling years as a young conductor. He had devoted himself to conducting after realizing that the world had nothing to gain from his composing.[16] But now he found his daily chores at the theater dull. The novelties in opera, he felt, were no better than his own work that he had discarded. Brahms was a revelation. Brahms, Levi soon realized, was able to do what he could not: to continue the tradition of Beethoven and Schumann while finding his own way to express himself. By devoting himself to this young genius, Levi realized that he was not called to write music, but to serve the cause of reproducing the works of others.

It was not only fascinating to experience Brahms as a composer; Levi was equally struck by Brahms's personality. Brahms taught him "what it means to be a true artist *and* a human being."[17] The revered composer came and stayed in the conductor's modest apartment in Karlsruhe and became his trusted friend. Suddenly Levi had someone with whom he could discuss all the things that moved him, and someone that in turn told him of all his plans. They spent August days together from dawn to dark, making music and attending concerts, taking long walks through the woods and exchanging thoughts. Brahms wrote to Joachim: "Despite all the conducting routine, this young man is so refreshing; he sees such beautiful acmes with such bright eyes, he makes everything a joy."[18]

How strong were Brahms's feelings for Hermann Levi? Brahms was Levi's senior by six years and at the age of thirty a confident, mature person. He already had an impressive reputation at composing and a wide circle of loyal followers and friends including the Schumanns, Joseph Joachim, Albert Dietrich, Otto Julius Grimm, and Theodor Kirchner. In every large city friends invited him to stay at their own homes when he performed there. And he corresponded with all of these dear friends.

And yet friendship with Hermann Levi gave Brahms something that he had hardly known before. This gifted and intelligent conductor put his artistic effort

Johannes Brahms. Courtesy of Frithjof Haas.

wholeheartedly at the service of the composer. Levi studied Brahms's works with care and empathy, rendering them with a musician's knowledge of skilled composition. Whether listening to Brahms's works, playing them on the piano, copying scores, or rehearsing and directing pieces, Levi identified entirely with the music.

Brahms never wore his heart on his sleeve and kept his deepest feelings to himself. He never clearly said what he thought of Levi. All the more startling, then, are the few sentimental greetings sent to Karlsruhe from Vienna: "Oh when will I see you flour sacks, you white pants, you woods and hills again!"[19]

Brahms hid his true feelings behind playful remarks and mischief, by inquiring, for instance, how Levi was coming along at entertaining Miss Elise

(Schumann) or whether he was looking for a Mrs. Kapellmeister. He sometimes even wrote humorous verse:

Den trefflichsten Balmung	He swang
Bei jeder Aufführung	Siegfried's surest sword*
Er schwung,	at every concert;
Und, ob zwar noch blutjung,	and though still very young
Doch fung	did fetch himself
Die schöne "gesicherte Stellung."	a fair, "secure position."
Um keine Bemerkung	For no comment (in the world)
Ich tunk	would I dip my pen
In schwärzliche Rundung!	in ink!
Sie wär' ihm 'ne Kränkung.[20]	He'd resent it.

* The conductor's baton, which at the time was rather large and heavy.

The friendship in Karlsruhe was actually a threesome. The third party was graphic artist Julius Allgeyer, whom Brahms had met among artists in 1854 in Dusseldorf and with whom he had corresponded ever since. Allgeyer was again four years Brahms's senior and of a frank nature typical for people from the Black Forest: a friend of solitude, but trusting and kind. After training with Joseph Keller, a professor for copper etching in Dusseldorf, Allgeyer went to Rome on a stipend and for four years lived next door to classicist painter Anselm Feuerbach. This pivotal encounter made him a glowing admirer of Feuerbach's work for the rest of his life. After Feuerbach's death, Allgeyer wrote the painter's biography. In 1860 Allgeyer returned from Italy and entered his father's business in lithographs. Meanwhile, however, the demand for lithographic copies of oil paintings by either old or new masters had dwindled. Allgeyer quickly switched to photography and soon became a well-known portrait photographer. His portraits of Brahms, Clara Schumann, Levi, and Feuerbach show artistic talent.

Allgeyer was an ideal friend for the other two men. He was generous, committed, and always open minded about their music activities. His serene and soothing manner reconciled differences. Levi said he was "a sweet old chap, true gold; an evening with him [was] like taking a bath."[21]

Allgeyer remained loyal to both Brahms and Levi for his entire life, even after the two others went their separate ways. When Levi died, Allgeyer said that "every bit of him was real love and kindness."[22]

The three friends adored Clara Schumann. When Brahms stayed in Baden-Baden, they met at her home. And Clara often visited them in Karlsruhe, where her oldest son, Ludwig, was in school, lodging with the family of Karl Will, the court orchestra's concertmaster. Levi and Allgeyer looked after the boy. When Levi had time after orchestra rehearsal, he picked Ludwig up from school.

Julius Allgeyer, portrait by Anselm Feuerbach. Bayerische Gemäldesammlungen, Munich, inv. no. 9496.

Together the friends tried to steer the vulnerable, sensitive boy toward a useful career. Elise, Schumann's second-oldest daughter, also came to Karlsruhe once a week to look after her brother. She was twenty-one and when people saw her often with Levi, rumor spread that they might soon be engaged. Levi liked Elise, but at the time he was much too involved in music to consider a commitment.

Brahms stayed at his summer residence, boarding at Mrs. Becker's in Lichtental. The little house on the hillside, where he rented the two rooms of the upper floor, suited his needs. Behind the house, hidden paths led to the nearby woods. When Levi had time, he visited Brahms in Baden-Baden and the two hiked through the outskirts of the Black Forest. They met every Wednesday anyway when Levi and the entire company from Karlsruhe took the train to Baden-Baden to perform there. Then they sat together until late at night and Brahms walked with Levi to the station in Baden-Oos, where the conductor caught the 1 a.m. train back to Karlsruhe. Brahms then walked the six kilometers back to his rooms in Lichtental. On one of these long evenings, Brahms offered the younger of the two, Levi, the privilege of addressing him with the personal form, "Du." He did so in writing—a manner that was so very typical of Brahms. Max Kalbeck wrote that Levi told him:

> Once Brahms had a packet with him. I was curious because he would have to take it back with him, but neither would he discuss it, nor would he let me carry it. Just as the train moved out of the station he tossed it into my wagon. It contained his first three piano sonatas and on the title page of the first one he had written "in cordial friendship, Dein Johannes." (Until then we had always used the formal address "Sie.")[23]

During the second week of October, Brahms stayed with Levi for a few days in Karlsruhe before returning to Vienna. It gave him an opportunity to see the premiere of Weber's *Euryanthe* directed by Levi at the court theater on October 11.

During their many hours together in the late summer of 1864, they surely also spoke of Brahms's current project, the Quintet in F Minor, op. 34. In July Levi and Clara Schumann had played the version for two pianos in Baden-Baden. They both liked its brilliant combinations and wealth of musical ideas. And yet they all agreed that this second version of the original string quintet was not quite the right form for the piece. Levi suggested that Brahms rewrite it for one piano and four strings. Brahms found the advice so good that he gave Levi the autograph of the draft for the two-piano version.[24]

In early November Brahms sent the piano manuscript for the finished quintet to Karlsruhe and in nightlong sessions Levi and his assistant Paul David wrote the string parts. On Sunday, November 6, the revised opus was performed for the first time—in Levi's apartment. Clara Schumann, who had come to Karlsruhe to hear Levi's production of *Fidelio* on November 3, played the piano. Musicians from the court orchestra played the string parts. Reporting on this private little premiere, Levi wrote to Vienna: "I wish you could have seen our faces during this first rehearsal. Clara smiled and rocked the piano bench more than usual. Afterwards David, Allgeyer, and I went to [the tavern] Erbprinz and I got drunk on champagne."[25] Two days later concertmaster Koning rehearsed the quintet in Mannheim. Clara Schumann said these were "hours of bliss." Levi and Allgeyer went to see a rehearsal in Mannheim, which roused some Karlsruhe friends to joke that Levi had become Brahms's *commis-voyageur*.[26] The adventures with Brahms and Clara Schumann gilded Levi's first months in Karlsruhe that otherwise seemed bleak.

> If Karlsruhe weren't so close to Baden-Baden—not a dog would want to live like this. At the theater they just keep grinding the same old organ, leaping from the sublime to the silly, today Shakespeare, tomorrow Birch-Pfeiffer.[27]

Actually, Levi had no reason to complain about the court theater's program. The young conductor perhaps felt unchallenged, had extra time on his hands, and was impatient to propel his career. Devrient rehearsed his troupe for their round of Shakespeare plays, but tried also to offer less demanding people in his audience a bit of light entertainment.

Of all the operas performed then we do not know exactly which ones Levi conducted because it was uncommon to mention the conductor on the printed

Clara Schumann, around 1868, photograph by Julius Allgeyer. Stadtarchiv Überlingen.

program. We know for certain that in September Levi presented a new production of Gluck's *Iphigenia in Tauris*, and in November repeated a performance of *Fidelio*. Between these two pieces there were premieres and repeat performances of Gluck's *Armida*; Weber's *Freischütz, Euryanthe,* and *Oberon*; Marschner's *Der Templar und die Jüdin*; and Wagner's *Fliegender Holländer* and *Tannhäuser*. Levi perhaps thought little of other operas in the troupe's repertoire, like Flotow's *Martha* and *Alessandro Stradella*, Conradin Kreutzer's *Nachtlager von Granada*, and Boïeldieu's *La dame blanche*. But he would have been grateful that the repertoire also included Bellini's *Norma*, Rossini's *Wilhelm Tell*, and Meyerbeer's *Huguénots*.

Karlsruhe's concertgoers watched Levi and Kalliwoda vie for the top position. It was the first time they had two conductors with equal rights. Of course, conducting was then much less spectacular than it is today. At the opera the conductor was hardly visible, standing down in the orchestra pit; even printed concert programs rarely mentioned the conductor by name. Levi and Kalliwoda nevertheless cooperated. They split the conducting tasks equally among themselves, including the Museum Concerts[28] and musical events organized by the Philharmonic Society.

At the museum Levi conducted Beethoven's fifth and eighth symphonies and Schumann's *Manfred* music. Kalliwoda presented Mendelssohn's overture *Das Märchen von der schönen Melusina* (The Myth of Melusina) and Schubert's sixth symphony. At a concert organized by the Philharmonic Society, the two conductors together played Robert Schumann's *Andante* and *Variations*, op. 46, at two grand pianos and then—together with Karl Zahlberg (a court violinist very gifted at composing)—played Johann Sebastian Bach's Concert in C Major for three pianos. These social gatherings were followed by dinner and dance. Coffee was served at midnight, and afterward the good-humored music directors sat down at the pianos again to improvise and provide music for dancing.

Ida Lessing, wife of the gallery director, sang in the Philharmonic Choir. She attended all of these events, reporting them faithfully to her friend Ferdinand Hiller in Cologne: "This winter we're reeling with music. Karlsruhe's getting nicer all the time, like Dusseldorf used to be; the painters throw little parties and organize performances—shadow plays, circus riders, and tightrope acts."[29]

People spoke of the rivalry between Kalliwoda and Levi, hoping both would stay in Karlsruhe. Each had something to offer: Kalliwoda was sensitive, Levi was dynamic. The two did not shun public comparison—they even took turns conducting in one and the same concert. Together they rehearsed Bach's *Passion of Matthew* with the Philharmonic Choir; the theater director had asked each of them to direct one of the performances. In his first year, Levi refused because his idea of the piece differed considerably from Kalliwoda's.

Levi constantly urged theater director Devrient to finally promote him to the higher position of Grand Ducal Court Conductor. The two had meanwhile often worked together closely. While preparing Gluck's *Iphigenia in Tauris* and reproducing *Fidelio*, Devrient had convinced himself of Levi's artistic skills. He found Levi an excellent orchestra conductor, but lacking an understanding of the stage: "[It is] the [same] old struggle with him; he separates the music from the drama."[30] Devrient wanted to appoint Levi to the position of first conductor, but was afraid it might go to his head. He did not want a soaring autocratic "king of music" next to himself. Finally, after Levi threatened in 1865 to accept a position in Paris as director of a new conservatory for music there, Devrient found a diplomatic solution. He made both Levi and Kalliwoda chief conductors, letting them appear to remain equal. But he raised Levi's pay to an annual 2200 guldens, 400 more than his colleague got. He also gave Levi the first choice of which operas and museum concerts he wanted to conduct. Levi accepted the solution—in the end he had gotten what he wanted, as the future would show. Kalliwoda was also pleased with the new title and took the financial inequality in stride.

At the end of the first season, Levi tackled a new production of Rossini's *Il barbiere di Siviglia* (Barber of Seville). Together he and Otto Devrient, son of the court theater director, retranslated the piece into German, including original recitatives that until then had not been delivered on German stages. Famous prima donna Pauline Viardot-García was engaged to sing the virtuoso coloratura role of Rosine.[31] Pauline was married to Parisian theater director Louis Viardot and had lived in Baden-Baden since 1862. Her singing voice was past its prime but still a big attraction for Karlsruhe's operagoers. She brought the flair of the grand world of Paris to the provincial court stage, but being a moody diva, she also caused a few problems. She wanted star treatment and she refused to learn Levi's new recitatives. The theater director made it clear that she had to sing the new version, and only the new version, of the text. The premiere was successful and proved the worth of Levi's new arrangement: in its now more correct German translation, critics found that Rossini's masterful opera ranked among the highest in musical theater. Until then, the widespread dialogue version had reduced it to burlesque.

With new enthusiasm, in August 1865 Levi delved into a second playing season in Karlsruhe. Now as an officially appointed First Ducal Court Conductor, he pledged to Grand Duke Friedrich, and therewith to the entire grand duchy, to be loyal, trustworthy, and prepared. After listening to the long text that ended with "so help me God and His Holy Word," Levi signed the oath, but not without first putting the last four words in parentheses. As a Jew he could not be sworn into office on the New Testament.[32]

Under Levi's musical direction, Gluck's opera *Alceste* was put on the agenda once more and performed on August 23 in Baden-Baden. Clara Schumann, Brahms, and Joseph Joachim and his wife sat in the audience. Brahms, who was now spending the summer in Lichtental, had already seen the performance once in Karlsruhe on May 27. He had plans for composing an opera of his own and now showed increased interest in the court theater's productions. During the summer Brahms probably also saw Bellini's *Sonambula*, Halévy's *La Juive* (The Jewess), and the new production of Ferdinand Hiller's *Der Deserteur* (The Deserter). Hiller, who thought of himself as Levi's protector, came to Karlsruhe for the final rehearsals and met many old friends there like Brahms, Schroedter,[33] and Devrient. The latter found Hiller's new opera music "lacking innovation," but was happy to welcome the composer and reminisce of times with their friend from youth, Felix Mendelssohn.

In the late summer of 1865, Brahms and Levi met more often. Their relationship became deeply sincere and emotionally charged. On Clara's forty-sixth birthday, when the entire Schumann family gathered to celebrate at her house in Lichtental, Levi turned up unexpectedly with a bottle of champagne. Parties in these circles were musical and jovial. Levi played *On the Beautiful Blue Danube* as if the piano were poorly tuned by playing the right hand half a note lower than the left. Later he hid in a closet and when Brahms passed by he sang out from behind the coats "O Freunde, nicht diese Töne!"[34]

On 19 December 1865, Levi directed a "Grand Concert" in Baden-Baden given by the court orchestra. Clara Schumann played her late husband's piano concerto. Pauline Viardot-García sang an aria from Mozart's *Titus* and songs by Schubert and Schumann. Levi began the program with Beethoven's first symphony and ended it with one of his favorite pieces: Cherubini's overture *Les Abencérages* (The Abencerrages).

In May 1865 Allgeyer introduced Levi to painter Anselm Feuerbach and his stepmother Henriette, who were spending restful weeks in Baden-Baden. Levi and Henriette became friends immediately and remained so even after Anselm's tragic early death in 1880. He liked Feuerbach's art with its ancient motifs that seemed to reflect his own classical ideals. After Feuerbach's death, Levi advised Henriette on how to preserve her stepson's paintings and writings.

In the late 1860s, Levi tried to persuade benefactors in Karlsruhe to purchase Feuerbach's *Medea* for their gallery. He had been the first to see the painting when it was unpacked and wrote to Brahms:

> All my life I shall remember how chills ran down my spine and I could not pry myself away from the picture, though I longed to fetch Allgeyer to heighten my pleasure with his. And how I finally, after galloping through the streets, brought him and we stood before the painting in silent awe and were united in the hope that the time of struggle had come to an end and that the picture would travel triumphantly throughout Germany.[35]

Levi's attempt to support Feuerbach failed because on the advice of Carl Friedrich Lessing, the grand duke refused to put out the money. He found the perspective wrong.

Anselm Feuerbach, copper etching by Julius Allgeyer. Anselm Feuerbach: Sein Leben und seine Kunst *by Julius Allgeyer, Bamberg, 1894.*

At the end of October, Brahms came to Karlsruhe and stayed with Levi in his new home at 1 *Grünwinkler Allee* (today 31 *Bismarck Strasse*). The house, owned by auditor Franz von Poetz (and that still stands today) was at the time completely surrounded by greens, very close to the palace gardens and the Hardt forest where Brahms took morning walks. At Levi's home Brahms prepared for an important concert performance. On November 3 at the season's first subscription concert, directed by Levi, Brahms played his Piano Concerto in D Minor, op. 15. It was a significant evening for both of them. For Levi it was the first opportunity to present himself in a museum concert to the public as the newly appointed First Ducal Court Conductor. For Brahms it was the first time he publicly performed this concerto after it had failed to please at the Gewandhaus concert in Leipzig six years earlier. They had taken great care in selecting the pieces for the program. Besides the concerto, Brahms played two piano pieces by Schumann, *Romanze* and *Novelette*. Four opera soloists, Henriette Wabel, Magdalena Hauser, Benno Stolzenberg, and Joseph Hauser sang two quartets by Brahms, op. 31. Levi began the concert with Cherubini's overture *Faniska* and ended it with Beethoven's Symphony no. 3.

The chief editor of Karlsruhe's newspaper, Heinrich Kroenlein, reported on the evening. He attested to Brahms's "superior artistic effort" but found fault with "the dialectic of thought that paints everything in shades of gray, the continuous unfolding of musical arabesque, the development of phrase in width instead of depth." He lauded Brahms as "a capable virtuoso," but regretted "constant arpeggios in slow passages." Levi, he commented, "led the orchestra with confidence and verve, stirring the crowd to rousing applause."[36]

Brahms was apparently satisfied with the concert. He penned to his friend Dietrich: "The people were surprisingly so friendly as to call me back on stage, praise me, and such."[37] Three days later Brahms and Levi attended a chamber music concert in Karlsruhe given by Clara Schumann and Joseph Joachim. Joseph Hauser sang two of Brahms's *Magelone* songs. Afterward they celebrated Levi's twenty-sixth birthday. Levi and Joseph Joachim offered one another the cordial address "Du."

The day before Brahms left for concerts in Switzerland, he and Levi went to Baden-Baden to plant shrubs in Clara Schumann's yard. Once Levi had seen Brahms off the next day, he felt, as he wrote to Clara, a void he had never known. He felt unworthy. He had nothing, he said, to give to his friends, especially Brahms, and got so much from them. He was disheartened. When with his friends Clara Schumann, Brahms, and Joseph Joachim, he felt that he mattered; on his own he felt worthless and insignificant. It was a fear that was to overcome Levi many times in the years to come.

He sought temporary distraction by attending Devrient's readings of *Emilia Galotti* for the troupe of actors and then heatedly debating Lessing with him.

In early December Brahms returned to Karlsruhe. In a concert on December 4, Brahms and musicians Ludwig Strauss (violin) and Ferdinand Segisser (French horn) from Karlsruhe played Brahms's new Trio for the Horn, op. 40, which he had presented six days earlier in Zurich. Brahms then left Karlsruhe to play the trio in several other cities with varying musicians, but was back by the end of January. He seems to have felt nowhere as comfortable as in Karlsruhe during this time.

For the duration of this, his longest visit to Karlsruhe, Brahms stayed with his old friend Julius Allgeyer, who had put his garden cottage in the *Lange Strasse* no. 233 at the composer's disposal. In the quiet abode, over the next few months Brahms worked entirely undisturbed on his *Ein Deutsches Requiem* (*A German Requiem*). We know that he finished the third movement and also composed the song *Mainacht* (May Night) there.

CARLSRUHE.

Freitag, den 3. November 1865.

Erstes

dem allgemeinen Publikum zugängliches

Abonnements-Concert

des

Grossh. Hof-Orchesters

im

grossen Museums-Saale.

PROGRAMM.

Erste Abtheilung.

1. **Ouverture** zur Oper „Faniska" von Cherubini.
2. **Concert** für Klavier und Orchester von Johannes Brahms, vorgetragen vom Komponisten.
3. **Zwei Quartette** für vier Singstimmen mit Klavier von Johannes Brahms:
   a. **Der Gang zum Liebchen** (Böhmisch),
   b. **Wechsellied zum Tanze** (Goethe),
   gesungen von Fräulein **Wabel**, Frau **Hauser** und den Herren **Stolzenberg** und **Hauser**.
4. { **Romanze** / **Novelette** } für Klavier von Rob. Schumann, vorgetragen von Herrn Joh. **Brahms**.

Zweite Abtheilung.

5. **Sinfonie** (Nr. 3) **eroica** von L. van Beethoven.

Anfang 7 Uhr. Ende 9 Uhr.

Abonnements-Preise:

Das Abonnement für alle „sechs" Concerte beträgt:
Für einen reservirten Platz im Saal . . . . 6 fl. — kr.
Für einen nicht reservirten Platz im Saal . . . . 4 fl. 48 kr.
Auf die Gallerie . . . . 3 fl. 36 kr.

Die Familienbillets auf die reservirten Plätze sind vergriffen.

Billete für sämmtliche Concerte sind zu haben im **Billetverkaufs-Bureau des Grossh. Hoftheaters** Morgens von 10—12 und Mittags von 2—4 Uhr.

Auch kann man noch Abends an der Kasse abonniren.

Eintrittspreise an der Kasse.

Ein reservirter Platz im Saal . . . . 1 fl. 20 kr.
Ein nicht reservirter Platz im Saal . . . . 1 fl. — kr.
Auf die Gallerie . . . . — fl. 48 kr.

Die Billete sind, mit Ausnahme der Karten auf die Reserveplätze, für jedes Concert gültig.

Zur Sicherung der reservirten Plätze ist geeignete Vorkehrung getroffen.

Chr. Fr. Müller'sche Hofbuchdruckerei.

Subscription concert in Karlsruhe on 3 November 1865. Johannes Brahms premieres his concerto for piano and orchestra, op. 15, and plays two piano pieces by Schumann. Hermann Levi conducted the ducal court orchestra on this occasion but goes unmentioned in the printed program. Generallandesarchiv Karlsruhe.

In the evening, Brahms enjoyed going to the theater. Devrient's stage offered *Wallenstein* and *Wilhelm Tell*, Schiller's fragment *Demetrius*, and Goethe's *Tasso*. The opera offered *Le nozze di Figaro*, *Così fan tutte*, *Freischütz*, *The Merry Wives of Windsor*, *Tannhäuser*, Méhul's *Joseph*, and *König Ezio* by Stuttgart's court conductor Johann Joseph Abert. The most successful new production of the season was Meyerbeer's *L'Africaine*. The crowd cheered, but Levi was dismayed by the piece's "ruinous success."

At museum concerts Levi conducted Schumann's second symphony and Beethoven's fifth, sixth, and ninth. Concert evenings normally lasted at least three hours. Beethoven's Symphony no. 9, for example, filled only the second half of the program. The first half included an overture by Joachim Raff, Berlioz's duet from *Beatrice et Benedict*, and Robert Schumann's piano concerto played by Württemberg's royal court pianist Dionys Pruckner (who often guest-performed in Karlsruhe). Symphony concerts normally included instrumental soloists and singers performing selected parts from operas, or other songs accompanied often only by the piano.

That spring they repeated Bach's *Passion of Matthew*, directed by Kalliwoda, except on Good Friday, when Levi did it for the first time. Pauline Viardot-García sang the alto part; Brahms played the organ. One of the orchestra players who did not recognize Brahms later remarked to Levi: "The young man [at the organ] did a fine job!"[38]

On their evenings off, Brahms, Allgeyer, and Levi frequented the tavern *Nassauer Hof* at the corner of *Kronen Strasse* and *Lange Strasse*. It was run by the Jeremias Reutlinger family. Brahms particularly enjoyed the kosher cooking. Mrs. Reutlinger and her music-loving daughter pampered him, once even sending their homemade goose liver to Vienna just for him. Meanwhile Ida Lessing complained that Brahms never attended her Thursday evening open house events. But he did befriend her sister, wife of painter Adolf Schroedter, professor for ornament drawing and aquarelle at the polytechnic school. Alwine Schroedter drew lovely floral patterns. Brahms sent her four canons with a request to "sing them with ardor and fondness" and adorn them with "pretty illustrations."[39]

Levi introduced Brahms to the arts-loving family of Veit Ettlinger who lived on *Zähringer Strasse* near the city's main marketplace. Veit Ettlinger was one of Karlsruhe's most prominent citizens and he loved having guests. He was among the first Jews that Grand Duke Karl permitted to study law, was head of the synagogue's advisory council, a member of the city of Karlsruhe's municipal council, and an ardent German patriot. His wife led an active social life and saw that their numerous children—three sons and six daughters—all took music lessons. Their oldest daughter, Emilie, who later married bank director Kaula and established her own private school for song in Munich, had met Hermann Levi during her student years in Paris. There she had been introduced to him by her cousin Friedrich Gernsheim. Levi was a frequent guest at the Ettlinger home. His father had already known advocate Veit for many years.

The Ettlinger daughters were eager members of the Cecilia Association, but once they had gotten to know Hermann Levi better, they switched to the Philharmonic Choir, where they had the opportunity to sing Brahms's newest compositions. Levi brought both Brahms and Allgeyer to their house. The three confirmed bachelors let the Ettlinger girls fuss over them, particularly the three younger ones, Anna, Rudolfine, and Emma. Anna was the brightest and the most artistically talented of the sisters; she became a writer and in her memoirs tells of delicious hours spent making music with Brahms and Levi at her parents' home. It must have been fun when the two played waltzes and Hungarian dances

Anna Ettlinger, around 1870. Brahms-Institut der Musikhochschule Lübeck.

four-handedly at the piano. They loved practical jokes, once improvising four-handedly on the then popular waltz *Il bacio* (The Kiss) by Luigi Arditi.

At birthdays and Christmas, the Ettlinger daughters wrote bantering poems and drew colorful pictures to chide the bachelors Brahms and Levi. Many years later they still sent sweet little poems to Brahms in Vienna and Levi in Munich. Some of them were kept for posterity, a sign of how well they pleased. For his fortieth birthday, Anna Ettlinger penned Brahms a rhyme making fun of his failed attempts to lose weight.[40]

During the first months of 1866, Brahms felt very comfortable in Karlsruhe. In Allgeyer's garden cottage he could compose undisturbed. When he needed diversion, his friends were good and stimulating company. Before he left he played in a concert at the palace directed by Levi. Between Mendelssohn's *Hebrides Overture* and Beethoven's overture *Leonora* no. 3, Brahms played a march by Franz Schubert and his own piano arrangement of the second movement of String Sextet, op. 18, *Theme and Variations*.

Brahms left two days later. An hour before he departed, the postman delivered a package from publisher Simrock containing the printed edition of the second sextet, op. 36. Levi forwarded it immediately, as Brahms had requested, to Clara Schumann, adding a song by Brahms that he had copied by hand. It was beautiful *Mainacht* (May Night), that Brahms had written recently in Karlsruhe. Levi sighed:

> You know the void that his departure leaves in me. What a man! . . . We cannot judge him by the norms that we use for ourselves. . . . As long as minds like his are among us, the materialism of our times will not win; let us rally around him, those of us that belong together; close the circle, that the truth of art may shine ever brighter.[41]

FROM *A GERMAN REQUIEM* TO *THE MASTERSINGERS OF NUREMBERG*

> For my part, I have nameless respect for every creative artist, because I know from experience, how disproportionate criticism is to the ability to produce.
>
> —Hermann Levi to Ferdinand Hiller

Brahms's absence made Levi melancholy. Life with Brahms had been exhilarating—making music together for hours on end, talking through the night, sharing spirited ideas. Their friendship had buoyed him through the long winter. Now there was this void that no close friend could fill. Fortunately Clara Schumann came to town in late May to check on her son Ludwig and see Meyerbeer's *Huguénots* under Levi's direction. It was her company more than any other that comforted him.

The winter's erratic life with Brahms and Allgeyer had left its mark on Hermann Levi. Rarely had they gotten to bed before three in the morning. And Kalliwoda's poor health meant more and more work for Levi: Levi directed not only every concert, but most of the operas as well. By the end of the season, he was exhausted and went to the resort town Bad Rippoldsau to rest. From there he sent lonely words to Brahms in Switzerland, using song titles by Schumann and Brahms: *In my dream I cried—And my soul spread wide its wings—Oh bury your sorrow.*[42] The summer months passed. Levi did not see Brahms again until a brief encounter in September at Clara Schumann's home in Baden-Baden. Something had changed: "I had already sensed that Brahms had estranged himself from me and I know enough to know why. I'll admire him all of my life. But as Goethe said somewhere: 'If I love you, what do you care?'"[43] Their exchange petered and Levi had to accept the fact that Brahms preferred a less intimate kind of friendship.

Levi tried to keep in touch with Brahms through Clara Schumann. She had been the soloist for the first museum concert of the winter season, playing her husband's piano concerto and a few solo pieces by Kirchner, Schubert, and Weber. The evening began with Cherubini's *Anakreon* overture and ended with Beethoven's Symphony no. 2. In between, Levi accompanied tenor Wilhelm Brandes at the pianoforte for Beethoven's round of songs *An die ferne Geliebte* (To a Distant Love), op. 98. Levi took great care in choosing pieces for the Museum Society's subscription concerts, systematically presenting all of Beethoven's and many of Haydn's symphonies, and Schumann's symphonic works that were practically unknown in Karlsruhe. From the living composers he presented Niels W. Gade, Louis Theodor Gouvy, and particularly Max Bruch.

Levi had known Bruch since the winter of 1857–1858 when they both studied in Leipzig under Julius Rietz and Moritz Hauptmann. Bruch had settled in Mannheim, taken lessons in conducting from Vincenz Lachner, and spent time with Levi's relatives, the Ladenburg family. He visited Karlsruhe often, going to Levi's concerts and to the nearby Black Forest on days that they both had off. There they also met up with Brahms, whom Bruch then valued so highly that he considered taking instruction in counterpoint from him. When Levi left the German Opera in Rotterdam, Bruch had tried in vain to get the vacant post. Now he hoped that his colleague in Karlsruhe would at least perform a few of his pieces. He had already once proposed to have his opera *Loreley*, op. 16, staged in Rotterdam, but Levi had refused: he was too familiar with Mendelssohn's brilliant fragment for Geibel's libretto to appreciate Bruch's weaker version.[44]

After initially hesitating, Levi finally did present a few of Max Bruch's works in Karlsruhe. In 1867–1868 the Philharmonic Choir sang the ballade *Schön Ellen*, op. 24, and scenes from *Frithjof*, op. 23, at an annual extra concert for the benefit of widows and orphans. On 20 February 1869, he premiered Bruch's Symphony no. 1, op. 28. Bruch had meanwhile become court conductor in

Sondershausen and planned to write another opera. Levi put him in touch with Otto Devrient, the son of Karlsruhe's theater director, to ask him to write a libretto based on Schiller's fragment *Demetrius*. They discussed it, but the project never transpired. Levi's friend Naret-Koning suggested that Bruch write a violin concerto. He did, and sent it to Levi, writing, "[N]o one's opinion is more valuable to me than yours. . . . I want nothing more than to always be on equal standing with you." Levi made some objections to the piece and the composer reworked it. It became famous as Bruch's Violin Concerto no. 1.[45]

Although Bruch wanted Levi's opinion on every new piece that he wrote, he was hurt when Levi was overly critical:

> You make that very German mistake of demanding that one person master everything. . . . One and the same musician must write the most beautiful operas, the most excellent symphonies, the most wonderful songs, the most profound chamber music. . . . I really don't appreciate being compared to Brahms all the time. . . . Brahms has some qualities that I don't, I agree. And I have some qualities that he lacks.[46]

Bruch sent his second symphony to Levi, but they had lost trust in one another. After a long silence, they first met again twenty-five years later in Berlin, when both had become acknowledged authorities in music: Max Bruch directed a master class in composition at the Berlin Academy and Hermann Levi had become Bavarian General Music Director and conductor for the festivals at Bayreuth.

At Karlruhe's court theater, theater director Devrient and his young conductor Levi worked well together, continuously improving the quality of performances, and giving particular attention to works by Mozart. Gustav Wendt, the director of Karlsruhe's lyceum and a man with considerable knowledge of music, found the local presentation of *Le nozze di Figaro* as good as that of any other German stage. They used Eduard Devrient's translation that reincorporated original recitatives, partly accompanied by a string quartet. During the season of 1866–1867, they not only produced *Figaro*, *Così fan tutte*, and *Die Zauberflöte* (The Magic Flute), but *Die Entführung aus dem Serail* (Abduction from the Seraglio), *Don Giovanni*, and *Titus* as well.

Occasionally Devrient found that Levi failed to understand the needs of stage scenes and focused too much on the music.[47] But he was very pleased with Levi's rendition of Marschner's *Hans Heiling*, saying that he had made its music clear and interesting. The two did not, however, agree on the importance of the piece itself. Levi backed it, but Devrient found the music "nondramatic and dry," despite the fact that he had written the text himself. Perhaps he still resented having ruined his own singing voice by singing the premiere of Marschner's *Der Templer und die Jüdin*.

After hearing Schumann's overture *Genoveva* in one of Levi's first orchestra concerts, Devrient made plans to present the whole opera at the court theater.

Max Bruch's letter to Hermann Levi (page 1), dated 9 January 1867, discussing Brahms's German Requiem (see appendix for translation). Bayerische Staatsbibliothek, sign. Leviana I.53, Bruch, Max.

Max Bruch's letter to Herman Levi (page 2).

The piece had only been performed twice since its first showing in Leipzig in 1850, and that had been in 1855 in Weimar under the direction of Franz Liszt. Levi welcomed the project; it meant fulfilling an implicit wish for Clara Schumann. They began rehearsals in the fall of 1867. But first they had to premiere *Lucia di Lammermoor* on November 13, leaving just three weeks to prepare *Genoveva* for December 3. Ten days before the performance, Levi wrote to Clara, thanking her for a birthday present (an autograph of Brahms's song *Herbstgefühl* (Autumn Feeling) and reported on the progress of rehearsals. He was worried about the first rehearsal that evening because of problems with scene changes. He would have liked to have entirely changed the opera's dramaturgy. But then, he wrote,

> I was boggled by the size and responsibility of such an undertaking—and dropped the idea in the conviction that love and piety and my bit of knowledge of the stage gleaned from six years of working in the theater are insufficient for the task. As it stands, the work will please, but not excite.[48]

Devrient was distraught by this "failed work that lacks dramatic expression."[49] Nevertheless, Levi's perseverance made the premiere a success and appeased the theater director. In celebration of the grand duchess's birthday, the entire theater stood in "grand illumination," every corner of the house lit brightly, even the spectator seats that were normally in the dark. Levi described the spectacle to Clara, who was unable to attend because she had concert obligations in Dresden and Leipzig:

> We stand before this music like none other since Weber's death and cannot fathom why the German public allowed a twenty-year pause between its first and second performance (not counting the one by the Composers Association). For me December 3 means not only the high point of my work as a conductor, but also a day of the most intense pleasure that I can recall, engraved into my heart for all time, and I am deeply grateful that I had a small part in reviving this opera. . . . After the performance Allgeyer, Will, Wendt (the very musical director of the lyceum) and I went to [the tavern] Erbprinz—and found no end to our rhapsodizing. We would have sent you a telegram immediately, but were afraid we'd disturb your sleep.[50]

Lyceum director Gustav Wendt was a diligent concertgoer and loved theater performances.[51] His wife, a capable pianist, often played the piano four-handedly with Levi, who in turn introduced the couple to the newest pieces of the theater's repertoire. Wendt later became a friend of Johannes Brahms, whom he joined for summer vacations at Lake Thun and in Bad Ischl.

The final act was rearranged for the third performance of *Genoveva*. This time Clara Schumann came. She said that her husband Robert had never seen such beautiful opera. Impressed, she wrote to her friend Rosalie Leser:

Gustav Wendt, friend of Levi and Brahms and grandfather of Wilhelm Furtwängler. Courtesy of Frithjof Haas.

The Genoveva performance was wonderful, it was one of the greatest pleasures I've had in years. It reminded me of so many things—a large part of my life is bound to that work. The performance was exceptionally beautiful and all evening I kept thinking: if only I could do something nice for Levi.[52]

In the spring of 1868 Levi began rehearsing Charles Gounod's newest opera, *Roméo et Juliette*. It had been premiered just a year earlier by the Théâtre Lyrique for the World Exhibition in Paris. After Dresden and Vienna, Karlsruhe was the third city to present it in German. The public had great expectations, especially since Gounod's *Margarethe* had been staged in so many other German cities, but not yet in Karlsruhe. Karlsruhe's newspaper (which had already printed two detailed previews of the performance) thoroughly reviewed the premiere, finding it apparently more significant than the performance of Schumann's only opera: "In terms of the singers and our distinguished orchestra, conductor

Levi's carefully rehearsed and exquisitely conducted production was also very laudable."[53]

Apparently, Heinrich Kroenlein, chief editor and music critic at the Karlsruhe newspaper, did not hold a grudge. Early in the season, he had sent his own work called *Magelone* to theater superintendent Devrient, hoping it would be performed. He had, he said, worked on it for four years and in his own opinion—with the exception of Wagner—nothing had been composed since Weber, Spohr, and Marschner that his work did not surpass thirty times over! Levi was critical of it, and Kalliwoda was, too. When even Vincenz Lachner condemned it, Devrient asked Kroenlein to please withdraw it.

During these months Hans von Bülow was rehearsing Wagner's new opera *Die Meistersinger von Nürnberg* (The Mastersingers of Nuremberg) at the Royal Bavarian Theater in Munich. Besides the pre-published text, Liszt and Bülow wrote promotion articles for the press ahead of the premiere on 21 June 1868 to attract fanciers and Wagner followers from across Europe. Although at the time Levi was wary of Wagner's works, he traveled to Munich for the performance, where among an illustrious crowd he witnessed Wagner's first huge success since *Rienzi*. The dazzling premiere directed by Hans von Bülow made a lasting impression on Levi. Once back in Karlsruhe, he aroused superintendent Devrient's curiosity and the latter journeyed to Munich, too, along with his son Otto, to see the final performance of *Meistersinger*.

Devrient was reluctant to stage the extremely difficult work (which he did not particularly care for) in Karlsruhe. But when the new playing season began, the grand duke ordered that the theater rehearse the work during the winter. Levi, too, hesitated: Karlsruhe's ensemble, he thought, was not up to the task. But then again, his long report to the superintendent, explaining why it was impossible to stage *Meistersinger* in Karlsruhe, was perhaps simply a strategy to expand the orchestra. In closing he wrote:

> Of course, operas *can* be arranged for two flutes. In Germany it has become common to amputate works of art for small stages that lack personnel. But I believe that an institution such as ours has only a choice between either properly complying with the composer's intentions or abstaining from the undertaking altogether. . . . Nonetheless, I do feel that it is our duty to let our audience judge a new work by a man such as Wagner for itself, and that we must make sacrifices to enable a good performance. But if we mutilate the opera, failure will be attributed to us and not to the composer.[54]

Levi was convincing. It turned out that four years earlier the grand duke had already advanced 930 guldens to Richard Wagner to write this opera. Thus it had to be performed, come what may. The grand duke increased the budget to add to both the choir and the orchestra and ordered that rehearsals commence immediately.

Later Levi came to admire *Meistersinger*, but when rehearsing it for Karlsruhe, he had some doubts. Naturally, he was not yet entirely free of Vincenz Lachner's influence. Lachner had conducted Wagner's early operas reluctantly, but now, while Levi was rehearsing *Meistersinger* in Karlsruhe, Lachner was doing the same in Mannheim. Besides having an aesthetic aversion to the work, he worried about managing the technical side of it: "I've had the score now for three days, and for three nights I've hardly slept a wink. Every night this cruel 570 folio weighs down my chest like one hundred pounds and haunts me for hours."[55] His solution was to condense the work for performance.

Levi would have none of that. Although he was hesitant to stage the work, he did respect every single note of the score and would present it to the public unabridged. He set vigorously to work, no effort being too great for success, motivating his troupe to tackle the extraordinarily difficult task and seeing them through a total of eighty-seven rehearsals.

He was simultaneously working on another large project: Brahms's *Requiem*. Although Levi had not heard from him in a long while, in August 1868 Brahms wrote that he'd be coming from Frankfurt to Karlsruhe on the afternoon train and did not plan to travel on immediately. We do not know how long Brahms stayed in Karlsruhe, except that it was long enough to discuss *Deutsches Requiem* (*German Requiem*) that had been premiered on April 10 in the cathedral in Bremen. Levi felt slighted for not having been asked to premiere it in Karlsruhe, where at least some of it had been written. But Brahms's reasons for premiering *Requiem* in Bremen, closer to his own hometown, had little to do with Levi. Brahms found the cathedral in Bremen the ideal site for his deeply religious work.

At the advice of Karl Reinthaler, the conductor of the premiere, Brahms reworked the fifth movement with its soprano solo "Ihr habt nun Traurigkeit." When he saw Levi that summer, he agreed that Levi should conduct the entire work the next spring. Thus, throughout the winter of 1869–1870, Levi had two new productions on his hands: during the day he worked with the theater troupe on *Meistersinger* and in the evening he had choir rehearsals with the Philharmonic Society working on *German Requiem*. These challenging tasks raised his self-confidence; he was encouraged by growing recognition for his achievements at both the opera house and the concert hall—recognition not only from his own superintendent and the local public, but from external sources as well. Ida Lessing, ever chronicling cultural life in Karlsruhe, wrote: "Levi is an Arabian horse that storms into gatherings, tosses ingeniously paradox balls of fire into conversation, and sparks off red and blue fireworks."[56]

January 1869 brought the final preparations for *Meistersinger*. Reserving as much time as possible for rehearsals, two weeks into the year the theater offered no other evening program. On January 19, during rehearsals for the second and third act, Karlsruhe's knight Stolzing, Wilhelm Brandes, got hoarse. They had to do without him for a couple of days. Nearing completion of the work, Levi himself was so exhausted that he ended the last rehearsals abruptly several times. When premiere day arrived, Brandes could not perform. Devrient put an emergency plan into action and wired Munich to get their knight Stolzing, Franz Nachbaur, for Karlsruhe. The grand duke communicated with the king of Bavaria for permission to borrow his subject. After days of anxiety in Karlsruhe, Nachbaur finally was allowed to do the guest performance, but for a salary of 55 Louis d'or, which was more than twice Levi's own monthly salary. On February 4, a final costume rehearsal, including Franz Nachbaur, was given in the presence of members of the ducal court. The next day the long-awaited premiere could finally take place. Devrient noted in his diary: "At last this nerve-wracking *Meistersinger von Nürnberg* is done."

After Munich and Dresden, Karlsruhe was the third German court stage to produce Wagner's most sumptuous work. Lit for festivity and honored by the presence of the grand duke and numerous visitors from afar, the house was a spectacular sight. The prominent guests included the court conductors from Mannheim and Stuttgart, Vincenz Lachner and Johann Joseph Abert, and singers Julius Stockhausen and Pauline Viardot-García. Skeptical about the first and second act, the audience eventually burst into ovations for the soloists and for conductor Levi, cheering him back onto the stage again and again. The next day, Karlsruhe's newspaper wrote that the orchestra and choir, never before set before such a daunting task, had surpassed itself. After the performance a circle of friends gathered around Levi at the tavern *Erbprinz*. Art historian Wilhelm Lübke from Stuttgart and Karlsruhe's lyceum director Gustav Wendt argued over the significance of the work they had just seen. Lübke attacked it. Levi defended the work, adding, however, that pruning it someday after Wagner's death might increase the dramatic effect.

Pauline Viardot-García rushed to report the triumph to Richard Wagner. But Levi had already written to him, too. An Augsburg newspaper said it had been an "outrageous success." Thus, Wagner was not at all upset by an anonymous claim that the performance had been a failure. Two days later the work was delivered again with Nachbaur singing the part of Stolzing. Despite the expenses for the star from Munich and for choir and orchestra extras, the production made a profit of 1168 guldens from those two performances alone. Baden's grand duke doled out bonuses in thanks for the stellar feat: Conductor Levi received a diamond ring worth 360 guldens; each soloist received a bonus of 100, the concertmaster 50, and each musician and the prompter 10 guldens. Wages for three copiers who had copied individual instrument and choir parts from the score were raised from 15 to 20 kreuzers per page.

The intense preoccupation with *Meistersinger* changed Levi's mind; initially critical and reserved, he now reverently admired it. We see this in the letter he wrote to Wagner immediately after the performance and in a letter to Brahms:

Pauline Viardot-García (1821–1910). Stadtarchiv Baden-Baden.

"Singing masterly kept me out of breath this winter; considering our means, the performance was exquisite. My feelings are mixed and I'd like to discuss it sometime."[57] Levi's new appreciation for *Meistersinger* cannot have clouded his friendship with Brahms because Brahms also thought highly of the work.

Having happily come to terms with *Meistersinger*, just one month remained to rehearse the *German Requiem*. Brahms and Levi reassumed correspondence. Levi reported progress to Vienna: every rehearsal thrilled him. Many of their mutual friends were loyal Brahms followers and sang in the choir, including the Ettlinger sisters and Julius Allgeyer. Brahms's growing recognition gave Allgeyer great personal satisfaction because years before he had battled claims that the times knew no real artists by pointing out his friends, Anselm Feuerbach and Johannes Brahms. Allgeyer also wrote to Brahms in Vienna, describing *Requiem* practice in Karlsruhe; it was, he said, "art of great style." Allgeyer wanted Brahms to return to Karlsruhe to conduct the performance: "I fear only that our capacity for worthy presentation is much less than you might desire."[58] Levi pleaded with Brahms to return to Karlsruhe:

> If you feel yet the slightest loyalty to the place where you wrote the work, the slightest friendship for me, then do conduct the performance. We are prepared—just name the day of your arrival! The board will follow up with an official invitation. An angel of a voice (and she's pretty, too) sings the soprano solo; our choirs are small, as you know, but well-rehearsed. . . . Ceterum censo—let me play the kettledrum in the Requiem—you know I'm a trained timpanist and will do it better than the chap in Vienna![59]

Brahms, however, was unable to attend any of the first performances in Karlsruhe because he had concerts scheduled in Vienna and Budapest with singer Julius Stockhausen for those very weeks. He expressed his regret to Allgeyer and Levi:

> It would be odd to hear or conduct my Requiem in Karlsruhe, the only town where the latter is certainly not necessary and nota bene the former would be a great pleasure! I've written off Basel, Hamburg, Cologne, and Leipzig, where they do whatever they want with my poor piece.[60]

On 9 March 1869, in the hall of the Museum Society, *German Requiem* was performed for the first time in Karlsruhe. The solo parts were sung by young Marie Hausmann (soprano), a student of Viardot-García, and Joseph Hauser (baritone) from the court theater. In reviewing the evening, the editor of Karlsruhe's newspaper said that while Brahms was well known to the locals, and certainly was one of the most ambitious, diligent, and skilled composers of the current young generation, one wonders why he did not leave it in Latin or use a German rendition of the Latin text.[61] He particularly disapproved of the *point d'orgue* at the end of the third movement. Pocketwatch in hand, he had clocked it as lasting two minutes. Finally, he thought that the applause was probably more for the performance than for the work itself.

The appraisal set off a feud in the newspapers. Baden's regional paper published a riposte signed by friends of music in Karlsruhe.[62] One could tell it was written by Brahms disciples surrounding Hermann Levi. The other paper's opinion, they said, did not reflect that of Karlsruhe's music *cognoscenti*. Brahms's brilliant piece had been the first one in a long time to make such a powerful impression. Later the same paper published a retort by some members of the Philharmonic Society saying that Brahms's newest composition left them just as cold as his other works.[63]

These feuds over the work of his friend angered Levi. He canceled a second performance scheduled for Palm Sunday, but not—as some claimed—because of the press, but because of illness. Delivering works by both Wagner and Brahms within such a short period had taken its toll. This was to occur time and again: under enormous emotional pressure, Levi's health failed. He needed rest and wired Vienna asking Brahms to conduct the Palm Sunday performance. But Brahms had already left Vienna for Hungary.

Finally, after postponing it several times, Brahms did return to Karlsruhe to conduct a repeat performance of the *Requiem* on May 12. Anna Ettlinger, who sang in the choir, recalled:

> We were pretty excited when Brahms came to the second performance. Will he be pleased with our little choir? Thanks to rehearsals with Levi, he was. But under his direction we were more self-conscious than usual. Unfortunately he had a cold when he arrived and was hoarse and had to take great pains to make himself understood. I still see him at the conductor's stand, his face red with excitement, his flashing blue eyes, flying blond hair, swinging back and forth in the most energetic way that he gave us the beat. . . . As a young man he was clean-shaven, his mouth with its slightly pouting lower lip was particularly expressive, his fine lips testified to great vigor. Yet they could also have such a serene, amiable look, and all kinds of elfish thoughts seemed to prance at the corners of his mouth.[64]

Levi sat overjoyed in the audience. In selfless admiration for Brahms, this time he found the performance freer and more nuanced than under his own direction. Clara Schumann later noted in her diary:

> On the twelfth we all went to Karlsruhe for the Requiem. Johannes conducted it nicely; Levi had rehearsed it with devotion and care. But I missed the effect of the massive choir that had been so wonderful in Bremen.[65]

The next day, Levi and Allgeyer accompanied their friend Brahms to Baden-Baden, where he began his summer stay at the home of Mrs. Becker in Lichtental.

The spring of 1869 ruffled Karlsruhe's court theater. Eduard Devrient, now sixty-eight and having directed there for seventeen years, was offered the position of superintendent for the Royal Theater of Württemberg in Stuttgart. The entire principality of Baden buzzed with alarm at the thought of losing their popular theater director. Levi, one of the first to hear the news, immediately began circulating a petition. The duke was to persuade Devrient to stay in Karlsruhe, no matter what. But the ducal court of Baden sulked in the belief that Devrient had negotiated with Stuttgart without consultations with them. In reality, Devrient had been wooed by Stuttgart and now tried to exploit that in an attempt to improve his standing in Karlsruhe one last time before retiring. He had long resented that he was subject to supervision by the court's director of finances,

Adolph Kreidel, and that he had no direct access to the duke himself. The duke feared losing his cherished theater director and made his officials negotiate. Devrient declined their initial offer of an additional 1000 guldens annually. He wanted not more money, but higher status. He requested the title of General Director and the authority attached to it. On four pages the duke expressed his esteem and generosity and awarded the coveted title. It had taken two anxious weeks of careful negotiation to satisfy Devrient. Eventually he was made an immediate senior magistrate and appointed to the newly created position of General Director of the Grand Ducal Court Theater. It gave him considerable authority and left him free to decline the royal proposition from Stuttgart.

Shortly before his fiftieth anniversary of working with the stage, news quickly spread that Devrient would stay in Karlsruhe after all. On the eve of the jubilee in his honor, Liederkranz, the choral society, sang a round of songs for him. Neighbors and friends sent flowers. On the festive day, Levi, the soloists, and the choir of the court theater serenaded him again in the morning, closing with *Abschied vom Walde*, a song by Mendelssohn, Devrient's friend since their youth. The evening was filled with festivity at the ducal theater, a ceremony in Devrient's honor, and a banquet at the museum followed by a surprise performance of a piece Devrient had composed as a young man.

Unfortunately the new General Director only fulfilled his function for a short while. Soon after the jubilee, Devrient became seriously ill and needed months of medical treatment in Baden-Baden. In the fall of 1869, he returned to the ducal theater with diminished gusto, opening the playing season with a repeat performance of Franz Lachner's *Catharina Cornaro*. Next came new productions of two operas by Daniel-François Auber: *Le premier jour de bonheur* and *Le domino noir* (in German). While repeating rehearsals for *Meistersinger* in October, problems once again arose with tenor Brandes, who was basically overtaxed by the role of Stolzing. Once again, a guest performer had to help out. This time it was Josef Schloesser from Mannheim. Levi had heard him sing the part for the first time in March, when Lachner had produced the work.

Devrient's very last opera production was *Undine* by Albert Lortzing, lavishly presented with the brand-new, first-time-ever, electric lighting. Wilhelm Kalliwoda directed the performance. Seventeen years earlier, Devrient had engaged him for the theater, but more recently poor health kept Kalliwoda from conducting. Magdalene Murjahn was triumphant in the title role. She was a newly engaged lyric soprano from Viardot-García's school and one of Levi's favorites. In December Devrient's physicians suggested that he retire. He tried to persuade well-known author and stage-writer Gustav Freytag to take his place.

But before retiring, Devrient had a promise to keep. He wanted to produce an operetta that Pauline Viardot-García had composed for a text by Ivan Turgenev. Three years earlier this one-act piece, *Le dernier sorcier*, had been performed at the Théâtre du Thiergarten, a small private enterprise run by Pauline and her husband in Baden-Baden. Family members took on parts, and her neighbor and friend Turgenev himself was the librettist, director, and main actor all in one. Richard Pohl in Weimar had rendered the text in German (*Der letzte Zauberer*) for performance there. Franz Liszt offered to write the piano arrangement, but for lack of time commissioned the task to Weimar's court conductor Eduard Lassen. In Baden-Baden, in the summer of 1869, Brahms had directed a repeat performance from the piano where he sat playing. Karlsruhe's performance staged by Otto Devrient, son of the new General Director, turned out to be only moderately successful. The audience perhaps missed a personality like Turgenev, who in Baden-Baden played the part of Napoleon III himself. That evening Eduard Devrient said farewell to his privileged loge and office. He found the music full of character and expression but the libretto "a tasteless nothing."

The next morning, on 1 February 1870, the sixty-nine-year-old director said good-bye to his ensemble. He recalled how he had presented himself to his troupe seventeen years earlier with "Stand by me as I stand by you!"—and now said that both sides had kept their word. They had shaped and performed theater as His Highness had wished, free of current fashions and frivolous trends, and had made a commitment to present to the public the best of what the poetic arts and musical composition had to offer, bringing it to life with the greatest perfection. In closing, Devrient introduced his successor, superintendent Wilhelm Kaiser. This renowned actor from Hanover and Berlin had accepted the offer that Gustav Freytag had turned down.

Tears were shed over Devrient's parting. Levi, too, wiped his eyes as he spoke of these events at a repertory meeting. He certainly sensed that he would never again work as closely with any comparable personality of the theater. Devrient gave the court conductor advice for the future, admonishing him to keep Gluck's operas an active part of the repertoire.

Levi's own era in Karlsruhe was coming to a close. He found it difficult to work with Wilhelm Kaiser, the new director, who had little interest in opera. If it weren't for Brahms visiting Karlsruhe more often, he would have felt entirely lost.

During his visit to Karlsruhe in May 1869, Brahms had stayed with Levi at his home at 1 *Grünwinkler Allee*. He had shown Levi his newest compositions, including a series of waltzes for four voices and four hands at the piano. Levi found them charming and agreed to rehearse them soon with his soloists. On August 24, following the summer break and trips to Berlin, Munich, and Salzburg, Levi held a group practice for Magdalene Murjahn, Mr. and Mrs. Hauser, and Benno Stolzenberg. They had asked Brahms to come, but on that day he was directing Madame Viardot-Gracía's operetta *Le dernier sorcier* at her theater in Baden-Baden. Clara Schumann, however, came to this rehearsal and found the group's work delightful, particularly Magdalene's lovely voice. "To see Levi working with this music is an exceptional pleasure!"[66]

Julius Allgeyer, Johannes Brahms, and Hermann Levi, 1869. Photograph by Ludwig Allgeyer. Brahms-Institut an der Musikhochschule Lübeck.

On September 21 Clara's circle of friends gathered in Baden-Baden for her daughter Julie's *Polterabend*[67] on the eve of her wedding at the Catholic church of Lichtental to Count Marmorito. Young people played the *Toy Symphony* (Haydn), and Clara and Brahms played Brahms's *Hungarian Dances* and waltzes by Johann Strauss four-handedly. Pineapple punch was served. Allgeyer, Levi, and Brahms together brought Julie an expensive dish. In a photograph taken in Karlsruhe in 1869, we see this trio of friends grouped around a table, beholding their gift. Allgeyer points to something on the dish, as if explaining a detail. Levi sits comfortably, listening attentively. But Brahms seems to pout and stare at the floor. Julie Schumann's wedding was bitter for him. No one realized that he loved her. He had secretly written *New Love*

Julie Schumann (1845–1872), around 1865. Brahms-Institut an der Musikhochschule Lübeck.

Songs, op. 65, for Julie, leaving them without any dedication when they went to print. In the summer of 1869, when Clara told him of Julie's engagement, he left the house in silence and stayed away for a week. When he returned he brought Clara his *Alto Rhapsody*, op. 53, based on verses from Goethe's *Harzreise im Winter*, exclaiming "Here is my song for the bride!" Clara confided to her diary:

> This profound pain in verse and music shook me more than anything had in a long time.... I cannot think of this piece as of anything other than an expression of his hurt. If only once he would use words for such personal things![68]

Brahms once told his publisher, Simrock, that *Alto Rhapsody* had been "a wedding gift for Countess Schumann."

The program for Karlsruhe's first Museum Concert of the fall season was obviously meant to honor Schumann and Brahms. Clara played Beethoven's fourth piano concerto and three piano pieces from Robert Schumann's op. 12 and op. 23. Levi ended the program with Schumann's fourth symphony. In between they presented Brahms's *New Love Song* waltzes, Levi and Clara playing them four-handed from the manuscript. Of these eighteen waltzes later published as op. 52, on 6 October 1869 they only played seven, along with a soprano solo from what was later published as op. 65. The audience called for encores, and they played two more of the waltzes.[69] The audience called for the composer, who was in the room but refused to go on stage alone, so Clara joined him. At the dress rehearsal, Levi had let Amalia Boni (contralto) sing the *Alto Rhapsody* from the manuscript especially for Clara. In her diary she notes: "What a deeply touching piece!"[70] A few days later, Levi took the vocal quartet on tour and presented the waltzes in Heidelberg and Mannheim.

Brahms stayed on two weeks longer at his summer residence in Lichtental, coming once again to Karlsruhe on October 19 to play his piano quintet, op. 34, the next evening with musicians from the court orchestra. Five years earlier the work had been presented for the first time in its final version at Levi's home. In late October Brahms returned to Vienna via Munich.

His successful productions of *Mastersingers* and *German Requiem* had increased Levi's reputation as a conductor, and offers came pouring in from other large opera houses. Vienna inquired whether he would like to have the position currently held by court conductor Heinrich Esser. It would have meant sharing authority with two other conductors, Heinrich Proch and Otto Dessoff. Levi asked Brahms whether Vienna would be an improvement at all, since he had fought so hard to get the lead position and the freedom to work as he pleased in Karlsruhe. Though Brahms felt that his friend from Karlsruhe was superior to the two colleagues in Vienna and would soon be awarded the lead position there, Levi could not decide to move to Vienna.

The next year, Munich knocked with an enticing offer to rehearse Wagner's *Walküre* (*Valkyrie*). In August 1869 Levi had been to the public dress rehearsal for *Rheingold* (Rhine Gold) directed by Franz Wüllner in Munich and knew of the uproar caused by the premiere: off in Lucerne, Wagner had prohibited the production; at home in Bavaria, King Ludwig had demanded it. The conductors that Wagner wanted, Hans von Bülow and Hans Richter, remained loyal to the composer and refused to direct the work. The indignant king ordered the director of his royal choir, Franz Wüllner, to take over the performance. Wüllner grabbed the opportunity to set foot in the opera house, despite Wagner's threat: "Keep your fingers off my score! May the devil get you, if you ignore my words!" Wüllner, incidentally one of Brahms's good friends, was unimpressed. He later even attended the first festival in Bayreuth, where Wagner received him well, and went on to fight bitterly for the privilege of conducting the entire *Ring* in Munich, though that did not come about.

Thus, in the spring of 1870, there was talk in Munich of whether Wüllner should also conduct *Valkyrie*. Theater director Baron von Perfall did not want Wüllner for the *Valkyrie* production and exploited the situation to win the successful conductor from Karlsruhe for his stage. He met Levi in Stuttgart and tried to make working on *Valkyrie* palatable. Levi began studying the score, electrified by the prospect of conducting Munich's huge orchestra for a Wagner premiere. But at the same time, he was worried about insulting the composer by accepting the offer. Thus he wrote to Wagner that he was prepared to conduct *Valkyrie* at any time, but only with the support of the Master. And that in order to accommodate the latter's wishes he would gladly travel to Lucerne. Wagner promptly replied that he didn't mind Levi conducting his work, but please don't pester him with it. He then congratulated Levi on the *Meistersinger* performance in Karlsruhe, about which he had—compared to Dresden—heard only the best.

Levi kept his word and turned down the offer from Munich. He reported these negotiations to Brahms, sending him copies of the correspondence with Wagner. It was important to him to avoid any misunderstanding on this point, particularly with his sensitive friend. He also tried to justify Wagner's publicly criticized behavior by mentioning that he had once defended the composer's article "Judaism in Music." And he felt that Wagner's reply to him, too, commanded respect. In closing Levi tried to set Brahms at ease about his appreciation of Wagner:

> But enough kept me from packing my things and deserting to his camp, just as the most profound Valkyrie intoxication is undoubtedly followed by a considerable hangover. But it would have been fun to hear such an orchestra surging and swelling around me and to wave my baton through it.[71]

Neither did Levi take up Perfall's offer of contracted employment with the Bavarian Royal Theater. Conditions in Munich seemed too uncertain with such "an erratic king and that ever-threatening Jupiter Tonans in Lucerne." Levi had done nothing to offend either Brahms or Wagner and could calmly await Munich's second try at some later time.

And yet, without openly admitting it, Levi was gradually drifting toward Wagner. Studying *Valkyrie* had drawn him into the fascinating world of musical drama. To keep his undivided attention, Brahms would have had to have written something comparable to Wagner's stage works. It was Levi's mistake of a lifetime to imagine that Brahms might compose opera.

Their mutual friend, Allgeyer, also tried to find a suitable opera text for Brahms. He contributed a libretto of his own based on Calderon's zarzuela *El secreto a voces*.[72] Brahms kept it in his drawer for ten years without putting a note to a word of it. Allgeyer even asked Henriette Feuerbach, mother of his painter friend, what in her opinion might make good material for an opera for Brahms. She suggested taking Wolfram von Eschenbach's *Parzival*, long before anyone knew that Wagner envisioned using that tale. Brahms's friends did not give up. Allgeyer introduced Brahms to Swiss writer Joseph Victor Widmann. But Widmann's *Der geraubte Schleier* and *Iphigenie zu Delphi* seemed unsuitable. Levi borrowed every book of old opera texts from the theater's library for him; Brahms particularly requested the book for *Figaro*, but probably not to write new music for it; he was more interested in the structure of an ideal libretto and thinking more along the lines of a "numbers opera" à la Mozart,[73] but without recitatives: Brahms wanted music to set in at the story's high points. This, he felt, would distinguish his opera from Wagnerian musical drama.

Brahms was also interested in the libretto from Méhul's opera *Uthal* that Levi had produced in December 1869 using Devrient's new arrangement. Levi was skeptical: when working with the piece he had felt that this sort of material in this form was no longer viable and that one should not think that delightful epic or lyric matter can be made into drama.

Levi, too, had made that mistake. He had sent Brahms a manuscript for *Melusine* by an anonymous author who turned out to be Anna Ettlinger. Brahms returned it, saying, "Continue to be so kind!" Taking that literally, Levi then sent him a libretto for the biblical story of *Sulamith*, written by Emil Zittel, the protestant pastor at Karlsruhe's town church. Brahms replied: "Now I know what you think of me and opera texts."[74] Levi gave up: "Then bury the stillborn trouble-maker. May he rest in peace—or be resurrected someday."[75]

For the time being, that was the end of discussing Brahms and opera. But the idea soon resurfaced when Levi became closer friends with poet Paul Heyse. And later, as Bavaria's royal conductor, Levi still believed he could persuade Brahms to compose opera. As he gradually fell for Wagner's notion that the symphony was dead and the only future for grand classical music was in musical drama, his persistent attempt to win Brahms over for the musical stage became a desperate struggle to save their friendship.

FAREWELL TO KARLSRUHE, *TRIUMPHLIED*

> You're right that I really had to return to Germany. I wanted my share of the elation. Nothing could keep me in Vienna.
>
> —Brahms to Levi in April 1871

By the summer of 1870, Levi was exhausted. Besides the commotion of Devrient's celebrations and the exciting negotiations with Munich, the work on a large opera and repertoire for the orchestra had eroded his strength. Although he had turned down the offer to conduct *Valkyrie*, negotiations did continue and superintendent Perfall tried to win him for Munich. But as Levi told Adolph Kreidel, Karlsruhe's court treasurer, he ultimately cut off the talks because the salary for a Royal Bavarian Kapellmeister was disappointing. And yet he was unhappy. He felt that he had negotiated poorly and would now be stuck in Baden's royal residence town forever. The recent season's program choices he had found mediocre, as he complained to Brahms: "Classical opera was nonexistent. Not a trace of novelty. Out of desperation I fell for Holstein's 'Haideschacht.'"[76]

When the summer's off-season began, Levi took a leisure trip, disclosing his destination to neither Clara Schumann nor Brahms. In mid-July he wrote to Brahms from Westerland on the isle of Sylt in reply to Brahms's request that they meet:

> If the matter is not urgent, I would like to devote two more weeks to the lovely North Sea and remain here until the twenty-first. I will then take a fisherman from Hamburg's boat to Helgoland and with favorable wind may arrive within twelve hours. If the weather's nasty, it may take two days; if it's stormy I may never arrive at all.[77]

Brahms had been offered the post of Artistic Director of the Society of Vienna's Friends of Music and asked Levi what he thought. Levi was honest:

> I know from Karlsruhe that you are more skilled at conducting than any other. But you are not made for dealing with the immense petty obnoxiousness inevitably tied to that kind of public obligation; I fear you would quickly go under and—bitter and hurt—return to solitude.[78]

Upon leaving Helgoland, Levi had planned to stop in Bremen, Wolfenbüttel, and Giessen and then travel on to Karlsruhe in mid-August. Newspapers were late in arriving on the isle of Sylt, and he therefore had no idea of the political events that would stymie his plans. Just one day before Levi had written to Brahms, Bismarck had published the Ems Dispatch that challenged the French government and caused France to declare war on Prussia.

Karlsruhe lay a stone's throw from the showplace of war. The city bustled with inconceivable enthusiasm. Ida Lessing wrote to Ferdinand Hiller: "How wonderful it is to be German, I'm so proud to give our nation two capable officers that rush out gladly as if to a ball and can hardly wait to measure themselves against the enemy."[79] Clara Schumann saw things differently:

> These victory cries everywhere frighten me. How much life will it cost? For weeks now we can hear bombardments from Strasbourg, it's horrible! How many of our young men this war will claim, how much grief it will cause.[80]

In Karlsruhe the mobilization of divisions from Baden was ordered immediately after the French declared war. Crowds thronged to see the Crown Prince of

Prussia take command of his southern troops. From the city's market square one could hear the cannon thunder from Alsace. As soon as news of first victories arrived at Baden's capitol, people gathered in front of the palace singing "The Watch on the Rhine." The grand duke and duchess stepped out before the portal and asked the crowd to sing "Now Thank We All Our God."

People from every social stratum volunteered to support the troops. Friends even had difficulty keeping Brahms from returning to Germany and reporting for military duty. His friend, Viennese surgeon Theodor Billroth, had volunteered on the first day of the war and oversaw the military hospital in Wissembourg. He wrote home:

> Indeed, you must be smack in the middle of war to understand the horror and the splendor. . . . My work here with Czerny is extremely fortunate and a boon. . . . I can do what I want and help and learn.[81]

After hearing news of the war, Levi cut short his vacation in the North and went straight to Karlsruhe. On discovering that Karlsruhe's theater was to remain closed for some time, he volunteered as a paramedic. Notes from his war diary describe his front line experience:

> 8/18. 4 a.m. to Maxau. 8/19. On to Hagenau, night quarters on hay, met Hübsch,[82] sudden attack, 30 injured. 8/22. Trip to Pont à Mousson bringing injured to Metz. 8/23. Loaded injured, drove 4 heavily injured to Nancy. 8/24. Cared for dysentery patients, assisted at bandaging. 8/25. Helped make limb casts. 8/26. Masses of injured die, no water. A member of parliament sent to Metz to record names of injured and a trumpeter were killed. Emptied bedpans for dysentery patients. 8/27. Attended an interesting resection. 8/28. A soldier came in with both eyes shot through. 9/1. News from Karlsruhe that the theater will re-open.[83]

In mid-September the battle at Sedan and victory at Metz ended the war. Levi could go home. To the extent that his weak constitution allowed, he had done his duty. Once he returned to Karlsruhe, one of the first things he did was to visit the Schumann family in Baden-Baden where he learned with relief that all of his friends had survived the war uninjured. The beleaguered city of Strasbourg had capitulated just a few days earlier. Levi persuaded Clara and two of her daughters, Marie and Eugenie, to take the train to Alsace with him and visit the city they considered now "liberated" from French rule. With them thousands of people crossed a makeshift bridge over the Rhine at Kehl. They strolled along the city's crumbled walls, paths still strewn with shell splinters. Levi and the ladies admired the unscathed cathedral. Taking a packed train—people even sat on the roof—they returned to Baden-Baden late at night.

Despite her French citizenship, Madame Viardot-García had spent the weeks of war in Baden-Baden. She and her daughters had sewn uniforms for the German soldiers. But when she heard of the French defeat at Sedan and that Napoleon had been seized, she moved back to Paris and never returned to Baden-Baden.

In Karlsruhe things gradually returned to normal. On October 9 Levi opened the new playing season with a new production of Mozart's *Don Giovanni*. In the weeks that followed, the troupe presented operas that they already knew well: Bellini's *Norma*, Kreutzer's *Nachtlager von Granada*, Rossini's *Barber of Seville*, Cherubini's *Water Carrier*, Verdi's *Troubadour*, Donizetti's *Favorite*, Mozart's *Abduction from the Seraglio*, and Flotow's *Alessandro Stradella*. Levi took particular care with Cherubini's *Medea*. He and Eduard Devrient had retranslated and rearranged the piece. And Levi had not forgotten his former colleague's advice. He gave priority to Gluck's operas, producing *Armida* in December 1870 and preparing *Iphigenia in Tauris* at the end of the season using a new translation by Otto Devrient; the next season, he produced *Alceste*. On the eve to Beethoven's one hundredth birthday, the company played Goethe's *Egmont* to Beethoven's stage music; on December 19 the orchestra gave a festive symphony concert. Besides increasing professional obligations, Levi also had heartache. His stepsister "Gustchen" had moved to Karlsruhe in 1867 where she lived with her husband, merchant Jakob Mombart.[84] Brahms described her as a particularly sweet, but delicate, even frail young woman. After the birth of her second child, at the age of twenty-five she caught tuberculosis. Brahms looked after her when she stayed in Baden-Baden with her father to restore her health. Hermann, who in the summer of 1871 took treatments in Alexanderbad near Wunsiedel to boost his own health, was relieved that Brahms wrote him soothing reports of her recovery. Since early childhood he had been close to Gustchen and could not deal with her grave condition. Although her doctors gave up in 1871, she lived another two years and died during the first off-season following Levi's commencement of work in Munich.

On 4 April 1871, regiments from Baden marched into Karlsruhe, led by Prince Wilhelm. The next day Levi performed Brahms's *German Requiem* at the Protestant City Church in memory of the fallen. Soloists Magdalene Murjahn and Julius Stockhausen sang without pay and Levi, who had just recovered from an illness, conducted "ailing, but with saintly fervor" as Stockhausen said.[85]

In late April Brahms announced by wire that he would arrive in Karlsruhe at 1 a.m.: "Perhaps you night owls will be hanging around the station." In his valise he brought drafts for two new choral works, the *Schicksalslied*, op. 54, based on text by Hölderlin, and a *Bismarcklied* that was later published as *Triumphlied*, op. 55. He stayed a few days at Levi's home on *Grünwinkler Allee*, which after the formation of the Reich was—at Levi's suggestion—renamed *Bismarck Strasse*. They both agreed that Levi should present *Schicksalslied* in the fall. Taking Levi's advice, Brahms altered the final act, eliminated the last choir segment, and let the orchestra end the piece.[86] Levi wrote out a piano arrangement and made a few suggestions for improved orchestration.

While finishing the score for the *Schicksalslied* at his summer quarters in Lichtental, Brahms kept in touch with Levi. He asked him for advice in practical matters of music and found inspiration at opera performances. On May 24 he heard Cherubini's *Medea* at the court theater and was, as he noted afterward, fascinated. He ordered four tickets for the performance on May 28 in Baden-Baden in order to hear *Medea* again, this time taking Clara Schumann and her daughters Marie and Eugenie. Brahms prepared carefully for hearing this opera by studying the score beforehand in one of the theater's rehearsal rooms.

While Levi was away at the health resort Alexanderbad during the months of July and August, Allgeyer brought the manuscript for the *Schicksalslied* to Karlsruhe's copier, Joseph Füller, who then wrote out the parts for the orchestra and choir. In September Levi began rehearsing it, using the handwritten piano arrangement and a copy of the score that he had made for himself. The composer's original had been sent in late September to publisher Simrock for etching.

The presentation was "based on the manuscript," as the program explicitly notes, and took place on October 18 at the first fall concert of the Philharmonic Society. Brahms conducted the performance that Levi had prepared. The program also included *Scenes from Goethe's Faust* by Robert Schumann, with the participation of Johanna Schwarz (soprano) and Julius Stockhausen (baritone). The latter also sang two songs by Franz Schubert, "Old Man's Song" and "Secrets" with orchestral accompaniment composed by Brahms.[87]

Brahms gave Levi the original score of the *Schicksalslied* in gratitude for his thorough rehearsal of the work. Fifty years later the valuable manuscript and other autographs were bought by a private American collector from Levi's widow's estate.[88]

While Brahms spent October days with Levi, the two discussed the selection of songs based on texts by Friedrich Daumer that were being prepared for publication. Brahms made a present to Levi of no. 7, *Die Schnur, die Perl an Perle* (Pearl by Pearl), which, together with the other songs, was published by Simrock as op. 57. Levi had gotten to know the Daumer songs the summer before and played them often for his friends.

A few months later, another guest stayed with Levi: composer Ferdinand Hiller from Cologne, who conducted his fifth symphony, op. 67, at the fifth subscription concert on 6 January 1872, and also performed three of his own piano pieces as a soloist. Since the days of Karlsruhe's productions of Hiller's operas *The Catacombs* and *The Deserter* they had continued to correspond. And Hiller's old admirer, Ida Lessing, kept him always informed of the music scene in Karlsruhe. During his first years of work there, Levi had not been given a budget for inviting guest conductors. Meager profits made from concerts were distributed among the musicians. But meanwhile he had gained so much respect that he could ask the ducal treasury for money to host renowned guests. For the first subscription concert in the fall season of 1871, Levi invited Leipzig's Gewandhaus Kapellmeister Carl Reinecke, under whose auspice he had presented his own piano concerto, op. 1, back in 1861.

Levi had explained the budget situation to Hiller. Hiller performed for the honor of it, saying that he had wanted to travel to southern Germany anyway to visit his daughter Tony, an actress in Freiburg. He would be content with a medal from the duke and to play the piano for the duchess "for as long as she can take it." While Levi's friendship with Reinecke turned on music alone, his tie to Hiller was cordial. They respected one another and had—for the time being—similar views on music. Ferdinand Hiller was the son of Isaac Hildesheim from Frankfurt and came, like Levi, from an old, Jewish family with a long tradition. And like Levi, he had begun his career as a composer and pianist but ultimately shaped the musical taste of a whole city. For decades he led the Lower Rhine Music Festival. In Dresden he often met with Wagner, even supported him financially. That did not stop Wagner, however, from disqualifying Hiller's compositions. Later Hiller turned away from Wagner's works, while valuing those of Brahms. In January 1872 he certainly spoke with Levi about how to evaluate Wagner as a composer. During those weeks Levi was working with Wagner's music. His program for the February concert began with Mozart's late Symphony in G Minor and ended with Wagner's prelude and closing song from *Tristan and Isolde*. He had heard them two months earlier, directed by the composer himself.

Hermann Levi's first personal encounter with Richard Wagner happened on 20 December 1871 in Mannheim. Music store proprietor Emil Heckel had founded the first Richard Wagner Association and invited Wagner to conduct a concert at Mannheim's National Theater. It took the combined orchestras from both Mannheim and Karlsruhe to be large enough. A huge circle of disciples gathered around Richard and Cosima Wagner who stayed at the Hôtel de l'Europe for five days. Friends from out of town started arriving as soon as rehearsals commenced: Alexander Ritter from Zurich (whose mother donated 500 talers to Wagner every year); Baden-Baden's author of music literature, Richard Pohl; and Professor Friedrich Nietzsche from Basel, at the time one of Wagner's most ardent admirers. Prior to the first rehearsal, court conductor Vincenz Lachner introduced Wagner to the orchestra. Cosima found Lachner's words ridiculous: the conductor that normally schemed against him now compared Wagner to the German Kaiser. On December 20 Baden's grand duke and duchess attended the festive concert and during intermission summoned Wagner to their loge. Wagner irritated them by touting the king of Bavaria for sponsoring the completion of the *Ring*. The grand duke took offense because he had been unable to bind Wagner to Karlsruhe with the *Tristan* project. The concert lasted from six to nine in the evening and included Wagner's *Kaiser March*, the overture from *Magic Flute*, and Beethoven's Symphony no. 7, and then, after an intermission, Wagner's preludes to *Lohengrin* and *Meistersinger* as well as the prelude to *Love Death* from *Tristan and Isolde*. Of this musical event in

Mannheim, Nietzsche wrote that it was exactly what he meant by "music" in the Dionysian sense of the word.

It was certainly also a Dionysian experience for Hermann Levi, who sat in the audience with perked ears. He, too, was invited to the banquet afterward, where many toasts were spoken for Wagner until finally the exhausted and hoarse master found words of praise for the city:

> The people of Mannheim have confirmed my belief that my plans can be made to work. The very name of the city itself, Mannheim, designates a place where "men" are "at home." Bayreuth has not yet been consecrated by culture; it is truly virginal ground for the arts. May a new, young and strong cultural life be born of this union.[89]

The next morning Levi took the train with Wagner, Cosima, and Nietzsche. When he got off in Karlsruhe, Wagner kissed him good-bye. As the train moved on toward Switzerland, Wagner remarked that he respected this conductor at least for using his real name, "Levi," and not changing it to Loewe or Levin as many Jews had done.

Cosima noted in her diary that many Jews had attended the performance in Mannheim. This and other entries reveal how frequently Cosima and Richard discussed Jews and the influence they had on music. Two decades earlier Wagner's essay "Judaism in Music" had been published under a pseudonym, but its author was quickly disclosed.[90] Although the publication aroused widespread disgust, Cosima encouraged Wagner to have it printed a second time in March 1869 under his real name. This all occurred during the very years that legislation was finally passed to cement the equal civil status of Jews in Germany.

Levi was uncertain of how to react to Wagner in light of Wagner's anti-Semitism. He and Brahms often discussed what they thought of Wagner, especially after becoming familiar with *Tristan* and *Meistersinger*. Brahms valued Wagner as a composer, but wanted nothing to do with him personally, particularly because of his anti-Semitism. Though Wagner sought it, artistic rivalry was entirely foreign to Brahms's nature.

Levi, on the other hand, knew that as a conductor of music for the stage there was no way of getting around Wagner. His own morals let him look for Wagner's positive, human, traits and present them favorably to Brahms. On 3 May 1870, he wrote: "You will remember that I once defended his pamphlet on Jews because I thought it was written by a serious artistic mind."[91] In a much later comment to Cosima, Levi spoke even more favorably of the essay. When we read "Judaism in Music" today, we find it very difficult to understand how Levi—coming from a family of rabbis—could defend Wagner's anti-Jewish views, particularly opinions such as: "Historically, we must call the period of Jewishness in modern music one of complete idleness, of degenerated stagnation."[92] Not once in the essay did Wagner mention Meyerbeer by name, but

Meyerbeer is clearly the composer "who writes operas for Paris and has them performed everywhere else." Wagner's devastating verdict on Meyerbeer downplays the dark chapter of his own years in Paris when he had flattered Meyerbeer in the hope that Meyerbeer would use his influence to draw attention to Wagner's own compositions.

Levi accepted Wagner's negative opinion of Meyerbeer because it confirmed his own view of the man. But what might he have thought of Wagner's opinion that Yiddish is "hissing, shrieking, buzzing, and bungling"? How could he tolerate Wagner's haunting words to "remember that only one thing can spare you the curse you bear, namely Jehovah's own salvation, which would be your ruin!"?[93] Levi came from a liberal, reformed Jewish community. As a youth at the organ he had accompanied chorales sung in German in the synagogue. He considered himself a secular representative of German culture; he was as well read in verse by Goethe and Schiller as he was familiar with the Old Testament. He felt that one must abandon orthodoxy and embrace modernity, meaning assimilation, becoming less a Jew and more a worldly citizen. This he saw confirmed by the second printing of Wagner's pamphlet. It mentioned that Wagner had truly congenial friends that fate had delivered to him out of Jewry, friends that stand with him on equal ground. Levi wanted to be one of them.

In December 1871 Levi had no idea of the sorrow he would bring upon himself by taking to Wagner. And it was an attraction that beset him to his very last breath. Ferdinand Hiller wrote bitterly in January 1782: "You didn't tell me that Wagner kissed you. So he wasn't afraid of Jewish contagion!"[94] But it was Wagner who was contagious.

During that season the Karlsruhe Court Theater presented *Meistersinger* three times. Levi found it strangely ironic that he professionally had to work with that piece at a time when "entirely different music" deeply moved him. By that he meant Brahms's *Triumphlied*, the score of which had been in his hands since November for copying. His enthusiasm for it was boundless. To Brahms he wrote, "Hail and praise and thanksgiving for the hour you were born to the nation!"[95] To Clara Schumann he wrote that Brahms's *Hallelujah* combined Handel's simplicity with Bach's polyphony and that nothing greater had been written in sacred music for a century. While Karlsruhe's copier Füller wrote out the parts, Levi was busy planning a grand music festival for the first presentation of the work. Clara Schumann and Joachim and his wife were to participate. Levi suggested to Brahms that it be performed in the Protestant Town Church, whose good acoustics would let the small choir sound full and mighty.

But it was not meant to be. Once again Bavaria's Royal Theater expressed a desire to hire Levi. Sophie Stehle, a dramatic soprano at Munich's court opera, had guest performed at the Karlsruhe opera from 18 January to 4 February 1872 where she sang eight different parts, including Elisabeth from *Tannhäuser*, Marie from *The Daughter of the Regiment*, and the gypsy Azucena from *Troubadour*. She was thrilled by the work of Karlsruhe's conductor and upon her return to Munich immediately insisted that theater director Baron von Perfall reassume negotiations with Levi. Perfall was disgruntled over orchestra conductor Wüllner's recent promotion to opera conductor. He also wanted to prevent Hans von Bülow from gaining influence in Munich. So he acted fast. In late March he invited Levi to Würzburg for talks and made him a definite offer. On April 1 Levi sent a request to the grand duke of Baden asking for release from his position at the end of the playing season. He said he was unable to work properly with stage director Kaiser. He enclosed a copy of the offer from Munich: an annual salary of 3800 guldens plus eight weeks of paid summer holidays and the prerogative to conduct all new opera productions.

The duke offered him an equal salary, almost twice what Levi had earned before, and unlimited authority in opera operations. But Levi replied: *Too late!* He could not pass up the opportunity to lead an orchestra twice the size of that in Karlsruhe, to conduct *Tristan* soon, and the entire *Ring* later. He accepted the offer from Munich, taking the resentment of his former royal employer in stride. "Wow," he wrote to Ferdinand Hiller, "how I look forward to the orchestra! I suppose I should be nervous, but when I look at my German colleagues, none of them are multi-talents either, and I'm not even the worst!"[96]

Levi's petition for release was granted promptly, but his request for an audience with the grand duke was denied. He wrote to court treasurer Kreidel in an attempt to disperse bad feelings by once more listing the reasons that left him with no choice: 1) in Munich he would lead an orchestra of over one hundred musicians, 2) he would have great influence on the musical trends not only of a major city, but of entire Southern Germany, 3) Munich had knocked thrice at his door, and that seemed like fate calling. It would have been indecent, he said, to use Munich's offer merely to improve his position in Karlsruhe. He added that he had requested an audience with the duke particularly because he wished to explain what he felt needed changing in Karlsruhe, and to express his heartfelt gratitude for all the benevolence His Highness had bestowed on him during his work under His Highness's auspice.[97] Shortly before leaving Karlsruhe, Levi was given an audience by the ducal family.

Levi sent stage director Kaiser a list of conductors that he considered qualified to take over his position. These included Brahms's suggestion (Ernst Frank from Vienna), Alfred Volkland from Leipzig, Joachim and Bülow's suggestion (Moritz Moszkowski), and Max Zenger from Munich. Max Zenger got the post, but held it just one year. He was followed by Josef Ruzek. An adequate replacement for Levi was not found until 1875 when Otto Dessoff[98] from Vienna raised his baton in Karlsruhe.

Congratulations came from all sides. Ferdinand Hiller, who, to his great satisfaction, had received the Order of the Zähringer Lion for his concert in Karlsruhe, wrote to Levi: "I hope in thirty years to see a statue of you in Munich next to that of Orlando di Lasso."[99] Richard Wagner's telegram read: "Congratulate Munich, pity you!"[100] In his next letter, Wagner asked Levi to help him get five musicians released from Karlsruhe as extras for the performance of Beethoven's Symphony no. 9 on the occasion of laying the cornerstone for the Festival House in Bayreuth on Whitsuntide. Karlsruhe's stage director Kaiser refused because he needed his players for the premiere of Gounod's *Margarethe.* Wagner snorted: "Then let Gounod have his Pentecost." On Levi's switch to Munich he wrote:

> Munich! Well, well! If you believe in a personal God, may He help you!—I shall be pleased to learn that after they are performed in Bayreuth you will present my *Nibelungen* in Munich.[101]

Brahms was the first that Levi informed of his decision to go to Munich, asking in the same letter whether during the "interregnum" in September and October they might not take a trip to Italy together. The plan for the music festival in Karlsruhe had fallen through and Levi suggested in its place having a farewell concert at which Brahms would direct the *Triumphlied.* As in his reply regarding the *German Requiem*, Brahms once again wrote that in Karlsruhe he would rather sit in the audience. He refused to indicate metronome settings that Levi had requested, saying that he didn't know how to use a metronome and that Reinthaler had written them into the score for *Requiem.*

Alongside dress rehearsals for Karlsruhe's premiere of Gounod's *Margarethe* on May 9, Levi prepared his farewell concert in high spirits. The date was set for June 5, the first day of the theater's off-season. Carl Will, concertmaster and speaker of the orchestra, applied for ducal permission to use the theater for this purpose. The request was granted, but the musicians had to pay for lighting and ushers out of their own pockets. In other words, it was the orchestra, not the administration, that organized the farewell concert. The Philharmonic Society and the theater choir agreed to help out in premiering the *Triumphlied.*

The evening's solo performers were Levi's friends, Clara Schumann and Julius Stockhausen. Joachim canceled because his wife Amalie was ill. The poster announcing a "Grand Farewell Concert in Honor of Ducal Court Kapellmeister Hermann Levi, sponsored by the Court Orchestra" mentioned not only the solo musicians and the choirs, but also the "kind support of local amateurs." The program attested to Levi's love of Beethoven, Schumann, and Brahms. It began with Beethoven's Symphony no. 8, followed by Clara Schumann playing her husband's piano concerto. Stockhausen sang an aria from *Ezio* by Handel and songs by Franz Schubert. Clara then played a gavotte by Gluck as arranged by Brahms and the scherzo from Mendelssohn's *Summer Night's Dream.* After intermission they presented Brahms's *Triumphlied.*

It was a festive evening. The theater was filled to the last seat. Levi was greeted with a fanfare, a shower of flowers, and endless ovations. There were many speeches. Clara Schumann was very pleased with her own performance that evening and found everyone in high spirits. Finally the audience called Brahms onto the stage, continuing the applause until he came down from the second-level balcony.

A few guests had taken great pains to come: publisher Simrock came from Berlin; men of letters Franz Gehring and Ottilie Ebner came from Vienna. Court Councilor Billroth was unable to attend and sent instead a silver cup to Brahms with the inscription: "For the Master of German Composition Johannes Brahms, in Memory of 5 June 1872." Following the concert Levi celebrated with Brahms, the solo performers, and all of his friends at the inn *Erbprinz*. Many more speeches were given in honor of the composer and the departing conductor. Levi was too moved to speak. "My friends, I can't," he said, and the whole crowd merrily raised their glasses. Then Brahms and Clara Schumann sat down at the piano and played four-handedly to let everyone else dance.

At the time, the premiere of this piece that we rarely hear today, the *Triumphlied*, was considered a national event. Based on passages from the Bible, Brahms considered it primarily a religious work. But carried by the national enthusiasm of the day, he wanted to dedicate it to the German emperor. Franz Simrock and Joseph Joachim applied for permission for him to do so and that permission was granted, although the emperor showed no interest in it at all. Brahms wrote:

> To Your Highest and Most Powerful, Most Merciful Emperor and Lord: The accomplishments of recent years are so grand and glorious that anyone unable to enter combat for Germany's greatness must feel all the more a need to say and show how happy he is to have experienced these times. Indeed, urged by these sentiments of gratitude and joy I have tried to express them by composing a triumph song. I have put music to words from the Revelation of John and although no one can miss what it celebrates I cannot suppress the desire to indicate that special occasion and intention of this work by dedicating it to Your Majesty. Thus I respectfully dare to ask whether I may dedicate the *Triumphlied* to Your Majesty when it is in print. Your Imperial Royal Majesty's most loyal subject, Johannes Brahms.[102]

This significant work, a piece "of compositional quality thoroughly equal to all other choral works by Brahms,"[103] has been all but forgotten and is rarely performed today. More than 125 years later, we can barely grasp Brahms's and Levi's joy at Germany's victory and the humiliation it caused France. Today we would not tolerate using passages from the Bible to glorify patriotism. As a hymn, as a spiritual chorale work, this composition with its splendorous polyphony might be rediscovered, if it were taken only for its religious significance and *Hallelujah* were meant to celebrate the reconciliation of all peoples. But that was not Brahms's intention.

After his farewell concert, Levi left for Munich where he soon saw *Tristan* directed by Bülow, held meetings with theater director Baron von Perfall and his future colleague Franz Wüllner, and signed the lease on a handsome apartment

Hermann Levi, portrait in oil by Franz von Stuck. Regina Heilmann-Thon (Baldham, Germany).

on *Arcis Strasse* (no. 32). In July he took water treatments in Alexanderbad; in September he traveled to Italy without Brahms. But first he stopped in Bayreuth on August 17 and 18 to visit Richard Wagner, who at the time was practicing the *Valkyrie* role of Siegmund with tenor Albert Niemann. The next day Wagner played fragments from *Götterdämmerung* (Twilight of the Gods) on which he was currently working. At dinner there was a slight dissonance when Levi criticized Bismarck's law regulating Jesuits. In leaving, Levi commented to Cosima that he was relieved to go because now he felt like a complete *null* and would have to try to find himself again. To which Cosima remarked: "I think that one finds oneself by comparing oneself to the great and then surrendering."[104]

In the years to come, Levi would *surrender* often enough at the Wagner home. In early October he returned to Karlsruhe one last time to pack his belongings and celebrate his promotion with Julius Allgeyer and Clara Schumann. For Levi it meant not only leaving a beloved circle of friends, it also closed a chapter of his life.

NOTES

1. Joseph Strauss, born 15 May 1793 in Brno, died 1 December 1866 in Karlsruhe, violinist and conductor, studied in Vienna with Seyfried and Schuppanzigh, was concertmaster in Prague and Mannheim and as of 1824 in Karlsruhe. From 1825 to 1864, he was Karlsruhe's ducal Kapellmeister. He wrote music for plays and operas. Richard Wagner said of him: "Everyone followed his orders as they would for a man who accepted no nonsense and kept his people under control. Strangely, this elderly gentleman is the only renowned conductor I have met to have true fire." Richard Wagner, *Gesammelte Schriften* (Collected Writings) (Leipzig, 1914), 9:155.

2. Friedrich Walter, *Briefe Vincenz Lachners an Hermann Levi* (Vincenz Lachner's Letters to Hermann Levi) (Mannheim, 1931), 15ff.

3. Ibid.

4. Wilhelm Kalliwoda, born 19 July 1827 in Donaueschingen, died 8 September 1893 in Karlsruhe, son of composer Johann Wenzel Kalliwoda. He studied at the Leipzig Conservatory, finishing in 1845, then became music director in Aarau (Switzerland), and afterward director of music at St. Stephan in Karlsruhe. As of 1853, he was music director at Baden's court theater. As of 1864, his position was coordinated with that of Hermann Levi, and in 1865 he was granted the title of Kapellmeister, having to accept being second to Levi. In 1875 he resigned from the theater and became head of the Philharmonic Society. He composed masses and choir music and wrote notes for lieder and some—in part—virtuoso piano pieces, stylistically reminiscent of Mendelssohn.

5. At the time, the first conductor was the "Kapellmeister," the second conductor was called the "music director."

6. Rolf Kabel, ed., *Eduard Devrient: Aus seinen Tagebüchern* (From the Diaries of Eduard Devrient), 2 vols. (Weimar, 1964), 2:99.

7. Historical Archive of the City of Cologne, letter dated 31 December 1863.

8. Generallandesarchiv Karlsruhe, no. 57/236, letter dated 4 January 1864.

9. The cast for *Lohengrin* on 7 August 1864, included: Karl Brulliot (King Heinrich), Wilhelm Brandes (Lohengrin), Anna Braunhofer (Elsa von Brabant), Joseph Hauser (Friedrich von Telramund), Amalia Boni (Ortrud), and Mr. Schmid, first name unknown (as the King's Herald).

10. In 1864 Baden's court orchestra consisted of eight first and six second violins, four violas, three cellos, two basses, three sets of woodwinds, four horns, three trumpets, three trombones, one bass tuba, one harp, and one kettledrum.

11. A. Kessler and F. Hofmann, eds., *Almanach und Adressbuch des Grossherzoglichen Hoftheaters* (Almanac and Directory of the Grand Ducal Court Theater) (Karlsruhe, 1865), 101ff.

12. Brahms, vol. 6, letter dated 29 August 1864.

13. Devrient, vol. 2, notes from 26 August 1864; list of the orchestra concerts given by the Association of Composers. Unless otherwise noted, Max Seifiz, Royal Kapellmeister for Hohenzollern-Hechingen, conducted all concerts. The grand ducal court orchestra was augmented by members of court orchestras from Stuttgart, Löwenberg, and Sonderhausen; the Grand Ducal Court Theater choir was fortified by local amateurs. First Concert: Eduard Lassen—Festive March (directed by the composer); Prolog spoken by Ludwig Eckhardt. First Section: Heinrich Strauss—Overture "Tasso's Complaint" (directed by the composer); Robert Volkmann—Concert for cello (solo by David Popper, conducted by the composer); Johann Joseph Abert—Symphony (conducted by the composer). Second Section: Youri Von Arnold—Overture "Boris Godunow" (directed by the composer); Joseph Joachim—Concert for violin in a Hungarian style (solo Eduard Reményi); Hans von Bülow—"The Singer's Curse," a ballade for the orchestra. Third Section: Franz Liszt—Psalm 13 for solos, choir, and orchestra. Second Concert: First Section: Heinrich Gottwald—March "Maria from Hungary" (conducted by the composer); Wilhelm Freudenberg—Dramatic scenes for soprano and tenor from the opera *Diana* (directed by Heinrich Strauss); Friedrich Kiel—Concert for piano and orchestra (solo Otfried Rötscher); Adolf Jensen—"Song of the Norns" for solos and women's choir (directed by Heinrich Strauss); Franz Liszt—"Mephisto Waltzes" for orchestra. Second Section: Max Seifriz—Overtures; Hector Berlioz—"Reverie and Caprice" for violin and orchestra (solo Heinrich Kömpel); Otto Bach: Wedding music for Hebbel's *Nibelungen* (directed by Heinrich Strauss); Adolf Jensen—Bride Song for solo, choir, and instruments (directed by Heinrich Strauss); Franz Liszt—"Festive Sounds."

14. Summer 1861, indicated by Max Kalbeck, is incorrect.

15. Louis Schindelmeisser, born 8 December 1811 in Königsberg, died 30 March 1864 in Darmstadt, was theater Kapellmeister in (among other places) Hamburg from 1847 to 1848, Frankfurt/Main from 1848 to 1851, Wiesbaden from 1851 to 1853, and then again in Darmstadt, where he particularly promoted Wagner's works, to whom he had been a close friend since 1831. In a letter to Clara Schumann, Levi calls Schindelmeisser "a pitiful specimen of a kapellmeistered musician" (Litzmann, 3:145).

16. Litzmann, vol. 3, letter dated 1 August 1863.

17. Litzmann, vol. 3, letter dated 12 October 1864.

18. Brahms, vol. 6, letter dated 29 August 1864.

19. Brahms, vol. 7, letter from December 1864. *Flour sacks* alludes to bakers that lived in the same house as Levi; *white pants* were the favorite garb of Levi and his assistant Paul David.

20. Brahms, vol. 7, letter dated December 1864. Brahms's ditty twists words to make them all rhyme by ending with "-ung," which sounds rather comical.

21. Litzmann, vol. 3, letter dated 20 December 1866.

22. Leviana; Julius Allgeyer writing to Clara Schumann on 27 June 1900.

23. Kalbeck, 2:560.

24. On 25 July 1899, Levi wrote to Landgravine Anna of Hesse: "At my suggestion Brahms rewrote the F-Minor Sonata (of which I own the manuscript) to become a quintet." (Archive of the Kurhesse Foundation, Fasanerie Palace near Fulda. This archive also has a hand copy of the score for two pianos, parts of which Brahms himself filled in.)

25. Brahms, vol. 7, letter dated 6 November 1864.

26. Traveling salesman.

27. Actress and stage-writer Charlotte Birch-Pfeiffer, born 23 June 1800 in Stuttgart, died 25 August 1868 in Breslau. From 1837 to 1843, she directed the City Theater of Zurich; afterward she acted at the Royal Theater in Berlin. She wrote seventy-four dramas, most of them based on French novels (Dumas, Hugo, Sand), popular tearjerkers that were performed often during her lifetime.

28. Until the end of the nineteenth century, symphony concerts given by Karlsruhe's Court Orchestra took place in the large hall of the "Museum Society." The Museum Society was a group of intellectual and artistically interested citizens that met regularly for lectures, talks, and performances. In 1813 they built a handsome building in the middle of town, based on plans by architect Friedrich Weinbrenner. It was destroyed by fire in 1918. The building that the Deutsche Bank later erected in its place corresponds approximately in size to the "Museum" that was never a museum in today's sense of the word.

29. Sietz, vol. 3, letters dated 2 January and 22 February 1865.

30. Devrient, 2:560.

31. Pauline Viardot-García, born 18 July 1821 in Paris, died 18 May 1910 in Paris, came from a famous family of singers: she was the daughter of Manuel García and sister to Malibran. She debuted in 1839 in London in the role of Desdemona in Rossini's *Othello* and sang (in St. Petersburg and Moscow, and as of 1859 in Paris) all of the grand roles for mezzo soprano (Rosina, Cenerentola, Fides, Orpheus, Sonnambula). As of 1862 she lived in Baden-Baden, establishing a renowned school for song; after 1871 she lived in London and Paris. She composed lieder and little operas (libretti by Ivan Turgenev) that were performed in her private theater in Baden. Her circle of friends included Chopin, Gounod, Flaubert, Maupassant, and Delacroix. Robert Schumann dedicated to Pauline Viardot-García his *Liederkreis*, op. 24, on poems by Heinrich Heine.

32. GLA no. 57/236, 21, dated 4 September 1865.

33. In 1859 painter Adolf Schroedter (1808–1875) had been called from Dusseldorf to Karlsruhe's polytechnic school as professor for ornament drawing and aquarelle.

34. Eugenie Schumann: *Erinnerungen* (Memories) (Stuttgart, 1927), 183ff. "Oh friends, not these [sad] notes!" by Schiller, as used in the finale of Beethoven's Symphony no. 9.

35. Brahms, 7:57. Feuerbach had hoped that the purchase of *Medea* would establish him in Karlsruhe. Gallery director Lessing's refusal crushed that hope. (See also Julius Allgeyer, *Anselm Feuerbach* [Bamberg, 1894], 277ff.)

36. *Karlsruher Zeitung* from 9 November 1865. Brahms had small hands and could not grasp large chords, thus he had to "unravel" them.

37. Florence May, *The Life of Johannes Brahms* (London, 1905), 367.

38. Anna Ettlinger, *Lebenserinnerungen* (Memories from My Life) (Leipzig, 1920), 59.

39. Canons no. 1, 10, and 11 from op. 13, *Göttlicher Morpheus* (Goethe), *Töne der Brust, Ich weiß nicht, was im Hain die Taube girret* (Ruckert), and an unpublished canon *Töne lindernder Sang* (Von Knebel). The original manuscripts preserved by the City

Archive of Karlsruhe deviate considerably from later published versions. (Illustrations thereof can be found in the exhibition catalog *Brahms in Baden-Baden and Karlsruhe* [Karlsruhe, 1983], 44f.)

40. "Wenn gleich es besser wär für sein Glück, Er setzte den Suppenkaspar in Musik, Weil daraus erhellt, wie es geht auf Erden, Wenn man mit Gewalt will magerer werden." [It would be better for his happiness to write music for (Heinrich Hoffmann's) Soup-Kasper, because it shows what happens when you force yourself to diet.] Anna Ettlinger, "For May 6, 1873," Archive of the Society of the Friends of Music, Vienna.

41. Litzmann, vol. 3, letter dated 18 April 1866. The last sentence quotes Schumann's essay "*Neue Bahnen*" (New Paths) (*NZfM* 28 October 1853), with which Schumann had heralded the appearance of the young genius Brahms.

42. Ich hab im Traum geweinet—Und Meine Seele spannte weit ihre Flügel aus—O versenk dein Leid. Texts by Heine, Eichendorf, and Reinicke.

43. Litzmann, vol. 3, letter dated 20 December 1866.

44. As Bavarian court conductor, on 28 October 1887, Levi critically reviewed Max Bruch's opera *Loreley*: "Overall, the way it is, the textbook is simply pitiable. The music is good inasmuch as the composer is an excellent musician, but bad inasmuch as he has no idea of drama and effect" (Leviana).

45. Leviana, letter dated 6 January 1867.

46. Leviana, letter dated 26 April 1868.

47. Devrient, vol. 2, entry for 2 December 1869.

48. Litzmann, vol. 3, letter dated 23 November 1867.

49. Devrient, vol. 2, notes from 22 and 27 November 1867.

50. Litzmann, vol. 3, letter dated 5 December 1867.

51. Gustav Wendt, born 24 January 1827 in Berlin, died 6 March 1912 in Karlsruhe, classical philologist, studied with Ritschl in Bonn and after working in Posen, Greifenberg, and Hamm became director of the lyceum in Karlsruhe in 1867, where he supervised the new building of the high school for humanities. Gustav Wendt was a friend of both Paul Heyse and Brahms, with whom he spent summer vacations as of 1886 at Lake Thun and in Bad Ischl. Wendt published works for use in schools. His Sophocles translation (1884) is dedicated to Johannes Brahms. He was the maternal grandfather of Wilhelm Furtwängler.

52. Litzmann, vol. 3, letter dated January 1868.

53. "Badische Chronik," *Karlsruher Zeitung*, 29 March 1868.

54. GLA no. 57/438, O5, letter dated 7 August 1868.

55. Lachner to Levi, letter dated 16 September 1868.

56. Sietz, vol. 2, letter dated 26 March 1868.

57. Brahms, vol. 7, letter dated 22 February 1869.

58. Orel, 47.

59. Brahms, vol. 7, letter dated 22 February 1869. In Vienna the kettledrummer had ruined the performance by playing too loud.

60. Brahms, vol. 7, letter dated 22 February 1869.

61. *Karlsruher Zeitung*, 14 March 1869. Editor and music critic Kroenlein.

62. *Badische Landeszeitung*, 18 March 1869.

63. *Badische Landeszeitung*, 21 March 1869.
64. Anna Ettlinger, *Lebenserinnerungen* (Karlsruhe, 1920), 61ff.
65. Litzmann, vol. 3, entry dated 12 May 1869.
66. Litzmann, vol. 3, entry dated 24 August 1869.
67. A party before a wedding where porcelain is smashed to bring good luck to the couple.
68. Litzmann, vol. 3, entry in late September 1869.
69. The waltzes were played in this order: op. 52, no. 1, 2, 4, 5; op. 65, no. 9; op. 52, no. 11, 8, 9. The singers were not the same as at rehearsals in August. This time they were Luise Hausmann, Magdalena Hauser, Benedikt Kürner, and Karl Brulliot.
70. Litzmann, vol. 3, entry for 6 October 1869.
71. Brahms, vol. 7, letter dated 3 May 1870.
72. A comic operetta translated roughly as "an open secret."
73. A numbers opera (*Nummeropera*), very common in the eighteenth century, consists of individual vocal or instrumental pieces that are complete in themselves but tied together by spoken dialogues or recitatives.
74. Brahms, vol. 7, letter from January 1872.
75. Brahms, vol. 7, letter dated 15 January 1872.
76. Brahms, vol. 7, letter dated 17 July 1870. Franz von Holstein, born 26 February 1826 in Brunswick, died 22 May 1878 in Leipzig, studied at the conservatory in Leipzig under Moscheles and Hauptmann. He composed piano music, vocal works, and operas with his own libretti: *Der Haideschacht* based on Hoffmann's *Die Bergwerke von Falun* (Dresden, 1868) was played on forty-six stages (premiering in Karlsruhe on 10 March 1872). Less successful was his opera *Der Erbe von Morlay* (Dresden, 1872), conducted by Levi in Munich in 1874. Holstein's third opera, *Der Hochländer*, was a failure in Mannheim in 1876.
77. Brahms, vol. 7, letter dated 14 July 1870.
78. Brahms, vol. 7, letter dated 14 July 1870.
79. Sietz, vol. 3, letter dated 5 August 1870.
80. Litzmann, vol. 3, letter dated 8 September 1870.
81. *Theodor Billroth: Briefe* (Letters) (Hanover/Leipzig, 1897), letter to his wife dated 12 August 1870. Billroth (1829–1894) was a prominent physician who as of 1860 held a chair for surgery in Zurich and as of 1867 in Vienna, and made decisive progress in surgical methods (ether-chloroform anesthesia, gastric resection). He played piano, violin, and cello and had well-founded knowledge of music. Billroth was a lifelong friend of Brahms, who dedicated Two Quartets, op. 51, to him. Vincenz Czerny (1842–1916) was Billroth's assistant in Vienna and as of 1871 professor for surgery in Freiburg, and as of 1877 in Heidelberg.
82. Probably cavalry captain Heinrich Hübsch. Whether he was related to architect Heinrich Hübsch (1795–1863), architect of Karlsruhe's Art Museum and Court Theater, we do not know.
83. Leviana; diary with entries from the military campaign of August/September 1870.
84. Auguste Levi, born 22 June 1846 in Giessen, was the daughter of Benedict Levi's second wife, Gitel Worms, who died a month after giving birth. Auguste often

visited Karlsruhe, staying with the Veit Ettlinger family. There she met Jakob Mombert, uncle of poet Alfred Mombert. They had two children, Henriette and Moritz. Auguste Mombert died of a lung disease on 4 June 1874 in Karlsruhe.

85. Sietz, vol. 3, letter dated 4 August 1871. Stockhausen wrote to Hiller in French: *Levi, quoique très souffrant, dirigeait avec son feu sacré à vous connu.*

86. Kalbeck, vol. 2. Page 366 shows a facsimile of the first version of the coda published in Levi's handwriting.

87. In 1862 at the wish of Stockhausen, Brahms arranged for the orchestra the piano parts of the songs *Greisengesang* and *Geheimes* by Schubert.

88. *Johannes Brahms, Thematisch-Bibliographisches Werkverzeichnis*, edited by Margit L. McCorkle (Munich, 1984), 225ff.

89. Richard Wagner, *Gesammelte Schriften* (Collected Writings), edited by Julius Kapp (Leipzig, 1914), 2:252.

90. K. Freigedank, "Das Judentum in der Musik" (literally "Jewishness in Music," commonly known, however, as "Judaism in Music"), *NZfM* (New Journal for Music), no. 19 (1850): 101.

91. Brahms, 7:58.

92. See note 90 above. *NZfM*, no. 19 (1850): 106.

93. See note 90 above. *NZfM*, no. 20, 112.

94. Sietz, vol. 6, letter of January 1872.

95. Brahms, vol. 7, letter dated 30 November 1871.

96. Sietz, vol. 3, letter dated 10 April 1872.

97. GLA no. 56/348, letter dated 13 April 1872.

98. Otto Dessoff, born 14 January 1835 in Leipzig, died 28 October 1892 in Frankfurt am Main. Dessoff studied at the conservatory in Leipzig and became conductor in, among other places, Dusseldorf, Aachen, Kassel, and (as of 1860) in Vienna. There he was also the director of the Philharmonic Concerts and given a chair for composition at the conservatory. In 1875 he became court conductor for Karlsruhe and, in 1880, for Frankfurt am Main. His pupils included Heinrich von Herzogenberg, Richard Heuberger, Felix Mottl, and Arthur Nikisch. Heinrich Ordenstein, a pianist and the director of the conservatory in Karlsruhe wrote: "Dessoff's and Levi's artistic natures differed fundamentally. Dessoff had much less fiery temperament and inspirational might. But he was unsurpassed at carefully working out every detail to the highest standards of artistic intellect." (Heinrich Ordenstein, *Musikgeschichte der Haupt- und Residenzstadt Karlsruhe bis zum Jahre 1914* [Karlsruhe, 1915], 28). On Dessoff, see also Joachim Draheim, *Johannes Brahms und Otto Dessoff*, catalog for the exhibition "Brahms in Baden-Baden und Karlsruhe," at the Badische Landesbibliothek Karlsruhe (Karlsruhe, 1983), and Joachim Draheim, Gerhard Albert Jahn, and The Friends of the Vienna Philharmonics, *Otto Dessoff, ein Dirigent, Komponist und Weggefährte von Johannes Brahms* (Munich, 2001).

99. Sietz, vol. 6, letter dated 12 April 1872.

100. Richard Wagner's letters to Hermann Levi, *Bayreuther Blätter 1901*, telegram dated 26 April 1872.

101. See note 97, letter dated 29 April 1872.

102. Kalbeck, 2:351.

103. Christian Martin Schmidt, *Johannes Brahms und seine Zeit* (Regensburg, 1983), 86. On the *Triumphlied* see also Klaus Häfner, *Das Triumphlied, eine vergessene Komposition von Johannes Brahms*, in *Johannes Brahms in Baden-Baden und Karlsruhe*, catalog for an exhibition at the Landesbibliothek Karlsruhe (Karlsruhe, 1983), 83ff.

104. Cosima, 2:563. The "Jesuit Law" passed in 1872 prohibited new Jesuit settlements, forced existing institutions to disperse, and restricted the residence of Jesuits in the Reich.

Second Intermezzo

The Conductor Hermann Levi

Enlightened by the spirit of the arts.

—Felix Weingartner

"His head on a slender, agile body, his posture calm, he knew with ideal mastery of his task to impart to every musician a large part of the burning enthusiasm that was the essence of his musical being."[1] That is how Eugenie, Clara Schumann's daughter, described Hermann Levi. A newspaper article from 1873 found similar words: "With extreme outward serenity he manages a sharp beat and directs entries with his hand and glance, keeping his eye on the stage and orchestra more than on the score."[2]

Similar reports tell us how the audience perceived him: a man of physical control and tranquility paired with an inner fire that flashed from his eyes. Years later, after working and preparing many productions together with Levi, Munich's superintendent Possart recalled:

> By lifting his ingenious head for a second, with a flash from his eyes he lit the singers on stage, and the quick change of his facial expression told the musicians more than all the pompous gestures of our common conductors ever could.[3]

As early as 1864, music lovers in Baden's royal residence town had seen in young Levi a new kind of conductor. One with a changed attitude about the importance of conducting: "A director at the conductor's stand, skillfully playing into the hands of the stage director."[4]

Until then, hardly a musician made a full-time career out of conducting. A conductor was in the first instance a solo instrumental performer, a concertmaster,[5] or a composer—some did all three. Composers Weber, Mendelssohn, and Berlioz conducted their works themselves. Often a conductor got his job based on his ability to write music. That was how Felix Mottl, Richard Strauss, and Felix Weingartner got started. As scores became increasingly more complicated and orchestras grew ever larger, the task of conducting became more sophisticated and attractive, too. Some composers gave up composing for the more glamorous work of leading an orchestra.

Hermann Levi, Felix Mottl, Arthur Nikisch, and later Wilhelm Furtwängler all made that career choice. As masters of the orchestra, they were to become the masters of musical life. They arose from the dark, anonymous orchestra pit to become "stars," replacing instrumental virtuosity by playing "their instrument"—the orchestra. As late as 1875, one music journal still complained that programs neglected to mention the conductor, and demanded that they should, because, after all, "the public could tell a good from a bad conductor." Until then even concert reviews rarely mentioned the conductor, ignoring his contribution to the performance by simply stating that a work had been, for instance, "rehearsed and presented by Court Kapellmeister Levi."[6]

In an essay "On Conducting," Richard Wagner had called for a "new kind of conductor." Wagner was less concerned with getting the beat right; he wanted a conductor to have intimate knowledge of musical rendition and to represent it with authority. Many music reviews from the late nineteenth century put it similarly. A survey for the musical scene in Munich from December 1888 says: "We want conductors that in general have significant personalities; not just that they can command entries accurately and keep time, we want them to hold the reins of drama in their hands."[7] The survey concludes that Hermann Levi met those demands.

Levi could be measured by that standard because he himself contributed to defining it. Most reviews noted that his command of the orchestra was highly intellectual. Upon arriving in Munich, in 1872, he was recommended to composer Rheinberger as follows: "He is the most intellectual musician we know and reminds us much of Mendelssohn."[8] It was apparently uncommon for a conductor to not only understand music, but to be knowledgeable in literature and the arts as well.

Levi was skilled at grasping music analytically, "at mentally understanding the whole work with a clear and vivid idea of the thematic structure of a composition."[9] Through suggestion he compellingly conveyed both his complete identification with a piece of music and his own sense of brilliance to musicians and the audience. Following the premiere of Anton Bruckner's seventh symphony, Heinrich Porges wrote: "It was as if a magnetic stream of enthusiasm flowed from the conductor to the players and from them to the audience."[10]

The fascinating aspect of Levi's rendition was that he was so fully absorbed in the music, as if he had written it himself. Once he had chosen to stop composing, he felt a strong desire to identify with the creativity of those who did, particularly the great composers. For almost ten years that was Johannes Brahms; then it was

Richard Wagner. After Wagner died, all other composers were compared to him. Levi turned to Bruckner and Berlioz, but also to Cornelius, Humperdinck, and Chabrier. Prior to performances he used every opportunity he could to demonstrate—at the piano—to his friends and colleagues his latest "discoveries" and to promote novelties. One year before the very first performance of *Parsifal*, even before the piano arrangement appeared in print, Levi played parts of the work by memory on the piano for a visitor, Hans von Bülow.

It was this focus on and love for the composer that took Levi to aesthetic heights. *Parsifal* marks his absolute peak. After conducting *Parsifal* Levi could no longer perform Brahms's symphonies successfully because he no longer believed in them. He nonetheless promoted many other contemporary composers, even though he found them second rate: Friedrich Gernsheim, Hermann Goetz, Karl Goldmark, Joachim Raff, Joseph Rheinberger, and Robert Volkmann, though he rarely presented works by his former teachers, Julius Rietz and Vincenz Lachner.

In classical music Beethoven was at the top of his list. He and his friend of later years, Adolf von Hildebrand, both thought that Beethoven had been the ultimate genius of European music. Symphony no. 3, *Eroica*, was the work he conducted most often. He also had a certain preference for Symphony no. 8 with its classical brevity. In March 1894 he presented it at a guest performance with the Colonne Orchestra in Paris. His vigorous Beethoven rendition shocked the traditionalists.

Alvin and Prieur's book *Métronomie expérimentale* provides a remarkable report on that performance.[11] The two French authors measured note values in symphony concerts and opera performances in Munich, Bayreuth, and Paris and came to conclusions for fundamental questions of how to render music. Their report on Levi's conducting of Beethoven's Symphony no. 8 mentions the heated controversy that his rendition triggered in Paris. The metronome settings tell us much about the nature of those performances.

First Movement: ♩. = 50; a measured tempo that allows the clear articulation of details (original metronome setting: ♩. = 69).

Second Movement: ♪ = 96; a flowing tempo that emphasizes the scherzo nature of the movement (original metronome setting: ♪ = 88).

Third Movement: Levi's tempo is not indicated precisely, but is said to be a quarter-note slower, therefore much slower than the original metronome setting of ♩ = 126.

Fourth Movement: Here, too, we do not find Levi's tempo, but it was said to be very much slower than the original metronome setting of 𝅝 = 84. Beethoven's metronome instructions are impossible to play.

Since the accuracy of Beethoven's metronome directions is controversial, we cannot compare Levi's performance to them. But the tempi do reveal something of Levi's grasp of Beethoven. His bridled measures that permit the precise articulation of detail refute the claim that he was always too fast. When we compare them with those of more modern conductors, for instance those of Wilhelm Furtwängler, we find that Levi's tempi, inasmuch as they were recorded, come very close to modern notions. We find here an enduring tradition of rendition.

Métronomie also notes Levi's tempi for *Ring* performances from September 1893 in Munich and for two repeat *Parsifal* performances on 8 August 1892 in Bayreuth and on 23 March 1894 in Paris. Although these were distinctly different performances at different places and with different orchestras, Levi's tempi remained constant. In making the transition from 4/4 to 6/4 in the prelude to *Parsifal* Levi carefully followed Wagner's instructions. Humperdinck once said that Levi's *Parsifal* prelude was too hurried for him. But the authors of *Métronomie* measured Levi's timing (measure one: ♩ = 32; brass entry at measure 39: ♩ = 40) as being quite stately.

When compared to the fragments performed half a year later in Paris, the metronome values recorded for Munich's *Ring* performance show that while Levi's tempi remained constant, for some passages he did take the liberty to be agogic, without ignoring Wagner's directions. He sped up the instrumental onset for *Valkyrie* from ♩ = 110 to ♩ = 136 and retarded the measure before Siegmund sings "wes Herd dies auch sei" to drop below the initial tempo of ♩ = 103.

At the end of *Rheingold*, when the palace of the gods appears above the rainbow, Levi created a festive mood by making ♩ = 62 in the orchestra measures just prior to Wotan's closing song, "abendlich strahlt der Sonne Auge."

For all modification of tempi, Levi certainly adhered to Wagner's instructions with which he was familiar from rehearsals in 1875–1876 and 1882. For him the composer's intent and written directions were absolutely binding. He frowned on arbitrariness. When he first performed new works, he invited the composers to final rehearsals and eagerly took their advice. Brahms, Bruckner, Gouvy, and Chabrier all came.

Levi had exceptional traits for a conductor: empathy, spiritual passion, a strong sense of responsibility, and modesty. His self-appraisal at conducting is disarming: "As a conductor I have no shining traits whatsoever with which I might impress an orchestra or audience; my strong points take a long time to emerge."[12]

NOTES

1. Eugenie Schumann, *Erinnerungen* (Stuttgart, 1927), 184f.
2. *AMZ*, no. 24 (12 June 1873): 379; review of a *Fidelio* performance in Munich.
3. Ernst von Possart, *Hermann Levi: Erinnerungen* (Munich, 1901), 48f.
4. Heinrich Ordenstein, *Musikgeschichte der Haupt- und Residenzstadt Karlsruhe bis zum Jahre 1914* (Karlsruhe, 1915), 26.

5. They often used the bow as a baton. See "Conducting with Violin and Bow," in Percy A. Scholes, *The Oxford Companion to Music*, 10th ed., edited by John Owen Ward (Oxford, 1998).

6. *Karlsruher Zeitung*, 14 March 1869; review of the Brahms premiere of *German Requiem*.

7. *NZfM* 56, no. 1 (2 January 1889): 1.

8. Letter from Hedwig von Holstein to Mrs. Rheinberger, in Harald Wanger and Hans-Josef Irmen, eds., *Joseph Gabriel Rheinberger, Briefe und Dokumente seines Lebens*, 5 vols. (Vaduz, 1984), 4:119.

9. Arthur Hahn, "Hermann Levi, ein Tonkünstlerporträt," *Nord und Süd* 71, no. 212 (1894): 195f.

10. Heinrich Porges in *Münchner Neueste Nachrichten*, 12 March 1885.

11. H. Alvin and R. Prieur, with a foreword by Hermann Levi, *Métronomie expérimentale: Etudes sur les mouvements constatés dans quelque exécutions musicales en France et en Allemagne—Paris, Bayreuth, Munich* (Paris, 1895).

12. Leviana, letter to Robert von Puttkamer dated 7 March 1887.

Chapter Three

Bavarian Court Conductor Levi

An artist feels in Munich as in no other German city.

—Hans Thoma

The four-room apartment that Hermann Levi leased in June on the first floor at 32 *Arcis Strasse* was situated in Munich's residential quarter preferred by artists and writers. Poet Paul Heyse lived on the same street at house number 9. A few steps away, Levi's colleague Franz Wüllner lived on the corner of *Karolinen Platz*. From there it was a fifteen-minute walk to *Brienner Strasse*, across *Odeon Platz*, past the royal residence, to the court theater.

In 1872 Munich was not much larger than the old downtown area. The *Sieges Tor*, the Maximilian Palace on the river Isar, the *Sendlinger Tor*, the train station, and *Stiglmayer Platz* made up the city boundaries. The suburbs of Schwabing, Bogenhausen, and Sendling had their own local administrations and were far out in the greens. The Isar had yet to be straightened and was lined with amiable gardens and rustic taverns, rafts from Tölz and Lenggries tied at their docks.

The city had grown rapidly in the 1800s. In 1830 it counted 80,000 inhabitants; by 1872 it had 170,000. During that period Munich was connected to the railways. In 1840 a train went to Augsburg and Stuttgart, in 1860 from Munich to Vienna, and a few years later a train went from Munich to the Brenner railroad, enabling direct travel to Italy.

Under kings Ludwig I and Maximilian II, Munich had raised magnificent buildings that gave the Bavarian capital the grand look it still has today: expansive *Ludwig Strasse* with the university, the Ludwig Church, and libraries (Heinrich Wölfflin called it Europe's most monumental street); the Odeon Concert Hall, the art museums called the Old and New Pinakothek, and the temple-like

Propyläen Gate were all built during that time. The king's extravagance perhaps mirrored the Bavarian people's sense of pride.

While devoted builder King Ludwig I emptied his own pockets to give Munich monuments to science and the arts, a half of a century later Ludwig II built mostly costly luxury castles that the public was not permitted to enter. The people of Munich took it in stride, proudly identifying with their Bavarian royalty—as they still do today.

In Munich the intermingling of all social strata was taken for granted. Beer—the national beverage—united the high and low. Carriage drivers, high officials, farmers, and university professors all frequented the brewery halls to down a mug. In Levi's time, too, artists and literati sat at the Hofbräuhaus discussing politics and art.

Levi totally immersed himself in the atmosphere of the city. Only at Christmastime in 1872 did sentiment lead him back to Karlsruhe and his old friends, the Poetz family, and take him to the bedside of his ailing sister Gustchen Mombert. He soon became an enthusiastic resident of Munich and felt at home there for the next twenty-five years. His friend Julius Allgeyer had moved to Munich, too, taking up work with court photographer Joseph Albert. Before finding his own accommodations, Allgeyer stayed for a few weeks with Levi on *Arcis Strasse* and wrote to their mutual friend Brahms:

> Levi's a very busy chap, his days organized in terms of meetings, rehearsals, meals, and sleep. From the first moment on, he's found his new position so indisputably fortunate and more pleasant than expected that now, on his thirty-third birthday, nothing remains to be desired—except perhaps a wife.[1]

On October 15 Levi took up his work as the royal Bavarian conductor and began rehearsing Mozart's *Die Zauberflöte*. Awe might have filled him at entering the theater for the first time as its new musical leader in the footsteps of conductors Franz Lachner, Richard Wagner, and Hans von Bülow. Franz Lachner,[2] an older brother of Levi's musical master from Mannheim, Vincenz Lachner, had managed Munich's entire musical life since 1836 and conducted all major musical events: glamorous opera performances at the National Theater, symphony concerts at the Musical Academy, and the concerts of the Royal Choir. In 1868 Franz Lachner retired. Being conservative at heart, he felt brushed aside when Richard Wagner appeared in Munich to direct *Der fliegende Holländer* himself and was then followed by conductors Hans von Bülow and Hans Richter.

Lachner had been a powerful, commanding figure for the orchestra, a well-versed musician who had known both Beethoven and Schubert personally and felt at home with Vienna Classic. For thirty years he shaped Munich's music scene and made what Wagner called "a wonderful court orchestra" out of the little ensemble he had started with. The concertgoers of Munich loved and respected Franz Lachner, particularly his renditions of Beethoven symphonies. He was welcomed with ovations when, after retiring, he occasionally returned to the stage to conduct.

Now that Wagner's followers Bülow and Richter had retreated after quarrels over *Rheingold*, and their substitute Franz Wüllner could not convincingly direct opera, Hermann Levi was considered the true successor to Franz Lachner. But when he took up the post, it was by no means clear whether he would succeed at shaping the entire musical life of the city.

The sheer size of the orchestra was enough to thrill thirty-three-year-old Levi. It had seventy-eight full-time musicians and nine permanently available extras, almost twice as many players overall as in Karlsruhe.[3] The orchestra had twelve first violins and enough brass and wind players of its own to perform the *Ring* operas without outside help. The ensemble included excellent solo performers like tenors Franz Nachbaur, Heinrich Vogl, and Max Schlosser as well as baritone August Kindermann, all of whom took on major parts in the premiering of Wagner's *Ring*. The ladies included famous soprano singers Josephine Schefzky, Therese Vogl, and Sophie Stehle, who after guest performances in Karlsruhe had insisted that Baden's Court Kapellmeister Levi be contracted for Munich.

Levi now had much work to do at his new post. Papers for the court theater administration show that he worked on forty operas from the repertory, all of which were to be performed during the running season and, if necessary, rehearsed beforehand. These included Wagner's *Rienzi*, *Meistersinger*, and *Tristan*; Gluck's operas; Mozart's operas; Meyerbeer's *Huguénots*, *L'Africaine*, and *Robert the Devil*; Marschner's *Hans Heiling*; and Franz Lachner's *Catharina Cornaro*, in addition to Beethoven's stage music for *Egmont*, Schumann's *Manfred*, and many French comic operas.

Most of these works Levi had already conducted in Karlsruhe; new for him were Wagner's *Tristan* and the *Ring* that was expected to be performed in its entirety.

On October 20 Munich's new conductor presented himself to the public by conducting *Zauberflöte*. The papers wrote:

> Right after the first rehearsals the most reserved of our court musicians spoke favorably of the new conductor. The performance was anxiously anticipated; it had contrasts, fervor, and momentum that we have not heard for a long time.[4]

After Levi's death, Ernst von Possart, at the time an actor but later to become the theater's superintendent, recalled Levi's first performance:

> At the dress rehearsal for *Die Zauberflöte* the stage personnel had a first opportunity to observe the eminent skills of the new conductor. I stood behind the curtain talking to Heinrich Vogl when the overture began. Three monumental E-flat major chords sounded in powerful width, swelling with force; Vogl was suddenly silent

and looked up. The tingly allegro began, pianissimo but crystal clear, so delicate and yet so determined in its rhythmic accents that you could feel it: this competent and commanding conductor understood style. . . . Franz Lachner sat in the auditorium. . . . When I ran into him the next day at Max-Joseph's Square I told him how happy I was that a promising conductor has come from his school (being his brother's pupil) and that I could tell by his face that he was quite pleased with yesterday's debut. *Ja, ja*—the old gentleman whirred, and an endearing smile fluttered about his lips—a smart chap, he'll have a great career, but for now he's in a bit of a hurry.[5]

On Beethoven's birthday, December 17, Levi presented *Fidelio* and music from *The Ruins of Athens* as edited by Otto Devrient. On December 23 he conducted a carefully prepared *Meistersinger* performance. To Brahms, who then was conducting first concerts in Vienna as their new Director of the Society of the Friends of Music, Levi reported:

I'm an exhausted beast and will be glad to escape for a few days at Christmas to visit my sister. But the incredible work load is the only thing I can complain about. Otherwise everything enormously exceeds my expectations. The orchestra is wonderful and thoroughly devoted to me; Perfall fulfills my requests, the singers here are more serious about their work than at other operas. So I think we can move something forward. After Christmas I will also be conducting the concerts at the Odeon. I get along with Wüllner just fine and considering that he has been almost entirely eliminated from theatrical operations, I give him credit for not being angry.[6]

Since Levi had to handle the greater part of the repertory, his colleague Franz Wüllner did feel displaced from his position as opera conductor.[7] After all, he had rescued the *Rheingold* premiere. After also premiering *Valkyrie* the next year, he felt a right to conduct these works, and the tetralogy as well. This was embarrassing for Levi because for many years Wüllner, too, had been a good friend of Johannes Brahms.

Franz Wüllner was a well-educated, highly cultivated musician from Westphalia, a person of integrity and a devout Catholic. He had an often pointed, brusque manner, but could also be humorous and genuinely cordial. He had known Brahms much longer than Levi. Through the care he took in leading the choir and large choral concerts he had made his mark on Munich's music life. And he had gained acclaim by taking it upon himself to premiere Wagner's works.

Ultimately, it would have overtaxed Wüllner to take on the work of the lead opera conductor in addition to the work he already had running the school of music, directing the choir, and being responsible for all public oratorio performances. And yet he would have felt slighted if behind his back a man seven years his junior was appointed to the position and given the prerogative to stage

Franz Wüllner (1832–1902). Courtesy of Frithjof Haas.

all of the great operas, including the upcoming complete performance of Wagner's *Ring*.

For Levi, it was déjà vu: without fault of his own and simply because he was better qualified, a merited colleague had been forced to give up his position. Wüllner continued to direct the school of music and the choir for another five years alongside Levi. He was then honored by a call to Dresden. As Levi had mentioned in a letter to Brahms, as of 1873 he and Wüllner split the conducting of concerts in the Odeon Hall among themselves. At a general assembly of the Musical Academy on 16 January 1873, the majority decided that Wüllner would handle the non-subscription concerts from October to December with choral works and oratorios, and Levi would do the subscription concerts during Lent.

On March 5 Levi introduced himself by conducting his first Academy Concert in the Odeon. His carefully selected program included Beethoven's *Eroica*, a concerto grosso by Handel, a scene from Brahms's cantata *Rinaldo* starring Munich's tenor Vogl, and Wagner's *Faust* overture. His debut went well:

> They played Beethoven's Eroica with more brilliant novelty, keen understanding, and precision than we have heard in years. The greatest boon was Court Kapellmeister Levi, who, directing a concert for the first time in this hall, from the very first to the last movement justified the high expectations placed in him and in the end was energetically called back onto the stage twice.[8]

Paul Heyse, too, sat with his wife in the audience at that first symphony concert, and later noted in his diary that the evening had given him "quite unique pleasures."[9] Cordial friendship had grown between Levi and this respected poet from Munich who lived just a few steps away. While he was still working in Karlsruhe, Levi had written to Heyse on 1 January 1872, asking him to improve two texts by August Kopisch for which Brahms had written music as op. 58. Heyse sent his prompt reply directly to Brahms without knowing him personally, and Brahms made those changes in the next new edition. In the letter from January, Levi had also mentioned that he and Brahms were both delighted by Heyse's libretto for the opera *Der Rothmantel* (The Red Coat) composed by Georg Kremplsetzer.[10] Levi had hoped that the poet would want to write a libretto for Brahms, too.

In the fall of 1872, Heyse and Levi became close friends. They spent evenings discussing the arts and tried to find an appropriate libretto for Brahms. Heyse had a few drafts that Levi told Brahms about: *Knight Bayard*, or *The Money Seeker*, a Californian gold-digger story, and material by Gregorovius about Pompeii, called *Euphorion*. Brahms stalled. If he were to have a libretto, then yes, only Heyse could write it for him. But he was no friend of big opera. Couldn't Heyse write something like Gozzi's fairy tales? Heyse replied that it was time that they finally met in person. A five-minute talk would get them further than writing back and forth via Levi. Little did he know that years earlier Brahms had stood often at his door but never found the poet home.[11]

Finally, in May 1873 the two met several times when Brahms spent the summer near Munich. Now that his friends Allgeyer and Levi no longer lived in Karlsruhe, Brahms no longer spent every summer in Baden-Baden. In early May he rented a modest place in Tutzing on Lake Starnberg on the first floor of an inn run by Conrad Amtmann. The region, he said, was more beautiful than he had imagined: "The lake is blue, darker blue than the sky, and there is a scent of snow-covered mountains." Brahms wrote to friends, and then, during those very days, put music to a poem by Karl Simrock: *Blauer Himmel, blaue Wogen, drüber blauer Berge Bogen.* [Blue sky, blue waves, and above them an arc of blue mountains.] When Brahms needed company, he visited the Lachner brothers in nearby Bernried or singer-couple Mr. and Mrs. Vogl, who had a pavilion on a bit of land reaching into the lake. There Brahms wrote the songs of op. 59, practicing them with tenor singer Vogl.

When he came into town to visit friends, Brahms stayed at Levi's home on *Arcis Strasse*. In early May the two of them once again stood at Heyse's door, but the poet was out. The next day Heyse returned the visit and invited the composer and Levi to come to his home on May 5. This time they had a long conversation about possible opera projects. Heyse noted in his diary: "Brahms and Levi at my place, with all kinds of libretto talk."[12] During the next weeks, Brahms and Heyse met often. Together they hiked through the landscape surrounding Munich, stopping for a beer at the pub *Zum Federstabler*. Brahms seemed seriously interested in the material for *Knight Bayard*, so Heyse drafted a libretto for it. When Levi was too busy with stage operations, Allgeyer handled the communication between Brahms and Heyse, bringing messages from Munich to Tutzing, and back again.

Once they had decided to do a joint project, it seemed reason to celebrate. On June 3 a sizable group gathered at Heyse's home. Besides Levi and Brahms, Michael Bernays, a historian of literature, Arnold Böcklin, a painter, and Moritz Carrière, a philosopher (and Justus Liebig's son-in-law), came. Heyse served May Wine[13] and the mood was good; Brahms played the piano and the guests lingered until early morning. Heyse made a toast to the "opera composer." But it was hopeless. Brahms never wrote music for either *Knight Bayard* or *The Island*, a libretto that Heyse wrote for him in the spring of 1874 based on a short novel by Hermann Kurz.

Yet for a long time Brahms did fancy that he might write opera music. He often discussed it years later with his Swiss friend Josef Victor Widmann. But one day he abandoned the thought entirely, saying that he would just have to give up opera as he had given up the idea of marrying.

After the opera house closed in late June, Levi left for Karlsruhe and the Mombert family, staying a few days with his fatally ill sister. He then traveled on to Giessen to comfort his distraught father, but after just another few days returned to Karlsruhe for his sister's funeral. After a short visit to Clara Schumann in Baden-Baden, he then journeyed to Helgoland for rest. He was back in Munich at the end of August. While spending the summer in Tutzing, Brahms had completed the second version of both string quartets op. 51. At Levi's home, the Walter Quartet[14] tried them out for Brahms. Levi rehearsed the works with the quartet and then invited guests to a house concert. Among them was a specialist for German literature, Rochus von Liliencron, who thanked the composer the next day for creating "two children that would one day become famous men."

That summer in Tutzing Brahms completed another significant work. He sent a score to Allgeyer asking him not to be bothered by his scribbling but to give the "nonsense" to a copier for a clean copy. If that were too much trouble, then just "toss the whole thing in the corner." The *nonsense* that he told Allgeyer to throw out was nothing less than the *Variations on a Theme by Joseph Haydn*, op. 56, in the arrangement for two pianos. The clean copy was meant for Levi, who presented it at his home in Brahms's presence in September.

The *Haydn Variations* stoked the competition between Wüllner and Levi. Each wanted to be the first to present the orchestra arrangement. Levi joked: "Then play the *Variations*, if you can get your hands on them!" Wüllner immediately wrote to Brahms and asked for the orchestra score. Brahms wrote right away to Simrock to speed up printing so it could be played by fall. And thus Munich's first performance of the *Haydn Variations* was conducted by Wüllner on 10 December 1873. Allgeyer wrote to Brahms that this work made him indescribably happy. But regarding the conductor, he said: "With all due respect for Wüllner's determination and ability, he lacks something, some spark that he could impart to the piece and to the listener."[15]

Levi was home in bed with a cold. If he hadn't been ill he would have taken a trip elsewhere to not be in Munich that day. To Brahms he wrote:

> The fact that the *Variations* issue so vexes me might suggest that my own vanity is more important to me than the cause. But that is not true. If I were certain that Wüllner could present any of your works—especially for the orchestra—as well as I, I would have kept silent and accepted it. But I remember the torture with the Triumphlied.
>
> I assure you that being kind and considerate of others is not as easy as it looks. Obscure relationships like this always depress me. That one claim by Wüllner's wife (told to me incidentally by C. Schumann), namely, "another affront, and I don't know what will become of my husband" ties my hands for all time and cements the current, untenable way things are.[16]

Brahms did not reply, as was his custom in matters such as this. But Levi did not stop tirelessly championing Brahms in Munich. He rehearsed the A major quartet, op. 51, no. 2 with the Walter Quartet for public performance. He rehearsed four of Brahms's lieder with tenor Heinrich Vogl for a concert at Frankfurt's museum, including the song written in Tutzing, *Auf dem See* (On the Lake) that had not yet been published. At the end of the year, Brahms was awarded the Bavarian Maximilian Medal, together with Richard Wagner. In a congratulatory letter, Levi said that he found the idea of "Brahms-Wagner" not all that bad. Nine years earlier Wagner had refused to accept the award. This time he did, but it irked him to be honored together with Brahms. Brahms was twenty years younger, and Wagner did not entirely respect him.

Then Brahms presented himself for the first time to the people of Munich as a pianist and conductor. Levi had invited him to do the second concert at the Odeon, on 13 March 1874. After weeks of letters, they finally settled on the following program:

- Joseph Haydn: Symphony no. 104 in D major
- Franz Schubert: Aria for Hérold's *Les Clochettes*
- Johannes Brahms: *Variations on a Theme* from Haydn, op. 56a and piano concerto in D minor, op. 15
- Four Lieder
- Three *Hungarian Dances*, nos. 1, 3, and 10.[17]

Brahms played his piano concerto, conducted the Variations and the Hungarian Dances and accompanied tenor Heinrich Vogl at the piano for the four songs he had already sung in Frankfurt: "The Wreaths," "On the Lake," "Rest My Sweet One," and *Falkenstein*. Levi conducted the Haydn symphony and the piano concerto. The next day the Walter Quartet gave a soirée for the Museum Society in the Portia Hall and Brahms played the piano part of his A major piano quartet, op. 26, followed by the string sextet, op. 36 in G major.

These two concert evenings brought Johannes Brahms lasting renown as a composer. Munich's audiences dropped their reserve about his music. The *Augsburg Evening News* wrote: "Johannes Brahms, one of the leading living masters of composition, was welcomed, accompanied, and seen on his way with distinction."[18]

Friends had arranged an entire program of social events for the days that the composer would stay in Munich. On the day of the concert in Odeon, Levi, Bernays, Heyse, and Brahms dined at Café Maximilian. The next day, before the chamber music concert, the Wüllner family invited Brahms, Levi, Lachner, Heyse, and Liliencron to lunch. After the meal, Brahms and Levi played Brahms's *Variations on a Theme by Robert Schumann*, op. 23, for four hands. In Brahms's presence, Levi and Wüllner kept their disagreements to themselves.

Brahms's friends in Munich also included composer Joseph Rheinberger.[19] He had excellent repute as a professor at the school of music. As a master of counterpoint and conservative in taste, he had much in common with Brahms who sought him out for the first time in 1864. A few weeks after taking up his post in Munich, Levi introduced himself to Rheinberger and promised to use the latter's opera *Daughter of the Tower Man*; he premiered it on 23 April 1873. Levi also had Rheinberger's first opera, *Seven Ravens*, re-performed in November 1873.

We don't know why Levi made an effort to promote these less significant operas by Rheinberger; perhaps it was because except for works by Wagner there was not much new on the market and it would still take years to complete the entire *Ring*. Ten years also lapsed before Mottl and Levi rediscovered Peter Cornelius's *Barber of Bagdad*.

Levi next presented Franz von Holstein's *Erbe von Morlay* two years after it had been premiered in Leipzig.[20] Levi had become acquainted with Holstein

Josef Rheinberger (1839–1901) and wife Franziska (Fanny) von Hoffnaass, née Jaegerhuber (1832–1892). Photograph dated 1869. Josef-Rheinberger Archiv/Liechtensteinisches Landesarchiv, Vaduz, Liechtenstein.

while preparing the composer's most successful opera, *Haideschacht*, for Karlsruhe. Holstein was an amiable musician marked by a chronic ailment since childhood, well respected in Brahms's circles, but not to be overestimated. When it came time for the first showing, Levi invited Holstein to final rehearsals and paid for a week's stay at a hotel. During the rehearsals Levi came down with bronchitis and from bed sent a grateful letter to the ensemble: "If the people on stage are merely half as pleased with the conductor as he is with them, neither side will find any fault."[21]

Besides these new pieces, the most important premieres in Levi's first years in Munich were Gluck's *Iphigenia in Aulis* on 25 January 1874 (with well-known Joseph Hauser from Karlsruhe playing Agamemnon) and *Iphigenia in Tauris* on 25 August 1874, as well as Robert Schumann's *Manfred* and *Genoveva* a year later. The most recent staging of Byron's *Manfred* with music by Schumann had taken place five years earlier. The production had been a catastrophe. Actor Ernst von Possart, later to become the theater's superintendent, had played the leading role. His memoirs say that back then the greater part of the audience left the building before the first performance was over. And just before the last act the concierge sent someone with a huge key backstage saying that the audience had left and as soon as Possart finishes his last monologue he should lock up the house. In 1873 theater director Perfall, and—once again—protagonist Possart, and conductor Levi worked enthusiastically and hard to revive the problematic opera, and this time it went well. To Clara Schumann Levi wrote of the opening night: "It was one of the most beautiful evenings I have ever had at the theater ... I can't explain it, you have to see and hear it. It's worth a trip from America, not to mention from Baden-Baden or Berlin."[22] And to Brahms he wrote:

> You can imagine the effect—not on music lovers or those educated in music, but on the commoners. I myself am always shaken through and through, although I know all of the work's weaknesses and why it actually cannot properly be considered a work.[23]

Clara Schumann did travel to Munich to see *Manfred* and loved it. But she was not happy with actor Possart, finding that his acting displayed much thought and diligence, but little empathy. To Levi's disappointment she could not stay to see *Genoveva*. He would have liked to have heard her opinion on how it compared to the Karlsruhe performance of five years ago. He himself was now much more critical of the work, writing to Brahms: "The performance was a pleasure. But

Munich's Royal and National Theater on Max-Joseph Platz, 1839. Painting by Heinrich Adam. Münchener Staatmuseum, Sammlung Graphik/Plakat/Gemälde, inv. no. GM 28/562.

the work itself is untenable, although the audience was kind and respected it. The book is really bad."[24]

Around this time, Levi began having serious health problems. They were to worsen during his years in Munich, when the rush of professional and social life was burdened even more by worries. This time Levi was in bed with "a sore throat and the obligatory nervousness, a result," he admitted to Brahms, "of working, and drinking at taverns." On his thirty-fourth birthday, he vowed to become "respectable and lazy" and to "take care of my *cadaver*." But their friend Allgeyer had doubts. He thought that Levi simply loved to make good resolutions and in order to have reason to do so, would exploit his own health time and again.

During Levi's second year in Munich, his authority as a conductor of orchestra concerts had become so firm that disregarding objections from the press, besides Brahms's works he was also able to include other new works in the subscription concert program. In March 1874 he presented *Harold en Italie* by Berlioz with Anton Thoms at the viola, closing the evening with the Fantasy Overture from Tchaikovsky's *Romeo and Juliette*—both were first performances for Munich. When a music critic questioned these choices, he replied: "Since I cannot decide to perform works by Hiller, Reinecke, and their friends, I feel justified in adding one of Berlioz's yet unknown pieces to the program every year. We cannot stop at the year 1827" [the year of Beethoven's death].[25] A journal for music had written:

> The concert ended with an overly long, shapeless overture by Tchaikovsky on the theme of Romeo and Juliette, the author supposedly being a teacher from the conservatory in Moscow. In terms of rhythm and harmony, part of the musical ideas in this work might not be uninteresting, if only the composer had presented them in some orderly fashion, free of many dissonances, and with intelligent orchestration. As it is, this work is downright unpalatable and the fact that it is on the program can only be attributed to the conductor's very odd, extreme enthusiasm for it.[26]

For many musicians of that time, the year of Beethoven's death, 1827, meant the end of a great era in music. Many composers, like Hiller and Reinecke, thought it wrong to stray from Beethoven by following new trends in music. In Mannheim and Leipzig, Levi had been instructed in that vein also. But meanwhile his musical horizon had widened. He had quit composing because he felt incapable of creating a door to the music of the future with pieces of his own. But he did expect Berlioz and Wagner, and until the mid-1870s even Brahms, to do so. The concert programs that Levi organized throughout these years show that he was open for all novelties and put his skill at conducting to the service of very diverse composers. In February 1875 he presented Serenade no. 3 by Robert Volkmann, and in March he conducted a premier performance of Joseph Rheinberger's Symphony no. 2.

For the annual Easter concert on Palm Sunday, Levi conducted for the first time in Munich Beethoven's Symphony no. 9, preceded by a Munich premiering of Brahms's *Schicksalslied*. At the court theater, he directed the first performance of *Uthal* by Étienne Nicolas Méhul, followed by Charles Gounod's *Le médecin malgré lui* (The Doctor in Spite of Himself) based on the text by Molière. Levi had known the piece since his studies in Paris when it was showing at the Théâtre Lyrique in January 1858. He translated it for its staging in Munich. We shall later return to discuss Levi's translations of operas by Berlioz and Mozart. At the time he produced *Nozze di Figaro* and *Così fan tutte* using a translation by Eduard Devrient. On 28 October 1874, conductor Wüllner staged *Don Giovanni* using a new edition made by Munich's director Franz Grandaur.

But the new work that moved Levi most was Wagner's *Tristan*. He directed it for the first time on 10 May 1874. It was a huge task that he only mastered after first waiting for a long time, and then preparing meticulously. Hans von Bülow had directed the sensational premiere in Munich on 10 June 1865, and then repeated the performance twice, in June and August 1872, just shortly before Levi took up his post. Levi had seen the performances directed by Bülow and had convinced himself of Bülow's excellent work. What it would mean for him to work on *Tristan* became clear to him during the performance: he wrote Wagner that he loved *Tristan* more than anything and that the day he met *Tristan* changed his life.

Clara Schumann had gotten an utterly different impression. In September 1875 she and her children had come to Munich to see *Manfred*. Her sick son Felix had come up from Italy, and their mutual friend Joachim came, too. The day after seeing *Manfred* they all went to see *Tristan*. Clara was appalled:

> That is really the most disgusting thing I have ever seen or heard in my life. To watch and hark to such lovesickness all evening, without a bit of decency.... Levi says Wagner is a much better musician than Gluck! And Joachim has not the courage to disagree.[27]

They argued about it, but that did not harm their friendship. Levi improvised, arranging an orchestra matinée three days later at which both Clara Schumann and Joseph Joachim played their instruments. Levi was particularly happy.

After the pivotal experience of directing *Tristan*, all the misgivings that Levi's friends Heyse, Joachim, and Clara Schumann had about Wagner and his dangerous propensities could not prevent Levi from being mysteriously drawn to the Master of Bayreuth. He did everything he could to meet Wagner personally— inviting him to a *Tristan* performance in Munich, offering to help find appropriate singers for the festival.

Still angry that *Rheingold* and *Valkyrie* had been staged against his will, Wagner wanted to engage performers from every other German stage, *except* Munich. But faced with financial ruin in January 1874 he had to admit that without help from Munich his festival would fail. His plea was heard by King Ludwig II, who responded: "No! No! And no! That's not how it shall end! Help will be found!" He promptly loaned Wagner 100,000 talers. Despite latent animosity between Perfall and Wagner, Perfall's troupe then had to make solo singers, orchestra musicians, and choir groups available for Bayreuth. But because after the break the opera in Munich resumed operations in early August, it could spare only a few to participate in rehearsals at Bayreuth in August 1875 and in the festival of 1876. These included soloists Josephine Schefzky (Sieglinde), Hedwig Reicher-Kindermann (Grimgerde), Heinrich Vogl (Loge), and Karl Schlosser (Mime). Levi also sent a few choir singers and what he called an "elite deputation" from the orchestra: Hieber and Venzl (violin), Thoms (viola), Schieber (cello), Sigler (bass), and Tombo (harp).

Levi wanted to participate, too. If visitors were not allowed at rehearsals, he would gladly play the kettledrum in the orchestra or help out backstage! Wagner readily accepted the offer and began letters to Levi with "Most Valued Friend." It seemed natural to him that the future conductor of the *Ring* should assist at Bayreuth. It had also flattered him that Levi had refused to conduct *Rheingold* and *Valkyrie* in Munich before they were staged in Bayreuth.

On 9 August 1875, Levi left for Bayreuth for five days to witness rehearsals of *Siegfried* and *Götterdämmerung*. He found the unique acoustics of the Festival House intriguing. Every morning a different act was practiced with the orchestra alone. The solo singers came for afternoon rehearsal. In the evenings Levi was Wagner's guest at Villa Wahnfried from 9 to 11 p.m. Levi wrote his father of the impact of those few days:

> I was totally overwhelmed by the impression that the works, hall, and performance made on me. Having taken a detour and having struggled with myself to become a Wagnerian, I, of all people, have perhaps more independent judgment than others. I am old enough not to be fooled—and I can tell you that future events at Bayreuth will radically change the world of art. Wagner's works may be forgotten, but not his reformative, or rather, reactionary ideas. I say "reactionary" because he returns to music its truest rank, as Gluck had done. And the fact that this man, a simple German minstrel, has been able to turn his ideas into action, well, that's what impressed me most about Bayreuth. . . . "Wagnerian" is a stupid word, people only associate radicals with it, to whom I shall never belong. I shall continue to shun that clique.[28]

On August 13 Levi attended a garden party held in the park surrounding Villa Wahnfried. One hundred and fifty guests were invited to celebrate the end of rehearsals. A band of musicians from the orchestra played on a platform. Buffets were arranged under arbors. Wagner asked Liszt to play *The Legend of Holy Francis* for his guests. Bengal lights were lit late in the evening and the crowd moved in a torchlight procession. To crown the event, Wagner stood above those gathered and spoke of the ideals of art that slumber in many but can only be awakened in special times such as these. Three cheers for art and an orchestra fanfare ended the festive evening.[29]

Now there was no stopping regular involvement at Villa Wahnfried for Hermann Levi. The place became for him a source of both aesthetic exaltation and painful humiliation. Through the first year of rehearsals for the festival he had no idea what he was headed for. He was simply thrilled to work with Wagner, side by side, and to know that they were making something very special materialize. It became pivotal for his future work as a conductor.

In the fall of 1875, letters flew back and forth between the Master of the *Ring* and his now entirely subservient Royal Bavarian Kapellmeister. To raise money for Bayreuth, Levi suggested having a concert where two of his best singers, Heinrich and Therese Vogl, would present works composed and conducted by Wagner. Wagner dismissed the idea. He believed to already have sufficient funds for the festival (he was wrong). Neither did he want to run into any old enemies in Munich. It also peeved him that Munich's court theater director insisted on beginning the playing season for 1876 on August 15, right after the summer break. That would certainly collide with the festival at Bayreuth.

In the spring of 1876, Levi requested that the theater director officially commission him to begin rehearsing the *Ring* tetralogy. It would, he said "establish an authoritative tradition for the future of German opera." To Wagner he wrote that the stage in Munich was the only one called to continue what had begun in Bayreuth. He rehearsed the part of Mime with Karl Schlosser and that of Sieglinde with Josephine Schefzky, demanding that solo performers memorize every detail of their roles. He requested extra pay for his tenor, Schlosser, because Schlosser had so little money that he could afford no household help and turned up at rehearsals absentmindedly, with the piano score in one hand and a shopping net of vegetables in the other.

Levi officially took vacation from July 1 to August 15. But by mid-June he had already left for Bayreuth, eager to participate in rehearsals. He worked together with twenty-year-old Felix Mottl from Vienna, and they became friends for life.[30] Every person working on the project felt himself a member of a select community, unconditionally serving the composer and his work. Levi helped out wherever help was needed, practicing with the singers, playing the piano for stage rehearsals. Ludwig Strecker, manager of the Schott publishing house in Mainz, witnessed Wagner's unbridled temper during a rehearsal for *Siegfried* with Levi at the piano. The composer ranted and raged, clenched his fists and stamped his feet, mimicked a clown, stuck Siegfried's horn on his own head, and then rammed it into the stomach of someone who just happened to come through the door.

In Bayreuth Levi met many old friends, but also colleagues and artists that orbited Wagner and became his new friends: besides Felix Mottl, the conductor

Signed photograph of Hermann Levi. Courtesy of Frithjof Haas.

of the *Ring*, Hans Richter from Vienna, and Heinrich Porges, a piano teacher at Munich's School of Music who also wrote for various newspapers. Cosima once said of Porges (one of Wagner's most devout disciples) that he was an extremely kind person and certainly the noblest Jew she had met.[31] Porges published articles with quips that Wagner had made during stage rehearsals:

> The aim of these performances is to blend realistic Shakespearian style with ideals from ancient tragedy. . . . The masters of the performing arts tried to achieve ideal naturalism and natural idealism.[32]

The words could have been spoken by Friedrich Nietzsche, if only he hadn't been extremely disappointed with the festival. Levi met him, too, in Bayreuth. They had known one another since Wagner's concert in Mannheim in December 1871 and both admired Brahms's *Triumphlied*, the piece that sparked the first

Herman Levi. Courtesy of Frithjof Haas.

fierce quarrel between Wagner and Nietzsche. The professor from Basel stayed in the background at the festival. Not only migraines kept him from attending the opening performance; he was disappointed by all the "ugly and overwrought things" he saw happening around Wagner and on the stage and turned away in disgust.

In Bayreuth Levi also met Munich's philosopher of aesthetics Conrad Fiedler, to whom he would later become close. Fiedler's opinion of Bayreuth was the exact opposite of Nietzsche's. At first he scorned it, then liked it. His report on Bayreuth contains the remarkable comment:

> Even though I would never admit to him that his is the only genuine music, indeed, that his work means that we have now finally discovered true art (as he and his followers claim), I do nonetheless believe that he has found a unique and legitimate form of expression for a true, primal need.[33]

These thoughts were certainly backed by discussions with Levi in which newlywed twenty-two-year-old Mary Fiedler, who years later was to become Levi's wife, also participated.

Wagner's own view of the festival was critical. Despite all the satisfaction of being honored as no artist before him by visits by His Majesty, Wagner found fault in many aspects of the event. He not only found Hans Richter's tempi often wrong, the overall performance disappointed. It was all much less wonderful than he had imagined, and he told Cosima that he never wanted to see it again. He had created an invisible orchestra, he said, and now he would need to invent an invisible opera performance.[34] It was a brilliant vision that half a century later became reality with the advent of sound recording.

Amid all the controversy, Levi felt himself a member of a select group of people working enthusiastically to reach a goal. An untiring aid at rehearsals and an enraptured listener at performances, in July he had arrived in Bayreuth as a tentative admirer, and in August he returned to Munich a servant devoted to Wagner and the idea of Bayreuth. The transformation that had begun when he conducted *Tristan* for the first time was completed by experiencing the *Ring*. The Bavarian Royal Court Kapellmeister had become Wagner's loyal vassal. And through Hermann Levi, Wagner had once again taken hold of Munich's opera.

AN END TO FRIENDSHIP WITH BRAHMS

> Until a few years ago I would have thought it impossible to lose friends by anything other than death; but since then I have had to learn to mourn the living dead.
>
> —Hermann Levi to Paul Heyse

In early 1875 Julius Allgeyer replied to Clara Schumann's inquiry about "our little dark curly-head Levi" (who meanwhile had his first gray hair) that they no longer had much in common because "before I knew it, Levi had been bewitched by Wagner's muse."[35] He hoped nonetheless that future concerts would show Levi the difference between "musical intoxication and true, noble art." Many of their mutual friends felt the same and considered it their duty to rescue the Royal Bavarian Kapellmeister from Wagner's snare. Levi stubbornly justified his priorities to Clara:

> I can't help that my views seem paradox and people find my way of thinking (about my past) a crime. . . . As a musician Brahms surely towers just as high above Wagner as Mozart did to Gluck. . . . But in making music for the stage, Wagner achieves effects like no other. . . . Thus I cannot see why an honest, sincere appreciation of his work would be incompatible with the same for Bach, Beethoven, and Brahms.

I, anyway, think no less of the *Schicksalslied* or the sextet in G major just because I find *Tristan* a tremendous work of art.[36]

Taken by themselves, these views could never have clouded Brahms's friendship for Levi, let alone destroyed it, because Brahms, too, openly admired Wagner's work. Twenty years Wagner's junior, Brahms never considered himself Wagner's rival in music. The fact that as a composer of chamber music, lieder, and symphonies Brahms got stylized as the antipode to the master of Bayreuth was not Brahms's doing. It was the work of fanatic followers of both of the composers.

At first Wagner simply dismissed the young genius heralded by Schumann. But it was not until Brahms published his first symphony in 1876—the very same year that the *Ring* was performed in Bayreuth—that Wagner began writing malicious articles about him. In an essay titled "On Writing and Composing," published in 1879 in the monthly *Bayreuther Blätter*, Wagner vented:

> Well, then, compose music—if you can't imagine what else to do. Why else would it be called composing—arranging things—if it took imagination, too? The more boring you are, the more you need an obvious mask. I know famous composers masquerading today as a ballad monger, tomorrow wearing Handel's hallelujah wig, the next day acting like a Jewish czardas player, and then dressing up in Number Ten[37] pretending to be a downright dignified writer of symphonies. Mendelssohn's great word that every composer composes as he can is a wise norm that truly can never be violated. The fault lies in wanting to compose better than one can; and when that does not work, one must pretend that it does: that's the masquerade. It's harmless, except when it deceives many superintendents and so on, leading to things like fine banquets in Hamburg and diplomas in Breslau.[38]

Surely Brahms did not read the *Bayreuther Blätter* and was unaware of Wagner's slander. He would not have thought less of Wagner's music, but even less of the man. Brahms sincerely admired Wagner's music, but condemned his behavior.

When Brahms came to visit Levi, Wagner was a frequent topic of conversation. As long as Levi had no personal involvement with Wagner's family at Villa Wahnfried, Brahms felt comfortable discussing the music with him. But when Levi decided to assist at Bayreuth in 1875, he cautiously asked Brahms: "Where do you stand on Wagner?"[39] What he certainly meant was "What would you think, were I to befriend Wagner?" He mentioned that two years ago Wagner had played *Götterdämmerung* for him, leaving him "tremendously impressed." Brahms understood the allusions. Levi's affection was shifting. Brahms's response was cool, stating simply that when in Vienna he intended to hear parts of *Götterdämmerung*.

A few weeks later, on the evening of 30 April 1875, they had a serious quarrel. Brahms had stopped in Munich on his way from Vienna to Ziegelhausen

Johannes Brahms in 1874. Courtesy of Frithjof Haas.

near Heidelberg, where he would spend the summer. We can only guess what was said from hints that Levi made later. The quarrel was definitely about Wagner. Levi saw himself as the future conductor of the tetralogy and argued passionately for the composer of musical drama. The next morning Brahms left the house without a word and took the train to Heidelberg.

Levi was shocked. He had planned to spend the entire morning with Brahms discussing concert plans and personal matters. He had canceled all of his appointments for Brahms. He now felt misunderstood, rejected, abandoned. Some years later he wrote Paul Heyse what he had felt that morning, the first of May:

> A friend, to whom I owe everything I am and have, deserted me because he would have nothing to do with a Wagnerian. It was the most painful experience of my entire life.[40]

Piles of mail arrived for Brahms at Levi's address. He forwarded it with a letter of his own, mentioning the quarrel. He had, he wrote, once chosen to devote himself to a cause. And he would continue to do that, continue to do his part as best he could—but only with his whole heart. Anyone that had heard his recent rendition of *Schicksalslied* could never imagine that any new work by another composer could diminish what he had truly loved before. In closing he said: 'If you ever need anyone to risk everything for you, turn to me. Why should you care that I love you."[41]

Levi's love for Brahms was very deep, much deeper than merely appreciating the composer's works. Their friendship gave him orientation and a hold throughout the multifarious everyday chores of a court opera conductor. He could not imagine mastering future challenges without Brahms's support, and thus succumbed to the illusion that he could restore their friendship without changing his mind about Wagner. Ignoring the hurt, he did everything he could to keep in touch with Brahms and to avoid an irrevocable break.

On his summer trip in 1875, Levi first went to Karlsruhe and then to Ziegelhausen with Otto Dessoff, who meanwhile had become Baden's court conductor. By making the visit a threesome, Levi avoided personal conversation, allowing for time to cancel the dissonance that had arisen in Munich. They spoke of Brahms's long-awaited symphony that each of the conductors wanted to be the first to present. Wüllner, too, had mentioned that desire in letters, saying that Brahms ought to write two symphonies so that each of them, he and Levi, would get one to premiere. After spending the afternoon in Ziegelhausen, Levi took the train on to Mannheim and Giessen and then up north. He stayed for two days in Kiel, attending the Schleswig-Holstein Music Festival, where Joachim conducted Handel's *Samson*, Mendelssohn's *Walpurgis Night*, and Schumann's piano concerto with Clara Schumann at the piano. On June 28 they celebrated Joachim's forty-fourth birthday. Levi later recalled that he had not had such pleasant days in a long time. He traveled on to Helgoland and stayed there for the month of July. The sea attracted him and seemed to requite his love. The tension that had built up over the year receded and Levi found new strength. The musical life of Munich was far away; it bothered him little that Wüllner was now conducting Brahms's *German Requiem*.

He had other sorrows. His "fiancée" Marie Reizenstein had tuberculosis. Only a few friends knew of his tender relationship with her. We know little about her. She seems to have combined fragile beauty with lasting affliction in a particularly endearing way: a sickly, yet lovely woman. In an attempt to satisfy Brahms's curiosity, Allgeyer wrote:

> Aside of all gossip, the only thing I can say is that if she were in good health, we would envy Levi for winning her affection. But the way things are, for our friend this affair is a disaster. With some luck his flexible nature will help him get over it.[42]

On his trip back to Munich, Levi stopped in Badenweiler to visit Marie. He wrote to his father that he expected the worst, but that he forgot everything when he was with her and abandoned himself to her charm.

Under this emotional strain, in the fall of 1875 Levi began his fourth playing season, a time when he would become increasingly chained to Wagner. On 13 February 1876, he conducted Munich's first viewing of Hermann Goetz's comic opera *The Taming of the Shrew* that a year earlier Brahms's friend, conductor Ernst Frank, had premiered in Mannheim. Brahms had been to one of the performances and shared Levi's respect for the composer. The libretto based on Shakespeare's text had been written by Josef Victor Widmann, whom Brahms still hoped might someday send him a suitable opera text. In Munich the stars Theodore Reichmann and Cornelia Meysenheym played Petruchio and Catharine. The work was kindly received but not a real success. The *Allgemeine Musikzeitung*'s review sounds remarkably current:

> The work is sound and conservative and can therefore not get support from advocates of the music of the future. For most people it is too delicate, and other friends of music tend not to express their approval as excessively as has become rote for the musicians of the future.[43]

Levi began the series of fall concerts with Beethoven's Symphony no. 7. On 27 November 1875 at the second concert in Odeon Hall, his friend from youth, Friedrich Gernsheim, guest conducted his own first Symphony, op. 32. Gernsheim had come from Rotterdam, where, as the concert director for the Society for the Promotion of Composition, he made every effort to promote Brahms. From the time that Gernsheim had played Brahms's piano concerto in Vienna, Brahms favored and guided him. Gernsheim's appearance in Munich at least brought him respect. Levi began the series of Lent Concerts on 10 March 1876 with Beethoven's *Eroica*. And he introduced his Munich audience to Brahms's *Alto Rhapsody* with singer Josephine Schefzky. Marie Reizenstein lay dying while Levi conducted this solemn music that Brahms had written for Goethe's verses "Who can heal the pain of one whose balsam has become poison?"[44] Being an admirer of Goethe, Levi seems to have deliberately made this choice for Brahms's music to the *Harz Journey*. The poem ends with words of consolation:

Ist auf deinem Psalter	If your psaltery,
Vater der Liebe, ein Ton	Father of Love, has but
Seinem Ohre vernehmlich,	One tone he can hear,
So erquicke sein Herz!	Oh, refresh his heart!

Julius Allgeyer sensed Levi's grief during that performance and mentioned the *Alto Rhapsody* in an attempt to persuade Brahms not to forsake Levi:

It almost looks as if we finally must accept that you will steal away through the underbrush. . . . Let me believe that you are too great and noble to brutally turn away from a man that through all the changes of his enthusiastic nature and exciting career always made and always will make you and your art his most important cause. He needs twice the care now. While conducting the Rhapsody he knew from a telegram that he might be called at any hour to the deathbed of one to whom he remained loyal, though it cost him considerable human strength. If only he could bring her a tiny sign of your old sentiments for him, it would soothe her, be balsam for him, and fulfill a sincere wish of mine.[45]

Marie Reizenstein died four days later. Levi was unable to be near her because he had a concert to conduct on March 15. It included Mozart's Symphony in G Major and Heinrich Hofmann's *Frithjof Symphony*.[46] He mourned alone for several days, letting his friends know that he would tell them when he could speak with them again. Ever-loyal Clara Schumann comforted him: "Don't be discouraged, dear friend! Don't you have music? How privileged we are among millions of people!"[47]

A few weeks later, Levi went to Bayreuth for the first performance of Wagner's *Ring*, while Brahms, far away on the Isle of Ruegen, was just completing his first symphony. From the island in the Baltic Sea, Brahms wrote to Levi's brother Wilhelm Lindeck that after a stay in Bayreuth Levi would "be in dire need of Helgoland or something."[48] He suspected what Bayreuth was going to do to Levi. For its first performance, Brahms gave his long-awaited first symphony neither to Levi nor to Wüllner, but instead to Otto Dessoff in Karlsruhe, a city, he said, where one finds "a good friend, a good kapellmeister, and a good orchestra."[49] Since the quarrel with Levi, Brahms came more often to Lichtental near Baden-Baden where he wrote the last note of Symphony no. 1. Brahms appreciated Karlsruhe's careful and empathetic conductor, Otto Dessoff, under whose direction he had given his first piano concert in Vienna. He considered Karlsruhe's concertgoers most suitable for hearing his first symphony. They were fond of him and he had presented so many new pieces there before.

As we know from correspondence to and fro between Karlsruhe and Baden-Baden, Dessoff—who had experience in composition—considerably influenced the way the symphony finally looked. Brahms welcomed all of the conductor's suggestions. He trusted Dessoff when it came to the practical side of performing. He would sometimes hand the baton over to Dessoff and take a seat in the hall to make final improvements from the vantage point of a critical listener. Recent research shows that Brahms entirely rewrote the slow movement after the work had been performed publicly.[50]

Following the premiere in Karlsruhe on November 4, Brahms conducted the symphony again on November 7 in Mannheim. On November 9 he arrived in Munich with the manuscript of the score and the orchestral parts copied by hand in Karlsruhe. He went to Julius Allgeyer first, but in order to hurt neither

Levi's nor Wüllner's feelings he stayed at Hotel Marienbad on *Barer Strasse*. In the mornings Brahms and Levi rehearsed the symphony and other parts of the program with the orchestra. The afternoons and evenings were reserved for all kinds of activities with their friends. But during the very first days, Brahms and Levi argued. Depressed by the unfortunate mood, Levi consulted Heyse. They tried to cover up the tension by arranging many social events. On November 13 Rheinberger invited Brahms, Heyse, and Wüllner to dinner; the next day Heyse invited all to his home, including Franz von Lenbach and Michael Bernays, and others. On Wednesday, 15 November 1876, Brahms stood at the conductor's stand at the Musical Academy and presented his first symphony as part of an Odeon concert. The second half consisted of cellist Sigmund Bürger playing Bernhard Molique's concert and a sonata by Luigi Boccherini. The Royal Choir sang two a cappella chorales by Brahms for the first time: *Maria's Churchgoing* and *A Quiet Night*, and three romances by Robert Schumann: *Little Boat*, *Sad Hunter*, and *Pretty Rothraut*. Levi closed the program with Beethoven's *Fidelio* overture and Wüllner probably directed his choir, but except for Brahms the printed program lists no other conductor. Max Kalbeck, going by hearsay, reported that the symphony's first three movements were failures. Only the finale got some applause and a few calls back onto the stage. A newspaper from Augsburg wrote of the concert:

> The whole symphony is marked by the principle of "saying much about little." It makes bold and clever use of the orchestra and has a few salient passages. But this coloristic face makes no lasting impression and it is hard to believe, when compared to the two chorales for four voices performed in the second half of the concert (that we must praise in terms of style and mood as being real pearls of choral literature), that the incredible lack of style that we see in the monstrously broad wasteland of the symphony was written by one and the same composer.[51]

Another paper, the *Allgemeine Musikalische Zeitung*, noted that many other new works had been played with more precision.

Levi thought differently and remained untroubled by the audience's reserved reaction. He found the performance excellent and that he had learned much from Brahms. But his opinion of the piece is interesting:

> The final movement is the best yet that Brahms has written for instruments; followed then by the first movement. But the two middle movements, as beautiful as they are, seem more suitable for a serenade or suite than for a symphony of this length.[52]

Perhaps Levi's objections, along with those of Clara Schumann, contributed to Brahms's entirely rewriting the second movement the next year.

The day after the concert, Wüllner invited Brahms and Heyse to lunch. Then they all met at Levi's home where the Walter Quartet played Brahms's String

Quartet, op. 67, that Joachim had premiered in Berlin just two weeks earlier. Everyone was in a good mood; shortly beforehand Brahms and Heyse had toasted to their friendship. Brahms was pleased because he thought he had reconciled the two court conductors. Levi was touched and grateful because he had the impression that his relationship to Brahms had not only been restored, but become even "more lovely" than before. But he did avoid talking things out, basing his opinion simply on what Allgeyer had spoken with Brahms.

The next day, Brahms traveled back to Vienna without mentioning the problem between him and Levi. Levi had avoided all personal conversation and Brahms was not a man of many words anyway. The relationship had grown cold. Levi ignored it and continued to campaign for Brahms's works. In a concert on 9 March 1877, he delivered Brahms's Serenade in D Major that had been written twenty years before. It was a belated first performance in Munich. But it was not overly successful. Levi had engaged Magdalene Koelle-Murjahn for the solo, a highly respected soprano that he knew from his days in Karlsruhe. When she accepted the part, he wrote back: "Well! The audience in Munich will be surprised and I will smile as I lead you to the podium with your innate grace and I shall remember past times while accompanying these songs."[53] In Karlsruhe under the direction of Levi, Magdalene Koelle had been the first to sing many of Brahms's lieder from their manuscripts. At the concert in Munich, she sang Susanna's aria from *Figaro* and lieder by Mozart, Schumann, and Brahms. As an encore she sang Rosine's cavatina from the *Barber of Seville*, with Levi at the piano. It was her last public performance. After that she performed only privately. Years later and at Levi's recommendation, she sang *Christmas Songs*, op. 8, by Peter Cornelius at a reception in Villa Wahnfried in Bayreuth.

Brahms had assets that through Levi's intervention were managed by the Ladenburg Bank in Mannheim. In May 1877 Brahms wrote to Levi's brother, Wilhelm Lindeck, asking him to transfer his stocks and bonds to the Bank of Prussia. He said he was no longer interested in profit. He apparently wanted to avoid future business dealings with Levi's relatives.

In the summer months of 1877, Levi took a long vacation trip. Along the way he visited Allgeyer's mother in Überlingen on Lake Constance and author Gottfried Keller in Zurich. He then visited the Mombert family in Karlsruhe and his relatives in Ladenburg and Mannheim. He traveled restlessly from one place to another. Finally he stopped for a longer while in Alexanderbad for curative treatments. In the future it was to become his preferred vacation retreat. Wilhelm Lindeck wrote to Brahms that his brother felt so ill and broken that he had stayed with the family in Mannheim for only one single day. Brahms replied:

> What you write of your brother does not come unawares, but it sounds sadder with each year that passes. And what would seem most desirable, namely marriage and domesticity, unfortunately looks less likely, year after year.[54]

Brahms's heartfelt concern was not without reason. Levi was in poor health. Diagnosed as having "head congestion" he took sick leave from the court theater until mid-September. The demands of his profession and his extreme nervous tension exhausted him. Henceforth he was constantly sick and could only keep up by taking regular curative treatments in the summer. Clara Schumann knew his habits well and the burdens that devoured him. She warned him: "If only you would take it easy and take time to restore your health, but alas, you will behave as ever, you will smoke (you surely do), stay out late in the evening with friends, and never take walks."[55]

While Levi rested in Alexanderbad, back in Munich his colleague Wüllner, who was in the process of accepting a call to Dresden, took over the entire repertoire for August and September and rehearsed the new piece, *Golo*, by Bernhard Scholz.[56] Levi returned to Munich in late September. A festive farewell ceremony was done for Franz Wüllner; the philosophical faculty of the University of Munich gave him an honorary doctoral degree for his achievements as a composer and teacher and for his theoretical and historical work in music. Joseph Rheinberger was then made director of the royal choir.

Now Levi alone was responsible for all of the subscription concerts at the Odeon. He worked with a large choir for oratorios, consisting of the royal choir, the theater choir, and the best singers from the school of music, with amateurs as extras. On All Saints they performed Haydn's *Creation*, at Christmas Handel's ode *Alexander's Feast*, and on Palm Sunday Handel's *Saul*. For this last work he would have liked to have used Brahms's arrangement from Vienna. But Brahms disappointed him, saying that the arrangement would only work for him.

The orchestra concerts for the winter of 1877–1878 included a number of solo attractions. On November 26, Spanish violinist Pablo de Sarasate played Mendelssohn's concerto and *Preludio, Menuetto e moto perpetuo* by Joachim Raff. The acrobatic virtuoso was better than any violinist they had heard in years. His sheer gypsy-like presence fascinated Munich's concertgoers:

> A short, thin, and very agile little person with jet black curly hair that falls deep into his face from both sides of his brow; a huge moustache, stumpy nose, bushy eyebrows, intelligent shiny eyes and an oddly yellowish complexion.[57]

Many thought he was a reincarnation of Paganini. At the next concert, on December 5, Camille Saint-Saëns from Paris played his Piano Concerto in G Minor, op. 22, and some solo pieces by Bach, Beethoven, and Liszt, and then in closing the evening conducted his orchestral piece *Danse macabre* that was already well known in Munich.

Brahms had completed his Symphony no. 2 during the summer in Baden-Baden and had it premiered by Hans Richter on December 30 at the hall of Vienna's Music Association. On January 10 he conducted it himself in Leipzig and then again in February in Amsterdam. In late fall Levi had already asked whether he might bring the new piece to Munich, if possible with Brahms conducting it, but a date could not be found. Then suddenly Brahms sent a telegram: the date for the premiere in Vienna had been postponed and he could come to Munich any time in December. It would have meant premiering Brahms's second symphony. But Levi did not have the courage to cancel the Christmas concert with Beethoven's *Pastorale* and Handel's *Alexander's Feast*. He would rather, he wrote, perform the new symphony during Lent. Brahms was insulted and retracted the offer entirely. It was hard to say no, Brahms said, because he had already agreed to let Wüllner present it in Dresden, and "what's good enough for Fafner is good enough for Fasolt."[58]

Levi was devastated. He and Wüllner compared with the two giants fighting over the golden treasure? And that Brahms sarcastically quoted—of all things—Wagner's *Ring*, the very piece that Levi during those months was preparing for its first showing in Munich, was a slap in the face. He felt more rejected than ever, left in the lurch by his best friend. The end of their friendship was inevitable. Levi replied: "I'll see how I manage." And that was the end of their correspondence.[59]

For the time being, Levi dispensed with Brahms's Symphony no. 2 and instead repeated Symphony no. 1 on 27 March 1878. The performance was the worst failure of his life, haunting him like a nightmare for years to come:

> I have never experienced anything more embarrassing. After the first movement the hall was silent. After the second a few claps and then loud hissing, and the same after the third. . . . I would have ignored it if the orchestra had backed me, but I could not name one musician whose eyes met mine at any beautiful passage in the piece. After the performance the newspapers ranted and anonymous subscribers threatened to cancel their subscriptions. One group went so far as to compel the Academy to publish the program ahead of the season so that they need not subscribe if one of Brahms's symphonies is planned![60]

Was the orchestra really so unreasonable and narrow minded about the compositional qualities of Brahms's symphony? Or was Levi so insecure that he could no longer excite his musicians for the work? To Clara Schumann Levi suggested that perhaps he had presented too much Brahms within too short of a time. (Shortly beforehand pianist Eugenie Menter had played Brahms's Piano Concerto in D Minor.) Besides, he argued, the protest had not come from avant-garde Wagnerians, it came from Rheinberger's and Lachner's philistines. There was some truth to it: the papers never compared Levi to Hans von Bülow, but regularly compared him to their old favorite, Franz Lachner, whose prowess at rendering the classics Levi could not attain.

Levi did not let the failure with Brahms's Symphony no. 1 keep him from doing a first performance for Symphony no. 2 in Munich on 20 March 1879. This time he put the new piece at the end of the program that began with Beethoven's overture *Coriolanus*. Between the two main pieces, French violinist Emile Sauret played Heinrich Wilhelm Ernst's *Concerto pathétique*, Beethoven's *Romance in F Major*, and Henri Vieutemp's *Fantasy* and *Caprice*; and the ladies Schefzky and Schulze sang a duet from *Beatrice and Benedict*. In other words, Levi's plan was to first give the audience lots of diversity. But it didn't help. After intermission, people found the new symphony dull. Augsburg's newspaper critic complained that the reception of Brahms's symphony had been disproportionate to the significance of the work. In Munich the wind simply blew unfavorably for Brahms.

Apparently Levi found it even more difficult to grasp Brahms's pastoral, second symphony than the more dramatic first symphony. He told Clara Schumann: "I do not yet fully understand the Adagio, it leaves me cold."[61] At the time Levi was surely so captivated by Wagner's *Siegfried* that he was preparing for its first performance in Munich, that he lost a feeling for Brahms's more delicate "Pastorale." The end of their friendship also ended his enthusiasm in championing Brahms. He was tired of putting so much effort into something that neither the public nor the composer appreciated.

Nevertheless, in the years to come Levi would include Brahms's orchestral works in the Odeon concerts: *Haydn Variations* (in 1881 and 1890), *Tragic Overture* (in 1881), *Academic Festival Overture* (in 1882), the violin concerto (in 1886), Piano Concerto no. 2 (in 1883 and 1886), Symphony no. 3 (1884), Symphony no. 4 (1886), Symphony no. 2 (1888), Symphony no. 1 (1893).

For the rest of his life, Levi guarded the many manuscripts, compositions, and letters from Brahms in his possession. Precise information that he was able to give Brahms's biographer Max Kalbeck shed much light on the middle years of Brahms's creativity. At heart he remained loyal to Brahms, even after they lost touch. Neither of the two ever tried to reconcile their differences. Too much hurt had been caused on both sides, too much said, the reason for their friendship was gone. They would have met once more later, if Brahms, as he had planned, had attended *Parsifal* in Bayreuth with Bülow. But when the time came, neither had the courage.

Only once did Levi sell a Brahms manuscript that he owned, in 1897. It was a piece from their time in Karlsruhe, when the friends sent riddle canons to one another. Levi donated the proceeds to Bayreuth's stipend fund. Attacked from several sides for doing so, he said: "There's a deeper meaning to one of Brahms's pieces enabling a few poor chaps to attend the festival in Bayreuth."[62]

In later years Brahms's friendship with Wüllner flourished, particularly because Wüllner (in his function as conductor for Cologne's Gürzenich Concerts) promoted Brahms's symphonic works. Brahms also found an excellent conductor and fanatic follower in Hans von Bülow, who took his Meiningen Court Orchestra on concert tours to many German cities giving exemplary performances.

The latter's career took the exact opposite direction of Levi's: von Bülow turned away from Wagner and found his way to Brahms.

And yet, the break with Levi left a gap for Brahms that could not be filled. His time with Baden's enthusiastic, fresh-baked court conductor was now irretrievably a thing of the past. Despite his growing success, Brahms got lonelier, quieter, more resigned. He withdrew from almost all of their mutual friends. He even lost touch with his loyal friend Julius Allgeyer. They had no contact again until 1884 when Allgeyer asked for financial support for a new printing method he had invented. But when Allgeyer sent Brahms a dedicated copy of his biography of Anselm Feuerbach, Brahms thanked him so effusively that it moved Allgeyer to tears. Two years before he died, Brahms wrote to Allgeyer: "It is my habit to take friendship very seriously and in simple terms, and thus I close with a bright, pure, chord."[63]

When Levi thought of Brahms, he no longer heard that clear chord. A fine string of his heart was broken. He suffered under the loss that was partly his own fault. Neither the aesthetic nor the personal tie to Wagner could ever make up for the lost friendship with Brahms. Despite his entanglement with the Wagner family, at Bayreuth Levi always only felt tolerated, never accepted. It took years for him to realize the price he would pay for choosing to become a conductor there.

SOCIETY AROUND PAUL HEYSE AND FRANZ VON LENBACH

> Believe me, the love and interest of others cannot be measured by the number of letters exchanged or the promises they contain.
>
> —Levi to Heyse

Levi's mental and emotional well-being depended on the sense of security and welcome he felt around good friends. He never sought a woman with whom to share his life. When he met charming Marie Reizenstein, whom he called his fiancée, she was already terminally ill and their relationship had no real future. The few leisure hours that remained for Levi after strenuous work at the theater and studying texts and scores, he spent socializing. On afternoons off, and at lunchtime, he sought intellectual conversation with like-minded friends. On evenings without concerts he would invite guests to his home, or accept invitations to others. He enjoyed discussing aesthetics, music, literature, and painting, and often made provocative claims just to get a debate going.

During his first years in Munich, Levi was able to find friends by looking up people he had met in the past. Julius Allgeyer, who moved to Munich the same time Levi did, remained his closest friend almost until he died. He had met

Emilie Kaula through his lady friend from Karlsruhe, Anna Ettlinger. Emilie was Anna's sister who married a banker from Munich and lived there, where she established and ran her own school of song. She had studied singing in Paris together with Levi's brother Wilhelm and had sung there in a choir directed by Julius Stockhausen. At the Kaula School of Song, pupils sang Brahms's newest lieder; some of which were heard there for the very first time. Levi was always welcome for lunch at the Kaula home, even unannounced. He would dish out the soup to prove that he could do it tempo presto.

When singers from the theater ensemble had problems with their voices, Levi sent them to Emilie Kaula. In the 1880s she organized a musical club that performed entire operas. The accompanying orchestra was directed by Wilhelm Kienzl, the composer of *Evangelimann*.

Levi rarely socialized with members of his own orchestra or opera troupe, with the exception of Therese and Heinrich Vogl, a married couple who, as dramatic soprano and heroic tenor, were indispensable for the Wagner repertory. Heinrich Vogl, who also wrote a bit of music himself, must have been a good singer of lieder. Accompanied by Levi at the piano, he often sang solos between the orchestral works presented at the Odeon concerts. These were mostly things such as Beethoven's round of songs *To the Distant Beloved* or lieder by Schubert, Schumann, or Brahms. In Tutzing, on Lake Starnberg, the couple owned a summer residence with a pavilion on the shore, where friends often met to play instruments and sing. In 1875 Heinrich Vogl took up farming in nearby Deixlfurt. He soon had 120 cows, 18 oxen, and 12 horses. In Munich people said, "Today he'll sing Tristan, for sure; tomorrow bring out the manure!"[64]

When she sang the part of Brynhild, Therese Vogl galloped across the stage on her own horse. It did not impress Richard Wagner. Although Heinrich Vogl would have made an excellent Mime for the *Ring*, for *Parsifal* Wagner did without him because the singer agreed to participate only on the condition that his wife was hired, too.

At Deixlfurt the couple always kept a room reserved for Levi if he needed rest. When Brahms spent his vacations in Tutzing, they often met and made music together there. Late in life Levi stayed at the Vogls' rustic idyll several times to calm his nerves, appreciating his hosts' Bavarian ways. The couple made pleasant outings with the conductor in the horse buggy. One of their favorite destinations was the pilgrimage church in Andechs above Lake Ammer. Once they got there, Heinrich Vogl would play the organ and then brewery master Father Jakob would serve them wine from his vast monastery cellar.

In these hours of leisure, Levi seemed like an entirely different person. Relaxed, chatting and joking, he took part in innocent pleasures and entertained his friends with amusing stories, of which he always knew plenty. He enjoyed rustic Bavarian hospitality. The Vogls appreciated that their court conductor stood 100

Poet Paul Heyse (1830–1914), photograph of an oil sketch portrait by Franz von Lenbach, around 1893 or 1894. Courtesy of Frithjof Haas.

percent behind them. At first Heinrich Vogl had had a rough time making his way onto the stage because King Ludwig II disliked his rural look and refused to attend either *Tristan* or *Siegfried* when Vogl sang the lead part.

The most important personal acquaintance for Levi during his first years in Munich was poet Paul Heyse, who lived in his neighborhood. In 1873 Heyse and his wife had purchased a beautiful villa in *Luisen Strasse*, just five minutes away from Levi's apartment.

Paul Heyse was a fascinating person. He has been called "Munich's poet laureate of the burgher era."[65] A sophisticated and cultivated aesthete and a master of discipline in speech, Heyse was seen by many as a worthy successor to Goethe. His friend Theodore Fontane found that "even people who grudgingly surrender their right to talk craved to hear Heyse, and the vainest of them enjoyed it."[66] Levi, too, was among Heyse's admirers and was thrilled to become his friend.

Paul Heyse had had a classical education. His father was a professor for classical philology in Berlin and, as a private tutor, had taught Felix Mendelssohn at home. His Jewish mother was a cousin to Lea Salomon, Felix Mendelssohn's mother.

On recommendation by Emanuel Geibel, in 1853 little known Paul Heyse was called to Munich by King Maximilian II. For an annual salary of 1000 guldens, his job was to take part in the king's symposiums and hold a few lectures at the university. Together with poet Emanuel Geibel, writer Count von Schack, historian Heinrich von Sybel, and painter Wilhelm von Kaulbach, Heyse was considered one of the "Northern Lights," a name given the group of scientists, artists, and poets that King Maximilian brought to Munich from northern Germany in an attempt to raise the intellectual level of the city. How strange it might feel for someone from Berlin to live in Munich, we know from one of Heyse's carnival verses:

> Until the day you die, man of Berlin,
> No bock, no Isar can wash you clean.
> Though she may burn for daughters of the south,
> Resemble she does, your muse,
> What they here call a cool blonde.[67]

A jovial circle of poet friends who nicknamed themselves "The Crocodile" met to read their verses to one another. Heyse felt so comfortable in this setting that he stayed in Munich for the rest of his life. By the time Levi came to Munich, though, Maximilian's successor King Ludwig II had long discontinued the royal symposiums. Some of the "Northern Lights" had moved away. Heyse stayed. His success at writing novellas and pieces for the theater allowed him to live as an independent author, without royal support. In Munich he had become a well-known, highly respected person. When he strolled through the English Garden arm in arm with his pretty and very young second wife, everyone tipped their hats and whispered "the famous poet!"

Important writers of the time—Theodor Storm, Gottfried Keller, and Theodor Fontane—thought much of Heyse. Fontane thought that one day their epoch of literature might be named after Heyse. Johannes Brahms considered him the best possible choice for writing a libretto, should he ever get around to composing an opera.

As soon as he had settled in Munich, Levi made a conscious effort to become acquainted with Heyse, visiting him several times a week, when the Heyses held open house for guests in the afternoon. They met for conversation and for social events in the afternoons and evenings. Levi was well versed in both classical and more recent literature. This made him an interesting conversational partner for Heyse. Heyse knew and understood much about classical music. He liked to have Levi play for him and explain the new pieces on the program. In May 1874 Levi was among the few guests (Joseph Rheinberger, Moritz Carrière,[68] Arnold Böcklin, and Michael Bernays) invited for coffee to celebrate the Heyse family's move to a new home at 49 *Luisen Strasse* (now house number 22).

The Heyses' grand house stood next to the Propyläen Park, behind the trees of a large front yard. One entered through a portico and up a wide outdoor staircase, decked to the left and right with replicas of Greek statues, to arrive at the first floor, and the family study and music room. The walls were covered with paintings by Menzel, Lenbach, and Böcklin. After the festive housewarming, Levi often came to the Heyses' new home for music making and conversation. In late 1874 the two men decided to confirm their friendship by allowing each other to use the personal form of address, "Du." Heyse confirmed it again in his next letter: "It's what I always wanted, from the first hour that we spent together, because I liked you the first time we met."[69] Levi was at first reserved about getting too close, as we know from a letter written from Helgoland in the summer of 1875:

> Besides my feelings for you, I have, namely, also horribly huge respect and since I have had similar experiences with others like you and have been aware of an almost unbridgeable chasm, I'm frightened by the prospects for our relationship, if it should turn out that you are not so different from all the others. But I don't want to lose all hope. Give me some time and continue to be as kind to me as you have been so far.[70]

Between the lines we see Levi's extreme sensitivity, his permanent fear of not being respected because he was a Jew. In Heyse's case, that fear was certainly unfounded. Levi should have wondered more whether he would in the long run be able to follow Heyse's conventional line of art. But at the time that thought escaped him, and he even considered spending the following year's vacation together with Heyse at the North Sea. Heyse, who preferred what Levi called "the charmingly coquettish, but passionless Mediterranean," tried for his part to lure his friend to Rome. Neither trip was ever taken, nor was a planned joint trip to Paris.

Perhaps their habits were just too different. Levi, the bachelor, rushing from one activity to the next, loved the stormy North Sea. Heyse, happily married for a second time, considered his family the center of his life and felt drawn through his poetry to the Mediterranean world. Nonetheless, their friendship grew, at least as long as Levi had not entirely defected to Wagner's camp. Heyse attended the Wagner performances that Levi conducted, even standing in line for tickets to the first Munich performance of the *Ring* because he wanted to study the work seriously. But he did not like musical drama. It contradicted his idea of art entirely. Despite endless debates, the conductor was unable to change the poet's deepest convictions. Heyse defended his view with derisive remarks, such as that his friend's "Wagneritis made it impossible to keep him on the narrow path of virtue."

Levi could tolerate criticism of Wagner's work, but he was sensitive about mocking the "Master." When Wagner stayed in Munich in late 1880, Levi evaded Heyse for months. At the end of the year, Heyse asked Levi to explain himself. Levi penned his answer, feeling inferior to Heyse when it came to verbal argument:

> During Wagner's presence of three weeks I did not see you because being with him was intoxicating. You've known for long that I am addicted to the man with body and soul. But you know equally well that I do not judge people by how much they love Wagner, and that on the contrary, I have very close relationships to people that cannot accept Wagner at all, such as Mrs. Schumann, Busch, and Lenbach. But during those November days it would have been impossible for me to hear one disparaging or ironic word about Wagner.—If from all this you understand that I still love you, you will know what I mean.[71]

Heyse would not have it. To him the situation questioned their friendship:

> If the passionate exclusivity with which you devote yourself to a man about whom we differ in opinion could destroy in you every desire to see me for nine long weeks, I shall have to prepare myself for unpredictable interruptions in the future, and that goes against my nature. I need dependability. Your aesthetic enthusiasm for a man whom I, despite all recognition of his unusual talents, consider an ominous phenomenon would in itself never have divided us. But the ground under my feet sways when you confess that you are addicted with body and soul to a man for whom I feel deep moral antipathy, a man who—based on facts you cannot deny—lacks true nobility of mind and has no respect for what binds people to others. . . . I ask myself, what do I still have to offer? . . . How could the son of your fine father succumb to and put himself at the mercy of a man who takes every opportunity to express his fanatic hate of people with your roots? . . . I have no idea what we might mean for one another in the future. . . . Perhaps the time will come when the person for whom you have fallen turns his mastery of perfidy against you, too. Then you will find that I have preserved your undiminished Self. Silently stepping aside, your Paul Heyse.[72]

We do not know what Levi replied to this letter; it was probably not in writing. They saw each other much less often, though still holding one another in esteem. But occasionally Heyse did—as he wrote—silently step aside. He attended *Ring* performances in Munich, but he eschewed Bayreuth. He did not swerve from his aesthetic views. It was a maxim he had formulated for himself: "To thy own self be true." It was for him the fundamental prerequisite for being truly human; inner conflict brought catastrophe. By the time Heyse was honored with the Nobel Prize for Literature in 1911, modern developments in literature had long left him behind. His friend's transition from Brahms to Wagner remained a riddle to him. But his esteem for Levi's accomplishments and his feelings for Levi were not lessened by it.

A few weeks before he died, Levi wrote last, very personal words on the occasion of Heyse's seventieth birthday:

> I remember with heartfelt gratitude the great kindness with which you always tried to reach out to me despite the abyss that separated our views on art, and how I always clasped that hand with the equal warmth. And when a relationship has not only luckily survived such crises, but become all the firmer because of them, we can very well say that it was built on a mysterious ground of sympathy and affection, something that cannot be explained rationally, and that by absolute necessity will last forever.[73]

Certainly Heyse's steadfast friendship helped Levi not to despair when Brahms broke with him, and to endure the abuse and abrasion he got from the Wagnerians. At Heyse's home he did meet other Wagnerians. One of them was professor for literature Michael Bernays, who had come to Munich a year after Levi. Michael Bernays was the son of a prominent rabbi in Hamburg and a younger brother of the professor for philology in Bonn, Jakob Bernays. At the age of twenty-one, Michael had converted and become a Protestant. His godmother was Henriette Feuerbach, the stepmother of painter Anselm Feuerbach. Thus he had an old tie to Levi, who collected Feuerbach's paintings and corresponded regularly with Henriette. Michael Bernays was a talented speaker and reciter. He traveled to many German cities giving lectures, speaking on Goethe, Schiller, and Lessing, and reciting from their works. King Ludwig II called him to Munich and in 1874 made him professor for modern languages and literature. It was the first professorship of its kind at any German university. Bernays taught with priestly earnestness and theatrical pathos. He never used notes and his students said he was omniscient in literature. He certainly had a unique memory. He could recite by heart poetry by Goethe and Schiller and texts by Homer and Dante for hours.

As an admirer of Wagner, Bernays was a frequent guest at Villa Wahnfried, reciting literature there for Richard and Cosima. At the time he was the sole professor in Germany who dared to discuss Wagner from the lectern. He called the devisor of musical drama a representative of the idea of "what a man with determination can do." Although Bernays was devoted to Wagner, the Wagners took this "fiery, wonderful man" (Cosima's words) and his visits at Wahnfried as cause for vicious anti-Semitic remarks. Cosima's diary entry for 27 July 1880 says: "Richard discusses the peculiar nature of the Jews, prompted by an anecdote about Prof. Bernays; he is a strange element, foreign to us." On 18 December 1881, Richard says of Bernays: "One feeds their pride by dealing with them." This is followed by Cosima's macabre note: "He joked that all the Jews in a performance of *Nathan* should burn."[74]

Of all people, Bernays, who had disavowed Judaism and deliberately adopted the Christian faith, elicited—by his "peculiar Jewish nature" (Cosima)—ridicule and antagonism from the Wagners.[75]

Enthusiastic for Wagner's works and out of friendship for the court conductor, Bernays hardly ever missed a Wagner performance in Munich. From his years in Karlsruhe, Levi was already somewhat familiar with Bernays because in Karlsruhe he had played the professor's arrangement for the connecting passages of Beethoven's music to Goethe's *Egmont*. He encountered Bernays at social events at the Heyse home and invited him to his own home for house music. Bernays and Levi discovered similarities in many aspects of their lives. Like the court orchestra conductor, the professor for philology came from a rabbi family and had reached a respected position in the intellectual scene of the nascent German Reich. In contrast to Levi, Bernays converted. But even conversion did not spare him the difficulty of assimilation. Levi consulted Bernays on questions in philology. For the premiere of Wagner's *Ring* in Munich, he hired Bernays to work with the soloists on the phonetics of Wagner's texts.

Levi not only introduced his friend Bernays to the Wagners, he also introduced him to Franz Liszt when Liszt visited Munich for a few days in late August 1878. Since Levi was not one of Liszt's disciples, he may have been grateful that Bernays entertained the composer for a while. He had no idea how thoroughly Bernays would fulfill the task. They were supposed to talk for thirty minutes. But Bernays stayed at the hostel talking with Liszt from 11 a.m. to 5 p.m. With his flood of words Bernays held the patient composer's attention for six hours.

Levi's contact with Bernays lessened after the latter retired and moved to Karlsruhe in 1890 in order to take up writing. He was well received at Baden's court, but lived only a few years longer. Teaching students had been the true purpose of his life.

Most of the contacts Levi made through Heyse were of a literary or philosophical nature. At Heyse's home he met philosopher Moritz Carrière, Liebig's son-in-law, with whom he could reminisce about Giessen. Another regular guest was poet Wilhelm Hertz,[76] who as of 1869 had a professorship at the newly founded Polytechnic College. Hertz became known for his free adaptations of medieval epics like the *Rolandslied*, *Tristan and Isolde*, and *Parsifal*. After Bernays left Munich, Wilhelm Hertz became Levi's adviser in literary matters. At the Heyse home Levi also met Max Kalbeck, who later became Brahms's biographer. At

Wilhelm Busch and Hermann Levi. Wilhelm Busch Gesellschaft, Hanover.

Heyse's recommendation Kalbeck had come to Munich to study under Joseph Rheinberger and Franz Wüllner. Kalbeck became a music and theater critic in Vienna and later revived his contact to Levi to get data for his long biography of Brahms.

Anyone with a name in Munich's intellectual circles was a guest at Heyse's home. Unannounced visits were always welcome in the afternoon. The evenings were reserved for big social gatherings with illustrious personalities. And music was often a part of it. Levi and Rheinberger, Franz Wüllner and Robert von Hornstein,[77] they all made music there. When in Munich, Brahms was the guest of honor and everyone gathered around him. But after his break with Levi in the late 1870s Brahms shunned Munich and did not return to the Heyse home.

Levi found another, entirely different circle of friends in the society of artists called "Allotria,"[78] where he was an honorary member. It was a club for the visual arts with members like Arnold Böcklin, Lorenz Gedon, Friedrich August Kaulbach (Wilhelm Kaulbach's nephew), Franz von Lenbach, Karl Piloty, and Michael Wagmüller. They caroused and debated, went bowling and had parties. Vital to the club was Franz von Lenbach who quickly became friends with Levi. A greater discrepancy is hardly imaginable as that between intellectual and elite Heyse and lusty, jovial Lenbach. Lenbach came from an Upper Bavarian agricultural family, had no academic background, and had at the age of fifteen completed an apprenticeship as a mason. As an autodidact he painted bright pictures of nature and might have become a second Liebermann if he had not in Munich entered the school of historical painter Karl Piloty. There was a demand for copies of paintings by the older masters from Rome and Madrid. While on these lucrative commissions from Count von Schack, Lenbach discovered his talent at portrait making à la Titian. His reputation as a gifted portrait painter quickly spread through Europe: emperors, kings, church dignitaries and worldly princes, poets, composers, bank directors and industry magnates, politicians, council members, and pretty young ladies sat in his ateliers in Munich, Berlin, and Rome to have their portraits painted wearing luxurious costumes, set before dark brown backgrounds. With his clients and friends, Lenbach spoke rustic Upper Bavarian dialect sprinkled with words of Italian.

Lenbach's favorite model was Bismarck. He painted almost eighty portraits of him. He was Bismarck's guest for weeks on end at the prince's residence in Friedrichsruh. When he got bored, Lenbach organized parties and invited his friends from Munich, including Levi, to Bismarck's home. In Rome Lenbach lived in Palazzo Borghese. In Munich he had architect Gabriel von Seidl build him a grand villa in Renaissance style where he lived like a high priest of the arts with his first wife, Countess von Moltke, below golden-paneled ceilings in rooms papered with damask. This extravagant lifestyle could only be maintained by painting thousands of portraits, often in a hurry. In order to produce faster,

Lenbach hid a photographer behind a black curtain and later used the pictures to complete the portrait.

Levi, too, was won over by Lenbach's ebullient and warm attention. Certainly Lenbach was not one for profound literary or philosophical talk. But he lavished his friendship on the conductor and remained loyal, even through difficult times. For years they met at least once a week at Lenbach's villa to play tarot cards; the round included Levi's physician Dr. Solbrig and royal court secretary Mr. Von Bürckel. When Lenbach was out of town he sent hurried scribbled greetings in large letters to his "dear little Levi, longing to get back to tarot, with a tender hug, Your Lenbacio." Or he advised his friend to "quit that exasperating conducting in Bayreuth and go for a walk" with him instead. He generously told Levi to "take whatever you like from my studio!"

Levi appreciated Lenbach's kind attention, a man who didn't care whether he loved Brahms or Wagner. He ignored Lenbach's petty weaknesses, superficiality, many love affairs, and pomp. He got Lenbach valuable portrait orders from Richard and Cosima Wagner, Franz Liszt, Clara Schumann, and the Ladenburg family. In thanks Lenbach painted a portrait of Levi's eighty-year-old father in oil. He also made several paintings of Levi. The best portrait shows Levi at about the age of forty-four. The view is from the front and against a neutral background, his pale face entirely framed by his beard and hair. Expressive eyes gaze at the observer. We see courage, and yet also woe. The portrait might just as well be the print of Jesus on St. Veronica's cloth. Levi owned another painting by Lenbach that shows Salome triumphantly presenting the head of John the Baptist on a platter. John's head strikingly resembles Hermann Levi.

In June 1890 Lenbach created a stir by inviting Bismarck, who, a few months earlier, had been ousted as chancellor to Munich. At his own cost, Lenbach ordered an entire train to bring the ex-chancellor to visit Bavaria's capital. When the train rolled in at night, a cheering crowd lined the streets from the station to Lenbach's villa. Lenbach had organized it, of course, and even Levi had to help out. Levi was also among the few invited for a personal audience with Bismarck at the Villa Lenbach. And he was with the "Allotria" when they presented Bismarck with a huge mug of beer. Bismarck said he was too old to drink it all, but if it would save the country, he would follow the example of the major of Rothenburg and empty the stein. Heyse told Lenbach it was like having Zeus among them. To commemorate Bismarck's visit, Lenbach organized a drive to collect money for a Bismarck Tower on Lake Starnberg. Donators got free portraits by Lenbach.

Among the company at "Allotria" Levi met and befriended their regular guest, painter Wilhelm Busch. Busch had studied at the Munich Academy and returned to the city after 1873 to paint among a circle of like-minded artists. He saw painting as his true calling. His famous picture books starring *Max and Moritz*, *Teacher Lempel*, and *Painter Kleksel* were just for fun. Their successful publication made the painter famous and secured him a life of financial independence. In 1873 Busch shared an atelier in Munich with Lenbach; later, architect Lorenz Gedon[79] set up a studio of Busch's own. He worked there every year for a few months until 1881. The rest of his time he spent in his hometown of Wiedensahl, near Hanover.

Busch and Levi became good friends and addressed one another with "Du." After Busch returned to Wiedensahl for good, they wrote letters and met when Levi traveled north. They met in Wolfenbüttel or Kassel, visiting galleries and libraries and discussing religion. They had much in common: their main careers were of an artistic nature, but beyond that they were avid readers and thought about the philosophy of religion. Busch's storybooks display a considerable amount of anti-Semitism; the questionable, ridiculous figures in his illustrations often look Jewish. It didn't seem to bother Levi. He often spoke with Busch about problems of being a Jew in a Christian environment, particularly during the years he spent working on *Parsifal* and when Richard and Cosima Wagner wanted him to convert. Upon Levi's mentioning it, Busch replied in December 1880:

> Woe betide you! Whoever has seen an eye of quick bestiality flash, has a gruesome premonition that a single queer scoundrel on Uranus might bring deliverance to a halt, that a single devil might be stronger than a whole heaven of saints. Are Christians right? Do diehards end in hell? Across the river, St. Augustine stands on the other shore. He nods gravely to me: here is the boat of belief. Mercy is the ferryman. Whoever calls urgently will be brought over. But I cannot call, my soul is hoarse; I have a philosophical cold. And you, my friend? The last time I saw you, you were inhaling. I hope it helped.[80]

Busch was too much of a skeptic to be able to resolve Levi's dilemma. But he was earnest enough to respond to Levi's quest with sympathetic understanding. This was something Levi craved, especially after Brahms had dropped him. None of his friends in Munich—neither Heyse nor Bernays, neither Hertz nor Lenbach nor Busch could replace Brahms. Levi needed them to survive, to succeed in the world of the arts. But ultimately he was lonely, at least until he decided to marry.

THE SPELL OF THE GRAIL

> Levi is one of those who know no limit to generosity.
>
> —Houston Stewart Chamberlain

The year 1876 sealed Levi's fate: the music of Wagner's *Ring of the Nibelung*, enchanted, drew him into a trance. Even the prospect of premiering Brahms's Symphony no. 1 in Munich in a few weeks did not lessen his determination to

Hermann Levi, portrait in oil by Franz von Lenbach around 1893. Photograph courtesy of Frithjof Haas.

now put all of his artistic effort into perfecting Wagner's project. From now on, he was obsessed with the idea of serving Wagner. It so possessed him that neither the loss of friends nor grave humiliation stood in his way.

When Levi heard that the first festival in Bayreuth had been a financial failure, he immediately sought to help out. At a concert in Munich on 17 March 1877, he presented fragments of the *Ring*, making a profit of 3,863 marks that were donated to the Bayreuth Festival Fund.[81] He wrote Wagner that it had been a great concert and the singers had gotten twenty-four calls to come back out onto the stage. French horn player Strauss (Richard Strauss's father) complained, but played beautifully. Wagner accepted the donation. He also accepted invitations to conduct his own works in London in May. But those concerts only raked in 700 pounds, just one-tenth of the festival's deficit. Earlier in the year, Wagner had founded a "Club of Patrons" for the purpose of supporting and sustaining the festival. He petitioned to the German Reichstag for funding, but his request was denied. This, he said, made him "bury all hope for help from the German mentality." He gave up the festivals, and began writing *Parsifal*.

Levi made up a list of performers and set up a plan for rehearsing the entire *Ring* in Munich. Wagner had arranged with King Ludwig that after Bayreuth, Munich's court theater would be the next German stage to present the entire work. *Siegfried* was planned for April 1878; *Götterdämmerung* would come after the summer break. This was to be followed by a repeat performance of *Rheingold* and then *Walküre* (*Valkyrie*), completing the tetralogy in the fall. In December 1877 Levi submitted his plans to the theater superintendent. The proposal was accepted and other projects postponed, enabling the entire workings of the theater to concentrate on preparing the biggest opera project ever known.

However, the premiering of *Siegfried*, planned for 22 April 1878, was delayed. During a rehearsal the title role singer, Heinrich Vogl, had fallen into a three-meter-deep pit and been injured. After six weeks and additional rehearsals, on June 10 the performance finally took place with Mr. and Mrs. Vogl singing the major parts, Siegfried and Brynhild.[82] Wagner sent a congratulatory telegram to Heinrich Vogl: "If you discover that your wife has fallen asleep during the last act, wake her up and give her my best." King Ludwig did not attend the performance because he preferred not to see Vogl as Siegfried and his real preference for the role, tenor Nachbaur, could not learn the part fast enough.

Leipzig's conductor, Anton Seidl, saw the premiere and reported to Wagner that it had failed: the attempt had been too great to make the performance differ from that of Bayreuth. By this he meant particularly the stage directing by Karl Brulliot, with whom Levi had already been dissatisfied in Karlsruhe. Munich's press, however, wrote that this outcome of *Siegfried* was the result of a very unusual willingness to endure more sacrifice and effort than ever before, and that it had been a brilliant, memorable day for the court theater.[83] In a letter, Michael Bernays wrote of the premiere:

> Levi applied the complete range of his conducting skills, allowing individual flaws to vanish in the unity that his mind gave to the entire performance. His sublimity and defiant temerity made the work, every note of which I know well, greater than ever.[84]

Levi began visiting Villa Wahnfried in Bayreuth more often, reporting on performances in Munich and asking Wagner for advice on how to render his works.

At such meetings they also regularly discussed "Jewishness." Wagner found Levi "touching in his way, as an Israelite, a living Jewish anachronism." Once he saw him off with the words: "Good-bye, you odd person!"[85] The next time that Levi came, which was in August 1878, Wagner played for him and Cosima the prelude to *Parsifal* that he had just completed. Levi had read the printed text a few months earlier and told Paul Heyse that he found the extreme Christian nature of the work rather questionable. Were he ever to perform it, he would have no choice but to first be baptized.[86] He made a similar remark in a letter to Cosima: *Parsifal*'s theme, he said, gave Christian notions such power over him that he could hardly walk past an open church door without irresistibly feeling drawn in.

Thoughts like these went through his mind during rehearsals for the first performance of *Götterdämmerung*. The *Ring* operas became particularly difficult for him because he constantly feared comparison with Bayreuth and missing the mark. He also felt that he had not been allowed enough time for rehearsals. *Götterdämmerung* was scheduled to show in Leipzig on September 22, but the king of Bavaria wanted it shown in Munich first. Levi wrote to Cosima that despite the challenges, his solo performers labored zealously to enable the premiere on September 15.[87]

Newspaper reviews hailed the performance as one of the greatest successes ever seen on Munich's court stage. Overall it was seen as not simply equal, but superior to the performance in Bayreuth. Once again Heinrich and Therese Vogl sang the major roles of Siegfried and Brynhild. They got laurel wreaths for their performance. In the closing scene Therese Vogl had dashed through the flames on a steed and gossip had it that King Ludwig himself had lent her his favorite horse "Luitprant" for the purpose.

On 8 October 1878, the court theater celebrated its one hundredth anniversary. A banquet was given at Odeon Hall for all the members of the house. Levi was awarded the Knight's Cross First Class from St. Michael's Order of the Empire. A writer friend, Felix Dahn, congratulated him with verse on the back of a postcard:

Wer ist der Jüngling sonder Fehl?	Who is this strange young man?
Er trägt dem heiligen Michael—	Bearing the cross of St. Michael—
Ist doch vom Stamme Israel!	Though from the house of Israel!
Und mancher Christ sieht darob scheel.[88]	Cock-eyeing many a Christian.

The jest contained perhaps more truth than the secular royal conductor cared to realize. An alarming wave of anti-Semitism was spreading through society, churned by the pastor of the court in Berlin, Adolf Stoecker,[89] and historian Heinrich von Treitschke.[90]

For the first time since it had been shown in Bayreuth, between November 17 and 23 of 1878, the first total performance of Wagner's *Ring* took place in Munich. After a performance of *Valkyrie*, Wilhelm Busch said:

> I was delighted by what I heard and bored by what I saw. If a deaf person were to go, they would think it an embarrassingly long parody of the northern saga of the gods.[91]

In contrast, Michael Bernays thought that at the time there was no better place than Munich to stage Wagner's operas. All four evenings were sold out. At midnight, when the five-hour performances were over, there was no end to the applause. Some of the cast had already sung major roles in Bayreuth: Heinrich Vogl (Loge), Karl Schlosser (Mime), and Josephine Schefzky (Sieglinde). Theodor Reichmann sang the part of Wotan (he had sung Amfortas in Bayreuth), August Kindermann sang Fafner (in Bayreuth he had sung Titurel). Franz Nachbaur debuted as Siegmund.

King Ludwig II did not attend these first *Ring* performances in Munich. He was given private viewings between the twenty-second and the twenty-ninth of April, 1879. Afterward he conveyed his "most benevolent applause" by way of a letter. At the age of sixteen, Ludwig had seen *Lohengrin* and discovered the world of the theater. To him the theater came to mean the only true place of all that is noble and ideal. It let his fantasies become reality. What happened on stage was more real to him than the outside world of politics.

At first the king attended public performances. But he suffered so much from being stared at by the audience that as of 1872 he wanted separate, secret performances at night. He sat alone in the auditorium.

Few reports exist of these eerie nocturnal viewings because everyone involved had orders not to speak of it. The actors played to the vast blackness of an empty auditorium, never knowing whether the king was in his loge or not.

As many as twenty such performances were given every year. The king wanted to see works by Richard Wagner, but also other operas, like *Oberon*, *Les Huguénots*, and *Queen of Saba*—as well as plays and ballet, usually with fantasy themes that appealed to his romantic imagination.

Not a soul dared to complain about these extra performances—after all, they owed their comfortable incomes to their king's passion for the theater. Actor Josef Kainz once admitted that never again could he act as well as he did for that one viewer, one who understood every detail of the performance. Art meant worship; the theater became a temple of the arts.[92]

Despite the challenge of premiering the *Ring* in November 1878, Levi did not forget Clara Schumann. One week after the first showing of *Götterdämmerung* she came to Munich to play Beethoven's Piano Concerto in G Major and a few solo pieces by Schumann and Chopin at the Odeon's third subscription concert. The evening began with Robert Schumann's Symphony no. 2 and ended with

Beethoven's overture *King Stephan*. Theodor Reichmann (baritone) sang three songs from Schumann's *Liederkreis*. The audience honored Clara Schumann, now sixty years old, with ovations. She was awarded the king of Bavaria's golden medal for the arts.

A few weeks later, Schumann's youngest son Felix died in an institution in Frankfurt. Of all the Schumann children, he had been the most talented and promising. Brahms, who put music to a few of Felix's poems,[93] once said: "I don't know what I'd do out of joy at having a son like Felix!" In early January 1879 Levi had visited the sick young man in Frankfurt. He was very moved by Felix's death and asked Clara for some small token, a book that her son had enjoyed, or a personal item.

In early 1879 Levi traveled. First he went to Bayreuth and spent the evening of January 13 at Villa Wahnfried. Wagner went through Beethoven's *Pastoral* symphony with him and pointed out how Beethoven had grasped the relation of strings to winds like no other—saying that nonetheless, some passages did need rewriting (!). Then Wagner played fragments of *Parsifal*'s third act for him, the scene he had just finished composing, up until the worship of the spear. Late in the evening, after Levi had spoken of his father, the rabbi, they returned to discuss "the Jewish issue" and Wagner remarked that "the humane aspect that should have been born of German nature had been stifled by the premature invasion of the Jews." Levi then told him of a large movement against Judaism in Munich, with plans to remove Jews from the administration. He added (Cosima quotes him): "I hope in twenty years they'll be wiped out, branch and root, and we'll have entirely different viewers for the *Ring*."[94]

Did Levi say that? Why? Cosima certainly had no reason to quote him wrong in her diary. Her notes on words between herself and Richard often contain passages that today we find anything but flattering. Levi's remark on wiping out the Jews reflects a typical, though extreme form of Jewish self-abasement. Like many Jews in the age of emancipation and assimilation, he found his Jewish heritage a burden, a curse that at least in the eyes of his environment kept him from wholly identifying with German culture. Self-denial was a desperate, masochistic attempt to shake off the Jewish stigma, to just be rid of it.[95] Being with Richard and Cosima Wagner seemed to elicit that attitude. They repeatedly made it clear that without being baptized, a man from the house of the Levites would never count as one of them, never be one of the "initiated." For Levi, who tried with every ounce of his artistic soul to understand Wagner's works, it was an acutely painful situation. The tension grew from year to year until it became monstrous. His desperate cry for ruin was a hopeless attempt to rid himself of it.

Levi's musical assistant Felix Weingartner said that when Levi was with the Wagner family in Bayreuth, the otherwise confident and accomplished conductor became an entirely different person: "He kept bowing to them and it embarrassed me because I had never seen Levi, the superior musician and freethinker, behave like that."[96] When Weingartner once asked him about the weird prejudice at the Wagner home, Levi stammered: "You, naturally, have it better there—you Arian!" In his pamphlet "Judaism in Music," Wagner had left the question open as to whether a very few Jews might not assimilate to German culture. Levi wanted to belong. It made him very self-conscious at Villa Wahnfried and often led him to say recondite things. No wonder Wagner called him an "odd person."

Wagner's relationship to Jews was remarkably inconsistent. His personal dealings included many Jews; his house pianist was Joseph Rubenstein, and his second assistant for *Parsifal*, next to Levi, was Heinrich Porges. And in a letter to Jewish theater director Angelo Neumann, he said he would have "no part in the current anti-Semitic movement." And yet in a late piece of writing called "Erkenne dich selbst" (Know Thyself) he confirmed his anti-Jewish standpoint. There he also adopted Count Gobineau's theory of the races that considered Jews the most astounding paradigm of the consistency of race:

> Whether male or female, when a Jew mixes with other races, the result is always a Jew. . . . The Jew is a wonderful phenomenon beyond compare; the pliable demon of the degeneration of mankind in triumphant safety, and on top of it all a German citizen of Moses's faith, the darling of liberal princes and the guarantor of the unity of the Reich.[97]

Was court conductor Levi, a German citizen of Moses's faith, hired by the king of Bavaria to lead the royal orchestra, a demon of degeneration? In any event, he did not bask in "triumphant safety." He careened between the tradition of his heritage and the demands of his environment. He perused Wagner's writings and was always a compliant conversational partner for "the Master," letting Wagner teach him how to present his music. Wagner and Cosima trusted and relied on him. He looked after Cosima when she stayed in Munich. Following one such stay in February 1879 (Levi arranged a portrait sitting for Cosima with Lenbach), Wagner thanked his "dear friend" and included in the letter his outline for the score of *Karfreitagszauber* (The Magic of Good Friday), belittling it as "run of the mill music."

On April 10, the Thursday before Easter, Levi went to Villa Wahnfried and Wagner showed him his almost completed composition for *Parsifal*. Rubenstein played the piano arrangement for act 3 from a penciled outline and Wagner marked the song passages in the score. Glancing at Levi and Rubenstein so engrossed in their work, Wagner remarked to Cosima: "How touching!"[98]

On 22 May 1879, a sunny Ascension Day, Levi and Lenbach went to Bayreuth for the celebration of Wagner's sixty-sixth birthday. The children did a pantomime and tarantella that they had rehearsed for that day with ballet master Fricke. Prince and Princess Liechtenstein from Vienna and Countess Schleinitz from Berlin were guests at lunch. Ten-year-old son Siegfried said a toast to his father and directed his siblings in singing their congratulations. Toward the evening, Wagner took Lenbach and Levi to his favorite tavern "Angermann."

An evening at Villa Wahnfried. Album photo (on cardboard) of an oil painting by G. Papperitz, 1882. From left: Siegfried Wagner and Cosima, and sitting next to them Amalie Materna. Behind Cosima from left to right: Franz von Lenbach, Emil Scaria, Franz Fischer, Richard Wagner, Fritz Brandt, and Hermann Levi. At the piano Franz Liszt. Behind Liszt from left to right: Hans Richter, Franz Betz, and Albert Niemann. To the far right Paul von Joukowsky (seated), and in front of the piano Countess Marie von Schleinitz (seated) and Countess Usedom (standing). Nationalarchiv der Richard-Wagner Stiftung Bayreuth, sign. Bi 895 b/1982-7-45/RWG.

Lenbach went back to Munich the next day, but Levi stayed on for two days. The Wagners had the entire music to *Parsifal* played to entertain their guests.

Meanwhile Levi was so familiar with *Parsifal* that when Hans von Bülow saw him a few weeks later in Munich, Levi could play large passages of it by memory. Bülow saw a *Lohengrin* performance and later told his colleague Hans von Bronsart that he thought Levi was an excellent conductor. At the town hall's cellar Bülow and Levi discussed Wagner and Berlioz for four hours. Bülow later remarked that "a Jew getting bayreuthized is twice as strange!"[99]

What Bülow called slavery to Bayreuth, Levi called (writing to Joseph Joachim during those very days) the result of "years of study and contemplation." Asked by a violinist whether he was still a Wagnerian, Levi said:

> I don't know whether my change of view (compared to what I thought as a young man) means a lack of principles, a weakness, or a crime, or development and

progress. But I know this much: I praise the day that my eyes were opened (first a little by *Meistersinger* and then finally and crucially by *Tristan*), and that there is no way back. But it's as little use discussing Wagner as it is discussing religion. To each his own.[100]

August and September brought two public presentations of the entire *Ring*, and in November it was given again as a separate performance for the king. Levi wrote to Wagner that no other performance in Munich had impressed him as much as the one they did for a single viewer; it hallowed the performance, and everything seemed transfigured. Since the king did not want to see Heinrich Vogl as Siegfried, tenor Ferdinand Jäger was engaged for that role for the private performance. Levi had spent four days in Bayreuth going through the intentions of the composer with him.

On their way to Naples, Richard and Cosima Wagner and the children stopped in Munich on 31 December 1879. Levi, Lenbach, and court secretary Bürckel spent New Year's Eve with them at Hotel Marienbad, drinking punch and celebrating the new year. On New Year's Day, Cosima and the children saw *Tannhäuser*. Cosima found the performance "impressive and overwhelming, the first scene relaxing and sunny." Before the family left two days later for Italy, Lenbach sent them—as a gift—a portrait of Bismarck. "Dreadful," said Wagner, "so determined and dumb!"[101] He meant, of course, Bismarck's lack of appreciation for the arts.

In February Wagner wrote the score for *Parsifal* at Villa Angri on Posilippo in Naples, while Levi conducted an Odeon concert in Munich presenting the festive march written in commemoration of the *Independence Day of the USA*. It was a weak composition that Wagner had written on commission. In March Levi staged a new production of *Tristan*, in May a new production of *Meistersinger*. By the end of the season, he was exhausted and needed four weeks of rest at Alexanderbad. Hardly had he returned to Munich, when he set to work rehearsing *Haideschacht* by Franz von Holstein and a performance of *Carmen* for the first time in Munich (on October 24). After introducing it to his operagoers in Munich, Levi showed little interest in the piece and handed it over to his colleague for repeat performances. Did he really not like it, or simply fear Wagner's opinion?

From Italy Wagner corresponded with King Ludwig about *Parsifal*. He wanted the work, "the most Christian of all art," to be reserved solely for performance in Bayreuth. The king complied by ordering his own royal orchestra and choir to make themselves available for the festival in Bayreuth in the summer of 1882. Up until that point there had never been any mention of who would conduct *Parsifal*; in their many conversations, Wagner never brought it up. But in her diary Cosima had recorded Richard's remark that without being christened first, Levi could not conduct it; Wagner would have Levi and Rothschild baptized at the same time and then take them to communion.

On their return trip from Italy in late October 1880, the Wagner family once again stayed for two weeks in Munich. There were many organizational matters to settle for *Parsifal*, and Wagner wanted to see for himself how Levi was at conducting. Levi had arranged an attractive program just for him: November 1, Beethoven's *Missa solemnis*; November 4, *Der fliegende Holländer*; November 7, *Tristan and Isolde*; November 10, *Lohengrin*; November 11, *Zauberflöte*. Cosima jotted down her and Richard's impressions:

> Missa solemnis: Beautiful, though mixed impression.—Fliegender Holländer: Richard deeply moved despite the performance's deficiencies, broke out in tears several times.—Tristan and Isolde: Orchestra very good. Act Two was the highlight.—Lohengrin: [private viewing for the king] Richard sat in the King's loge with him. The children and I sat below. Otherwise the auditorium was empty. Richard was unhappy with the tempi, damned the conductor and the stage director.—Zauberflöte: Richard calls this sweet work the genesis of German character. (Cosima's Diary 1880)

For the afternoon of November 12, a separate performance of the prelude to *Parsifal* was to be given for the king alone, conducted by the composer. Lenbach and a few other loyal Wagnerians hid in the loges. Wagner was in ill humor from the start because he—a fanatic about punctuality—had to wait for the king. Once the prelude was over, a long silence filled the hall. Finally Levi brought Wagner the king's request to repeat the piece. Wagner grudgingly fulfilled his ruler's wish. But when His Majesty then asked that he play *Lohengrin* to allow a comparison, Wagner thrust the baton into Levi's hand and left.

The next day, Levi had to conduct a private performance of *Aida*. Out of protest Wagner went that evening to see the burlesque *Staberl's Travel Adventures* showing at the Garden Place Theater. On November 14 Richard and Cosima went to see Shakespeare's *As You Like It* but went home after act 2. Richard was outraged that actor Possart played Probstein "like a Jew." On November 16 Wagner missed the *Meistersinger* performance because of a cold. Levi had made plans for the evenings off, too. For November 3 he invited the Wagners along with Busch, Lenbach, and Gedon to his new apartment at 1 *Hildegard Strasse*. His guests admired the opulent interior and Levi's collection of valuable paintings. Besides a few by Lenbach, he also owned several by Anselm Feuerbach (including *The Death of Pietro Aretino*, *Nana Risi* in profile, an almost full-length portrait of J. Allgeyer, *Bachhantin crowned with wine leaves*, and a sketch made of Michelangelo's *Madonna and Child*).

During the day, Wagner sat for Gedon to have a bust made and for Lenbach for a portrait. The latter had organized an atelier party in Wagner's honor for Saturday, November 6. Everything went fine until late in the evening someone mentioned Lenbach's idol, Bismarck. Wagner hissed: "Enough of Bismarck! I can't stand his bulldog face!"[102] It ruined the party and everyone left. Lenbach felt insulted, Wagner had a "horrible night," and Cosima contemplated "the wretchedness and guilt of being." On the last day of their stay, Wagner went through *Lohengrin* once more with Levi because he had not been happy with the conductor's tempi. As they dined afterward, Wagner spoke of "the unfortunate influence that Jews had" on the current state of affairs. It left Levi melancholy. The next morning he accompanied the Wagner family to the station where their salon car was waiting to take them to Bayreuth.

While visiting Munich it had become clear to Wagner that he could, after all, accept Levi as the conductor of *Parsifal* and that from an artistic point of view none was better qualified. His reluctance to let this piece of work be directed by a Jew had been snuffed from the start by the king's having ordered his own royal orchestra and its conductor Levi to make themselves available for it, including assistant conductor Franz von Fischer. Wagner had no choice but to gratefully accept the offer without asking whether the conductor was Jewish or Christian. When the king made it final, Wagner felt a need to justify his initial refusal of a Jewish conductor:

> I can only explain Your Majesty's neutral stance by the fact that these people never wander into Your Majesty's realm; to Your Majesty they are theoretical, for us they are real. Since I deal with many of them out of kindness and pity I have learned that the Jewish race is the natural enemy of true mankind and all that is noble. That we Germans will be ruined by them is certain, and perhaps I am the last German that as an artist knew to reject the Judaism that has already taken over everything.[103]

The king did not respond. When Levi visited Villa Wahnfried in January 1881, Wagner first sang some ballades by Loewe to show him "what the Germans have had to do without." He then, to Levi's astonishment, announced that Levi would conduct *Parsifal*, but that "first we have to do something with you. I wish I could find a way to put it—something that will make you one of us, let you feel like you belong."[104] At this allusion to being baptized, Levi's face clouded and Wagner ended the conversation. In leaving, Levi silently kissed his master's hand. The master embraced him. He later remarked to Cosima that the Jews among us always have a wistful lot.

Perhaps Levi thought of all the good friends who had not followed him down this path, not only Brahms and Heyse, but his old teacher Vincenz Lachner, too. Lachner had written him a farewell letter a year ago:

> I see you then, called to be a priest of art, forever chained to a cause that I must consider a disease, indeed, a national calamity. It seems you are a victim of a clever, deceitful, profoundly false, ruinous mission![105]

Levi must have been very sure of his conviction to stand without fail for Wagner's cause despite rejection from Brahms, Heyse, and many other important artists.

The worst trial was yet to come. In late June 1881, Levi stayed for an entire week at Villa Wahnfried, taking every meal with the Wagner family. During the day he and Wagner discussed matters of organization; in the evenings they made music. Joseph Rubenstein played from the score for *Parsifal*. It contained only the vocal parts fully written out, the orchestra was merely alluded to by using three different systems. Wagner sang the solo parts. Levi preferably played Bach, among other pieces the last chorus from *Passion of Matthew*. One evening Wagner spoke enthusiastically of Mendelssohn's *Paul*. Music, he continued, was getting decadent: Mendelssohn had still had good ideas, Schumann was a fool, and now "this Brahms hasn't got anything." Levi was silent.

On the fourth day, Levi was in town doing errands and returned a bit late to lunch. Wagner waited for him at the house door, pocket watch in hand: "You are ten minutes late. Tardiness is second-worst to disloyalty. And now we shall dine, but first read the letter on your desk." In his room Levi found an anonymous letter from Munich addressed to Wagner, hinting at an intimate relationship between Levi and Cosima and warning Wagner to keep his work pure and not have it conducted by a Jew. Close lipped and disheartened, Levi came to the table. "Why so quiet?" Wagner wanted to know. Levi said that he could not understand why Wagner had not simply torn the letter to shreds. Wagner said it would have left something unclear, and this way he can now banish it from his mind. Levi said nothing, packed his bags, and left that evening for Bamberg. From there he wrote Wagner a letter begging for release from his duty to conduct *Parsifal*. Wagner replied by wire: "Friend, I beseech you to return to us immediately; we must get the main thing back in order." The "main thing" for Wagner was the performance of his newest work; everything else was secondary. He knew, too, that letting Levi go would have caused a scandal and that he had no suitable substitute. But Levi repeated his request for release. And Wagner wrote to him in Bamberg:

> Dear best friend! Your sentiments in honor, but you are not making things easier either for yourself or for us! Your dreary soul-searching makes dealing with you so nightmarish. We both agree that we should make this sh— public, and that means that you may not leave us, otherwise people will believe the nonsense. For heaven's sake, turn around and finally get to know us as we are. Keep your faith, but find courage! Perhaps there is a big turn ahead for your life. But at any rate you remain my Parsifal conductor! Now then: *Herauf, herauf!* Your R.W.[106]

Wagner, brilliant at letter writing and a virtuoso at luring people, knew exactly how to get his runaway conductor to return. "Keep your faith" means "you can conduct *Parsifal* without being baptized." Levi gave in. Wagner tried to patch things up by ordering kosher wine for lunch. Levi told him that in Bamberg he had visited the cathedral and felt drawn to Catholicism. Wagner praised the simplicity and ardor of Protestantism and mentioned that he had hoped Levi would accompany him to communion, but he realized it wouldn't happen. As they parted, he told his conductor to be brave.

It is difficult to understand Wagner's changeful attitude toward the Jews around him. It seems often to have been guided by spontaneous feelings and oscillated between sinister and hateful testimonials to effusive proofs of friendship. His views of Jews that he put in writing, like many other things he wrote, are obscure and contradictory. He liked to write and usually did so spontaneously, but his behavior contradicted his words. Initially his anti-Semitism focused on Meyerbeer and had been triggered by personal experience, disappointment, and rivalry. Later he continued the habit, making Jews responsible for every adversity that he encountered as a composer. This went so far that he mistakenly called his harshest critic Hanslick a Jew.

And yet he was surrounded by Jewish friends, acolytes, and benefactors: Samuel Lehrs and Carl Tausig were longtime companions. Bayreuth's assistants Joseph Rubenstein, Heinrich Porges, and Hermann Levi, theater director Angelo Neumann, and even his idol Judith Gautier—they all seemed mysteriously drawn to him. They put up with his anti-Jewish writing and his numerous outbreaks of hate for "the Jewish race, the natural enemy of true humanity." And yet he thought that a few "select" Jews should be allowed to embrace German culture entirely. His notion that this should be sealed by having oneself baptized was an idea that turned up for the first time in connection with Levi conducting *Parsifal*. Wagner attacked Mendelssohn and Joseph Joachim as "Jews" despite the fact that they converted.

Wagner was influenced by the theory of races advanced by Arthur Gobineau, an author with whom he spoke frequently. Wagner's late writing clearly reveals that influence. It had nothing to do with the radical anti-Semitic movement of the late 1870s. Wagner was not interested in denying the Jewish population material prosperity; he was out to protect "religion and art." In the behavior of the Jews that surrounded him, particularly Levi's, he saw his theory confirmed that ultimately the Jews were destined to die out.[107]

In October 1881 Levi once again got a message from his "good old friend Richard Wagner" claiming that in terms of musical preparations for *Parsifal* he considered Levi his "plenipotentiary," his "alter ego." This, Levi felt, now locked him into Wagner's cause for the rest of his life. His many later attempts to free himself from it were sham battles. The sight of the grail in *Parsifal* became for him a substitute for the cup of communion he could not share with Wagner. Remaining true to his rabbi forefathers forbade it. Levi's aged father, still an active rabbi in Giessen, stood by him, visiting him in Munich and at the festivals in Bayreuth. Hermann tried to explain what he felt for Wagner:

> He is the best and noblest person. . . . Someday the world will see that he was just as great of a person as he was an artist, as those close to him already know. And his struggle against "Judaism in Music" has the noblest motives.[108]

On November 2 Levi once again met the Wagners at Munich's train station where they stopped to see him on their way to Naples. Levi bought them breakfast. In Palermo Wagner—often interrupted by chest cramps—completed the score for *Parsifal*'s act 3. His house pianist Rubenstein meanwhile wrote the piano score. Levi wrote Wagner of the tedious preparations, there was so much to organize. Off in his idyll in Palermo, Wagner wanted to hear nothing of the petty details. He basked in Italian sunshine and let Auguste Renoir portray him, writing to Levi: "Oh Hermann!—Hermann!—Why make my heart so heavy?"[109] In reply Levi tried to comfort the composer with abstruse thoughts: "I'm no longer fainthearted; even my nose no longer bothers me."[110] Meanwhile he worked at getting everything taken care of. He negotiated with the Vogls to participate in the festival, selected actors for the pages, knights, and flower girls, and set up the orchestra. No task was too much because he wanted to prove his complete identification with the work and ideas of the master. Serving Wagner in this way made him happy: "The most wonderful experience of my life is being close to such a man, and I thank God daily for it."[111]

The Wagner family returned from Italy in late April 1882 and was welcomed in Munich by Levi who during that week had performances of *Tannhäuser* and *Meistersinger* to conduct separately for the king. In the evening Lenbach accompanied the couple and their children to a "spectacle with song, dance, the story and acts" for Jules Verne's *Around the World in Eighty Days*. The next day the family traveled on to Bayreuth, stopping in Nuremberg to visit the churches of St. Sebaldus and St. Lorenz. Five days later Levi arrived in Bayreuth to discuss the choir arrangement with Engelbert Humperdinck.[112] In early June he rented accommodations in Bayreuth. He got 500 marks monthly to compensate for expenses in Bayreuth. He refused payment for conducting because his salary from Munich continued throughout that time. He had lunch and dinner at Villa Wahnfried, where he ate not only with the Wagner family, but also with painter Paul von Joukowsky[113] and the children's private tutor, Heinrich von Stein.[114] The evenings were filled with music making. Wagner played parts of Mozart symphonies and sections of Weber's *Euryanthe*, Levi played from Bach's *Well-Tempered Clavier* and passages from Bach's organ works.

By the end of June, all of the soloists, choir members, and 107 orchestra musicians had arrived. The first horn player was Franz Strauss, father of composer Richard Strauss. Franz Strauss hated Wagner, but he was a master of his instrument and indispensable. To this event he brought his eighteen-year-old son Richard, who from then on became an enthusiastic follower of Wagner.

On July 1 Levi began the weeks of rehearsals by having the conductor's stand pompously put in its place. The orchestra pit could not be seen from the auditorium, so Wagner had a little window built in behind the conductor's stand from which he could give instructions and communicate with the conductor. The three weeks of rehearsals were scheduled such that each act could be studied for one week separately with each of the two casts. The end of each week saw a dress rehearsal for the act that had been worked on that week. Wagner himself directed stage scene rehearsals, assisted by ballet master Fricke.[115] Levi split the orchestra work with Kapellmeister Fischer,[116] who conducted the last major rehearsal for each act. Wagner came to hear most of the orchestra rehearsals, but sometimes he stayed home because of chest pain. One evening he instructed Levi on how to use the baton; he thought Levi should not use his arms, but make movements from the wrist only.

Assistants Heinrich Porges and Engelbert Humperdinck made considerable sacrifices to support the rehearsals. They often had to console one another when Wagner ranted and raged. During the main rehearsal for act 1, technical manager Fritz Brand, who had stood watch-in-hand timing the scenery switch, announced simply that the music was too short. Wagner lost his temper, shouting that he could not compose music by the yard, swore never to attend another rehearsal or performance and marched off. Levi suggested that just as they had often eliminated passages, they might just as well add a few by inserting repetitions. Humperdinck found the solution: overnight he composed a few transition passages that could be used to prolong the phase needed for changing scenery. Wagner accepted them and that is how it was done that first year. When the same problem turned up for act 3, Wagner agreed to Emil Scaria's (Gurnemanz) suggestion to simply close the curtains and skip the scene change. He sent a note to Levi: "No change of scenery!—If you don't like the decision, as seemed to be the case yesterday—then reverse it."[117]

The dress rehearsal for the cast of the premiere took place on July 24. While Wagner was bothered by the dragging tempi in act 1, he was deeply moved by his own work when it got to act 3. He told Cosima later that if he were an orchestra musician, he would not want to be led by a Jew. The next day he discussed all of the tempi once more with Levi. In the evening there was a banquet for everyone involved in the production. Wagner thanked them all for their loyal commitment. "Art is made by artists, but you, my friends, shall live!" He then turned their attention to Franz Liszt. Franz Liszt, he said, was the mediator between the world within him and the world out there: "Long live Franz Liszt! And people, tomorrow is going to be wild. If we don't all go crazy, we'll not have reached our goal."[118]

Wednesday, 26 July 1882 was foggy and rainy, but for the city of Bayreuth it was a red-letter day. All municipal buildings were decked in flags. Angermann's Inn, Wagner's favorite tavern, was decorated with green fir branches. It was a special day for Hermann Levi, too. As the conductor of the premiere of *Parsifal*, Bayreuth's "stage consecration play," he had reached the summit of his artistic career. It had been worth giving up composing. He served a composer that he believed would establish a new era in music. In this he did not err. One hundred years later the charisma of Wagner's works still enthuses.

The wonderful, mysterious sound of the *Parsifal* orchestra must have been an indescribable experience for all that attended, particularly for composers Léo

Delibes, Camille Saint-Saëns, Anton Bruckner, and Richard Strauss. The unique score, written after gaining experience with performance of the *Ring*, refines orchestral hues. The Festival House wraps its audience in a mystical cloud of sound. Felix Weingartner wrote of the first time he heard the sound of Bayreuth:

> The auditorium darkens entirely. Like a voice from another world, the first sweeping prelude theme begins. Nothing can be compared to it. Technology, orchestration, and acoustics here all combine in a unique manner that is found nowhere else. . . . Listeners that were not blind partisans could only later assess the extent of Herman Levi's achievement, because he no longer conducted.[119]

At the time, the building had gas lighting and the visual impression could not compete with the music. With the advent of electric lighting, Wagner's grandchildren were able to change that. In 1882 the first viewing was reserved for members of the Patron Club, whose contributions had guaranteed sufficient finances in advance. It pained Wagner that his royal benefactor, Ludwig II, did not attend.

The main roles of Kundry, Parsifal, Gurnemanz, and Klingsor were sung by the first cast that Levi had won for the project: Amalie Materna, Hermann Winkelmann, Emil Scaria, and Karl Hill. Wagner sat with Cosima and the children in their loge. When after act 1 the applause seemed to take no end, Wagner came to the ramp and asked the audience to please stop calling the actors back on stage. When act 3 was finished, part of the audience tried to suppress applause. Wagner stood up again to say that they need not eliminate applause entirely; they should merely stop calling the soloists out again and again. For decades it was then thought improper to clap at *Parsifal* performances. The incident peeved Wagner for the rest of the premiere evening, and it has been said that he complained that Wagnerians are dumb and they drove him up the wall. But the next day at Villa Wahnfried his mood had improved and he laughed with the soloists about it.

The second cast performed on July 28 with soloists Marianne Brandt (Kundry), Heinrich Gudehues (Parsifal), Gustav Siehr (Gurnemanz), and Anton Fuchs (Klingsor). Theodor Reichmann (Amfortas) sang at both performances.[120] At the end Wagner stood on stage surrounded by the soloists and once more thanked all the artists who had participated. It was their doing that *Parsifal* had turned out as he had imagined it. He especially mentioned the conductor, "my friend Levi," who had directed this work with extraordinary perseverance, knowledge, and enthusiasm.

Levi's particular accomplishment lay in having fully identified with the work. He thoroughly explored the aesthetic intentions of the composer. He had seen the composition evolve from scene to scene. He was as familiar with the score as if he had written it himself. He interpreted the theme that initially seemed so foreign to him by finding it parallel to his own religious situation: a desperate quest for rescue and redemption. Not by chance do so many descriptions of Levi's interpretation highlight his moving rendition of the prelude to act 3 when Parsifal searches for the grail. With every performance it seemed as if Levi suffered Amfortas's pain anew. At the end of each performance Levi was exhausted. On August 6 and 18, Kapellmeister Fischer took over the conducting and Levi sat next to Wagner in his loge, taking down ever more instructions on proper tempi. Wagner did not attend every performance. Later he usually only came for act 2 and shouted *Bravo!* from his loge at the end of the Flower Girl scene. Carrie Pringle, the third flower girl, was his favorite.

On August 25, the evening of the fourteenth performance, they celebrated King Ludwig II's birthday. The next day at the Catholic court church in Bayreuth, Blandine von Bülow, Wagner's stepdaughter, married Italian Count Gravina. For the ceremony, Levi had rehearsed a mass by Palestrina with the church choir. Cosima sat between Liszt and Wagner, surrounded by festival participants, listening to the song in a devotional mood.

Two days before the last performance, on a day the cast had off, Wagner threw a party for the performers in the garden of Villa Wahnfried. He found a kind word for each one. He joked with the Flower Girls, who now, "my children, will be queens and princesses on stages all year long." The old friends that Levi had invited to see *Parsifal* in Bayreuth included Henriette Feuerbach, a loyal admirer of Brahms. The day before the performance, Levi gave Henriette an introduction to the work so she could enjoy it "like someone familiar with it, first familiar with the entire work, and then particularly familiar with Act Three." To a girlfriend, the wife of philologist Ribbeck, Henriette wrote a little report showing what she had understood:

> This music consists from start to finish of motives that are so intricately interwoven that they present the idea not only musically, but as a narrative. Throughout the opera one hears the same sounds, individually, connected, whole, as halves, measure for measure, in other keys, major, minor. Our traditional composers could not have done it, they would have suffocated from the wealth, but in this half-human, half-artistic kind of presentation lies, I believe, the magic that enslaves those that fall for it. For my part, I believe that I understand the work better than many others because a day beforehand the conductor played it for me from the score, as only a conductor like Levi can.[121]

The sixteenth and final performance took place on August 29, a day of pouring rain. Levi had a bad cold and was worn out. During the music of the final act, Wagner turned up in the orchestra pit and took the baton, perhaps to relieve his conductor, perhaps to say farewell to his work. Levi stood behind him, in case he would need to intervene, and was surprised by how confidently Wagner directed the entire ensemble. Every performer gave his best for one last time. Reichmann,

Stage designer, conductor, and technician for the Parsifal *premiere: Paul von Joukowsky, Hermann Levi, and Karl Brandt. Bayreuth Festival Program for 1959. Courtesy of Frithjof Haas.*

who sang Amfortas, later said that only a true master can get a performer to spend so much breath and energy. At the end of the performance the crowd cheered. Wagner remained out of sight in the orchestra pit, joking with the musicians. Finally Levi shouted "Silence, silence!" The curtain rose and Wagner said a few words of thanks. Many wept.

That evening Levi collapsed from exhaustion. But after sleeping for a day and a night straight he felt refreshed and left Villa Wahnfried for vacation in Baden-Baden. On September 14 Wagner and his family left for Venice and took accommodations on the second floor of palace Ca' Vendramin Calergi on the Grand Canal. Pained by constant chest cramps, there Wagner wrote his essay "The Stage Consecration Festival in Bayreuth." Levi visited the family in Venice from October 3 to 6. He took gondola trips with them and visited old churches. The children's tutor Heinrich von Stein and house pianist Joseph Rubenstein were there also. In the evenings they made music, or Wagner read from works by Shakespeare. When he came to Portia's speech in act 2 of Julius Caesar, where she declares her boundless love for Brutus, Wagner's eyes filled with tears.

As the year drew to a close, Levi wrote Wagner a letter reviewing his own work and confessing his total devotion:

> Only one thing stands out in wonderful clarity against the blurred, indistinct background of my past—the awakening, and growing, and finally the fulfillment of my love for you and for everything that you mean to me and the world. I own nothing other than this feeling of love and adoration, but in it I feel immeasurably rich and blessed.[122]

Two days later Wagner replied from Venice: "Pain is short and joy is long. . . . What have I not already forgotten! I don't know! Just don't write so much, it's my death."[123]

As the winter season began, Levi started having nervous disorders. In the second subscription concert he had to step down from the conductor's stand shortly after the concert began and hand the baton over to concertmaster Abel because he felt unwell. But he returned to the stand to conduct the next piece, Mozart's *Requiem*. In early January 1883 he took a short vacation to relax in Arco, a winter spa north of Lake Garda that was popular at the time. Before returning to Munich he went to Venice to visit Wagner. But once he got to Ca' Vendramin Calgeri he fell ill and they had to keep him in bed. The physician summoned diagnosed a mental disorder. Cosima felt guilty, believing that life with them had made Levi gloomy. Richard dismissed his conductor's "annoying problem" and said it was better not to have anything to do with Jews: they were all either arrogant like Rubenstein or mentally unstable like Levi.

Levi lay in bed most of the day; Wagner visited him several times. On Sunday evening, February 11, Levi felt better and spent a few hours together with the family. The next morning he said good-bye and left. Wagner walked him to the stairs and kissed him repeatedly, obviously moved. Did he sense that it was for the last time? Twenty-four hours later, Wagner died in Cosima's arms of a heart attack.

On Friday of the same week that Levi had left Venice on Monday, he boarded the train in Innsbruck that brought Wagner's body and entourage via Munich back to Bayreuth. On a chain around her neck Cosima wore a key to the bronze casket that at her wish had been made with a glass window on the top. The funeral took place the next Sunday in Bayreuth. The funeral procession and the hearse drawn by four horses moved slowly to the entrance gate of Villa

Wahnfried. There twelve of Wagner's best friends, among them Hermann Levi, shouldered the casket and carried it to the burial site in the garden. In tears, Wagner's four children held the four corners of the pall. His dogs Marke and Froh wandered around the procession whining. The pastor spoke a few words. That day closed the happiest, but also most painful chapter of Hermann Levi's life.

NOTES

1. Orel, 83, letter dated 7 November 1872.
2. Franz Lachner, born 2 April 1803 in Rain am Lech, died 20 January 1890 in Munich. Lachner began as a musician at Munich's Isar Gate Theater, went to Vienna as an organist, studied under Simon Sechter, and joined the circle of friends surrounding Franz Schubert. In 1827 he became conductor in Munich and was awarded the title of General Music Director in 1852. In 1863 he was made Dr. phil. h.c. of the University of Munich, and in 1883 honorary citizen of the City of Munich. He composed orchestral works, chamber music, religious choral works, and four operas.
3. In 1872 the Bavarian Court Orchestra had 20 violins plus three extras, eight violas plus one extra, eight cellos, six contrabasses plus one extra, five flutes, four oboes plus one extra, four clarinets plus two extras, three bassoons plus one extra, seven horns, five trumpets, three trombones, one tuba, two harps, and two kettledrummers (*Hof- und Staatshandbuch des Königreichs Bayern*, Munich, 1873).
4. *AMZ*, no. 24, 11 June 1873, 378f.
5. Ernst von Possart, *Hermann Levi: Erinnerungen* (Munich, 1901), 30f.
6. Brahms, vol. 7, letter dated 15 December 1872.
7. Franz Wüllner, born 28 January 1832 in Münster/Westphalia, died 7 September 1902 in Braunfels. Wüllner studied under Beethoven's friend Anton Schindler in Vienna and Frankfurt, then continued his studies in Cologne, Berlin, and Leipzig. In 1854 he became a music teacher in Munich, in 1858 music director in Aachen, in 1864 director for Munich's Royal Choir, and in 1871 court conductor. Levi's appointment made him the second man. In 1877 he took over the direction of the Leipzig Conservatory and became conductor for the opera house there; in 1884 he succeeded Hiller as City Kapellmeister and director of the conservatory in Cologne. His encounter with Brahms in 1853 at the home of Deichmann in Mehlem was the starting point of a lifelong friendship. Wüllner successfully promoted Brahms's symphonic works. His *Etudes for the Choir* are still used for choir practice today.
8. *AMZ*, no. 30, 23 July 1873, 474.
9. Stabi, Paul Heyse Archiv, diary entry for 5 March 1873.
10. Georg Kremplsetzer, born 20 April 1827 in Vilsbiburg (Lower Bavaria), died there on 9 June 1871. Kremplsetzer was a pupil of Franz Lachner and from 1865 to 1868 Kapellmeister at Munich's Aktien-Theater (a stock-owned people's theater), then Kapellmeister in Görlitz, Magdeburg, Graz, and Königsberg. He composed the comic opera *Der Rothmantel* (The Red Coat) in 1868 for a text by Heyse based on a story by Johann Karl August Musäus, as well as smaller pieces for the stage, including *Vetter auf Besuch* (The Visiting Cousin) in 1863 based on a text by Wilhelm Busch.

178   *Chapter Three*

11. In the catalog to the exhibition *Brahms in Munich* (Munich, 1972), Robert Münster tells us many details about encounters between Brahms and Heyse. See also Münster's "Abseits, wer ist's? Brahms und das musikalische München in Unser Bayern," 32, no. 5/6 (Munich, 1983) and *Brahms-Studien*, vol. 7 (Hamburg, 1987), 51ff.

12. Stabi, Paul Heyse Archiv, diary entry from 5 May 1873.

13. *Waldmeisterbowle*, also known as May Wine, is a German beverage traditionally served on May Day. Sweet woodruff, a forest herb, is steeped in white wine, sometimes spruced with brandy and strawberries, and served from a punch bowl.

14. Joseph Walter, first violin, Franz Brückner, second violin, Anton Thoms, viola, Hippolyt Müller, cello. After Joseph Walter died in 1875, his younger brother became the first violinist. The Walter Quartet then consisted of Benno Walter, Michael Steiger, Anton Thoms, and Hippolyt Müller.

15. Orel, letter dated 10 December 1873.

16. Brahms, vol. 7, letter dated 3 December 1873.

17. Brahms had discovered this unknown aria by Franz Schubert, composed in 1821 as an insert for the Viennese performance of the comic opera *La clochette ou le diable page* by Louis Hérold. Shortly before the March concert, Brahms had premiered these three *Hungarian Dances* in the original version for four hands at the Gewandhaus in Leipzig.

18. See Robert Münster, note 11 above.

19. Joseph Gabriel Rheinberger, born 17 March 1839 in Vaduz, died 25 November 1901 in Munich. Rheinberger trained at Munich's School of Music. In 1860 he became the organist for St. Michael's Church, in 1864 director of the Oratorio Association, as of 1867 professor for the newly founded school of music. In 1877 he was appointed Director of the Royal Choir as successor to Wüllner, in 1894 raised to nobility, and in 1899 awarded an honorary PhD by the University of Munich. Brahms valued Rheinberger's organ sonatas and religious choral works with their fine counterpoint; they are sometimes still performed today. Humperdinck, Thuille, and Wolf-Ferrari were among his students.

20. See chapter 2, note 73. Reviewing the first performance, the newspaper for Augsburg wrote on 26 December 1874: "Holstein is rich in melodies, pleasant and noble. . . . But to be fair we must admit that a huge part of the success is due to how it was presented, namely, in the way the author intended, with all of its peculiarities" (*Augsburger Allgemeine Zeitung*, 26 December 1874).

21. Leviana, letter dated 28 November 1874.

22. Litzmann, vol. 3, letter dated 18 October 1873.

23. Brahms, vol. 7, letter dated 21 November 1873.

24. Brahms, vol. 7, letter dated 21 November 1873.

25. Leviana. The letter is written to an unnamed editor and dated 27 March 1874.

26. *AMZ*, no. 19, 10 May 1876, 298.

27. Litzmann, vol. 3, note dated 8 September 1875.

28. *Parsifal* program, Bayreuth, 1959, p. 6/7. Letter held by the Richard Wagner National Archive, Bayreuth.

29. Martin Gregor-Dellin, *Richard Wagner, sein Leben, seine Welt, sein Jahrhundert* (Munich, 1980), 689. The description is taken from a report by Susanne Weinert.

30. Felix Mottl, born 24 August 1856 near St. Veit near Vienna, died 2 July 1911 in Munich, pupil of Anton Bruckner. In 1876 Mottl became assistant in Bayreuth, from

1880 to 1903 he was court Kapellmeister in Karlsruhe, then in Munich where he was also the director of Academy concerts and director of the Academy for Composition. He delivered premieres of works by Berlioz and Cornelius. As conductor in Bayreuth from 1886 to 1906, Mottl was a close staff member for Cosima Wagner and she advised him on scenes for some of his productions in Karlsruhe.

31. *Briefe an Friedrich Nietzsche* (Berlin/New York, 1977), 2:159.

32. Heinrich Porges, *Die Bühnenproben zu den Bayreuther Festspielen des Jahres 1876* (Chemnitz, 1881). Heinrich Porges was born on 25 November 1837 in Prague and died on 17 November 1900 in Munich. He studied law and philosophy and took up music late in life. As of 1863 he, Cornelius, and Tausig belonged to the circle surrounding Wagner, whom he promoted through his position as editor of the *Süddeutschen Presse*. In 1886 Porges founded Munich's "Chorverein" and presented with its members works by Liszt and Berlioz. Porges was Levi's friend and admired him.

33. Bernhard Sattler, *Adolf von Hildebrand und seine Welt, Briefe und Erinnerungen* (Munich, 1962), 231f.

34. At the opera house in Bayreuth the orchestra cannot be seen by spectators, one can only see the opera stage. The music seems to come from nowhere.

35. Litzmann, vol. 3, letter dated 4 January 1875.

36. Litzmann, vol. 3, letter dated 3 November 1876.

37. Bülow had called Brahms's first symphony "Beethoven's Tenth."

38. Wagner alludes to the honorary doctoral degree awarded Brahms by the University of Breslau in 1879.

39. Brahms, vol. 7, letter dated 21 February 1875.

40. Stabi, Paul Heyse Archiv, letter dated 31 December 1879.

41. Brahms, vol. 7, undated letter, probably from early May 1875.

42. Orel, letter dated 24 September 1874.

43. *AMZ*, no. 17, 1876, 266.

44. "Ach wer heilet die Schmerzen des, dem Balsam zu Gift ward?"

45. Orel, letter dated 11 March 1876.

46. Heinrich Hofmann, born 13 January 1842 in Berlin, died 16 July 1902 in Gross-Tabarz, Thuringia. Hoffmann was a music teacher in Berlin, as of 1882 at the Academy of the Arts. He wrote the operas *Cartouche* (1869), *Armin* (1872), *Little Anna from Tharua* (1878), and *William of Orange* (1882), none of which were successful. Max Bruch also produced an oratorio based on the Frithjof saga by Esaias Tegnér.

47. Litzmann, vol. 3, letter dated 24 March 1876.

48. Michael Martin, ed., *Johannes Brahms: Briefwechsel mit dem Mannheimer Bankprokuristen Wilhelm Lindeck* (Stadtarchiv Mannheim, Heidelberg, 1983), 34.

49. Litzmann, vol. 3, letter dated 24 September 1877.

50. Frithjof Haas, "Die Erstfassung des langsamen Satzes der 1. Sinfonie von Johannes Brahms," *Die Musikforschung* 36, no. 4 (1983): 200–211.

51. Robert Münster, *Johannes Brahms und das musikalische München*, see note 11 above.

52. Litzmann, vol. 3, letter to Clara Schumann dated 22 November 1876.

53. Magdalene Koelle, née Murjahn, *Erinnerungen* (Karlsruhe, 1892), 95.

54. *Johannes Brahms: Briefwechsel mit dem Mannheimer Bankprokuristen Wilhelm Lindeck*; see note 48 above.

55. Litzmann, vol. 3, letter dated 24 September 1877.

56. Bernhard Scholz, born 30 March 1835 in Mainz, died 26 December 1916 in Munich. Scholz was conductor at theaters in Zurich, Nuremberg, and Hanover, directed the Cecilia Choir in Berlin and taught at the Stern Conservatory. As of 1883 he became director of the conservatory in Frankfurt. He composed, among other things, seven operas, including *Golo* (1875) and the *Trumpeter of Saeckingen* (1877). A friend of both Brahms and Joachim, he initiated the so-called Order of the Black Cat made up of like-minded musicians, including Perfall, Wüllner, and Stockhausen. In March 1860 he signed—along with Brahms, Joachim, and Grimm—a manifest attacking the "New Germans."

57. *AMZ*, no. 11, 1878, 172.

58. Brahms, 7:200.

59. Brahms, vol. 7, letter dated 20 February 1878. Levi mentioned to Heyse that he had written a farewell letter on New Year's Eve in 1878, but it has not survived.

60. Letter to Franz von Holstein, taken from Kalbeck, 3:116.

61. Litzmann, vol. 3, letter dated 6 March 1879.

62. Leviana, letter to Mr. Fritsch dated 31 October 1897.

63. Orel, letter from May 1895.

64. Heute singt er Tristan, morgen fährt er Mist an!

65. At an exhibition in his honor in Munich in 1981.

66. Theodor Fontane, "Ein Liebling der Musen," *Gartenlaube*, no. 36, 1867, 566.

67. Paul Heyse, *Jugenderinnerungen und Bekenntnisse* (Berlin, 1900), 219: "Denn es waschen dir, der Heimat echtem Sprössling bis ans Grab/Weder Bock noch Isarwasser jemals den Berliner ab. Deine Muse, ob sie stets auch für des Südens Töchter brennt/ Gleicht aufs Haar der Holden, die man eine kühle Blonde nennt."

68. Moritz Carrière, born 5 March 1817 in Griedel (Hesse), died 19 January 1895 in Munich. Carrière was a poet and philosopher, who in 1849 in Giessen acquired the right to teach at the university and in 1853 was given a chair in Munich. He married a daughter of Justus von Liebig and published poetry with her. Collected Writings in 13 volumes, Leipzig, 1886/1891.

69. Stabi, Paul Heyse Archiv, letter dated 15 December 1874.

70. Stabi, Paul Heyse Archiv, letter dated 22 July 1875.

71. Stabi, Paul Heyse Archiv, letter dated 31 December 1880.

72. Stabi, Paul Heyse Archiv, letter from January 1881.

73. Stabi, Paul Heyse Archiv, letter dated 13 March 1900.

74. Cosima, entry dated 18 December 1881.

75. Michael Bernays, born 27 November 1834 in Hamburg, died 25 February 1897 in Karlsruhe. As of 1874 Bernays was professor for modern languages and literature in Munich; after retiring he lived as of 1890 in Karlsruhe. Although he came from an orthodox Jewish family, at the age of twenty-one he converted and broke with his family. He was convinced that "Christianity is the greatest fact in the history of the people of the earth." For more on Bernays, see Erich Petzet in *Biographisches Jahrbuch und Deutscher Nekrolog* (Berlin, 1918), 2:338ff.

76. Wilhelm Hertz, born 24 September 1835 in Stuttgart, died 7 January 1902 in Munich. Raised to nobility in 1892, Hertz was a historian of literature shaped by Uhland, his teacher from Tübingen. He belonged to the circle of poets surrounding Emanuel Gei-

bel, Paul Heyse, and Felix Dahn, and wrote scientific papers on literature and medieval folklore, poetry, and epics. Hertz also translated Old-French and Middle-High-German poetry.

77. Robert von Hornstein, born 6 December 1833 in Stuttgart, died 19 June 1890 in Munich. Von Hornstein was a teacher at the Royal School of Music in Munich and a friend of Schopenhauer and Wagner. He composed the operas *Adam and Eve* and *The Village Lawyer*, piano pieces, and lieder. In 1896 his daughter Charlotte, nicknamed Lolo, became Franz von Lenbach's second wife.

78. Munich's society of artists called "Allotria" was established in 1873. One of its founding members, architect Lorenz Gedon, had done the artistic design for Munich's exhibit at the World Fair in Vienna in 1873. The president of the Artists' Guild rejected the work, saying, "We'll have no Allotria here!" (Allotria = skylarking, frolicking). The artists then formed their own association and called it Allotria.

79. Lorenz Gedon, born 12 November 1843 in Munich, died there 27 December 1883, was an architect and artisan of historicism style. In Munich he built, among other things, the facade for the Schack Gallery, Hotel Bellevue, and the Art Hall for Allotria. He designed the room for the German exhibit at the World Fair in Paris in 1878, too. In a letter to Levi, Wagner called Gedon *Munich's Benvenuto Cellini*. He died at the age of forty of illness. Upon Gedon's death, Wilhelm Busch wrote a poem for the friend, which begins and ends with the following verse: "So kernig schienst du uns so wetterhart / Ein köstlich Bild erfrischter Gegenwart . . . / Ach liebster Freund! Ein Teil von meinen Glück / Nahms Du mit fort und kehrst nie mehr zurück." [You seemed so hardy, so weatherproof, / A luscious image of refreshed presence . . . / Oh friend! You've taken part of my / Happiness with you and will never return.] (Wilhelm Busch, *Sämtliche Briefe*, edition and commentary in two volumes [Hanover, 1968], 2:244f.)

80. Wilhelm Busch, *Sämtliche Briefe*, 1:214f. Levi communicated the contents of the letter to Cosima Wagner, who in her diary reports on 19 December 1880 that Wagner disliked it so much that "he said he had once known the son of a brewer who wrote like that." (Cosima, 2:642.)

81. Program for the Wagner concert on 17 March 1877: *Walküre*, final scene of act 1 (Schefzky, Nachbaur); *Siegfried*, smithy songs (Heinrich Vogl); *Götterdämmerung*, duet from act 1 (Therese and Heinrich Vogl); Daughters of the Rhine Trio (Weckerlin, Kesch, Schefzky); Brynhild's final song (Therese Vogl).

82. Cast for *Siegfried* performed on Monday, 10 June 1878: "Scenes by Royal Director Mr. Brulliot / Cast: Siegfried—Mr. Vogl, Mime—Mr. Schlosser, The Wanderer—Mr. Reichmann, Alberich—Mr. Mayer, Fafner—Mr. Kindermann, Erda—Miss Schulze, Brynhild—Mrs. Vogl. / The voice of the bird in the woods will be sung by Miss Margarethe Siegler, pupil of the Royal School of Music. Costumes, workings, and props by engineer Mr. Denk." (The program also includes stage painters and members of the ensemble that were ill or absent. It does not mention Levi as the conductor.)

83. A detailed account of the performance was given in two parts in the *Münchner Neuesten Nachrichten* on 14 and 15 June 1878, no. 166 and 167.

84. *Letters from and to Michael Bernays* (Berlin, 1907), 45. This letter was from Bernays to Hermann Uhde and dated 16 June 1878.

85. Cosima, vol. 2, entry for 2 July 1878.

86. Stabi, Paul Heyse Archiv, letter dated 31 December 1877.

87. Cast for *Götterdämmerung* performed on Sunday, 15 September 1878. Scenes by Royal Director Mr. Brulliot. Cast: Siegfried—Mr. Vogl, Gunther—Mr. Fuchs, Hagen—Mr. Kindermann, Alberich—Mr. Mayer, Brynhild—Mrs. Vogl, Waltraute—Miss Schefzky, Three Norns—Miss Meysenheym, Mrs. Reicher from Graz, Miss Schulze, Three Daughters of the Rhine—Miss Riegl, Miss Meysenheym, Miss Schefzky.

88. Leviana, postcard dated 10 October 1878.

89. Adolf Stoecker, born 11 December 1835 in Halberstadt, died 2 February 1909 in Gries near Bolzano. Stoecker was the Protestant pastor for the court and cathedral in Berlin. In 1878 he founded the Christian Social Labor Party that had anti-Jewish tendencies. He was a member of the Prussian House of Representatives from 1879 to 1898, and a member of the Reichstag from 1881 to 1908, where he led the right-wing faction of the Conservative German Party. For him Israelites were a foreign people that could only be united with the German people by converting to Christianity. During the last years of his life, Levi kept in touch with Stoecker.

90. Heinrich von Treitschke, born 15 September 1834, died 28 April 1896 in Berlin. Von Treitschke was a historian and as of 1863 professor in Freiburg, as of 1866 in Kiel, as of 1867 in Heidelberg, and as of 1874 in Berlin. From 1871 to 1884 he was a member of the Reichstag, at first national liberal, but later belonged to no party. He published many writings under Bismarck and was a historical writer for the State of Prussia. His *German History of the 19th Century* (1879–1894) shaped the historical ideas of the nationally minded middle class. In 1879 he wrote in Prussia's Annals: "Anti-Semitism is a natural reaction of the German sentiment toward a foreign element. There is only one solution: Emigration and the founding of a Jewish state."

91. Wilhelm Busch, *Sämtliche Briefe*, 2 vols. (Hanover, 1968/69), 2:190. Letter to Marie Hesse dated 14 November 1878.

92. Kurt Hommel, *Die Separatvorstellung vor König Ludwig II von Bayern*, (Munich, 1963).

93. Three lied compositions, *Meine Liebe ist grün*, op.63 (5), *Junge Lieder II*, op. 63 (6), and *Versunken*, op. 85, (5).

94. Cosima, vol. 2, entry for 13 January 1879.

95. See Peter Gay, *Freud, Jews, and Other Germans—Masters and Victims in Modernist Culture, a Study in Service and Self-Hatred* (Oxford/New York, 1979). The book includes an essay on the issue of Jewish self-hate in Levi's relationship to Wagner.

96. Felix Weingartner, *Lebenserinnerungen* (Zurich/Leipzig, 1928), 1:264.

97. Richard Wagner, *Ausführungen zu Religion und Kunst, Erkenne dich selbst* (Collected Writings) (Leipzig, 1914), 14:189f.

98. Cosima, vol. 2, entry for 10 April 1879.

99. Hans von Bülow, *Briefe* (Leipzig, 1904), 5:582. By "bayreuthization" he meant becoming a slave to Bayreuth.

100. Johannes and Andreas Moser, eds., *Briefe von und an Joseph Joachim* (Berlin, 1913), 3:211f.

101. Cosima, vol. 2, entry for 2 January 1880.

102. Cosima, vol. 2, entry for 2 January 1880. At this late date Cosima mentions Wagner's fit over Bismarck at Lenbach's atelier party.

103. Winifried Wagner and the Wittelsbacher Ausgleich-Fond, eds., *König Ludwig II und Richard Wagner*, 4 vols., rev. by Otto Strobel (Karlsruhe, 1936), 229f.
104. Cosima, vol. 2, entry for 19 January 1881.
105. Lachner-Levi, 35.
106. Telegram from Wagner dated 30 June and letter dated 1 July 1881, in Carl Friedrich Glasenapp, *Das Leben Richard Wagners*, vol. 6 (Leipzig, 1912). The detailed description of events is given in a report by Levi printed in *Bayreuther Blätter* 24, 13f, and includes Wagner's letter to Levi. *Herauf, herauf!* is from *Parsifal*, act 3 (Klingsor calling Kundry).
107. See Manfred Eger, *Wagner und die Juden—Fakten und Hintergründe*, documentation for an exhibit at the Richard Wagner Museum (Bayreuth, 1985).
108. Hermann Levi's letter to his father dated 13 April 1882, printed in the program for *Parsifal*, Bayreuth Festival, 1959.
109. Wagner's letter to Levi dated 15 March 1882, printed in the *Bayreuther Blätter* 24, 1901.
110. National Archive at Bayreuth, letter dated 24 March 1882.
111. National Archive at Bayreuth, letter dated 13 April 1882.
112. Engelbert Humperdinck, born 1 September 1854 in Siegburg, died 27 September 1921 in Neustrelitz. As of 1890 Humperdinck taught at Hoch's Conservatory in Frankfurt am Main, and from 1900 to 1920 the master class for composition at the Academy of the Arts in Berlin. He wrote *Hansel and Gretel* (1893) and *Königskinder* (1897). As of 1880 he worked closely with Wagner in Bayreuth. His memories of that time can be found in *Parsifal Sketches* in *Die Zeit*, Vienna, 1907.
113. Paul von Joukowsky (1845–1912), Russian painter. As of 1880 Joukowsky belonged to the Wagner family's inner circle of friends. He designed costumes and (together with the brothers Gotthold and Max Brückner) the decorations for *Parsifal*. In Venice in December 1882 Wagner told him: "Friend, now that we've been through fire and water together, only death can separate us." (Martin Gregor-Dellin, *Richard Wagner* [Munich/Zurich, 1980], 833.)
114. Heinrich von Stein (1857–1887), philosopher and aesthetician. From 1879 to 1881 von Stein was Siegfried Wagner's private tutor; in 1881 he became a *Privatdozent* in Halle, in 1884 in Berlin. Cosima Wagner wrote to Chamberlain about von Stein: "I not only loved Stein, I adored him like an archangel walking the earth." (Mack, 843.)
115. Richard Fricke (1818–1903) was a dancer in Coburg, Danzig, and Königsberg and as of 1853 court ballet master in Dessau. Wagner made him his choreographer for Bayreuth: in 1876 for *Daughters of the Rhine* and in 1882 for *Flower Girls*. His diaries from Bayreuth were published posthumously. Richard Fricke, *Bayreuth vor dreißig Jahren: Erinnerungen an Wahnfried und aus dem Festspielhaus* (Dessau, 1906).
116. Franz von Fischer, born 21 July 1849 in Munich, died 8 June 1918 in Dresden. Fischer began as a cello soloist at the Budapest Opera. In 1877 he became court conductor in Mannheim, and in 1879 the first Kapellmeister under Hermann Levi. He was personally raised to the status of nobility. In 1875 Wagner made him a member of the Bayreuth "Nibelungen-Kanzlei" (the office for the production of the Nibelungen); he directed the choirs for the festival in 1876. As of 1882 he alternated with Levi at conducting *Parsifal*. Wagner wrote to Levi regarding Franz von Fischer: "Let him help you

well. If necessary, transfer your authority to him as if coming from me" (*Bayreuther Blätter*, 1901, 33).
117. *Bayreuther Blätter*, 1901, 37.
118. As related by Glasenapp, *Das Leben Richard Wagners*, 6:632.
119. Felix Weingartner, *Lebenserinnerungen* (Zurich/Leipzig, 1928), 1:131f.
120. The conductors were not mentioned on the printed program. In the *Wiener Neuen freien Presse*, Eduard Hanslick wrote: "Yesterday the premier performance of Parsifal was clearly a success. . . . In both its grand scheme and in every detail, Parsifal screams the character of its creator. Just like the Babylonian ruler that had his name imprinted on every single brick of his grand palaces, to make sure it lasts for thousands of years, so too has the author of Parsifal imprinted an invisible R. W. on every single measure of the music. Surely future researchers will recognize every single page torn out of the score. The individual parts of this extensive work touch us by swaying from fortunate to unfortunate, once strong and uplifting, then cold and oppressive. And through it all we feel the force of a powerful person and his own unshakably solid conviction. The strength of a powerful, undoubting will is always impressive, in art as it is in life. It commands respect and admiration—but not always sympathy" (Susanne Großmann-Vendrey, *Bayreuth in der deutschen Presse* [Regensburg, 1977]).
121. Hermann Uhde-Bernays, ed., *Henriette Feuerbach: Ihr Leben in ihren Briefen* (Berlin/Vienna, 1912), 408.
122. National Archive at Bayreuth, letter dated 31 December 1882.
123. *Bayreuther Blätter* 24, 1901, 38.

Third Intermezzo

Editor Hermann Levi

> What luck to be so close to such a fine intellect, such a sympathetic mind.
>
> —Cosima Wagner to Mary Levi

One of Levi's duties as a conductor of operas and concerts was to edit works to suit the needs of a planned performance. Often he had no usable scores for vocals and instruments, and the available German translations were often poor. Nineteenth-century musicians often found it reasonable to adapt older works to appeal to modern tastes: Mendelssohn and Schumann edited Bach; Liszt transcribed lieder by Schumann, Italian operas, Beethoven symphonies, and Wagner dramas for the piano; Gustav Mahler edited Mozart; Richard Strauss edited works by Gluck; Hans von Bülow published classical works for the piano with his own instructions for phrasing and dynamics. Musicians rendered works as they saw fit; urtext editions were unknown. The complete edition of Bach's works began appearing in 1850, but as late as 1900 Felix Mottl presented Bach's cantatas with a Wagnerian orchestra with its clarinets, trombones, and tuba.[1]

It was nothing unusual, then, for Levi to adapt and retranslate the operas he was to present. His work does show that he took great care to understand the composers' intentions. When retranslating texts he kept them as literal as possible, without changing notes. When he changed or shortened instrumental parts, his aim was always to achieve a better effect. It was typical of him to work anonymously, intuiting his way entirely into the composition and leaving himself out of the picture. He started doing it for works by Brahms and later continued to do so for Cornelius, Berlioz, Humperdinck, and Chabrier. Not until he had retired as an accomplished conductor did he have an opportunity to put his own name on his editions of Mozart and be paid for them. But he turned down remuneration. He put his versions of the works at the disposal of the opera in Munich free of charge and asked that royalties from other opera houses go directly to the Bayreuth stipend fund. Much of his selfless, anonymous work is no longer identifiable as such. We do not know how much of the new translation of Gluck's *Iphigenia*, done in collaboration with Devrient for production in Karlsruhe in 1871, can be accredited to Hermann Levi. His edition of Gounod's comic opera *Le médicin malgré lui* remained a manuscript, as did his new translation of Chabrier's *Gwendoline* and Berlioz's *Trojans*. Levi translated both of these in their entirety because the available German texts were poor. But neither of his renditions ever appeared in print.

In order to better rehearse Brahms's *Schicksalslied*, Levi wrote a piano arrangement for it. Brahms, in turn, reworked that arrangement and sent it to his publisher for printing—without any mention of Levi at all. That also happened with Wagner's early opera *Die Feen* (The Fairies). Levi wrote a piano score for its premiere in Munich in 1881. He became ill and Kapellmeister Fischer conducted the performance. When the score was later printed by Heckel in Mannheim, Levi's name was not on it.

And yet, these piano scores and arrangements were more or less routine tasks that Levi gladly took care of, but to which he could not bring much of his own artistic ability. Editing Cornelius's operas was a different matter. The original, it was felt, was impossible to perform successfully. Levi set to work to create a new version for both the orchestra and the stage. He also reworked the *Barber of Bagdad*, as mentioned above, undoing changes that Mottl had made to it, and returning it to its original state. Levi was the first to edit Cornelius's *Cid*, and here we can clearly see his influence in a copy of the score found in files of the Bavarian Court Theater.[2] In contrast to Mottl's entirely new orchestration for the *Barber of Bagdad*, when Levi reworked *Cid* he corrected only a few awkward instrumental passages. He did not change the work's characteristic sound, but made it more perceptible, leaving the musical form untouched. Unfortunately Aibl, a music publisher in Munich, printed Levi's reworked score without indicating which changes had been made; he especially neglected to indicate the omission of measures. The title page merely states that it is the version used by the Bavarian Court Opera. Levi was convinced that his version was in Cornelius's best interest and that he was making amends to an unsung composer. By leaving his own name off the final product, he merely intended to cast light on Cornelius. He could not know that a later, much more critical epoch would condemn the anonymous editing of an original.

By the time he began to re-edit Mozart, Levi's views had changed. Now it was important to reconstruct the original as well as possible. Superintendent Possart had begun a series of Mozart performances at the Royal Residence Theater in Munich that for decades was to become an established part of the city's musical life. At the time, Mozart's Italian operas were performed with more or less mangled German texts. Recitatives had been given string accompaniments or been replaced by dialogues. The exaggerated and pompous German used distorted the intent and style of Mozart's works. Some entire passages had been deleted arbitrarily.

The first Mozart opera that Levi translated was *Don Giovanni*. Possart needed it for a new stage production. In Munich a translation done by stage director Franz Grandaur had been in use since 1871. Possart felt that it needed reworking and commissioned Levi to do "this time-consuming chore that demands not only a thorough understanding of the value of the translated word, but also advanced knowledge and appreciation of musical phrasing and the most pious treatment of individual notes." Hermann Levi, Possart continues, "approached the task with the vigor and precision that comes only from true enthusiasm for the work."[3]

Levi's work at translating Mozart was also a topic of correspondence between his vacation site in South Tyrol and Possart back in Munich. They discussed different versions for some of the lines in detail, for instance, why "*dann schliess wieder Frieden*" is better than "*dann sei wieder gut*" for ending the recitative that comes before Zerlina's first aria. In contrast to earlier renditions, Levi changed as few notes as possible. Stage director Possart shared his view on it. When it came to the title, Possart insisted that it must be returned to *Don Giovanni* from—what was common at the time—*Don Juan*, because whenever the name is sung, two-syllable "Don Juan" simply does not fit the notes intended for the four syllables of "Don Giovanni." After 1900 it became traditional, then, for all German opera houses to use the original Italian title *Don Giovanni*, even though the opera was sung in German.

Levi's next translation, *Così fan tutte*, was a delicate and difficult exercise because for over one hundred years this opera had been performed on German stages using entirely disfigured texts. The libretto was considered so bad that many entirely new texts had been written to replace it: *Die Mädchen sind von Flandern* (Bretzner, 1794), *Die verfängliche Wette* (Herclots, 1820), *Peines d'amour perdues* (by Barbier and Carré, 1809, and based on Shakespeare's *Love's Labour's Lost*). In Karlsruhe, the opera had used a version by Eduard Devrient since 1860. Wilhelm Kalliwoda had eliminated some of the recitatives accompanied by string quartets and composed a few transitional passages of his own. A version published by Peters (that incidentally could still be purchased in 1980) contains many additions by Kalliwoda but omitted many passages of recitatives. Levi was familiar with this version from conducting it in Karlsruhe.

Levi liked the German texts for arias and ensembles so well that he adopted many of them. He put the recitatives back in place and translated them anew. Devrient had found suitable German phrases and expressions that were used in all subsequent renditions, for example, Despina's inquiry at the beginning of her first aria: "*Bei Männervolk, bei Soldaten, sucht ihr ein treues Herz?*" [You seek a loyal soul among *men*? Among *soldiers*?] But Devrient also made mistakes.

In the first finale, Despina cures lovesick men with one of Doctor Mesmer's magnets: "*Dringt Wunderkräfte durch Mark und Säfte, dies ist Magnetkraft, die neues Leben schafft.*" [Magic powers penetrate bones and blood, magnetic force creates new life.] Levi took recourse to the humorous original: "*Hier ein Magnetstein, den ich empfangen aus Doktor Mesmers Hand, der rings im deutschen Land Tote kurierte, und dessen Ruhm sogar in Frankreich strahlt.*" [This is a magnet given to me by Doctor Mesmer, who cured the dead all over Germany and is even famous in France.]

Levi labored over many a passage. When translating *Le nozze di Figaro*, he occasionally consulted Cosima Wagner: "How should I translate *Canzonetta sull'Aria*? Can you help me figure out how to continue my first two lines for Figaro's aria at the end of Act One—*non piu andrai*?"

Nun vergiß leises Flehn, süsses Kosen und das Flattern von Rose zu Rosen. [Now forget gentle pleading, sweet caress, and fluttering from rose to rose.]

Cosima had fun with verse and made several suggestions, among others:

Noch die Herzen bezaubern durch Schönheit ein Narziss, ein Adonis der Zeit.[4] [And charming hearts with beauty, Narcissus, today's Adonis.]

Levi finally found a better solution, the text as we know it today:

Du wirst nicht mehr die Herzen erobern, ein Adonis, ein kleiner Narziss.[5] [You shall no longer conquer hearts, you Adonis, you little Narcissus.]

In the early twentieth century, Hermann Levi's editions of Mozart operas were used on all German stages and considered the best available. After 1933 they were boycotted based on National Socialist race laws. Since no other good translations were available, musicologist Georg Schünemann[6] was commissioned to translate Mozart's operas again based on the Italian originals. The first page of his score for *Così fan tutte* bears, in large print, an homage to its Nazi sponsor: The Minister for Popular Enlightenment and Propaganda.[7] In a foreword to *Le nozze di Figarro*, Schünemann attacks Levi's rendition: "It has been all the more necessary to replace the edition presented by Hermann Levi (Jew), used for centuries [*sic*] on German stages, because he thoughtlessly changed Mozart's recitatives, improved them, and even changed the music."[8]

These unfounded claims sought to ruin Levi's repute in music for the sake of ideology. In reality, Levi had restored the original versions of Mozart's works. Only rarely had he altered notes within recitatives to make them accommodate the melody of the German language. Mozart himself had done that for his own German version (*Gärtnerin aus Liebe*) of *La finta giardiniera* (The Pretend Garden Girl).

From a philological point of view, Schünemann's rendition is flawless. It is literal, true to the original musical score, and based on previous translations, particularly Levi's. But where Schünemann strayed from former texts, his wording is stiff and lacks theatrical expression. A comparison of the first lines of recitative from *Figaro* reveals the difference between the version made by the musicologist and that written by the opera conductor. The Italian original reads: *Cosa stai misurando, caro mio Figaretto?* Schünemann's version reads: *Sag was hast du denn da zu messen, mein lieber Figaro?* Levi's version reads: *Sag was hast du da zu messen, mein lieber Figaro?*

The entire difference is the one little word: *denn*. Schünemann had stuck it in to maintain the original note values for the first measure. But that renders the emphasis wrong within the German sentence, putting emphasis on *da*. Levi changed the rhythm slightly to accommodate the natural beat of the spoken word, and this well suits the recitative's *parlando*. As a musician, Levi knew that when translating a recitative from Italian to German one must adapt the note values to the natural pulse of the language.

The Nazi law forced Levi's renditions out of opera house repertoires. Today one can still purchase his piano arrangements for Mozart, but besides Schünemann's version, other translations have meanwhile also been published, and modern stage directors often prefer to use them. In addition, today more and more German stages, even the smaller of them, present Mozart's Italian operas in Italian. This may change. An audience that understands nothing of the story will lose interest. Hermann Levi knew how important it is to keep operas intelligible. It was his main reason for translating many of them. But even though his renditions are no longer used for the stage, it was his great merit to have made Mozart's stage works more understandable for his German audience.

The complete picture of Levi as a translator and editor does not emerge until we take account of his late literary works—his translations from French and his studies of Goethe. Throughout his life, Levi was profoundly interested in literature. He spoke fluent French and read not only German literature, but kept abreast of new prose in French as well. He happened upon Anatole France and was thrilled by the novelist's command of language.[9] During the winter of 1895–1896, Levi translated two of the writer's novellas, *Le jongleur de Notre-Dame* and *Le procurateur de Judée* (from the collection *L'Etui de nacre* [1892]). The first of the two he sent to Cosima Wagner's daughter Eva with a note saying that he liked it so well he would think it worthy of being the eighth of Keller's seven legends and that if she should "find anything wrong with the translation, take a pencil and mark it for me."[10]

Levi viewed these smaller translations merely as practice for translation work on operas, which was much more important to him. Not until the last year of his life did he detach himself far enough from music to be able to concentrate solely on literary translation. He then went about publishing a set of short stories by Goethe. He consulted his writer friends Heyse, Hertz, and Chamberlain and got their approval for his plan: he wanted to take short narratives out of their contexts within Goethe's larger works of prose—*Conversations among German Emigrants*, *Elective Affinities*, *From My Life: Poetry and Truth*, and *Wilhelm Meister's Journeyman Years*—and publish them together. The foreword to the little book explains:

> It has been my experience that even the best Goethe scholars often cannot immediately say where one or the other tale can be found and that most of them have not been acknowledged and appreciated for what they are. I thus saw a need to take them from their contextual surroundings, which are often rather loose anyway, and combine them in one volume. Only a few, negligible changes were needed.[11]

Levi asked artist Hans Thoma for a lithograph of his painting *Flight from Egypt* to use for the title page, and paid 500 marks for it. He supervised every detail of going to press, insisting, for instance, that the printer retain Goethe's old-fashioned spellings for words such as *Maaß* and *Scepter*. He wanted to focus on Goethe and not draw attention to himself. He had planned to donate any profits made by the book to the stipend fund for Bayreuth, but the publisher refused because it cost too much to print.

Thus Levi's plan was to put even his literary work in the service of Bayreuth. And he had Bayreuth in mind, too, when he used quotes from Goethe, quips and sayings collected during the process of editing the tales, to adorn a calendar for the year 1900 that he sent to the Wagner family, adding: "As the year marches on, the sayings get more beautiful and rarer."[12]

Levi had gone from Wagner to Mozart and from Mozart to Goethe. In working with Mozart's music and Goethe's writings, he tried to find a way to express what he had been unable to express by composing. Had he lived longer, he would certainly have continued working on Goethe.

NOTES

1. Klaus Peter Richter, "Die Bach-Bearbeitungen im Nachlass von Felix Mottl," *Die Musikforschung* 42, no. 3 (1989): 247f.

2. Stabi, Music Department, St. Th. Nr. 118.

3. Ernst Possart, *Über die Neueinstudierung und Neuinszenierung des Mozart'schen Don Giovanni auf dem Kgl. Residenztheater zu München* (Munich, 1896), 21f.

4. Mack, 460f.

5. *Nun vergiß leises Flehn, süsses Kosen und das Flattern von Rose zu Rosen. Du wirst nicht mehr die Herzen erobern, ein Adonis, ein kleiner Narziss.* [Now forget gentle pleading, sweet caress, and fluttering from rose to rose. You shall no longer conquer hearts, you Adonis, you little Narcissus.]

6. Georg Schünemann, born 13 March 1884, in Berlin, died there 2 January 1945. Researcher of music, professor at the University of Berlin, from 1932 to 1933 director of Berlin's College of Music, in 1935 director of the music section at the Prussian National Library. He collaborated with Leo Kestenberg in reorganizing musical education in schools and private lessons.

7. Georg Schünemann in cooperation with Kurt Soldan, *Wolfgang Amadeus Mozart: Così fan tutte*, score and piano arrangement (Leipzig: Edition Peters, 1941).

8. Georg Schünemann in cooperation with Kurt Soldan, *Wolfgang Amadeus Mozart: Die Hochzeit des Figaro* (Leipzig: Edition Peters, 1941).

9. Anatole France, pseudonym for Anatole François Thibault (1844–1924), narrator and essayist after the tradition of French enlightenment. His works include *La vie de Jeanne d'Arc* (1908) and *Les dieux ont soif* (1912). In 1921 he was awarded the Nobel Prize for Literature.

10. Leviana, letter dated 28 November 1895. Here Levi cites *Meistersinger*, act 2, where Beckmesser says to Sachs: "Take your pencil and mark it for me."

11. Hermann Levi, ed., *J. W. v. Goethe: Gesammelte Erzählungen und Märchen* (Stuttgart: Cotta Publishing House, 1900). See also "Mozart and Goethe" in chapter 4.

12. Leviana, letter from January 1900.

Chapter Four

The Struggle over the Bayreuth Legacy

> Now that the Master is gone, we have a sacred obligation to cooperate and put our personal interests aside.
>
> —Hermann Levi to Gabriel Seidl

Once Richard Wagner's funeral in Bayreuth, with its huge crowds and ceremonial pomp, was over, his followers were undecided about what should happen next. Most large German theaters had already presented or planned to present Wagner's stage works, including the *Ring*, *Tristan*, and *Meistersinger*, and the acceptance and success of these works was growing. But what about *Parsifal*? Would it be possible to reserve the rights to perform the "stage consecration play" for Bayreuth? Wagner had not written a will determining how he wanted the administrators of his estate to proceed with the festival. Cosima withdrew and said nothing. Even Hans von Bülow's wired condolence: "soeur, il faut vivre," could initially not persuade her not to want to die, too. Her closest confidants doubted she would ever return to an active life.

Thus Hermann Levi, whom Wagner had called his "alter ego" when it came to *Parsifal*, and with whom he had discussed plans for the next festival just hours before he died, became an authority in managing Wagner's artistic legacy. He took on the huge responsibility immediately and found new courage. Suddenly the gloom that had beset him since Venice was gone. He not only found the strength to be a pallbearer for Wagner, over the next few weeks he was to develop astounding stamina when it came to protecting Wagner's interests.

Following the funeral on February 18, Levi stayed on in Bayreuth for a few days looking after Wagner's children. For this he had put the conducting of a commemoration concert in Munich in the hands of Franz von Fischer. It began with the funeral march from *Götterdämmerung* and continued with a performance of *Tristan and Isolde*. Traveling with Paul Joukowsky he soon returned to Munich, however, and headed a memorial service for Richard Wagner at the Academy on February 28. It included Beethoven's *Eroica*, the prelude and *Liebestod* from *Tristan*, and preludes to *Meistersinger* and *Parsifal*. On March 26 he began a cycle of Wagner commemoration performances. On ten evenings, ending on April 13, his stage in Munich would present all of Wagner's stage works from *Rienzi* to *Götterdämmerung*. It was a huge project that no other opera house in Germany could have managed. On March 15 Levi was given an appointment to speak with the king, whom he asked to continue paying Wagner's salary in full for the sake of Wagner's children. But the request was denied and the children received only 10 percent of the royalties flowing from future performances.

During these weeks Levi negotiated and corresponded with Bayreuth's banker, Adolf von Gross, on how to organize future festivals. Von Gross was a close friend of the Wagner family and the children's guardian. On March 7 Levi wrote confidently: "The performances shall be. May we be fortified by the spirit of our dear Master."[1] Everything was to remain as it had been in 1882 and as Wagner had planned it during his last days in Venice. Levi also wanted Heinrich Porges, Julius Kniese, and Engelbert Humperdinck to assist again. The only solo singer he wanted to replace was the third flower girl, Carrie Pringle. He found her "artistically incapable" and her behavior deplorable. She had enjoyed Wagner's special attention and on the morning of the day he died had caused marital distress between Richard and Cosima by announcing that she was coming.

Once the performances in memory of Wagner were over, in April the king asked for private nocturnal performances of the entire *Ring*. As usual, the auditorium was entirely empty and no one could see the royal viewer alone in his dark loge, silently remembering his lost friend to the sound of the tetralogy.

In early June a group gathered in Nuremberg to found the Richard Wagner Association. Levi, one of the most active supporters of the association, tried to convince his own father to join:

> Wouldn't you like to become a member of the Richard Wagner Association? Dues are four marks annually. Anyone whom Wagner has ever afforded a pleasant hour should join. For these four marks you get neither privileges nor obligations, and all that people say about Wagner and the tendencies of his writing in the Bayreuther Blätter—i.e., anti-Semitism—has nothing to do with it.[2]

Levi shared what was important to him with his aged father, still in office as a rabbi in Giessen. In an effort to persuade him to join the Wagner Association, he even trivialized the anti-Semitism among Wagner's followers, although he himself was a victim of it.

On 1 July 1883 rehearsals began for the first opera to take place in Bayreuth without Wagner's overpowering control. Assisted by Heinrich Porges and Julius Kniese, Levi worked with Emil Scaria (Gurnemanz) and Hermann Winkelmann (Parsifal), playing the piano as they practiced their parts. There was little discus-

Hermann Levi and his father. Courtesy of Frithjof Haas.

sion; everyone buried their grief in rehearsal work. But as the rehearsals came to an end, Levi's assistants noticed his sorrow. The new producers of *Parsifal* were tacitly united by the loss of their Master.

The tranquility did not last for long. Assistant Julius Kniese planted seeds of dissent by arriving at Villa Wahnfried with his own plan for organizing future festivals: Franz Liszt was to preside over the entire enterprise and Hans von Bülow was to preside over the orchestra. Hermann Levi's authority was to be curtailed as much as possible, in order to eliminate his "ruinous Jewish influence."

Levi had no idea of the machinations of his own assistant. While he worked to preserve Wagner's intentions, Kniese sought secretly to win over like-minded members of the troupe, particularly those who felt uncomfortable with *Parsifal* being conducted by a Jew. In two letters to his fiancée, Kniese wrote:

> Now nothing, nothing at all can be salvaged for Bayreuth. The crudest of his friends is Levi. I wish rehearsals were already over, simply because I can no longer stand

hearing his voice—the cry of a cattle drover. / Levi—as Wagner has often written of Jews in general—acts as if Parsifal were unfathomable.[3]

And yet two days later Kniese admitted that the premiere on July 8 was "good, indeed, very good." Apparently this time the performers felt liberated from the critical gaze of the composer that had intimidated them a year ago.

The play was performed twelve times; Levi conducted nine of the performances, the other three were handled by his assistant Franz von Fischer, while Levi watched from the loge. At the end of his stay in Bayreuth he wrote to his father:

> Never in my life have I experienced such happiness as now while reminiscing of that wonderful time. From the first hour of the first rehearsal until the last note of the final performance, I found myself in an exalted, celebratory state of mind. Everything went as planned; I cannot name a single mishap. The play's visible success equaled my personal satisfaction; from performance to performance my pleasure grew at this most beautiful, most profound work of all, and at my pride in being called to interpret it.[4]

He seems to have had no idea of what was going on behind the scenes. Levi spent time with Wagner's offspring almost daily. They sat in on performances and had dinner with him during second intermissions. Cosima withdrew from the public, but she did listen to her children's reports on the shows. Daniela, her oldest daughter, wrote to Engelbert Humperdinck: "It all went wonderfully. Following the final performance, Siegfried spoke to the entire troupe, saying that they must remain friends and return next year."[5] (Siegfried had just turned fifteen.) Levi's letter to his father picks up where Daniela left off: "They all hugged one another and wept, and swore to continue the Master's legacy."[6] At the request of the administration, Levi wrote to Liszt, offering him the position of chief artistic director for the festival plays. At the same time, an appeal written up in the name of all artists participating at Bayreuth and addressed to the entire nation, asked for donations to keep the festival alive. Liszt refused the offer; and the call for support was never published.

In the fall Levi visited Julius Kniese in Frankfurt to discuss plans for the next year. He still had no idea of his assistant's intrigues. But at some point Daniela inadvertently mentioned them and Levi discovered that at the Wagner home Kniese had claimed that Levi's Jewish descent made him incapable of conducting *Parsifal*. Levi demanded that Kniese be fired. Kniese no longer wanted to work with Levi anyway and tried to apologize:

> Out of respect for the cause that we both shall honor for the rest of our lives, please forget all of our personal misunderstandings and allow me to greet you as I did the first time we met in Bayreuth.[7]

Levi and Wagner's daughters as "flower girls," from left to right: Eva, Biagio, Count Gravina, Isolde, Blandine, and seventeen-year-old Siegfried. Courtesy of Frithjof Haas.

Levi saw it as more than a simple misunderstanding. It touched his sorest spot—and came from one of his closest associates. The accusation that as a Jew he was incapable of correctly rendering Wagner's work fed his insecurities for years. Time and again he tried to shake off the responsibility that he felt Wagner had given him. After a long while, he finally replied to Kniese:

> From a thorough conversation with Miss Daniela, I know that my relationship to the Wagner family has by no means been altered by your strange opinion of me.

Now my heart is free of all animosity, just as in general from the very start I did not believe that your words came from a person who despises me, but represent a whole sort of people under whose bias it is my tragic destiny and that of all Jews to suffer. But I do not want to be reminded of it every time I step up to the conductor's stand in Bayreuth and therefore I must prevent ever encountering you again at work in the festival theater. If I should see you at some neutral place in Bayreuth, I will gladly shake your hand, because it is not my habit to take revenge; and by no means do I harbor the aversion for you that you do for me. . . . But you yourself can hardly desire to collaborate on Parsifal with someone whom you have declared incompetent and unworthy—in both artistic and personal respects—of directing it.[8]

Surprisingly, years later Kniese returned with Levi's approval to direct Bayreuth's choirs and school of style—and they got along well. Occasionally Levi even lauded Kniese, once calling him his "most conscientious coworker." As sensitive and vulnerable as Levi was about having his artistic ability questioned because of his Jewish background, he was forgiving.

The struggle between rivals for power in Bayreuth after Wagner's death was purely pretense. After remaining in the background in 1883 and for the most part of 1884, in the late summer of that year (and after a lack of discipline had become apparent among the solo performers) Cosima decided to take control. Ever utmost willing to propagate Wagner's work, in the past she had often taken unusual measures. For now she would suppress her greatest desire—to be united with Richard in death—and take command. Thus without being his legal heir, she rescued Wagner's legacy for posterity. One hundred years later, we realize that she was right in doing so. Without Cosima, Levi, Mottl, and Richter would never have carried the Bayreuth Festspiele into the twentieth century.

Gradually surrendering her wish to die, Cosima took the reins, at first through middlemen and then one after another, into her own hands. She certainly would not have been willing to take orders from her father, Franz Liszt. It is also improbable that she would have wanted her ex-husband, Hans von Bülow, to whom she felt morally indebted for the rest of her life, to preside over the music at Bayreuth. But out of a need to somehow make amends for the pain she had caused Bülow, she let him know that he was best suited to manage Wagner's legacy. She knew that despite his respect for Wagner, Bülow's pride would never allow him to accept the offer.

She had never wanted anyone other than Levi to conduct *Parsifal*. The Master had summoned him, and for Cosima, Levi was the "appointed one" for all time. Even though Mottl, of whom she thought highly, had conducted *Parsifal* one summer when Levi was ill, once Levi had recovered, she insisted that he return to the conductor's stand and continue. Cosima knew that she could find no better conductor for *Parsifal* than Levi.

Meanwhile, now that Wagner was dead, *Parsifal* had to be prepared for the stage in Munich, too. Eccentric King Ludwig claimed his right and demanded in the spring of 1884 not only private performances of *Tristan*, but three private performances of *Parsifal* as well. Engelbert Humperdinck came to Munich specifically to assist backstage, as he had done in 1882 in Bayreuth. He wrote detailed reports of the rehearsals and the first performance. By using the same troupe as in Bayreuth, he said, everything went smoothly and all the challenges had been met. But despite the troupe's fine performance, the house lacked the desired hallowed atmosphere. Act 3 had not begun until after midnight and everyone was tired. As the last note faded, the king rose from his throne and left. Humperdinck remarked: "Give me Roman Caesars and Spanish kings that at least share their gladiators and bullfights with the commoners!"[9] Between the first and second private performance the king did give a dinner for the entire troupe at hotel *Vier Jahreszeiten*, but that was all.

Rehearsals in Bayreuth began shortly afterward, in July 1884. The cast was the same as it had been a year before, except for Fritz Planck who now played Klingsor. Mottl had discovered him in Mannheim and hired him for Karlsruhe. Years later he also sang the parts of Kurwenal and Hans Sachs at Bayreuth. Cosima remained in the background, but she had a screen set up on the side stage from where she—out of sight for both the actors and the audience—could watch dress rehearsals and performances. She sent stage director Anton Fuchs and conductor Levi critical notes and suggestions. She followed the performance with the score in hand, had a clear idea of what it should be like, and registered every mistake. She was particularly unhappy with incorrect expression and blurred themes. "Please understand: I must repeat that tempi and themes are indicated by the score from the outset." But she was also willing to praise, especially the orchestra: "With explicit mention that the orchestra's work was beautiful and moving."[10]

Levi welcomed Cosima's critical notes, saying that he learned more from them about stage performance than he had in twenty years of conducting. That year Engelbert Humperdinck had returned to replace Julius Kniese as Levi's assistant. He, too, had a critical ear and made numerous suggestions for improvement.

Levi wrote to his father that all ten performances went smoothly. But by the end of the season his pockets were empty because this time he had refused to take any compensation; and after opening night he had treated the entire orchestra to beer from the Hofbräuhaus.

After a "farewell friendship feast" with Humperdinck and many others, Levi left Bayreuth in a triumphant frame of mind. Once more he had shouldered the entire responsibility for the music. In the future the three associates—Hans Richter, Felix Mottl, and Levi—were to direct the festival in collaboration with Cosima. They had agreed to interrupt performances for a year in order to start the Festspiele for 1886 with a well-prepared new production of *Tristan*.

From Bayreuth Levi left directly for vacation. He visited Conrad Fiedler and his wife Mary in Crostewitz[11] and spent September resting in Alexanderbad.

There he read Dostoyevsky and quietly celebrated twenty-five years of conducting.

FROM PERFALL TO POSSART— AND THE ADVENT OF ANTON BRUCKNER

> The boom at Bavaria's court theater was for the most part due to Baron von Perfall's dexterity and industry.
>
> —Ernst von Possart

When Court Kapellmeister Levi took up work in Munich in 1872, Baron Karl von Perfall had already been managing the court theater for the past four years. The charming grand seigneur ran his house with verve and prudence. He diplomatically coordinated the various interests of the king, the conductor, the soloists, and Richard Wagner, who constantly intervened from distant Lucerne.

Perfall had much less past practical experience with the theater than Karlsruhe's superintendent Devrient. He was the son of a Bavarian officer and born in Munich, a fact that has always been of certain importance for a career there. He had completed studies in law, and then taken training in music at Leipzig's conservatory. As a young musician, he directed Munich's Oratorio Society and in collaboration with Hans von Bülow he reorganized the school of music according to plans worked out by Richard Wagner. In recognition of these achievements, in 1864 the king made Perfall superintendent of royal musical affairs. Ludwig II had hoped that doing so meant winning a Wagner devotee for the management of his own theater. But he was mistaken. Perfall, who had studied composition under Moritz Hauptmann, remained loyal to the traditional school and was basically against Wagner. He was nevertheless amazingly cautious on aesthetic issues and open for novelty and let Wagner's works be shown on his stage. Wagner, far off in Tribschen, considered Perfall his personal enemy and tried to persuade the king to fire him.

But Ludwig II valued Perfall's strength of character and integrity. He had stood the test of dispute over premiering *Rheingold* and *Walküre* in Munich. Despite all resistance and angry protest from Wagner, who accused the superintendent of perfidy and incompetence, Perfall went ahead and made the premiering in Munich possible by letting conductor Wüllner step up to the challenge.

Although a musician and composer at heart, Perfall took over responsibility for the theater and did his job with great care. He extended an invitation to all authors of the German theater to submit their pieces for consideration. And he devised a new stage that came to be known as the Shakespeare stage: by covering up the orchestra pit, a scene could be continued at the front of the stage while preparing for the next scene at the back. During Perfall's era, Munich saw its first performances of Henrik Ibsen's *The Vikings at Helgeland*, *Pillars of Society*, *Nora*, *An Enemy of the People*, and *Hedda Gabler*. It began a new epoch in the theater history of Munich that was continued by Perfall's successor Possart.

When, in 1872, after years of attempts, Perfall was finally able to contract Hermann Levi for Munich's court theater, the conductor had the reputation of being a follower of Brahms. Perfall hoped Levi would support him in warding off the overpowering influence of Richard Wagner. But he soon realized that Levi was spellbound by Wagner's works. Thanks to the integrity of both men, that did not diminish their appreciation for one another's work. They respected and valued one another, without ever becoming friends. And Levi was clever enough to also perform some of his superintendent's inferior works.

They agreed on the most important issues regarding the musical stage, repertoire, and cast decisions and had few serious disagreements. In matters of public relations they always voiced one joint opinion. Over the years the newspapers became increasingly aggressive. The worst attack occurred in 1882 when shortly after opening night for *Parsifal* in Bayreuth one paper ran a series of articles titled *Lasciate ogni speranza* (Give Up All Hope) by Paul Warneck.[12] The campaign began when two of the public's favorite singers, Marie Basta (coloratura) and Theodor Reichmann (baritone), left the troupe. The paper accused Perfall and Levi of selecting soloists for reasons other than skill. It called the repertoire "monotonous beyond compare."

The press's accusations were not justified. During the first ten years under Levi's direction, the company had premiered not only *Siegfried* and *Twilight of the Gods*, but also Meyerbeer's *African Woman* in 1872, Rheinberger's *Türmer's Töchterlein* and Spohr's *Jessonda* in 1873, Holstein's *Erbe von Morlay* in 1874, Gounod's *The Doctor in Spite of Himself* and Kretschmer's *Folkunger* in 1875, Goetz's *Taming of the Shrew* and Rubenstein's *The Maccabees* in 1876, Verdi's *Aida* and Scholz's *Golo* in 1877, Massenet's *King of Lahore* in 1879, Zenger's *Wayland the Smith* and Goldmark's *Queen of Saba* in 1880, Verdi's *Rigoletto* in 1881, and Abert's *Ekkehard* in 1882. Statistics for the opera repertoire under superintendent Perfall for the years from 1867 to 1892—which coincide for the most part with Levi's tenure—contains works by seventy-two composers, forty of whom were living at the time.[13]

Works by Richard Wagner dominated the repertoire from 1876 to 1882, largely because the first-time productions of the *Ring* tetralogy and preparations for *Parsifal* in Bayreuth required so much time and effort. After Wagner's death the stage in Munich was the only one in Germany to present all of his works (and to stage *Parsifal* in separate performances for the king as well). In the following years, Munich staged first performances of operas by Cornelius, Humperdinck, Berlioz, and Chabrier. But occasionally Karlsruhe, under the direction of Felix Mottl, was a bit ahead in terms of new productions. Levi examined all of the new works submitted for consideration and wrote up assessments for the opera house director. Sometimes he had to openly disqualify works by composers of his own personal acquaintance, as in the case of Max Bruch's work *Loreley*, of which he wrote: "Not recommended for our stage!"[14] Exempt from criticism were exclusively the insignificant works of his own colleague, the superintendent of the house. In 1894 Levi staged Perfall's *Melusine* and *Junker Heinz*.

The most successful new production during the 1880s—which was actually a rediscovery—was the *Barber of Bagdad* by Peter Cornelius. The opening night, 21 October 1885, began with the one-act piece *Lazy Hans* by Alexander Ritter. The *Neue Zeitschrift für Musik* wrote: "Both composers were crowned with complete success. The arts put a laurel wreath on the head of the one and laurel sprigs on the tomb of the other."[15] During his first years in Munich, Levi seems to have known the composer Cornelius, who lived modestly with his young family in Schwabing: but he apparently underestimated him. He now wanted to compensate for the outcomes of that mistake by carefully preparing Cornelius's opera for performance.

Peter Cornelius, drawing by Johannes Niessen. Wissenschaftliche Stadtbibliothek Mainz, sign. PCA g7.

In Weimar, when Franz Liszt had conducted the *Barber of Bagdad*, the premiere had been sabotaged by a sinister intrigue meant to harm the conductor. As a result, it was taken from the program after its first showing. In 1877 Hans von Bronsart unsuccessfully attempted to revive the piece in Hanover. Karlsruhe's young opera conductor Felix Mottl, who since his days as a student of music in Vienna had been an ardent admirer of Cornelius, had also adapted the score and conducted the new version at Baden's court theater on 1 February 1884. But to his great disappointment the audience's response was tepid. The next summer, at Bayreuth, Mottl tried to get his friend Levi interested in the work. At first Levi was skeptical. But in late autumn when he began looking for something to put on the program to follow Ritter's *Lazy Hans*, he remembered it and asked Mottl for the score. Levi was enthusiastic. But he had some doubts about Mottl's revisions and said "if I hadn't been dependent on borrowing singers from Karlsruhe, I would have changed some passages back to the way they were originally."[16]

Based on plans that the composer had allegedly later made, Mottl had taken the opera of two acts and condensed it into one act, eliminating large sections and rewriting most of the score. Cornelius's original orchestration was lucid and written before the advent of the Wagnerian orchestra. Mottl had been subconsciously shaped by the sound of Bayreuth. He even wrote an overture based on a piece by Cornelius, filling it with typical Wagnerian sound.

Levi felt uncomfortable with it, but since no other scores were available, he used the arrangement written by Mottl. In Munich the performance was a great success anyway, perhaps also because Eugen Gura sang the title role.[17] The audience cheered and celebrated the discovery of a humorous German opera play as the sensation of the season. A major Munich newspaper, the *Münchner Neueste Nachrichten*, wrote that Cornelius's masterpiece had finally returned acclaim to the German stage. And that in taking up and conducting this forgotten piece, Levi had proven the rare skill of "penetrating this opera, made of the finest material, with truly intuitive congeniality." After the performance Levi welcomed Cornelius's widow and children and both Levi and Perfall gave speeches in Cornelius's honor. Levi expressed his regret at not having recognized Cornelius's merits while he was still alive; Cornelius had never spoken of his own works, and Levi had taken him for an ingenious amateur.

Franz Liszt attended the performance on the following day. He had been a fatherly friend and mentor for Cornelius and had premiered the *Barber* twenty-seven years ago. He also wanted to see the opera of his other favorite pupil, Alexander Ritter. But arriving too late, he missed the performance of Ritter's work and could only see the *Barber*, that "unfortunate child," which he had encouraged Mottl to bring back to life. The day after the second performance, Levi invited both Berta Cornelius and Franz Liszt to his home and together they celebrated that at last the piece had been successful. To see a breakthrough on the horizon for a masterpiece by one of his former favorites from Weimar gave Liszt late, but great, satisfaction.

The piece was successful on opening night, and as appreciation for it increased from performance to performance, other opera houses scrambled for the rights to stage it. Leipzig's publisher Kahnt wanted to print the score. Now there was the dilemma of which version to publish. Levi wrote to Mottl that Cornelius's original version was at most a "literary document" that could never be used to produce the work. He asked Mottl to revise it once more and reinsert the passages he had omitted, such as the entire first finale. In several letters, Levi urged his friend Felix to comply as soon as possible. Finally Mottl replied: "I don't have the time. Do what you want with the score and what you think is right";[18] so Levi began revising it himself. The plan was that Mottl would once again go over Levi's revision next year, either coming to Munich to do so, or writing a new score in Karlsruhe. But it never happened. Mottl fully trusted "Little Hermann." He had a high opinion of Levi's sense of art. Perhaps he was also a bit envious that the staging in Munich had been so much more successful than his staging of the work in Karlsruhe. In his last word on the *Barber* he could not suppress a nasty allusion: "Return it to its state of chaste simplicity, you Puritan! There's still *a trace of earth* on you from your days with Lachner."[19] Levi took it with humor. The two had become such good friends during their time at Bayreuth that when it came to music, they could rebuke one another without taking offense.

Levi thus worked his way through the entire score for the *Barber*, reverting it to a stage piece with two acts and eliminating some of Mottl's instrumental embellishments. Overall, he found Mottl's orchestration acceptable, even excellent in places, as he admitted in early 1900 after hearing it again at the Munich opera: "No one excels you at the art of orchestration, none living and none dead."[20] The score was printed as Levi had revised it and presented in a new production at the Bavarian Court Theater on 13 April 1887. For almost half a century, it remained part of the Munich opera's repertoire and was performed with success on every German opera stage. The original version, published in 1904, was not used in Munich until 1936, when it replaced Levi and Mottl's score. But appearances were deceiving. Experienced stage directors continued to consult the Mottl-Levi score for details, tacitly weaving improvements into that version.

Encouraged by music scholar Max Hasse, Carl Maria Cornelius, the son of the composer Cornelius, publicly accused Mottl and Levi of tampering with his father's original score, and having done so anonymously. Speaking also for Levi, who had meanwhile died, Mottl answered:

> We loved that opera. We gave our best to make it as well-known as possible and (thank heavens!) we did. If anyone could now convince me that the original orchestration is better and more suitable for the piece, I would gladly throw my score to the flames. Meanwhile, I prefer to save it.[21]

When they had taken the score to the press, Levi and Mottl had agreed to remain unmentioned because they felt that their work was negligible compared to the work of the composer. Once again, drawing the attention to Peter Cornelius was meant to make up for having overlooked him during his lifetime. From today's standpoint, it is inacceptable. But it was done in good faith and meant well. Both of the conductors refused remuneration and all royalties went to Cornelius's widow.

Levi's enthusiasm for the *Barber* led him to consider staging other works by Cornelius as well. On 1 March 1891, he presented Cornelius's second opera, *Der Cid*, which had not been performed since its premiere in Weimar in 1865. After viewing a performance of *Der fliegende Holländer* in Weimar, starring Feodor and Rosa Milde, Cornelius had taken the story of the idealistic love between Cid and Ximene and written *Der Cid* explicitly for that pair of singers. He left Wagner and Munich in order to complete the work; but he was unable to shake off Wagner's dominance. The premiere fell through and the work was forgotten until Levi rediscovered it.

Munich's press said of the new production of *Cid*: "Jubilant applause and eager ovations for Conductor Levi, who grasped the score with dedication and a sense of practicality, and directed the performance with delectable briskness, prudence, and vigor."[22] Felix Mottl came to the opening night and later called

Hermann Levi and Felix Mottl. Courtesy of Frithjof Haas.

himself a fool for not having been the first to produce it. He followed suit and presented it at Karlsruhe's court theater in May 1892.

Levi and Mottl were wrong about the merits of *Cid*. Despite its musical qualities, it was soon dropped from programs and repertoires because of its dramaturgical faults. Richard Strauss, who had seen a performance in Munich, said that he liked the first two acts, but that the third was "horribly botched." Cosima Wagner, for whom Levi had played the work on the piano, said the whole thing was a "stillborn story teeming with dilettantism."[23]

Cosima's crushing verdict was also informed by her dislike for Cornelius, who had witnessed too much of Wagner's past. In the spring of 1864, Cornelius had helped Wagner, dressed as a woman, to flee in the night from Vienna and his creditors. And during the following summer, as a guest at Wagner's residence in Starnberg, Cornelius had seen through the pretense and knew that the relationship between Cosima and Richard was intimate, although the couple denied it publicly and lied about it to the king. And yet, with her sense for theatrics, Cosima was right about the fundamental weakness of *Cid*. Cornelius had chosen the wrong material. He lacked the skill to master heroic opera. His was a delicate, lyrical personality, best described by Alexander Berrsche:

> Love does not shout or stomp, it does not pine or flail; it greets quietly, and intimately. One must have felt the bliss of silver poetry, ominously animated by the musician's sweet manner! It exudes a sense of Calderon, as if a mysterious stranger were to walk across the stage with a wondrous message, a person of times past, seeking the like-minded.[24]

Levi understood the wondrous message. Something about Cornelius's fate touched him, they seemed to have something in common: ardent idealism, an excruciating fascination for Wagner, surroundings that seemed not to understand, and finally, resignation. But Levi had not come that far yet. There was another big composer in the offing in need of his help: Anton Bruckner.

Ever since Brahms had withdrawn, Levi was on the lookout for symphonies that would meet Wagner's approval. His orchestra performed symphonies by Anton Rubenstein (op. 107 in 1882), Hermann Goetz (op. 9 in 1883), Friedrich Gernsheim (op. 46 in 1884), and Louis Spohr (op. 102 in 1884). But with these works he could hardly refute Wagner's claim that the era of symphonies was over. In the summer of 1884, at Bayreuth, he met Mottl and Weingartner's teacher from Vienna, sixty-year-old composer Anton Bruckner. Bruckner had just finished writing his seventh symphony and was in search of a conductor to play it. He approached Hermann Levi—the conductor of *Parsifal*—with "utmost respect."

Levi let him send the score for Symphony no. 7 to Munich. After reading it through once, he wrote back to Bruckner: "At first the work seemed strange, then intriguing, and in the end I found myself highly respecting anyone that can create anything so unique and significant."[25] But Levi decided to first only play the *Adagio* because he had qualms about confronting his audience in Munich with the entire, complicated symphony. Bruckner was overjoyed to have any of his work played in Munich at all and asked Levi merely to explain to his listeners that the reason for not presenting the rest of it was *not* because it was bad. "Don't disappoint me," he wrote, "you are my hope and pride, my supreme and noblest patron of the arts."[26]

While studying the score more carefully over the next few weeks, Levi decided to present the entire work. The decision was supported by Conrad Fiedler,[27] who had heard the first performance of the work in Leipzig, conducted by Arthur Nikisch. This symphony, Fiedler said, made a strong impression on him and revealed particular musical skill. Bruckner, he added (who was in Leipzig at the time), had "an incredible appearance, with a fantastic head: half hippopotamus, half galley slave."[28]

Levi scheduled the performance of the symphony for the second subscription concert, to take place on 10 March 1885. He invited Bruckner to final rehearsals and sent him money for the trip. Bruckner and one of his pupils, Friedrich Eckstein,[29] took the night train from Vienna to Munich, arriving on the morning of March 7 and surprising Levi at breakfast. The three ate together and then Levi sat down at the piano and played the symphony for Bruckner, asking for advice on how to interpret it. It was beautiful, he said, but the finale needed modification. Together they made some changes in dynamics and phrasing and then went to rehearse it with the orchestra. While working with the orchestra, Levi paused often to ask the composer what he thought, listening patiently to Bruckner's suggestions. The composer was delighted because in Vienna Hans Richter had not involved him in rehearsals at all, assuring Bruckner that he knew best how to present music. Following the rehearsal, Levi invited Bruckner and the student to his home for lunch and offered to let them stay with him. But both turned the offer down and took a room at Hotel "Vier Jahreszeiten" for the special rate of 2.50 marks.

Two of Bruckner's friends from Vienna, Josef Schalk and Ferdinand Löwe, came to the last rehearsal. Levi had also invited members of "Allotria," the club of artists. When the rehearsal was over, Bruckner sat down at the organ in Odeon Hall and improvised for the musicians and his friends. In the evening, the Fiedlers gave a dinner for Levi and Bruckner.

The first part of the concert program on March 10 included Méhul's *Hunting Overture*, Viotti's Violin Concerto no. 22 in A Major, a few solo pieces played by concertmaster Benno Walter, and Brahms's three romances based on Tieck's *Beautiful Magelone*, sung by Eugen Gura. The second half of the program consisted of Bruckner's Symphony no. 7. The applause was rapturous. After each movement the audience called the composer out onto the stage several times and at the end they presented him with two laurel wreaths. A funny thing happened during the adagio movement: when the cymbal was struck at the dynamic high point of the movement, Riehl, a professor for aesthetics, gasped "Ugh!" to which Levi turned around and hissed "Shush!" The newspaper *Süddeutsche Presse* found the concert a significant milestone in music:

> Writing today about the music academy's second subscription concert, we feel that a remarkable incident, something great, has taken place, and we are still captivated by it. Rapturous, enthusiastic applause escalated to an ovation. . . . The composer was called out on to the stage again and again to accept the audience's thanks. But they were thanking Royal Conductor Hermann Levi as well, who, with true congeniality, knew how to present this work. It is to his merit that we know of the work at all. Under his charming verve the orchestra performed very well, as if magnetic current flowed from the conductor to the musicians and from the musicians to the audience.[30]

After the concert a large circle of friends including Kaulbach, Defregger, Heyse, and Fiedler met at "Allotria." Levi praised Bruckner as "the greatest composer of symphonies since Beethoven." And he considered that day's performance the peak and pride of his career.

The next day Bruckner attended a performance of *Walküre* that Levi scheduled especially for him, taking the *Trumpeter of Säckingen* off the program. He had a chair for the composer put next to him in the orchestra pit and pointed out particularly nice passages during the performance. Bruckner's interest was in the music, not in stage play. During intermission Levi had the four tuba players repeat a few characteristic passages from the symphony. When the concert was over, Levi asked the orchestra to remain seated until the last concertgoer had left the auditorium. He then spoke to his musicians:

> In these halls we have often enough played for the king alone. We have among us today a prince of music. I ask you to please play once again the *Adagio* of his symphony, just for him.[31]

As the coda of the second movement sounded, the music of mourning written upon Wagner's death, Bruckner sat listening, with tears streaming down his face.

In gratitude for the presentation of his work in Munich, Bruckner decided to dedicate Symphony no. 7 to the king of Bavaria and asked Levi to intervene on his behalf. Levi turned to Perfall, and Perfall wrote to the king. A few weeks later, Levi was able to tell the composer that the dedication would be accepted. On May 10, Bruckner sent a letter of dedication to Ludwig II, "the truly royal benefactor of the immortal Master, the ideal German monarch," who was always in his thoughts. Levi suggested playing the symphony again in a private performance for the king, but never did because one month after receiving Bruckner's letter of dedication, Ludwig II was declared incompetent and deprived of the right to rule and Luitpold, the third son of Ludwig I, was made Prince Regent of Bavaria. On 13 June 1886, Ludwig II was found dead in Lake Starnberg.

Because of his imposing and unique features, Munich's artists were keenly interested in painting Bruckner. Fritz August Kaulbach made a life-size portrait, ignoring the composer's plea to "please make my nose a bit smaller!" Fritz von Uhde modeled an apostle in a Last Supper scene after Bruckner, although Bruckner felt unworthy of appearing in the company of apostles. The day before leaving Munich, Bruckner improvised on the organ at a church for all of his newfound friends. He left Munich a very happy man. From Vienna he wrote: "My mind is still wholly in Munich, it has become my artistic home."

Three weeks later the Walter Ensemble played Bruckner's string quintet in Munich. The day before the concert, Conrad Fiedler invited the musicians to a matinee at his home. There Levi went through the piece with them again and then let them perform it twice for him. He later wrote to the composer that the work was well received and had gotten a "warm-hearted review" by Porges. He planned to rehearse the piece soon in Florence with an ensemble there.

Levi had once again found a master to selflessly serve and honor. In Munich he and Conrad Fiedler founded a Bruckner Association that spontaneously collected 1000 marks to subsidize the printing costs for Symphony no. 7. Bruckner was touched by Levi's "unlimited favor and generosity." When performed in Munich, Bruckner's *Te Deum* got thundering applause, and Bruckner was said to be a composer of sacred works on equal standing with Berlioz and Liszt.

After this second triumph for Bruckner, Levi approached Bavarian duchess Amalie, asking her to intercede in Bruckner's favor and ask Austrian emperor Franz Joseph "for a small annual salary from the emperor's private treasury, which would enable Bruckner—the most important of living composers—to cease giving private music lessons and perhaps give the world a few more important works of music."[32] The composer was awarded the Knight's Cross of the Order of Franz Joseph and an annual salary of 300 guldens. The honor, along with knowing that his Symphony no. 7 had been successfully performed in Chicago, New York, and Amsterdam, fired Bruckner's creativity. In early September 1887, he wrote to Levi: "Hallelujah! Finally the Eighth is finished and as my artistic father, you must be the first to know."[33] He had already told friends that only Munich would get his permission to play his "Eighth." On 19 September 1887, he sent the manuscript of his score to Levi with the remark: "Have mercy!"

Without being familiar with the work, Levi invited the composer to come the next winter to hear it; he wanted Bruckner to plan a longer stay, and invited him to stay at his home. But the more he studied the score, the less he knew what to do. His premature promise to present the piece now put him in a predicament: he could not perform it, because he could not understand it. He found the beginning of the first movement grandiose, but could not understand the development, and found the finale a sealed book. In desperation he confided to Bruckner's friend from Vienna, Josef Schalk:

> I don't understand Symphony No. 8 and don't have the courage to put it on our program. Please tell me what I should do about Bruckner. If he were to think I'm dumb, or what's worse, disloyal, I could live with that. I but I fear something worse, I fear that this disappointment will crush him entirely. Help! I don't know what to do![34]

But without awaiting an answer, a week later Levi wrote to Bruckner personally that he could not perform the symphony the way it was. The themes were fantastic, but the development, particularly the orchestration, was impossible. This, he said, was not a verdict, it was merely his impression. "Please release me from my promise to perform the work. Don't be discouraged, rework it again, perhaps it can be redone."[35]

Were Levi's reasons for turning down the first version of Symphony no. 8 justified, or was it an error of judgment that needlessly made the composer doubt his abilities? Schalk tells us that Bruckner was hit hard by the news and could hardly be comforted. He sought the fault within himself and felt he could no longer write music. But on the other hand, he had years of experience with disappointment and setbacks that ultimately enabled him to overcome this crisis, perhaps the most bitter of them all. He soon began thoroughly rewriting his score. To Levi he wrote: "Naturally, I have cause to feel ashamed—at least now—because of the Eighth. How stupid of me. It looks entirely different now."[36]

Bruckner had taken two and a half years to rewrite the score, but at the same time he had already begun working on his "Ninth" while simultaneously revising his third symphony. An original version of Symphony no. 8 published in 1972 allows a detailed comparison with the second version. For the most part, Bruckner modified passages that Levi had found objectionable. He tripled all of the woodwinds to produce a more homogenous sound. (The original version had only two sets of woodwinds, except the finale, which had three.) The use of tubas, of which Levi had been particularly critical, was heavily reduced. The overall proportions were also altered by shortening some passages. The finale was cut down the most; the trio in the scherzo and the coda of the first movement were new compositions.

Today it is easier to appreciate the rougher, original versions of Bruckner's symphonies. And yet in terms of composition, the second version of Symphony no. 8 clearly *is* an improvement over the first. While it took pressure from others to get it changed, in the end Bruckner himself was convinced that revising it had ultimately made it a better work. He wrote an entirely new score for the first three movements. But for the finale he glued in new passages, covering up the old, and inserted new pages. This may have been simply to save time. In contrast to Brahms, luckily Bruckner did not destroy his original versions. We can look over his shoulder and see how much Levi influenced the final version of Symphony no. 8.

Meanwhile Levi had made an effort to find someone to perform it, if not in Munich, then elsewhere. He recommended it to Weingartner, now court conductor in Mannheim. Weingartner took Richard Strauss's tone poem *Death and Transfiguration*, op. 24, from the program, scheduled the symphony in its place for March 1892, and began orchestra rehearsals. But shortly before the date of the concert he was called to Berlin and left Mannheim without presenting Bruckner's work. Levi penned a good scold to him and urged him to present it in Berlin. But Bruckner's Symphony no. 8 was not premiered in Berlin. It was Hans Richter in Vienna who conducted it for the first time on 18 December 1892.

After Levi had decided not to present Symphony no. 8, he scheduled Bruckner's Symphony no. 4 for performance the next spring. At the end of February 1888, he got the new, revised score. But he had to disappoint Bruckner once more. A nervous disorder made Levi unable to conduct for six months. The performance was postponed. When Bruckner learned of Levi's poor health, he cried: "Now everything has gone dark!" Levi handed the academy concerts over to Franz von Fischer, and in December 1890 the latter conducted Munich's first performance of Bruckner's *Romantic Symphony*. Paul Heyse, who sat in the pleased audience, wrote to the composer: "You have now conquered Munich. Your friends will make certain that many other successes follow this great one."[37]

Although Levi was unable to promote Bruckner by conducting during these years, he did what he could to help him. Writing his professional opinion of Bruckner's music for the vice dean of the faculty for philosophy at the University of Vienna, he proposed that the composer be awarded an honorary doctoral degree for his achievements. "In my opinion," he wrote,

> Bruckner is by far the most important composer of symphonies since Beethoven. The fact that he has not yet been recognized as such has to do with the fact that our times have (to some extent) left the tradition of the great classics behind and today the concert programs are governed almost exclusively by the so-called romantic trend represented by Mendelssohn and Schumann (and Brahms). But Bruckner's time will very certainly come.[38]

To demonstrate his support, Felix Mottl signed the proposal, too, but asked that Brahms's name be removed from it.

Levi was right about the future of Bruckner's works, while he was wrong about Brahms, whom he considered entirely one of the Romantics. Perhaps he felt a need to justify himself, now that he stood fully on Wagner's side and rarely conducted works by Brahms. He also thought it unfair that Brahms was well paid for his pieces, while Bruckner was forced to finance his composing by giving music lessons.

Levi had discontinued conducting entirely for three quarters of a year. When on December 15 he returned to the conductor's stand at the court theater to present Gluck's *Iphigenia in Aulis*, the crowd cheered. For minutes the audience stood clapping and waving handkerchiefs, while laurel wreaths and flowers were thrown from up on the stage down to the conductor's stand. But for the next three years Levi left the conducting of concerts up to his colleague Franz von Fischer. As of 1892 he once again conducted the subscription concerts between Christmas and Easter that at his wish had been moved to the court theater. He felt more comfortable there, where he did not have to stand as conspicuously on a high platform. Fischer conducted the non-subscription concerts in the fall that still took place at the Odeon. When Bruckner heard that Levi was well, he cried out: "God has heard my prayer! Hallelujah! My artistic father has recovered."[39]

Levi presented Bruckner's Symphony no. 3 on 3 February 1893. The composer was forced to stay home in Vienna because of a water retention ailment. Levi reported that the concert had been beautiful. But the audience hadn't been too enthusiastic. That would change, Levi thought, once they had heard the symphony soon again. Munich's newspaper, the *Münchner Neueste Nachrichten*, wrote:

Franz von Fischer (1849–1918), as of 1879 assistant conductor under Levi in Munich. Courtesy of Frithjof Haas.

This often truly powerful music stimulates, but does not satisfy. By presenting this work of considerable difficulty with his own keen resolve, chief conductor Levi was able to hold the attention of the listeners to the very end.[40]

For the winter season 1893–1894, Levi's concerts were moved back to the Odeon. The room held fewer people, but the audience preferred the cozy concert hall atmosphere to the large auditorium at the court theater. Levi's physician, Dr. Solbrig, had asked a circle of music friends including Conrad Fiedler, Franz von Lenbach, and Moritz Guggenheimer to donate 1500 marks to rebuild the podium. At the first concert, Levi once again presented an early work of Brahms's: Four Songs—for women's chorus, two horns and harp (1860), op. 17. On 25 March 1894, Levi gave his last concert as the conductor of Odeon concerts, presenting Weber's *Euryanthe Overture*, Schubert's "Unfinished" symphony, and Beethoven's Symphony no. 5. In the fall Richard Strauss took over symphony concerts as Levi's successor.

On 31 March 1895, Levi stepped up to the conductor's stand at the Odeon once more for a Sunday matinee in honor of Bismarck's eightieth birthday. Center stage stood a monumental laurel-wreath-crowned bust of Prince Bismarck under a canopy. Ernst Possart opened the ceremony by reciting a poem that Paul Heyse had written just for the occasion. Then the orchestra played Beethoven's Symphony no. 9. At the end of the ceremony, there were ovations, cheers, and a wave of handkerchiefs for the former Imperial Chancellor. Levi had become a close friend of the Bismarck family after attending Bismarck's seventy-eighth birthday in Friedrichsruh at the invitation of Franz von Lenbach. And he was not the only prominent conductor to favor the former chancellor at the time. At the party in Friedrichsruh, he ran into Hans von Bülow, who was very ill. Bülow tried to play down the latent tension between himself and his successor in Munich and later said that when they met, he apologized to Levi, adding "by the way, the fact is, that of all my replacements [Richter, Mottl, Maszkowski], Levi has by far been the most successful, in terms of both quality and quantity."[41] Ten months later Hans von Bülow had died and Levi had the orchestra play Beethoven's *Eroica Symphony* in Munich at a concert in his memory.

In the beginning of 1893, management at the court theater changed. Perfall reduced his duties to supervising musical activities alone; Possart, his colleague of many years, took over supervising the activities of the theater. In 1864, after playing Franz Moor, Shylock, and Don Carlos as a guest actor, Possart had been given a permanent contract. In the course of four decades, he played all of the great roles in character and was especially celebrated as Mephisto, Hamlet, Richard II, and Richard III. He was great at playing intellectual figures, and less successful at convincingly portraying passion and emotions. The younger generation complained that he wallowed in pomp and pathos. Back when Levi had been hired, Possart had been promoted from his job as actor to stage director for plays; a few years later he was made general director for the plays. In 1887 he

Richard Strauss. Courtesy of Frithjof Haas.

went temporarily to work at the Lessing Theater in Berlin and traveled for guest performances to theaters in Russia and the United States. In 1893 he returned to become the court theater superintendent for Munich; two years later he was appointed as general superintendent.

Possart had many artistic talents and knew all the details of theater operations from his own practical experience. He had played hundreds of roles as an actor; as a director he had staged both plays and musical drama. He was a much-vaunted, brilliant speaker who could recite with theatrical thrust for entire evenings. Richard Strauss composed the melodramas *Enoch Arden* and *The Castle by the Sea* for Possart and accompanied him at the piano when the actor went on tour. Besides being a tireless actor, stage director, theater manager, and reciter, Possart also occasionally wrote poetry. One year when the press found the season's program miserable, Possart wrote:

> The director offering what's modern today
> Will read in the press, straight away:
> "What of the classics? The public yearns
> For programs with pieces on which its heart turns."
>
> If he then reaches for Goethe and Schiller,
> They'll say "Skip the ancients, the faster the better!
> Are you out to kill progress? Throw open the shutter
> And give us young authors, one after another."
>
> If he flirts with composers novel and chic,
> They print "Of course, he knows nothing of Gluck.
> And Marschner he seems to have totally missed,
> Has no Verdi, no Auber on his opera list."
>
> And if the man sighs, "okay, okay!"
> And puts Lortzing and Meyerbeer on the stage,
> The printer's ink will scream in rage:
> "No Schilling, no Strauss, no Pfitzner to play?"
>
> If the tenor stays home, without a regret,
> And Isolde has strep throat and lies in her bed,
> The papers will say "It cannot be—
> The theater—what an infirmary!"
>
> Day in, day out, he has to bear it,
> As if each work were out to swear it:
> The refrain for all eternity:
> "That's not how it used to be!"[42]

Levi admired Possart's acting, but during their first years of collaboration their personal dealings were somewhat strained, particularly because Possart had his own wife, Anna Possart, hired for the opera. She failed on the stage and felt that Levi neglected her. Later their relationship improved when Possart did the stage directing for operas that Levi conducted. Possart respected Levi's conducting skills and his musical authority, honoring him posthumously by writing his memories of Hermann Levi. Waiving occasional objections, Possart defended his lead conductor:

> Hermann Levi was a man of continual goodness of heart, a man of endearing kindness. Occasionally within the world of theater people one would hear doubts about his integrity; but whoever made an effort to carefully compare Levi's words

and behavior was convinced that at heart he was incontestably straightforward. In twenty long years and in situations that put his fairness to the test, I never heard him say a false word.[43]

Perhaps Possart had the letter in mind that Levi had written when the former took up the post in Munich: "Give me whatever you want to conduct; stage whatever you like. I will always assist and never be in the way."[44]

One of Possart and Levi's first joint decisions was to stage the premiere for Humperdinck's *Hansel and Gretel*. While working together closely in Bayreuth, Humperdinck and Levi had become good friends, calling one another by the nicknames "Bonus" and "Melchior." In the summer of 1891, Humperdinck had come to see *Parsifal* with Hugo Wolf and when he met Levi, he told him of his new fairy tale opera. Levi was interested and asked to have the orchestra part for a composer's festival in Munich. Humperdinck sent him the *Dream Pantomime*, but the score arrived too late for the concert.[45] Meanwhile Levi was soon so delighted by Humperdinck's music that he asked Possart to secure the rights for the first performance of the opera. Mottl from Karlsruhe and Strauss from Vienna also both wanted to perform it. But Humperdinck said that if "Melchior" were to conduct it, the first performance would have to be in Munich.

Time was of the essence because they wanted to perform *Hansel and Gretel* during the Christmas season. Young Hans Pfitzner and pianist Carl Friedberg volunteered to write out the parts. Humperdinck spent the last of his savings to make the trip to Munich in December and assist at orchestra rehearsals and play the piano for stage practices directed by Possart. After the first orchestra rehearsal he wrote to his sister: "I feel like Moses, who saw the Promised Land from afar." Lily Dressler[46] and Hanna Borchers[47] were ideal for the parts of Hansel and Gretel. Hanna Borchers, however, became ill during final stage rehearsals and the whole performance was postponed for two weeks. Since Richard Strauss had scheduled Weimar's first performance of the piece for December 23, it eventually was premiered there, although not in its entirety. The overture, namely, had arrived too late by mail. In Karlsruhe the theater troupe also came down with the flu and its premiere had to be postponed until January 5.

The performance in Munich on December 30 went unusually well. There were several curtain calls for the composer and the soloists. Music critic Oskar Merz wrote favorably of this "new kind of musical and scenic play," noting:

> It well suits the atmosphere of the world of fairy tales, a world that has here found the right artistic form through genuine feeling. This distinguishes it from many similar attempts.

From Weimar, Richard Strauss wrote to Humperdinck: "All are delighted by this masterpiece. The orchestra sounds enchanting. You're gigantic!"[48]

Hansel and Gretel proved to be the greatest opera success in years. Humperdinck was inundated with offers. The most prominent stage directors wanted the new piece: Ludwig Rottenberg from Frankfurt, Gustav Mahler from Hamburg, Felix Weingartner from Berlin. Fifty opera houses worldwide presented it that very first year.

Levi wrote that the house was sold out for every repeat performance. He sent Humperdinck six pages of notes for orchestration improvements meant to better highlight the vocal parts, saying that he had discussed the changes with Strauss in Weimar and the latter had agreed to them. Humperdinck replied that he had already planned to make several similar improvements.[49]

Humperdinck's later touch-ups for instrumental parts, at least those suggested by Levi and Strauss after having performed the work, could not be incorporated into the first version on time, before it went to the press. They were not added until one hundred years later, when publisher B. Schott & Sons issued a revised edition of the score in 1992.

During the last years of his career in Munich, Levi looked to France for new operas. He had remained in touch with his friends in Paris since his year of study there, all the more once Gaston and Henriette, children of his oldest sister Emma Moch, lived there. He exchanged letters often with his sister and kept an eye on musical events in the French capital, particularly interested in French composers that had come to Bayreuth because of Richard Wagner.

Léo Delibes,[50] who was more successful with ballet than with opera, had come to the festival in Bayreuth in 1876 and said: "I sense Wagner's enormous dimension, and this giant is frightening!" In 1889 Levi presented Delibes's opera *Le roi l'a dit* (The King Has Spoken).

André Messager[51] was another devoted Wagnerian, although he preferred to write light play operas and operettas. He came to Bayreuth for the first time in 1883, together with his teacher Gabriel Fauré, and thereafter returned frequently. In 1892 Levi presented Messager's opera *La Basoche* in Munich.

In Bayreuth Levi also met Emmanuel Chabrier,[52] who had already once been to Munich specifically to see the *Ring*. He was the most interesting of Wagner's followers in France. Paul Verlaine had written two operetta texts for him; in Paris he was acquainted with Édouard Manet and composers Henri Duparc and Vincent d'Indy. Levi found Chabrier's refined sound fascinating and recognized it as trendsetting for French music. On 10 November 1890, he presented *Gwendoline* for the first time in Munich. Its very first showing for a German audience had been a year earlier in Karlsruhe under Felix Mottl. Levi used the orchestra parts and piano scores in German that Mottl had passed on to him, but he found the opera text so poorly translated that he retranslated it himself.

Impressed by the composer's proximity to Wagner, Levi continued to promote works by Chabrier. Chabrier used leitmotifs, chromatic harmony with unresolved seventh and ninth chords, and—modeled after *Tristan*—wide-arching melodies for Harald and Gwendoline's romantic duets. His librettist for this work was Catulle Mendés, husband of Judith Gautier, who had been Wagner's great love late in his life.

The premiere of *Gwendoline*, with its wonderful cast starring Milka Ternina[53] as Gwendoline and Otto Brucks[54] as Harald met with enthusiastic approval. The newspaper *Münchner Neueste Nachrichten* wrote that now German musicians no longer had to be successful in Paris, the French composers themselves came to Bayreuth for inspiration.

Chabrier was welcomed warmly by artists in Munich when he came for the premiere. At the home of Conrad Fiedler he developed ideas for his next opera, *Briséis*. When it came time to leave, Levi gave him a plaster cast of Beethoven's death mask. Chabrier kept it in his studio in Paris as a souvenir of his days in Munich. Events in Munich stimulated him to write *Briséis*, but when he died in 1894 at the age of fifty-three, the opera remained unfinished. His musical ideas live on in the works of Debussy.

Ever in correspondence with Mottl, Levi turned to works by Hector Berlioz for his last years of stage work. Shortly after they premiered in Karlsruhe, he presented *Benvenuto Cellini* and *Les Troyens* in Munich. Mottl was fanatic about promoting Berlioz and tried to convince Levi of the composer's qualities:

> You must knock on the mysterious door to Berlioz's genius with all your might, your whole being and heart, and it opens to show you gardens of roses and magical palaces, where sober people see only thistles and cottages.[55]

The discussion on how to abridge the work almost cost them their friendship. Frustrated, Mottl called Levi an "old pruner." Levi was angry. "If you had to work in a big city, you would think differently. In Karlsruhe you are father and mother at once, producer and recipient in one!"[56] But when they met the next time in Munich they settled their quarrel. Mottl sent a card to Levi: "I'm still fond of you and always will be!"[57]

Levi worked diligently on *Benvenuto Cellini*, but was unable to bring it to the stage. Cosima Wagner attended the dress rehearsal and was very critical of the work's dramaturgy. She suggested rewriting it in collaboration with Levi and then dedicating the new version to "Cellini redivivus" Mottl.

All of the obstacles that presented themselves in rehearsing *Cellini* did not stop Levi from tackling Berlioz's most ambitious stage work, *Les Troyens*. During Berlioz's lifetime, in Paris this six-hour-long opera had only been shown in a mutilated version. In 1890 Mottl was the first to perform it in full length by splitting it in two and showing part 1 and part 2 on consecutive evenings in Karlsruhe. Part 1 (first and second act): The Destruction of Troy; Part 2 (third and fourth act): The Trojans in Carthage. Levi used this arrangement but translated the opera into German himself. In contrast to the opera in Karlsruhe that had rehearsed both parts simultaneously, Levi first produced part 2, which has a much greater impact, and premiered it in Munich on 29 January 1893. Two years later, on 17 March 1895, he presented part 1. About one week later, on March 23 and 24, he showed both parts.

The best description of the music of *Les Troyens* has been given by Berlioz himself: "Expressive passion, reserved fervor, rhythmic vigor, and unforeseeable twists" (l'imprévu).[58] In principle it meant further developing the theatrics of Gluck, whom Berlioz idolized. Since Levi had thorough experience at staging Gluck's works, he found it easy to find his way through Berlioz's opera. But he had to admit that the work's dramaturgy displayed little skill; it seemed almost amateurish. Yet he found that *Les Troyens* also contained unique moments of great opera theatrics like the septet in act 3 and the romantic duet for Dido and Aeneas that follows it.

Levi had a great cast for the main roles: Milka Ternina was Dido, Emanuela Frank[59] was Cassandra, and Heinrich Vogl sang the part of Aeneas. Munich's newspapers lauded their efforts and "the well-rehearsed choruses and the excellent orchestra led by Levi" but also noted that only a small circle of music lovers would appreciate the huge undertaking: it would be some time before this work made money.

To this day, Berlioz's opera works have not made much money. After Levi retired, Mottl continued to present Berlioz in Munich. But after Mottl died, Berlioz vanished from the theater's programs.

For Levi the courageous act of presenting *Les Troyens* was the final climax in his career as the Bavarian Court Kapellmeister. He was physically exhausted. Ever since 1893, when he reassumed conducting concerts at the Odeon, he had been looking for an appropriate successor. He saw Mottl, Weingartner, and Strauss as the only real options. Mottl had announced that if he were to come to Munich, the opera would also have to hire his second wife, Henriette Standhartner. Possart was against it and negotiations failed, although Strauss had already signaled an interest in following Mottl as the conductor for Karlsruhe. Weingartner was unable to leave Berlin. That left Strauss, who from 1886 to 1889 had already once worked as the third conductor for the Munich opera. Levi wrote to Strauss: "I long for you or someone like you like the stag longs for fresh water."[60] Negotiations were difficult. Levi's colleague Franz von Fischer had hoped for the promotion and was disappointed. Strauss had misgivings regarding the retirement of his own father, the orchestra's horn player, in 1889. Finally, in 1893 Levi traveled to Florence and was able to resolve the misunderstanding with Strauss. Richard Strauss remembered that it was Levi more than anyone who had introduced him to music and that Levi had conducted the premieres of his early symphony (in 1881) and his concert overture (in 1883). On 3 June 1893, Levi asked Possart to hire Strauss for an annual salary of 7000 marks, including two months off in the summer. He wrote:

> Strauss makes a very favorable impression. He is at least a real personality, is unique and interesting. He's not prone to compromise, appears to be of a solid

nature, and has firm artistic ambitions. All said, I doubt whether we can find anyone better.[61]

Strauss took up the position in Munich in August 1894. He began with a cycle of Mozart works after first presenting *Tannhäuser* in Bayreuth. Levi was pleased to have such an important musician as his successor. The two conductors were very different in nature and in their artistic goals. Strauss conducted in order to be an independent composer; Levi gave up composing in order to become a conductor. They didn't discuss their disparate views on music—but they did enjoy playing skat together.[62]

Tacitly, Levi had always hoped that his good friend Felix Mottl would succeed him as the Bavarian Court Kapellmeister. Four years after Levi's death, Mottl did.

COSIMA WAGNER AND HER "MAJOR"

> Your letters, my dear and respected madam, are like a mirror held up to me, in which I don't simply recognize myself, but learn to know myself.
>
> —Hermann Levi to Cosima Wagner

For Hermann Levi, preparing the festival in Bayreuth in 1886 meant a new phase in his life. From then on, a dominant person, his master's widow, Cosima Wagner, influenced his thought and work. They wrote hundreds of letters back and forth, documenting an intimate mutual tie under a constant flux of attraction and repulsion. Hermann Levi and Cosima Wagner were fatefully dependent on one another.

Levi was the oldest of the three conductors—Levi, Mottl, and Richter—that in the difficult year of 1886 all stood by Cosima Wagner in Bayreuth. It was Cosima's habit to give nicknames to everyone around her. She called Levi her "Major"—putting the emphasis on the first syllable, as she mentions explicitly in a letter dated 29 December 1886.[63] She called Felix Mottl her "Spielmann" (bandsman), and Richard Strauss her "Ausdruck" (expression). It was certainly not simply his age that made Levi her "Major" and ranked him above the others.

It had been the "Master" himself, Wagner, who originally under circumstantial pressure had declared Hermann Levi the musical administrator of his "stage consecration play" *Parsifal* and called him his "alter ego." Cosima was adamantly determined to execute Richard's legacy, and that meant keeping Levi. She could not release him from the duty. But even in moments of clear insight, neither did she want to lose him.

With the exception of Hans von Bülow, of all the conductors who had worked to promote Wagner's works, none had worked as hard as Hermann Levi. None

Bayreuth's first Festspiel *conductors: Hermann Levi, Felix Mottl, and Hans Richter. Courtesy of Frithjof Haas.*

had penetrated the *Geist* of Wagner's complete artistic works, both music and writing, with such empathy. Cosima was certainly aware of the fact that an artist of Jewish descent, trying to overcome the obstacles that kept him from the innermost circle of "the initiated" few, would seek to understand the work more zealously than any other.

Hermann Levi's misery intensified after Wagner's death. Both his physical ailments and his constantly recurring anxiety must be seen in terms of his disastrous bond to Cosima Wagner. Ultimately, it forced him to give up conducting.

Cosima became the mast he clung to when the storms of a hostile environment rattled him. He often tried to pry himself from her, but like a magnet she drew him close and held on. He was never able to remove himself far enough that she could not pull him back. Every now and then she would talk of "separation"—and achieve the exact opposite: Levi then felt closer than ever. This bitter ordeal began for Levi while preparing the Bayreuth Festival in 1886.

In late August 1885, Levi journeyed to Bayreuth to meet with Mottl and Richter. It was the first time since Wagner's death that he encountered Cosima, who had withdrawn from all activity for two years. She now proudly presented herself to her conducting advisers as the Mistress of Bayreuth. Roles were quickly divided among the triumvirate. Hans Richter had been a friend of the family since the days of Tribschen. He had directed the first *Ring* performances and copied Wagner's *Meistersinger* manuscript by hand. He was best at all practical matters. Felix Mottl had assisted at the festival in 1876. He was now a successful conductor in Karlsruhe and Cosima's explicit favorite. She saw him as the upcoming next conductor for the festival. Levi's higher standing followed from his intellectual advantage and skills at organizing. It became his duty for years to put together the cast for the Bayreuth Ensemble. Even after it was no longer possible to simply send Munich's entire opera troupe off to Bayreuth, Levi organized the choirs and orchestra for the festival. He not only knew all the singers and musicians, he was willing to tackle tedious negotiations and arduous correspondence to get them. He proudly reported to his father that he had been chosen for this "honorable" task. When it came to Wagner, Levi knew only the single words spoken by Kundry in act 1 of *Parsifal*: "Serve, serve!"

In late June 1886, Levi came to Bayreuth for rehearsals. His new assistant was twenty-three-year-old conductor Felix Weingartner, currently conducting in Danzig. Mentored by Franz Liszt, Felix Weingartner had been able to present his first opera, *Sakuntula*, in Weimar and had attained early fame. Levi had invited Weingartner to guest conduct his own, second opera, *Malawika*, in Munich himself. With his youthful charm, Weingartner soon won everyone's hearts at Bayreuth. He admired Levi and called him "Papa." For the rest of his life, Weingartner considered Levi the ideal conductor.

When rehearsals began, Hans Richter was unable to drop his obligations in Vienna and the team then consisted of Levi, Mottl, and Cosima. They worked together from dawn to dusk, preparing *Tristan*. Levi came to Villa Wahnfried at eight in the morning. He then drove with Cosima to the *Festspielhaus*, where rehearsals took place from nine in the morning until one in the afternoon. After the rehearsal Levi, Cosima, Mottl, and Weingartner had lunch in a restaurant. Afternoon rehearsals were from four to eight. Afterward Levi had dinner at the Wagner home. It was a wonderful time for him. The friendship and even love that he felt in this environment carried Levi to peak performance. He wrote to his father:

> This year things are the most beautiful imaginable. Mottl and I are like brothers. Madam Wagner trusts our decisions without limitation—in short, working like this is heaven on earth.[64]

Levi found the opening performance for *Parsifal* the best he had ever done. The *Tristan* premiere, he reported, sent the crowd reeling with enthusiasm. He wanted his father and brother to join him and experience the excitement and offered to set up extra beds in his room in Bayreuth for them. Not a single dissonance seemed to disturb the weeks of the festival; Levi, Mottl, and Cosima worked together like three "good comrades." Not even the death of Cosima's father, Franz Liszt, was permitted to lessen the ecstasy. Liszt had attended the opening nights for both *Parsifal* and *Tristan*, but suffered from a mean cough. His young friend Felix Weingartner sat next to him in his loge for *Tristan* and asked him at intermission what he thought of the performance. Liszt looked at him sternly and replied: "Under the circumstances, I don't think it could have been better." He died six days later. At his funeral Anton Bruckner improvised themes from *Parsifal* on the organ. Cosima ordered that the festival must go on without any outward trace of grief.

As the summer came to a close, Cosima and her Major wrote each other more and more often. They exchanged several letters every week, sharing their opinions on cast and directing decisions, discussing the stipend fund, the children's upbringing, literature, and all the practical details of life. Cosima asked Levi not only to clear up issues with the cast and rendition, but also to run all sorts of errands and even shop for her in Munich. She commanded and he served. But a recurrent theme is woven through all of their correspondence, at times barely noticeable, at others brutally blatant: Levi's stain—the fact that he was a Jew.

We know from a very early letter to Cosima, dated September 1878, when Wagner was still alive and before Levi was even appointed conductor for *Parsifal*, that Levi's faith was a frequent topic of discussion beginning with their very first encounter. There Levi mentions a serious conversation that bothered him:

> What would become of me if I were to approach *Parsifal* from a level higher than that of the arts, I do not know; for the time being I struggle not to let any such power get a hold of me, just as I often stoically walk past open church doors, although—or perhaps because—they irresistibly beckon me to come in.[65]

At some point Levi may have been willing to convert. But he could not bring it upon himself to hurt his father, a rabbi. At the same time, Wagner's insistence during *Parsifal* rehearsals made it impossible for him to comply. Cosima would not settle for anything less and kept probing and probing his conviction. Following the first dress rehearsal for *Parsifal* in June 1886, a short conversation ended in a serious huff. We can only guess what it must have been about by knowing what happened next: for the first and only time ever, Levi refused to dine at Villa

Wahnfried in the evening. In a later letter, Cosima returned to that dispute with offending aggressiveness: "Everyone dies a Christian, because Christianity is a fact. Blessed are those who may be it during their lifetime."[66]

We can only imagine how much Levi must have suffered from affronts such as these. His amazing reaction concealed the extent of his hurt: with labors of love he tried to bind the Wagner family closer to him than ever. At Christmastime 1886, when Cosima and her children were staying in Munich, he invited them all to his home and set up a Christmas tree. Cosima seemed delighted. She let him play passages from Wagner's early opera *Die Feen* at the piano, as a Christmas present to her. But in her thank-you note that followed, she pounded on Levi again: "It seems to me that the demonical part of you often directly (either inwardly or outwardly) contradicts what I want. This dark, demonic part of you that used to outright frighten me, now appears to be a cry for salvation."[67] Did she still think she could get him to convert?

The letters reflect conversations that were held more and more often in Munich because after Wagner's royal benefactor Ludwig II had died, Cosima was forced to come to the city to renegotiate the rights to Wagner's works. Finally, in February 1887 she signed a contract agreeing that the rights to Wagner's early works, *The Fairies* and *The Ban on Love*, would remain with the Bavarian National Theater, while the rights to all other works went to the Wagner family. She had achieved that the rights that Wagner had originally handed over to the king in exchange for a lifelong pension were returned to her.

Cosima was not inclined to travel to Munich often and implored her Major to come out to Bayreuth as often as possible: she needed both confidential and stimulating conversation with her most experienced artistic adviser. She suggested that he spend the summer off-season in Bayreuth, reading Dante's *Divine Comedy* with her. The proposal flattered Levi and reminded him of Richard and Cosima's intimate evenings of shared reading in the past. Her ulterior motive was perhaps to guide him through Dante's purgatory to arrive at the "paradise" of Christianity. At any rate, to her Levi was a well-read and valued conversationalist.

In mid-June 1887, Levi and Mottl met in Bayreuth to discuss the program for 1888 with Cosima and Adolf von Gross. Since her advisers had convinced her to skip 1887, Cosima wanted to present two new works—along with *Parsifal*—at the next festival. Once again, Levi's advice was crucial. In a detailed letter he wrote why it was impossible to do a new production of *Meistersinger*, to repeat *Parsifal* ("that must always be done"), and to do *Tristan*, too. Cosima gave in reluctantly. To contrast *Parsifal* and *Tristan* had always been one of her favorite ideas. She saw *Parsifal* as a reconciling answer to the terrible question posed by *Tristan*. Perhaps she also wanted to produce *Tristan* because it would give her favorite, Felix Mottl, an opportunity to conduct at Bayreuth. Hans Richter was to conduct *Meistersinger*, and Levi to conduct *Parsifal*. In the end that's not what happened, but of course, she could not have known what would transpire.

During the summer weeks of 1887, Levi tried to prevent a nervous disorder from getting worse. He took water treatments prescribed by Dr. Schweninger[68] and then went to Lake Tegernsee to recover. In early August he met Cosima in Munich. She had come to organize props and equipment for *Meistersinger* and to see about having electric light installed at the festival hall in Bayreuth. When it came time to leave, Levi took the train with her as far as Landshut in order not to interrupt the conversation they had begun in Munich.

We know how important that conversation was for Levi because he mentions it time and again in subsequent letters. The main point was probably the very grounds for collaborating with Bayreuth. The urgency of clarifying that point was brought about by a decision made by the superintendent in Munich, not to release his first conductor, Levi, for the entire duration of rehearsals in Bayreuth. Cosima was indignant. She thought the only clear response to that would be to give up Munich entirely and to live and breathe only for Bayreuth. Levi would not have dared taking that radical step and putting his entire existence at her mercy. "Separated by the curse of birth," he never felt wholly accepted in Bayreuth. The more Cosima insisted, the worse things became. The "stain" of his Jewish origins stood between him and Cosima at every encounter. He was not willing to throw away his heritage, or to deny it.

As he got off the train in Landshut, Cosima—in her own words—"left her Major in profound distress," so much so that she would have liked to have followed him back to Munich to continue their talk. Straightaway she sent him a long letter, in an effort to comfort him:

> You don't need any other [religion], and the fact that you serve [Christianity] despite your misery makes you her most chosen servant. . . . In truth, my friend, I cannot understand why Jewry should ever burden your mind. . . . You have devoted yourself with your whole heart to our cause and done it powerfully. How can you be so half-hearted? . . . The way nature has made you, no one can serve our cause better than you. I doubt whether the prelude to Act Three of *Parsifal*, for that matter, whether the whole of Act Three can ever again sound as it did under your direction. . . . Are you with us in paradise?—No, you're in your grave.[69]

What did that mean? A few years later, when Levi felt that he no longer had the strength to participate actively in Bayreuth, she was more explicit: it is better to perish in Bayreuth than to abandon it.

Cosima now began writing to Levi every third day. She was, she said, "worried about her sad friend and feared he might die." With beguiling phrases she wrapped her thoughts around him and spoke of "the religious view of our cause." She pointed out that Dante sent gloomy people to hell. But the ultimate comfort, she thought, was to be gained from the Master's own music—if only

Levi would conduct *Tannhäuser*. Cosima had finally found the right words to encourage Levi. He replied: "Your truly comforting letter will be the guiding star for the rest of my life."[70] She wrote back:

> I believe in God, Mozart, and Beethoven, in these and in their followers and apostles. I believe in the Holy Spirit and in The Truth of the One, Indivisible Art. I believe that all can be saved through this art.[71]

In other words, if you cannot be happy as a Jew, then let yourself at least be blessed by the music of God's "apostle," Richard Wagner.

Levi's friends in Munich seem to have been unaware of these exchanges and the emotional strain they caused. They simply thought Levi had become a Wagnerian and was now inseparably involved in the life of the Wagner family.

Sculptor Adolf von Hildebrand[72] complained to Conrad Fiedler that Levi was "forever trying to drag me to his heaven in Bayreuth." Levi had bitter debates with his old friends, Elisabeth and Heinrich von Herzogenberg. They were ardent followers of Brahms and could not understand his infatuation with Wagner. Similar debates also estranged Levi's former confidant, poet Paul Heyse.

In early September 1887, Cosima's daughters and her son Siegfried visited Munich. Levi chaperoned them, inviting them to the opera several times, for which Cosima wrote ebullient notes of thanks. In October Levi wrote up cast lists and rehearsal plans for Bayreuth while rehearsing *Die Feen* with the opera in Munich. The list of choir members also mentions the names of the musical assistants, including dependable Heinrich Porges and Engelbert Humperdinck, and surprisingly, Julius Kniese. For Cosima's sake, Levi had decided to include Kniese after he had apologized to her. Felix Weingartner was no longer interested in participating at Bayreuth. He was tired of Cosima's paternalism in all musical matters. Neither did he appreciate how two years before, the death of his beloved teacher Franz Liszt had been kept secret in order that the show may go on.

In early 1888, Levi received notice from his superintendent in Munich that he would not be given all the days off that he had applied for in the summer months, in order to be in Bayreuth. He wrote to Cosima that in light of "this whole ignoble fusion of the Bayreuth Festival with Munich's Court Theater," this year he would prefer not to conduct at Bayreuth. He did not propose abandoning Bayreuth altogether, but offered instead to help out with preparations for *Meistersinger* and *Parsifal*. But it is also possible that he wanted to use the new circumstances to free himself of responsibility for Bayreuth. It had become more and more of a burden. Once again, Cosima was angry:

> I must have a serious word with you, my dear friend, perhaps the most earnest word ever spoken since we started working on practical matters. . . . Listen to me: Since you got yourself into the predicament of having to decide between Bayreuth and Munich, and you have decided to stay in Munich, I, for my person, have considered

complete separation from you. I mean: complete. After which there shall never be any personal or artistic dealings between us.

But immediately after severing the bond so thoroughly, she returned to question the feasibility of that step: "Do you think we, you and I, have the courage to make that sacrifice?" And then suggested a compromise: "Well, then, conduct here as much as your work in Munich allows."[73] She threatened to exile him, but was incapable of following through.

Cosima's wavering pronouncements did not help to solve the dilemma and could not calm Levi's nerves. He avoided the conflict by throwing himself into his work. At the court theater he prepared Verdi's *Otello*. Between rehearsals he traveled to Leipzig for the opening night of *Die drei Pintos*, an opera fragment by Carl Maria von Weber that Leipzig's conductor Gustav Mahler had finished and then produced. This premiere drew prominent theater people to Leipzig: Superintendent Count von Platen from Dresden, Count von Hochberg from Berlin, Baron von Perfall from Munich, and the conductors Ernst von Schuch, Franz Wüllner, and Hans von Bronsart. Even music critic Eduard Hanslick came up from Vienna. Gustav Mahler wrote to his parents: "Kapellmeister Levi was there, too, and showed a lively interest in me."[74]

Once back in Munich, Levi continued rehearsals for *Otello*. A few days later he took the train to Karlsruhe to meet with Cosima, Adolf von Gross, Julius Kniese, and Felix Mottl. The latter was in the middle of producing the entire *Ring* for the first time at Baden's court theater. On the evening before their meeting, Levi and Cosima watched the *Siegfried* performance. At their conference the next day, the group decided on the program for next summer's festival without discussing whether Levi would participate. Cosima simply ignored Levi's retreat. In a letter to their mutual friend, Mary Fiedler, Cosima mentioned her concern for Levi's well-being and said that out of kindness she had decided to hold her tongue, although she used to give him her mind on everything. What she meant was that she would no longer mention his Jewish descent. "If he needs a vacation to improve his health, then for heaven's sake, he should take it and join us in Merano."[75] She perhaps sensed how ill Levi was. She discovered the whole truth a few days later.

At an Academy Concert on February 22, Levi had to step down from the conductor's podium in the middle of Beethoven's Symphony no. 5 and let his concertmaster finish conducting the performance. He had felt queasy and sought out his physician. He wrote Cosima that because of "an extreme nervous disorder and mental depression" he was unable to work artistically for several months. He thanked Cosima for her words on "the religious meaning of art" and then continued:

> I feel now that I need not leave you, as if through this profound insight into my heart and life you have recognized and sealed the fact that we belong together for

this whole life and the thereafter. . . . I believe I have now also learned how to pray![76]

Two days later he sent a complete list of the names of all orchestra musicians and the flower girls to Adolf von Gross in Bayreuth. It was his last act in preparing the festival for 1888, the first festival that he could not attend.

At the end of March, Levi began treatments at a curative water spa in Bad Cannstatt under the supervision of Dr. Fischer. He had daily medical treatments and the strictest orders to refrain from all artistic activity. At Cosima's request he nevertheless was willing to examine tenor Ferdinand Jäger at a private sitting. Jäger had been a member of the third cast in the year that *Parsifal* had been presented for the first time. Levi understood that the matter involved some diplomacy. When rehearsals for the festival began, he wrote Cosima his assessment of Jäger's qualities and expressed his good wishes for the rehearsals in which he could not participate for the first time ever:

> May the heavens bless the project! Without me it may even be easier; you've had much misery and useless anxiety because of me. I do know that you will sometimes think of me, not as of an outsider, but as of someone among you. And as often as your thoughts turn to me, they will meet with mine that incessantly flow in your direction. May God be with you and all the participants![77]

And now, far away from all theater operations, Levi let himself take a rest from music. In complete isolation and quiet he discovered a peace of mind he had never known and his self-confidence returned. Far from the hustle and bustle of the festival, he believed now to understand the true meaning of *Parsifal*. On July 22, the night of the premiere in Bayreuth, he entered a church in Heidelberg. Lying prostrate on the floor, he went through the prelude in his mind. The next day a telegram arrived from Felix Mottl, who had conducted *Parsifal* in his place: the performance had been beautiful. For Levi it was "as if a string drawn tighter and tighter year after year finally broke" and the tension that had built up for so long gave way to tears.

The reviewers were very critical of Felix Mottl's conducting *Parsifal*. In the journal *Nord und Süd*, Munich's critic Paul Marsop wrote that the latest production of *Parsifal* was inferior and Mottl too immature to render the work properly:

> There's something nervous about him, something unreliable, something effete. . . . This drama that takes us to the heights and depths of life demands a conductor like Munich's Court Conductor Hermann Levi, to whom Mottl cannot compare, though he may try.[78]

The polemic of this review flowed from the fact that it appeared six months after the event in reaction to controversy that had arisen in the meantime to the effect that at last "Jewish *Parsifal*" had been returned to the hands of a Christian conductor. Felix Weingartner, who had attended one of the performances conducted by Mottl, took part in the controversy. Years later he wrote to his "Dear Papa" (Levi):

> The noise he made of the music was indescribable. Right from the start, the prelude was torture. . . . In my opinion, you are the one that carried on the tradition, you are the conductor of *Parsifal* that continued the work's "spiritus sanctus" as the Master wished.[79]

Cosima defended her Major throughout the dispute:

> It's scandalous that some of his friends now think that they underestimated him and that they must compensate for that by finding fault with our [new] production of the work.[80]

Levi, too, was upset. He wanted nothing to do with Paul Marsop's *Parsifal* review because it favored him at the cost of a colleague that was also an esteemed friend, Felix Mottl. He was disappointed that Mottl had found no opportunity to visit him during his convalescence in Bad Cannstatt, which is not far from Karlsruhe. But he did welcome Siegfried Wagner's visit on Thursday before Easter, on his way home from Karlsruhe. Levi loved Siegfried like a son and did what he could to support the young man's training in music. During Siegfried's visit in Bad Cannstatt, Levi offered the man thirty years his junior the personal form of addressing one another with "Du."

In July Levi asked the director of Munich's court theater to extend his sick leave and then traveled from Bad Cannstatt to the island of Sylt to relax. He had always found the North Sea balm for his weak body. He spent his time there reading Schopenhauer. On his way home in late September, he stopped to see his friend Wilhelm Busch in Northeim and they spent an interesting day together at the painting gallery in Cassel. But once he was back in Munich, he still felt unable to return to conducting. A visit to Cosima in Bayreuth upset him once more. He accepted an invitation from the singer couple Heinrich and Therese Vogl to spend a few weeks at their country home in Deixlfurth near Tutzing. In these rustic surroundings that he had found so relaxing when he was well, he finally recovered entirely and felt strong enough to resume work.

In mid-November Levi returned to Munich, held a few rehearsals, and attended a few performances. But every stay in the theater felt like martyrdom. He nonetheless let Cosima know, via Adolf von Gross, that he was willing to conduct again next year in Bayreuth. She considered it a "sign of faith and strength" and recommended that her Major read Schiller to lift his spirits. In December he conducted his first performances again in Munich, among other works, Gluck's *Iphigenia in Tauris* and Méhul's *Joseph in Egypt*.

As every year, in 1888 Levi spent New Year's Eve alone, looking back over the year and writing letters. The last hours of the year were devoted to Cosima:

> New Year's Eve is my only holiday. . . . The other holidays when people are pious or merry, even Christmas, just make me very sad, even melancholy. . . . When I compare my festive feeling today with that of other New Year's Eves, I cannot recall one time in my life when I felt as serene, as harmonious as tonight. You alone, dearest Madam, know why, and what it means to me to have to use such shabby, time-worn phrases such as "thank-you" to express it. . . . Now you shall see how differently I plan to handle my task next year, indeed, I have the feeling that I will solve it better than any other [person], and this not despite the fact, but *because* I have had to take the detour of great suffering and every kind of self-torment to attain what others, the luckier, are given in the cradle. . . . I thank my respected, untiring, patient, and loyal guide, in unchanging love from my whole heart.[81]

During the first six months of 1889, most of their correspondence concerned *Tannhäuser*, which Cosima planned to produce next. She wanted to know from Levi whether Wagner had agreed to any abridgments. She would have liked to have consulted Hans von Bülow because in her mind he was the authority when it came to artistic issues regarding Wagner's works. But she was reluctant to write to him. Levi gave her a clear answer: the common omission of a verse for Tannhäuser from the scene "Venus Berg" was only acceptable if the singer was unable to sing it. Otherwise the form of the work forbade it. Neither was it acceptable to cut Walther von der Vogelweide's solo in the battle of the singers, although it had been omitted for Wagner's own production of the work in Paris.

Besides discussing music, Levi and Cosima's correspondence now moved on to discuss literature at great length. Levi continued to read works by Goethe and Schopenhauer, which he seemed always to have with him, but also read work by scientist Georg Christoph Lichtenberg and novellas by Gottfried Keller. He particularly recommended the latter to Cosima. They met again in Munich and Cosima was glad to see her Major "at the conductor's stand, commanding his orchestra." They spent happy hours at the home of their friends Conrad and Mary Fiedler, and Cosima said "it would be difficult to find four such nice people in the whole world."[82]

In Bayreuth Cosima now had a telephone and could settle urgent matters without coming to Munich. Levi rehearsed daily with Ernst Blauwaert who was to sing the part of Gurnemanz for the first time in 1889. As a precautionary measure, because of Levi's precarious health, they decided that Franz von Fischer would be ever ready to step in and conduct. Levi also recommended that his third conductor in Munich for the past three years, Richard Strauss, be hired as Cosima's assistant. Shortly before Levi was to leave for Bayreuth, the twenty-nine-year-old musical director of the opera in Budapest, Gustav Mahler, turned up at Levi's home and played "a very significant symphonic poem" for him. It was the *Todtenfeier* (funeral march), the first version of Mahler's first movement of his Symphony no. 2 (*The Resurrection*).[83]

Levi went to Bayreuth in early July. Standing in for Hans Richter, he and Felix Mottl went through the first rehearsals for the *Meistersinger*. Levi, Mottl, and Cosima ate all of their meals together. Once again, Levi's letters to his father say they were all in very high spirits and that the *Parsifal* performance was perfect: "As if God's blessing rested on every single note."[84] That year he invited his longtime lady friend from the circle surrounding Brahms, Elisabeth von Herzogenberg, to the performance. He had not yet been able to win her over for Wagner. She wrote a critical, ironic report to Adolf von Hildebrand, saying that Mary Fiedler and Levi had turned Bayreuth into a "sanctuary" and that they had become totally incapable of distinguishing debauchery from artistic pleasure:

> People like this go to *Parsifal* like Catholics go to the Holy Tombs on Good Friday; it has become a worship service for them. The whole bunch of them is in an unnatural, heightened, hysterically delighted frame of mind like Ribera's wide-eyed saints. They're breeding bloodthirstiness, the stench of incense, a muggy sensuousness with sacred solemn gestures, a grave and bombastic atmosphere unheard of in any kind of art; it's suffocating. To be truthful, one might say that the flower scenes are much cuter and much more innocent than they have been said to be, and that where it belongs, the sensuality is not part of the opera, but part of the spiritual hocus pocus that is nothing more than a sensual, mushy, dwelling on emotions and an unhealthy delight in the marks of wounds. For a stomach used to Bach, it's nauseating.

She was, however, surprised to find Levi in such good health:

> A moment of weakness that came over him during rehearsal was not due to a nervous disorder, but to a nameless emotion that grabbed hold of him when faced with his holy task.[85]

The festival days brought Levi uplifting highlights and honors. When he entered a restaurant after the second performance to dine with Mottl and Richter, the entire crowd of about two hundred people raised their glasses to celebrate him. Prominent guests came for the final performance: Bavarian Prince Regent Luitpold and German Kaiser Wilhelm II. At one reception, Levi wore a Bavarian uniform while conducting Weber's *Jubel Overture*. At an audience with the Kaiser he was awarded the Order of the Crown, third class. Bavarian Prince Regent Luitpold presented him with a baton of gold. Levi was overjoyed. Last year's crisis seemed a thing of the past. Was it?

During the next winter, Cosima visited Munich several times. She usually stayed with Conrad and Mary Fiedler, a home where Levi came and went daily. Richard Strauss often joined them. At the opera Cosima assessed the performance of the new tenor, Max Alvary, to see whether he could sing *Tannhäuser* and *Tristan* for Bayreuth in 1891. In Karlsruhe she helped design scenes for the staging of Franz Liszt's *St. Elisabeth*. Levi would have liked to have done that project in Munich, too, but the relationship between Bayreuth and the court theater's director was disturbed by the director's plans to stage Wagner in Munich. Cosima was unwilling to participate in rehearsals in Munich.

In 1890 there was no festival at Bayreuth. During the theater's off-season, Levi took a trip up north. From the North Cape he sent greetings to Cosima by wire to demonstrate his steadfast bond to her.

In the fall Cosima and Mottl came to Munich to meet Levi and discuss the agenda for 1891. They decided not only to repeat *Parsifal* and *Tristan*, but to make a new production of *Tannhäuser* as well, this time to be directed by Mottl. When Cosima stayed for a whole week in Munich the next March, they had a *Tannhäuser* rehearsal at Levi's home with Felix Mottl and Cosima's new favorite, Richard Strauss. Cosima recognized young Strauss's potential and would have loved to lure him permanently to Bayreuth as her own house conductor. His job for the moment was to assist Mottl at *Tannhäuser* rehearsals. Three years later he conducted the work himself at Bayreuth. When they met at Levi's home, the "Major" played passages from Peter Cornelius's opera *The Cid*, which had just shortly before been premiered in Munich. Mottl liked it; Cosima did not. But Levi, who meanwhile had become a fervent admirer of Cornelius, traveled in May to Weimar to hear the composer's opera fragment *Gunlöd*.

In July of 1891 Levi moved to Bayreuth, where he alone was to direct *Parsifal* that year. Mottl (assisted by Strauss) directed *Tristan* and *Tannhäuser*. But in contrast to the ecstasy felt the year before, this summer was unbearable. He felt tacit rejection from all sides. A talk with Mottl left him unsettled. He felt that he was in the wrong place. Mottl, Strauss, and Cosima seemed to work well without him. It took an effort to get through those dismal festival weeks. After the festival he went off to Bad Reichenhall in a very depressed mood and spoke with no one for a whole week. Once again, he persuaded himself that he must finally let go of Bayreuth. Again, he asked Cosima to release him:

> I have the distinct feeling that I can no longer shoulder both the work in Bayreuth and the rest of what I must endure and tolerate. I am sore and sick and long for peace. I ask and implore you: Let me go! You have so often said, in jest and seriousness, that I am the cross you must bear to the very end. But when is the end? Can't it be today?[86]

Cosima's reply was curt and determined. She was not in a position, she said, to release him from an obligation "to which he had been appointed." They each had a duty to tolerate one another. If he was sore and sick, well, then he should simply learn to see life as a wound; the cure lay in repentance or death! Levi wrote back begging, please "let me go!"[87]

Cosima's next letter was a masterpiece of persuasion. On the one hand she said straightforwardly: "If your physical strength is failing, it is better to perish in Bayreuth than to live anywhere else." On the other hand, she accuses herself of being unfair in not clearly showing how much she felt for him. In closing the letter she clearly states of what her anti-Semitism consists:

> The traits of yours that hurt me have to do with your ancestry, and everything about you that is good, even excellent is what you have made of yourself, and cannot be praised highly enough. For me it's the opposite: what is good about me, I have inherited . . . and my evil qualities . . . are all my own doing.[88]

By accusing herself she appealed to Levi to rescue her: Don't abandon me! And Levi withdrew his request for release. After a conversation in Munich, he agreed to try to do the festival in Bayreuth again.

Why did Levi reverse his decision a second time and decide to conduct at the festival in 1892 and again in 1894? He certainly had more reasons than ever to refuse. He was well aware of the increasing anti-Semitic tendencies in the German Reich; he felt that many of the festival guests and even coworkers rejected him for being Jewish. Even Richard Strauss thought that way and sought to influence Siegfried Wagner. When Strauss heard that Levi would conduct *Parsifal* again in 1892 he wrote to Cosima:

> Indeed, the Jews have come a long way among us. Poor *Parsifal* will never escape the Jewish torture chamber; why must the poor piece suffer for Levi's merits?[89]

Levi was too sensitive not to have known that such things were being said. And yet he did not have the strength to turn his back on Bayreuth once and for all, just as he had not been able to do so after Wagner profoundly insulted him in 1881. Like most of the Jewish artists of his time, Levi wanted to belong. He wanted to be fully accepted as he was, or sent away, released. Since that did not happen, he felt stuck. He stayed in his place and suffered a wound that broke open, again and again. It was as incurable as the wound of Amfortas: healed only by death.

Cosima was well aware of it. She knew how to treat her afflicted Major to keep him where she wanted him. At the year's end of 1891, she assured him that she could never repay him for all that he had done for her. In February 1892 she invited him to meet her in Nuremberg and when he spontaneously agreed, she cried out "Major, you're simply charming!"[90] Another time she quoted a friend as having said that for years she had not encountered any man as witty and kind as Hermann Levi.

Levi felt ready to direct the eight performances of *Parsifal* scheduled for the festival of 1892. He felt that he had learned a lesson from the previous year. Cosima might exclaim: "O Bottom, thou art changed!" Nonetheless, she did take precautionary measures, should Levi drop out: she asked Richard Strauss to be prepared to take over *Tristan*, if Mottl would have to take over *Parsifal*.[91] But Levi managed all of the performances without an incident.

On his way home, he had a remarkable conversation with Houston Stewart Chamberlain. The latter tells us that when he got to the train station he found Levi sleeping on a bench—he had fallen asleep reading something by Martin Luther and missed the night train. They traveled, then, together and debated. Chamberlain was one of the most stalwart followers of Richard Wagner. He attended the festival regularly and had known Cosima for a long time. In his second marriage, in 1908, he married Eva Wagner. Levi was familiar with him from fleeting encounters, was interested in his writing, and sought his favor. He once asked Cosima to praise him when she saw Chamberlain: he would like to get to know the man. Before the train even left the station, Levi asked Chamberlain what he thought that the final words of *Parsifal* meant: *Salvation to the Savior*. Chamberlain had no answer and could not come up with one immediately, so Levi answered the question himself: the grail is a symbol of the Savior; the knights that knew nothing of *Parsifal* were glad to finally get food and drink instead of fodder. Chamberlain certainly would have found a better explanation, but apparently at that moment he was disinclined to contradict the director of *Parsifal*.

Another crisis soon flared up between Levi and Cosima, caused by Oskar Merz, the royal Bavarian director of music and a music critic in Munich. As of 1882 he had assisted in Bayreuth. He was a cofounder of the "Order of the Holy Grail," an association of fanatic anti-Semitic Wagner enthusiasts. In early 1894 Levi told Cosima that because of Merz's anti-Semitism, he could no longer work with him in Bayreuth. When Cosima refused to fire Merz, Levi immediately asked to be dismissed:

> I had hoped that you would fulfill the only wish I have ever expressed since I began working for you. That you cannot comply is just as symptomatic as the other spotlights you focus on my character and my behavior and that taken together with other more recent experiences assure me that you only still tolerate me for the very same reason that you believe you cannot dismiss Mr. Merz, namely, for the simple reason that we were given the work in 1882. . . . Three years ago I stood at this same crossroad. And you called out "don't abandon me!" and those few words sufficed to make me reverse a decision that was already very firm. Today . . . I see no other option but to implore you to release me from your circle, where I will always only be a stranger, an intruder. I cannot imagine that my release would truly endanger the festival. If that should be the case, I would not retreat from the cause that is greater than you and me both. . . . God bless you and your works![92]

In light of these often repeated requests for release, one wonders what answer Levi actually expected. Did he want to hear that he was irreplaceable? If he were, he could justify to himself the fact of staying on. Certainly his love for

Richard Wagner, for Wagner's works, and the Wagner family at Wahnfried was more intimate than any other relationship he entered during his entire lifetime. He could not ease himself from that grasp and was desperate for the other side to find a solution.

This time Cosima's reply was even harsher than before. She accused him of collaborating with Munich's theater superintendent Possart in staging a new production of *Lohengrin*. And she said that she had many Jewish coworkers already signed up for the next festival. And then:

> Despite all our differences of opinion and ways, I will always remember that you have been chosen. We shall find some way for you to participate this summer, such that you need not suffer.[93]

In a reply letter, Levi once again summarized all of his reasons and apologized for doing so in writing, but in conversation she was simply more persuasive than he:

> I believe that the whole thing boils down to one issue: I am a Jew. And since at and around Villa Wahnfried it has become a dogma that a Jew looks this way and thinks and acts that way, and especially that no Jew is capable of selfless devotion, my words and deeds are constantly judged from that perspective. . . . Before me lies a copy of a letter I sent in 1881, in which I urged you, implored you to release me from my appointment to conduct *Parsifal* for the very fact that I am a Jew. And when I today reflect all that has happened in the past twelve years, and today repeat my urgent desire, it seems to me as if finally an untenable, unnatural relationship can be brought to an end that is favorable for both parties. And thus I request once more, esteemed Madam: Let me go!—Only one consideration could make me stay, namely the thought that my absence would, in some way, be detrimental to the festival. But that is not the case. . . . If Siegfried were to direct *Parsifal*, I would gladly be willing (if necessary) to support him during rehearsals, and in doing so to hand over *Parsifal* to him during my lifetime. That would seem the most beautiful end to my twelve years of misery and joy in Bayreuth.[94]

Cosima knew that she could not persuade Levi by mail, so she came to Munich and invited him to a guest performance by Eleonora Duse. We can only surmise what they discussed that evening and the next day. Levi, at any rate, immediately wrote to Cosima that he would like to always remember that beautiful afternoon. Cosima had moved her Major to change his mind again.

And thus Levi came to Bayreuth for one last time in 1894 to conduct *Parsifal*. Richard Strauss directed *Tristan*, and Felix Mottl took over *Lohengrin*. That year George Bernard Shaw was among the guests at the opening night of *Parsifal*. Under the pseudonym "Corno di Bassetto," he wrote a crushing review for London's journal the *World*. In a later conversation with Hermann Levi, he criticized the singers' talents, particularly that of Karl Grengg, who sang the part of Gurnemanz. Levi replied that Grengg's bass voice was the best in Germany and challenged Shaw to find a better one. Shaw offered to sing the part himself, and Levi thought he was crazy.[95]

During the festival year of 1894, Levi witnessed Siegfried Wagner's debut as a conductor at a concert in the Bayreuth Opera House. A letter from Levi's father, Rabbi Benedict Levi, to Cosima Wagner reveals how satisfying that event was for Hermann Levi. Benedict Levi had been to the very first viewing of *Parsifal* in Bayreuth and had been received by Richard and Cosima Wagner at their home. Without his son's knowledge and with the explicit request to Cosima not to mention it to Hermann, Benedict wrote:

> If I may measure your motherly sentiments by my fatherly ones, it may comfort you to know what Hermann wrote me about Siegfried Wagner's debut as a conductor:
> "Siegfried Wagner's debut as a conductor was a big event here. I have the greatest admiration for him. His whole way of conducting expresses an important personality; the orchestra has no choice but to follow him, and I had the feeling that rehearsals were unnecessary; he conveys his intentions to the orchestra immediately, as if it were only his spontaneous nature, his energetic will that elicits performance. He has strength, drive, an ability to change the tempo at the right time, to highlight the essentials, to drop what can be omitted. And all of this with youthful high spirits and naivety, in a word: charming. Add to this the touching similarity he has with his father, and the fact that in 1872 the Master stood on the very same spot (in the opera house) conducting Beethoven's Symphony No. 9. I was deeply moved and when at the end he came to our loge (reserved for members of the Wagner family), and I embraced him, I had to hold back the tears."[96]

This touching document written by the hand of the aged rabbi, the story of how the former conductor of *Parsifal* honors the son and heir of Richard Wagner, closes the chapter of Hermann Levi's life in his role as the Major, a servant to the Mistress of Bayreuth. Cosima Wagner never had to dismiss him. In 1896 *Parsifal* was not shown because of extensive preparations for a new production of the *Ring*. And a year later, Levi was retired. He remained friends with the Wagner family, but only as a guest and supporter, without the burden of operative responsibility.

LITERARY AMBITION: MOZART AND GOETHE

> One can never discover soon enough that one is indispensable.
>
> —Levi's notes, taken from Goethe's *Wilhelm Meister*

In the spring of 1895, Levi was again in poor health. Throughout his life he had struggled with illness. As early as 1867, Max Bruch advised him to live sensibly and stop turning night to day. But Levi ignored all warnings, even Clara Schumann's advice. He worked incessantly, and made music, and socialized—with friends, at restaurants, and by inviting guests to his home. If things could not be finished during the day he worked through the night: studying new scores, writing innumerable letters, reading, and reading more. Conducting the works that were particularly important to him—initially orchestral works by Brahms and subsequently music drama by Wagner—ended in total fatigue. During his very first rehearsals for *Meistersinger* in Karlsruhe, dizziness caused him to interrupt work several times. Later in life his health forced him to take sick leave at least once every winter. When not conducting in Bayreuth, he spent most of the summer in the curative spas of Bad Cannstatt, Alexanderbad, and Wörishofen. Besides nervous disorders, he also suffered from chronic bronchitis. In the mid-1880s, he began to suffer from swollen knuckles that made piano playing and conducting difficult. A few years later, he complained of intense pain in his hands.

Although he felt weak, in early 1895 Levi took on a challenging and heavy workload. Besides delivering *Les Troyens* by Berlioz and beginning a cycle of Mozart performances at the Residence Theater with *Le nozze di Figaro*, he directed a premiere for *Fledermaus*. Hildebrand said of that evening that the whole audience was waltzing and even Wagner's success would pale in comparison. Levi invited Johann Strauss to conduct the Overture at the third performance, writing that Lenbach wanted very much to paint the composer's portrait. But the seventy-year-old "King of Waltzes" turned down the invitation for reasons of health.

At Easter time Levi traveled. Edouard Colonne had engaged him to guest conduct two concerts featuring pieces from *Tristan* and *Parsifal* at the Théâtre de l'Odéon in Paris, followed by a Wagner program on April 25 at London's Queens Hall. Entirely exhausted, Levi then went to the seaside resort of Bournemouth in the south of England for medical treatments. Attaching a note from his physician, he wrote to Possart asking for sick leave that he intended to take in Bournemouth. He returned from England in mid-May. Still not quite well, in Munich he conducted several performances of the new production of *Le nozze di Figaro*, the only opera besides *Tristan* for which he had reserved the performance rights for himself when he had brought in Richard Strauss.

A few days later, a tragic accident affected the whole city of Munich. It was to change Levi's entire future. While pulling up the blinds one morning, his friend Conrad Fiedler fell out the window and hit his head on a stone plinth below. He lay unconscious in the yard and died minutes later.

Although not in the best of health himself, as a close friend Levi felt responsible for Fiedler's widow Mary. He went with her to arrange the interment in Crostewitz and helped her organize Fiedler's affairs. The summer off-season had already begun and he had not yet fully recovered from the illness from spring; he was in no condition to resume conducting in Munich. And so he asked again for sick leave, this time for the remainder of the year 1895.

His symptoms became so much worse, especially the arthritis in his fingers, that he feared never being able to conduct again. On 1 January 1896, he received notice of his "tentative retirement for reasons of health."

Forced to rest, Levi preoccupied himself with translation. From French he translated the story of *Le procurateur de Judée* by Anatole France, and he began a new rendition of Mozart's *Don Giovanni* based on the Italian original. Since he could no longer conduct, he offered Cosima to assist in Bayreuth, but she did not take him up on it. He felt responsible for Wagner's works and festivals and the Bayreuth stipend fund. At his initiative, steel producer Krupp donated three thousand marks to the cause, but Levi was disappointed because he had expected 100,000.

In the spring of 1896, Mary Fiedler accompanied him on a vacation to Gries near Bolzano, Italy. From there they together went to Partenkirchen, where they planned to settle. Levi's physician in Partenkirchen, Dr. Bock, confirmed that because of his poor heath Levi was unable to return to his position in Munich. The director of the court theater in Munich confirmed his permanent status of retirement.

Richard Strauss, who had already taken over Levi's work in operas and concerts, was not given Levi's position. His progressive programs had raised eyebrows. In the fall of 1898, he became the prime conductor at the opera in Berlin. This left Franz von Fischer and newly hired Bernhard Stavenhagen, neither of whom could take Levi's place. In 1901 Hermann Zumpe, an important conductor, took up conducting at the National Theater, but he died two years later. Finally, after ten years of negotiating, in 1904 the Bavarian Court Theater won Felix Mottl for the position. He became Levi's true successor. With excellent performances of Mozart, Berlioz, and Wagner, Mottl heightened the musical initiatives of his friend and predecessor Levi to represent a glorious era in Munich's opera.

Freed of professional obligations, Levi could now plan for the future. On 1 October 1896, he married Conrad Fiedler's widow Mary. Their witness was Adolf von Gross from Bayreuth. At the age of twenty-two, Mary, a daughter of art historian Julius Meyer (director of the Art Gallery in Berlin from 1872 to 1890), had married Conrad Fiedler, who was half a generation older than herself. At the wish of Fiedler's young wife, the couple spent much of the year in Munich and their summers in Bayreuth. Thus Mary, who was a Wagner enthusiast, had already known Levi, whom she admired as a conductor, for years.

When Mary wed Levi one year after Fiedler's death, she was, at the age of forty-two, a very attractive, elegant woman, poised in society, and interested in many of the arts. Since her early youth Wagner had been one of her favorites; to now marry a conductor from Bayreuth, one who had gone in and out of the

Hermann Levi after retirement. Courtesy of Frithjof Haas.

Wagner home, was the greatest thing to which she could aspire. At the time they married, Levi was fifty-seven years old. He felt old and sick, as he often said. But with all his varied ambitions in the arts and philosophy he remained intellectually unbroken. Despite his constant ailments and need for care, for his youthful wife he remained a fascinating and intellectually stimulating companion.

After Conrad Fiedler's sudden death, a bond emerged between Mary and Hermann that had certainly already existed for a long time. Without hesitation Levi stood by Mary, helping her through the difficult time of widowhood even though he must have felt that he soon would be dependent on her.

Levi wrote Cosima that he and Mary were wed in a civil ceremony because after thorough deliberation they had come to the conclusion that for them it seemed "more honest" than being married in a church. And that he had "formally detached himself from Judaism"—to which he "had always felt estranged anyway." This was not being entirely honest. Despite long years of pressure from the Wagner family he had never before chosen to deny the faith of his fathers. He took that step now because by marrying a Gentile woman, in the eyes of Jewish orthodoxy he had now excluded himself. We do not know what Rabbi Levi, his aged father, thought of his son's late break with family tradition, nor whether he understood him on the delicate matter. Benedict Levi died in 1899 and no correspondence has survived from the last years of his life.

Through marriage Levi had become financially independent. Mary had inherited her late husband's huge estate that allowed her to lead a privileged life, to travel and stay at the best hotels. Shortly after marrying, the Levis bought a large piece of property on Riedberg Mountain in Partenkirchen, high above the center of the old village and with an open view to the surrounding mountains. Their friend Hildebrand designed a castle-like villa for them in classicist style. A local constructor was commissioned for the work and until it was completed the couple stayed first in Gries near Bolzano (for the winter of 1896–1897) and then with the Hildebrand family in Villa San Francesco in Florence.[97]

As Fiedler's wife, Mary had already been closely affiliated with the Hildebrand family. In the years before Conrad died, Levi, too, had been introduced into their circle of friends. When Hildebrand came to Munich alone, he often met Levi for evening conversation. They debated art issues on which their opinions greatly diverged. Richard Wagner was one of those topics. Hildebrand abhorred Wagner's musical dramas outright, just as he abhorred Schopenhauer's philosophy. For him, as a sculptor trained in classical form, music ended with Beethoven. He once articulated his stance in a letter to Levi:

> Wagner's art links emotion directly to the intellect and leaves nothing for the imagination, nothing for fantasy. That's why his music is (now, don't scream) for the general public, but not for people with artistic imagination. I am an enemy of conquerors and tyrannical natures in all intellectual areas. I reject it, while you enjoy it.[98]

Levi thought that Hildebrand "says the strangest things about Wagner" but it did not lessen his value as a friend. He admired Hildebrand and his sculpture: "May the officials and artists in Munich finally realize what they have in you."[99] Levi said that Hildebrand's essay "On Proportions in Architecture" had touched him like the "crystal clarity of a snowy landscape."[100]

While staying at Hildebrand's home at San Francesco, Levi was delighted to discover the musical talents of Hildebrand's daughters. He wrote for them an arrangement based on the slow movement of Beethoven's violin concerto using the clown's text from Shakespeare's *Twelfth Night, or What You Will:*

> Come away, come away death,
> And in sad cypress let me be laid.
> Fie away, fie away breath,
> I am slain by a fair cruel maid.

When the Levis departed, the four daughters stood on the terrace singing the song in farewell. It was an unforgettable moment for Levi that he cherished for the rest of his life.

In June 1898 the Levis moved into their home in Partenkirchen. Cosima received a sketch of the house explaining the three guest rooms: one for Siegfried, one for Eva and Isolde, and one for herself. They would not really consider it their home until Cosima had paid them the honor of a visit. Levi also wrote to the mayor of Partenkirchen, expressing his will to work for the renown and good of the town.

The Levis had interesting neighbors: Adolf Stoecker, pastor to the court in Berlin, and writer Walter Siegfried. Stoecker's notorious anti-Semitism seemed not to bother Levi. On the contrary, Levi hoped for interesting talks with him. But the two never became close. Walter Siegfried,[101] who used to visit Paul Heyse, knew Levi from Munich. The Levis and the Siegfrieds often spent time together, sometimes reading classical literature together in the late afternoon.

In Partenkirchen Levi set to work translating Mozart's libretti. He had been able to stage his own rendition of *Figaro*. His renditions of *Don Giovanni* and *Così fan tutte* were staged by Richard Strauss. In a lecture given by Possart on the occasion of the premiere of *Don Giovanni*, he explained the new ideas that guided him and Levi in setting up their cycle of Mozart performances. These were later printed as a brochure.[102] The central idea was that "the person on the stage has an effect on the person in the audience." This meant that certain things needing changing: 1) All renditions and new productions were to be based on the original score and the original text. All modifications and abridgments that had become common were to be eliminated. Renditions were expected to reflect the Italian text and the melody of the Italian language as much as possible. 2) Performances were moved to the Residence Theater. The small hall there allowed working with a smaller orchestra that more correctly rendered the sound intended by Mozart. The actors' facial expressions could be seen clearly from every seat in the auditorium. 3) A newly installed revolving stage was to enable quick scene changes in sequence. Possart supported Levi's new text for *Don Giovanni*. In an introduction for it he wrote:

> Some of our older, loyal theater-goers will say to one another that they liked it better when everyone sang "and when the champagne makes us dizzy" and "My

Governor, mounted, I bow to the ground." That's what their grandfathers sang to them, and now it's all different. They'll say it is not the "Don Juan" they know.— And of course, it's not the "Don Juan" they know; it's Mozart's *Don Giovanni*. After one hundred years, to see it restored to its original authenticity and clarity is truly an end worthy of our best efforts.[103]

By working together on new renditions of Mozart's operas, Possart and Levi got to know one another better and the tension between them subsided. Possart visited the Levis in Partenkirchen and was thrilled by their gorgeous home. He wrote a ditty about their luxurious bathroom titled "On Visiting It on Tuesday at 8 a.m." The last lines go:

> A polished throne! The softest paper,
> The whole room soothes like paradise.
> Electric light! A small warm heater;
> All made to let your metabolism rise.
> And then the view of woods that roll,
> Seen from the seat of a toilette bowl!
> A sight to make intestines swell,
> O Hildebrand, you did that well.
> I'd gladly give one hundred villas,
> For what this little chamber has.[104]

Levi kept up on how rehearsals for new Mozart productions were going in Munich. He advised Richard Strauss to take more time to study the parts with the singers instead of concentrating exclusively on the orchestra. His deep concern was the proper phonetic treatment of his latest rendition. Levi was idealistic about compensation. He turned his translations over to the opera in Munich gratis for all time. Royalties from other opera houses were to go to the Bayreuth Stipend Fund.

When in Munich, Hermann and Mary Levi stayed at their furnished apartment at 17 *Arcis Strasse*, particularly during the winter months when in town for the theater or concerts or to visit friends. Paul Heyse, Wilhelm Hertz, or Adolf von Hildebrand occasionally joined them there. Richard Strauss came once in a while to play skat.

Levi kept himself informed of new pieces for the opera stage, like premieres at the National Theater for *Sarema* by Alexander von Zemlinsky, *Königskinder* by Humperdinck, and *Theuerdank* by Ludwig Thuille. He familiarized himself with *Genesius* by Felix Weingartner and *Der Rubin* by Eugen d'Albert by reading the scores. The stage event that moved him most was the first production of Siegfried Wagner's debut opera *Der Bärenhäuter* (The Bear Skinner) on 22 January 1899. Levi had made an effort to see this work put on the season's program and had been to all orchestra rehearsals led by Franz von Fischer. When one passage particularly pleased him he turned to Siegfried sitting next to him and kissed him on the forehead. The opening night, attended by Cosima and prominent musicians from Munich, was considered a *succès d'estime* for the young composer. Levi tried to get other opera houses interested in it and took offense at Heyse's complaints about the libretto. After a repeat performance on April 30, conducted by Siegfried Wagner himself, the Levis hosted a party at their apartment on *Arcis Strasse*. Among the many guests were Houston Stewart Chamberlain, Ernst Possart, Wilhelm Hertz, and of course, Siegfried Wagner.

Levi wanted to understand Richard Strauss's new orchestral works *Also sprach Zarathustra* (Thus Spoke Zarathustra), *Heldenleben* (The Life of a Hero), and *Sinfonia domestica* (Domestic Symphony). He had performed many of the early works of the son of his solo horn player. But he now realized that he could no longer follow the bold development of the mature composer:

> I cannot grasp Strauss's musical constructions with my inner ear; neither its rhythm nor its sound. I feel like Zelter must have felt about Beethoven and Weber, except that I'm not critical, I simply regret that I don't understand it.[105]

Levi sensed the genius of composer Strauss, but he could not comprehend the modernistic tendencies of his work.

Levi's impulse to understand what could be understood, to help where he could, and to enjoy serving others did not fail as he grew older. Now financial independence made him even more willing to help artists in need. As a young man he had borrowed money to buy paintings from little-known artist Anselm Feuerbach. Now he sent his old friend Julius Allgeyer 200 marks every month to write Feuerbach's biography. Brahms, too, donated a large sum to the cause.

At the age of sixty and in constant poor health, Levi devoted his leisure hours to Goethe. Since early youth he had enjoyed reading Goethe and owned a very large selection of his works; it was said that he owned the largest Goethe library around. He began compiling short narratives and tales found here and there within larger contexts of Goethe's prose, wrote a foreword to his collection, and offered it to the publisher Cotta in Stuttgart. Paul Heyse and Wilhelm Hertz gave him advice on difficult literary issues. Cosima, too, knew of Levi's plan to publish Goethe's stories, but she belittled her Major's literary ambitions, not knowing that toward the end of his life he would consider this work his intellectual legacy. In his letter to Cotta, Levi wrote: "I am old, my health is poor, and I would like to live to see the publication of the little book."[106]

Levi asked Hans Thoma, who shortly beforehand had designed a bookplate for him, for permission to use the latter's painting *Flight from Egypt* for the cover of his book of tales by Goethe. With Thoma's approval, Levi had graphic design studio Hanfstaengl in Munich make a print of it. Another small book resulted from the same Goethe studies; using 365 quotations from Goethe, Levi made a calendar for the year 1900 and gave it to Cosima for Christmas.

244   *Chapter Four*

Brahms's biographer, Max Kalbeck, asked Levi for details on dates and experiences that he had shared with Brahms. It reminded Levi once more of that lost friendship. In order to fill in some of the missing information, Levi contacted Countesse Anna von Hessen, who had often made music with Brahms in Baden-Baden. In reply, she asked him for his thoughts on Brahms. Without hesitation Levi wrote:

> Unfortunately I cannot compete with the loyalty with which you have preserved the ideals of your youth. My artistic development took me in an entirely different direction. Looking back now, I see my relationship with Brahms—which at one point was very intimate—as merely one station. When the transition occurred—under the tremendous impression that *Tristan* and *Meistersinger* made on me—my personal dealings with Brahms naturally came to an end. We went our separate ways around the year 1877, without discussing it, without a quarrel, simply in the knowledge that we no longer had anything to say to one another. And after that, I never saw him again.[107]

In mid-February Mary and Hermann Levi spent three days in Bayreuth celebrating Eva Wagner's twenty-third birthday. It was Levi's last visit to Villa Wahnfried, where he had come for the first time twenty-seven years ago. At the end of March, Levi participated in a gala evening for the dedication of the newly renovated House of Artists. One of Munich's chroniclers recalls Levi's last public appearance: "Tormented by pain, though he did look cheerful, he left the glamorous hall with his wife in the middle of festivities."[108]

In early April a serious kidney dysfunction kept Levi in bed. Mary wrote his correspondence regarding the printing of the Goethe tales. He read the first page proofs. When he felt the end nearing, he asked that Cosima visit him. But she was ill in Florence and could not fulfill her dying "Major's" last wish. On one of his last days, Levi told Mary that he had read sufficient Wagner and Schopenhauer to die in peace. On the morning of 13 May 1900, he died quietly in his apartment in Munich. His friend Hildebrand said: "His head looked beautiful, like a transfigured image of Christ."[109]

Levi was interred temporarily at Munich's East Cemetery in the family plot of his parents-in-law. Later Mary had a mausoleum erected on their property in Partenkirchen and Hermann's remains brought there. Hildebrand designed the slab. Years later Nazis destroyed the tomb and it was never reconstructed.[110]

Walter Siegfried handled the publication of Levi's book of tales and narratives by Goethe. Mary wrote a personal note and sent the little book to all of the couple's relatives and friends.

From among the many obituaries that appeared, two seem to have captured Levi's character the most clearly. Superintendent Ernst Possart published a series of articles in the *Allgemeine Zeitung*. These were later printed as a brochure

Conductor Hermann Levi by Adolf von Hildebrand, plaster cast tondo based on Levi's death mask, 1900. Bayerische Staatsgemäldesammlungen, Neue Pinakothek, Munich, inv. no. B 522.

with a dedication by Mary Levi. Possart's heartfelt words reflect his esteem for his friend and colleague:

> Hermann Levi's stimulating nature, his fascinating personality, had an irresistible effect on everyone who knew him only fleetingly. But whoever got to know him as a friend and looked deep into his bright brown eyes, would never again forget their captivating charm.[111]

At Cosima's request, Houston Stewart Chamberlain wrote words of appreciation for the *Bayreuther Blätter*. Later this appraisal was included in his book *Race and Personality*, where he tried to explain Levi's personality as resulting from a tension between his Jewish origins and his desire for assimilation, claiming that the figure of Hermann Levi provides a key to one of the highly complex general phenomena of the times:

> Levi's relationship to Wagner by no means exhausts our interest in him; it was only the pinnacle of one person's life whose every effort was meant to assimilate German culture and make it his own, true possession, indeed, to be absorbed by it, to blend with it. Levi was one of those who know no limit to generosity. . . . What was unique about his life was endless ambition and quest.[112]

And Cosima finished the thought: "His lot was to stray and search, and death was the place of his grail, his ultimate end."[113]

Hermann Levi, searching and straying, was an example of the selfless, dedicated artist. Just as his forefathers had devoted themselves to service in the temple, he devoted himself to music and the masters that he acknowledged and revered, above all, Johannes Brahms and Richard Wagner. For Levi that service meant to be entirely absorbed in the composer's work, to surrender his own ego to the point of extinction. The destiny that followed for him was one of infinite happiness, but also of endless agony. To truly grasp his happiness, but even more so to understand his ability to endure humiliation, is to really understand Hermann Levi.

NOTES

1. Leviana, letter to Adolf von Gross dated 7 March 1883.
2. Hermann Levi's letter to his father dated 13 April 1882, printed in the program for *Parsifal*, Bayreuth Festival, 1959. (See also chapter 3, note 105.)
3. Julius Kniese, *Der Kampf zweier Welten um das Bayreuther Erbe* (Leipzig, 1931), 69 and 71.
4. See note 2 above.
5. *Engelbert Humperdinck: Briefe und Tagebücher*, vol. 3, in *Beiträge zur Rheinischen Musikgeschichte*, no. 123 (Berlin/Kassel, 1983), 38.
6. See note 2 above.
7. See note 3 above, page 25, letter dated 17 May 1885.
8. Leviana; Levi's own hand copy of his letter to Kniese dated 27 July 1885.
9. Engelbert Humperdinck's letter to Hans von Wolzogen, in *Engelbert Humperdinck: Briefe und Tagebücher*, vol. 3, in *Beiträge zur Rheinischen Musikgeschichte*, no. 123 (Berlin/Kassel, 1983), 37.
10. Mack, 37f. Cosima's critical notes on the music were very precise, for example: "kettle drums, p. 61, measures 1 and 2: somewhat too slow (Act One). The trio accompaniment at 'sehend in Todesschmachten' is not very clear (Act Two). The oboe and horns could be more delicate at 'es dankt dann alle Kreatur' (Act Three)."

11. See note 38 below.

12. The articles were published in the *Bayerische Landeszeitung*. Later they were combined and printed as a brochure. Paul Warneck, *Ungeschminkte Briefe über das Münchener Hoftheater* (Munich, 1882).

13. Otto Julius Bierbaum, ed., *25 Jahre Münchener Hoftheater-Geschichte, ein Rückblick auf die 25 jährige Amtsführung des Freiherrn Karl von Perfall als Leiter der Münchner Hofbühnen* (Munich, 1892). The statistics for the number of staged performances per composer are headed by Wagner (731), Mozart (237), Lortzing (208), Weber (202), Verdi (168), and Auber (164).

14. Leviana. See chapter 2, note 44.

15. *NZfM* 52, no. 44, 30 October 1885. Alexander Ritter was born on 7 June 1833 in Narva (Estonia) and died on 12 April 1896 in Munich. In Weimar he was second concertmaster under Franz Liszt; in 1882 he joined the Meiningen Court Orchestra directed by Hans von Bülow. He belonged to the circle called the New-German musicians. His anti-Semitic attitude strongly influenced young Richard Strauss.

16. Carl Maria Cornelius, *Peter Cornelius* (Regensburg, 1925), 2:238.

17. Eugen Gura (1842–1906) studied with Franz Hauser in Munich and debuted in 1865 at the Bavarian Court Theater, moving on for roles in Breslau, Leipzig, and Hamburg but returning to Munich where he sang for the opera from 1886 to 1892. In Bayreuth he sang the parts of Donner and Gunther (in 1876), Amfortas (in 1886), and King Marke and Hans Sachs (from 1889 to 1892). He was also successful as a singer of lieder.

18. Stabi, Felix Mottl estate, letter dated 22 October 1885.

19. "Dir bleibt ein Erdenrest von Lachners Zeit zu tragen" means "you are not yet a perfect angel." *Erdenrest* is from Goethe's "The more perfect angels" (Die vollendeteren Engel) from *Faust II*: Uns bleibt ein Erdenrest / Zu tragen peinlich, / Und wär er von Asbest, / Er ist nicht reinlich." Johann Wolfgang von Goethe, *Faust II*, verse 11954. The angels are anguished to be soiled by a trace of earth, because even if it were asbestos (considered a wondrous fireproof element in antiquity), it would be impure.

20. Stabi, Felix Mottl estate, letter dated 10 February 1900.

21. *Süddeutsche Monatshefte* 1, no. 2 (July–December 1904): 697. (Munich/Leipzig).

22. *Münchner Neueste Nachrichten* 44, no. 183, 23 April 1891.

23. Mack, 233.

24. Alexander Berrsche, *Trösterin Musika* (Munich, 1942), 270.

25. Leviana, letter dated 30 November 1884.

26. Quoted from August Göllerich in *Anton Bruckner*, edited by Max Auer (Regensburg, 1936), vol. 4, part 2, 206f. Bruckner's letters to Levi can also be found in Franz Gräflinger, *Anton Bruckner. Leben und Schaffen* (Berlin, 1927), 319f.

27. Conrad Fiedler (1841–1895), philosopher of aesthetics, outstanding art collector. Financially independent due to a considerable inheritance, Fiedler sponsored many artists, including Hans von Marées. In 1876 he married Mary Meyer, who later married Hermann Levi. After 1880 he lived in Munich and occasionally at the manor Crostewitz near Leipzig.

28. Hildebrand, 280.

29. Friedrich Eckstein (1861–1939), philosopher, mathematician, chemist, and lover of music. In his memoirs Eckstein wrote a detailed story of his trip to Munich with his

former teacher, Anton Bruckner. See Friedrich Eckstein, *Alte unnennbare Tage* (Vienna 1936, reprint Vienna, 1988).

30. *Süddeutsche Presse* and *Münchner Neueste Nachrichten*, as quoted by Heinrich Bihrle, *Die musikalische Akademie München (1811–1911)*, Festschrift for the academy's one hundredth anniversary, Munich 1911.

31. August Göllerich, in *Anton Bruckner*, vol. 4, part 2, 284f.
32. August Göllerich, in *Anton Bruckner*, vol. 4, part 2, 486.
33. August Göllerich, in *Anton Bruckner*, vol. 4, part 2, 558.
34. August Göllerich, in *Anton Bruckner*, vol. 4, part 2, 558f.
35. Leviana, letter dated 7 October 1887.
36. August Göllerich, in *Anton Bruckner*, vol. 4, part 2, 563.
37. August Göllerich, in *Anton Bruckner*, vol. 4, part 3, 81.
38. August Göllerich, in *Anton Bruckner*, vol. 4, part 2, 181.
39. August Göllerich, in *Anton Bruckner*, vol. 4, part 2, 311.
40. *Münchner Neueste Nachrichten*, 5 February 1893.
41. *Hans von Bülow: Ausgewählte Briefe* (Leipzig, 1919), 562, letter to Eugen Spitzweg dated 2 April 1893.
42. See Alfred von Mensi-Klarbach, *Alt-Münchner Theater-Erinnerungen* (Munich, 1924), 27f.
43. Ernst von Possart, *Hermann Levi: Erinnerungen* (Munich, 1901), 36f.
44. Leviana, letter dated 18 January 1893.
45. On 27 May 1893, at the second concert of the composer's festival, Levi conducted the original versions of the "March" and the "Tale of the Grail" from *Lohengrin* by Richard Wagner, and the Adagio from Anton Bruckner's Symphony no. 7.
46. Lily Dressler (1857–1927) belonged to the troupe at the Bavarian Court Theater starting in 1883; her specialty was lyrical drama. She sang Pamina, Santuzza, Elsa, Elisabeth, Evchen, and many other roles, including Evchen and one of the Flower Girls in Bayreuth in 1889.
47. Hanna (Johanna) Borchers, born 1869 in Wiesbaden, died 1961 in Garmisch. From 1889 to 1900 she was a lyrical soubrette for the Bavarian Court Theater, singing, among other things, Cherubin, Zerline, Papagena, and Marie (Zar). In 1888 she was one of the Flower Girls in Bayreuth. She later married publisher A. Bruckmann from Munich.
48. Oskar Merz wrote for the *Münchner Neueste Nachrichten*. Richard Strauss's letter can be found in the Humperdinck Archive of the Library of the City and University of Frankfurt/Main. Letter dated 18 December 1893.
49. See note 48, letter dated 28 October 1894. The archive also has a handwritten copy of the score made by the composer with correction marks that are identical to suggestions that Levi made.
50. Léo Delibes, born 21 February 1836 in St.-Germain-du-Val, died 16 January 1891 in Paris. He was a pupil of Adam and Benoist. In 1881 he became professor for composition at the conservatory in Paris. He wrote two ballets: *Coppélia* (1870) and *Sylvia* (1876); his most successful opera was *Lakmé* (1883).
51. André Messager, born 30 December 1853 in Montluçon, died 24 February 1929 in Paris. He was instructed by Saint-Saëns and Fauré, began as a church organist, and was later the successful conductor of the Opéra Comique in Paris and at Covent Garden in London. In Paris he directed Wagner's works for the stage and was the first to deliver

Debussy's *Pélléas et Mélisande*. Messager wrote numerous operas, operettas, ballets, and pantomimes.

52. Emmanuel Chabrier, born 18 January 1841 in Ambert, died 13 September 1894 in Paris. Chabrier had studied law and was an autodidact at music; he had significant influence in shaping the style of musical impressionism. He wrote one operetta, *L'Etoile* (1883), two operas, *Gwendoline* (1866) and *Le roi malgré lui* (1889), and the orchestra rhapsody *España* (1883).

53. Milka Ternina (1863–1941) was from Croatia. She had played on stages in Leipzig, Graz, and Bremen before coming to Munich in 1890. At the Bavarian Court Theater, her métier was lyrical drama; she sang as Senta, Elisabeth, Leonore, and in other roles. In Bayreuth she sang the part of Kundry in 1899.

54. Otto Brucks (1854–1906) began as a trombonist in the opera orchestras of Vienna and Berlin. In 1890 he came from Dresden to the Bavarian Court Theater as a baritone, where he sang Holländer, Hans Sachs, and Wotan. In 1898 he married a daughter of Duke Ludwig of Bavaria and left the stage. For a short time he was director of the City Theater of Metz.

55. Stabi, Felix Mottl Archive, letter dated 3 December 1888.

56. Stabi, Felix Mottl Archive, letter dated 22 May 1889.

57. Stabi, Felix Mottl Archive, card dated 2 December 1889.

58. Hector Berlioz, *Memoiren* (Leipzig, 1905), 2:319.

59. Emanuela Frank (1868–1940), dramatic alto singer. Before coming to the Bavarian Court Theater in Munich in 1892 she had sung in Cologne, Cassel, and Dusseldorf. She sang, among other roles, those of Orpheus, Ortrud, Kundry, and Amneris.

60. Library of the City of Munich, letter dated 12 March 1894.

61. Leviana, letter dated 19 June 1893.

62. A German card game for three persons played with thirty-two cards, sevens through aces.

63. In German stressing the second syllable indicates the military rank of a lower staff officer, while stressing the first syllable indicates the comparative form of Latin *magnus*, namely, *maior*, or being greater in importance.

64. Hermann Levi's letter to his father dated 14 July 1886. See chapter 3, note 105.

65. Leviana, letter dated 3 September 1878.

66. Mack, 69.

67. Leviana, letter dated 15 January 1887.

68. Dr.med. Ernst Schweninger, born 15 June 1850 in Freystadt (Upper Palatinate), died 13 January 1924 in Munich. Schweninger was professor for dermatology and became known for his diet and water cure treatments. As of 1881, he was Bismarck's physician. Levi took several treatments with him, and through Levi Cosima Wagner also became one of Schweninger's patients.

69. Mack, 120f.

70. Mack, 785.

71. Leviana, letter dated 8 August 1887.

72. Adolf von Hildebrand, born 6 October 1849 in Marburg, died 18 January 1921 in Munich. Hildebrand was a renowned sculptor and created, among other artworks, a relief of Bismarck in Jena (1894), the Wittelsbach Fountain in Munich (1895), and busts of Conrad Fiedler, Arnold Böcklin, Cosima Wagner, Clara Schumann, Elonora Duse, and

Hermann Levi. As of the mid-1880s he and Levi were friends. Levi gave Hildebrand's daughter Eva piano lessons, Hildebrand designed the architectural plan for Levi's house in Partenkirchen. In 1904 Hildebrand rose to the status of nobility.

73. Mack, 137f.
74. Kurt Blaukopf, *Gustav Mahler, sein Leben, sein Werk und seine Welt in zeitgenössischen Bildern und Texten* (Vienna, 1976), 179.
75. Mack, 142.
76. Leviana, letter dated 17 March 1888.
77. Leviana, letter dated 25 June 1888.
78. *Nord und Süd, Eine deutsche Monatsschrift*, vol. 49, edited by Paul Lindau (Breslau, 1889), 81f.
79. Dietrich Mack, *Von der Christianisierung des Parsifal in Bayreuth*, a letter from Felix Weingartner to Hermann Levi, in *Neue Zeitschrift für Musik*, October 1969, 467f.
80. Mack, Cosima Wagner's letter to Mary Fiedler, 158.
81. Leviana, letter dated 31 December 1888.
82. Leviana, letter dated 20 January 1889.
83. Leviana, letter dated 20 January 1889. In his letter to Cosima Wagner, Levi describes young Gustav Mahler as having "a boisterous, gnarly and yet very amiable nature."
84. Hermann Levi's letter to his father dated 23 July 1889, National Archive in Bayreuth.
85. Hildebrand, 327f. Elisabeth von Herzogenberg's letter to Adolf and Irene von Hildebrand, dated 7 August 1889. Elisabeth von Herzogenberg, née Stockhausen, married composer Heinrich von Herzogenberg. At the age of sixteen she had been a pupil of Brahms and she remained one of his most loyal admirers for the rest of her life. The remark about Ribera's saints refers to Spanish artist Jusepe de Ribera (1591–1652), who painted saints with eyes gazing upward in ecstasy.
86. Leviana, letter dated 30 August 1891, quoted by Egon Voss, *Die Dirigenten der Bayreuther Festspiele* (Regensburg, 1976), 22f.
87. See note 82 above, letter dated 15 September 1891.
88. Mack, 261.
89. *Briefwechsel Cosima Wagner—Richard Strauss* (Tutzing, 1978), 108.
90. Leviana, letter dated 20 February 1892.
91. Richard Strauss, who that year assisted Hans Richter in preparing *Meistersinger* and was scheduled to conduct the two final performances, eventually canceled because of illness.
92. Leviana, letter dated 15 January 1894.
93. Leviana, letter dated 23 January 1894.
94. Leviana, letter dated 22 May 1894.
95. George Bernard Shaw, *Musik in London* (Frankfurt, 1964), 148f. Shaw grew up influenced by his mother's vocal teacher, George J. V. Lee, who was a passionate advocate of bel canto.
96. National Archive in Bayreuth, letter from Benedict Levi to Cosima Wagner, dated 7 August 1894.
97. In 1873 Hildebrand had purchased the buildings of the former monastery San Francesco near Porta Romana on Bello Sguardo in Florence and set up an atelier for

himself and Hans von Marées there. Later the Hildebrands and their children spent a large part of the year there. Their guests stayed in the little house called the "Villino," which had formerly been Marées's studio.

98. Hildebrand, 469f.
99. Hildebrand, 470.
100. Hildebrand, 470.
101. Walter Siegfried (1858–1947) was from Zofingen, Switzerland. He knew Levi as of 1880. Siegfried wrote novels and novellas, dealing mainly with psychological problems: *Tino Moralt* (1890), *Fermont* (1893), *Tag- und Nachtstücke* (1922).
102. Ernst Possart, *Über die Neueinstudierung und Neuinszenierung des Mozart'schen Don Giovanni auf dem Kgl. Residenztheater zu München*, (Munich, 1896).
103. See note 99 above, 35–36.
104. Leviana, Possart's poem dated 26 July 1898.
105. Leviana, letter from November 1899.
106. DLA, Levi's letter to Cotta-Verlag dated 30 December 1899.
107. Levi's reply to landgravine Anna von Hessen dated 25 June 1899; Kurhessische Hausstiftung Schloss Fasanerie near Fulda.
108. Heinrich Bihrle, *Die Musikalische Akademie München 1811–1911* (Munich: Festschrift, 1911), 125.
109. Hildebrand, 75.
110. The tomb slab made by Hildebrand included a portrait of Levi in relief. It is shown in Sigrid Esche-Braunfels, *Adolf von Hildebrand* (Berlin, 1993), 397, fig. no. 631.
111. *Allgemeine Zeitung* 15–20, October 1901. The series was published as a brochure by C. H. Beck'sche Verlagsbuchhundlung (Munich 1901), 41. See also Ernst von Possart, *Hermann Levi: Erinnerungen* (Munich, 1901).
112. Houston Stewart Chamberlain, "Hermann Levi," in *Rasse und Persönlichkeit* (Munich, 1934), 92f.
113. Mack, 530.

Epilogue
Levi's Religion

> Thus non-being is decidedly preferable to being: at the end of his life a man would hardly honestly want to experience it again.
>
> —Schopenhauer

From his deathbed, Hermann Levi sent a last message to Cosima Wagner: he would die well, he said, because he had read enough Wagner and Schopenhauer.

As he once told Brahms, at the age of twenty-six, when already the conductor for the Court of Baden, Levi had had a profoundly religious experience while visiting the cathedral in Cologne. At dusk he had entered the cathedral and listened spellbound for an hour to the prayers of a young priest. He might have committed himself to the priest, if only the latter had approached him.

Ever since that experience, Levi felt magically drawn in whenever he walked past open church doors. Twenty-five years later, while staying in Wörishofen with Pastor Kneipp to rest, he told Cosima Wagner of a "backslide into things Roman, the priest's mild eyes, May devotions, the nuns that sang so wonderfully, the transfigured faces of praying individuals, my apartment near the graveyard between the church and the monastery."[1]

For most of his life, Levi pondered converting to Christianity. Yet the most crushing pressure from his surroundings, ultimately even marriage with a Gentile woman, could not move him to deny the religion of his forefathers.

His parents and grandparents had welcomed measures taken under Napoleon to integrate Jews as full-fledged French citizens and to the east of the Rhine, too, assimilation had made quick progress. Jews began to identify themselves with their countries; some even became ardent nationalists. They laid aside outward signs of Jewry, gave up rituals of costume and meals, and wanted to be like all other citizens. For many the desire for complete assimilation led to religious conversion, as was the case for Heinrich Heine, Mendelssohn, and Joseph Joachim.

When Levi came to Bayreuth to conduct *Parsifal*, a new anti-Jewish movement had begun to spread throughout the German Reich. For a long time, he forced himself not to see it. And yet, as the conductor of what Wagner called his "stage consecration play," *Parsifal*, Levi experienced hostility of the worst kind. He might have put up with it, if he had not ultimately come to believe that members of the Wagner family and all the people around them felt the same. That triggered numerous crises, until—in the end—Levi resigned to his fate.

Wagner urged his conductor for *Parsifal* to convert; he wanted to take communion with Levi and Cosima. But the more Wagner pressed, the more Levi withdrew. He had come to terms with the fact that he was and would remain a Jew. His unfulfilled desire to belong nevertheless found its expression in his musical rendition of Parsifal, a man that wanders about "having learned the truth through compassion." Even critics observed how strongly Levi identified with that work, especially with the prelude to act 3.

Levi sometimes made peculiar remarks on Jewry. He acknowledged, even admired Wagner's pamphlet "Judaism in Music." After conducting an opera by a Jewish composer, he once ran in despair from the court theater to meet Hans von Bülow at the Hofbräuhaus, shouting that he could no longer take such "mumbled music." Late in life he made a conscious effort to befriend stalwart anti-Semites such as Adolf Stoecker and Houston Stewart Chamberlain. Levi's occasional outbursts against all things Jewish and his obscure behavior toward what provoked that animosity can only be understood against the background of his desperate struggle, his attempt to bridge what he saw as an abyss: he often oscillated helplessly between loyalty to his orthodox, rabbinical forefathers and a basically narrow-minded Christian environment.

The anti-Semitism of the 1880s that was directed particularly against converted Jews especially distressed Levi. He probably realized that even after conversion, for many people around him, he would always remain a Jew.

Brahms had responded with a kind smile to the proud Jewish attitude that Levi had as a conductor. Brahms made him feel accepted. But after their quarrel in Munich, Brahms remained silent and out of reach.

Levi's bitter experience made him so insecure that at first gradually, and then evermore earnestly, he began to withdraw from the spotlight in Bayreuth. He hesitated time and again to do so because every so often, optimism got the upper hand. Perhaps it was Cosima's word, that he "must bear and tolerate it" that held him back. He did not find peace of mind until he had given up conducting and withdrawn from public sight.

Levi's desperate search found solace in Arthur Schopenhauer's writing on death and the indestructability of human life. Reading Schopenhauer made him feel at one with Richard Wagner. The philosopher's words comforted him and gave him the strength to live his life to the end in remarkable poise:

> And if suffering itself has such a healing power, the same will be even truer for what we fear more than all suffering, namely, death.[2]

Levi's joy at reading Schopenhauer was heightened by what Schopenhauer wrote about music. No one, he found, had said it better:

> The unspeakable intimacy of music that allows it to waft past us like a wholly familiar and yet so distant paradise, so clear and yet so inexplicable, flows from reflecting all of the instincts of our innermost being, but entirely beyond reality, and far from its torment.[3]

Thus in the last years of his life, Levi gave up conducting and began wrapping himself in Mozart's music and books by Schopenhauer and Goethe. Here there was no tension between Jew and Christian. Perhaps he grasped the biblical message of the Old and New Testament far ahead of his times. Fifty years later and after the Holocaust, Pope Johannes XXIII prayed:

> We know today that for many centuries we were blind, we did not see the beauty of Your chosen people, nor recognize Your face in the traits of our privileged brothers.

The features of "privileged brother" Hermann Levi prompted painter Franz Lenbach to use them for the faces of John the Baptist and Jesus of Nazareth. Thus in the end Levi's appearance reflected both the Old Testament and the Savior, as it were, a message to future generations to reconcile these two religious worlds.

NOTES

1. Leviana, letter dated 27 May 1889.
2. Arthur Schopenhauer, *Die Welt als Wille und Vorstellung*, edited by A. Hübscher, (Wiesbaden 1972), 2, part 2, fourth book, chapter 49, p. 746.
3. See note 2 above, vol. 2, part 1, third book, chapter 52, p. 331.

Appendix
Works by Hermann Levi

PUBLISHED WORKS

Op. 1: Concerto for the Pianoforte and Orchestra

Dedicated to Court Conductor Vincenz Lachner.
Published by J. Rieter-Biedermann, Winterthur/Leipzig, plate no. 186.
Written in 1858–1859, published in November 1861.
Editions: for the pianoforte, for two pianos.
First performance on 8 April 1860 in Mannheim, conducted by V. Lachner, soloist was Hermann Levi.

Op. 2: Six Songs for One Voice and Pianoforte Accompaniment

Dedicated to Wilhelmine Szarvady, née Clauss.

1. *Der Mond ist aufgegangen* (H. Heine)
2. *Verratene Liebe* (from modern Greek by A. v. Chamisso)
3. *Auf dem Rhein* (C. Immermann)
4. *Die Glocken läuten das Ostern ein* (A. Böttger)
5. *Allnächtlich im Träume seh' ich dich* (H. Heine)
6. *Der letzte Gruß* (H. v. Eichendorff)

Published by J. Rieter-Biedermann, Winterthur/Leipzig, plate no. 187.
Written prior to 1861, published in November 1861.
Song no. 6 was also published in English as "The Last Greeting" by Schirmer, New York.

No Opus Number: Drei Gedichte von Goethe for One Voice and Piano Accompaniment

Dedicated to Mary Levi.

1. *Wanderers Nachtlied*, for mezzo soprano
2. *Frühling übers Jahr*, for tenor
3. *Dämmrung senkte sich von oben*, for mezzo soprano

Published by Otto Halbreiter, Munich, plate no. 21.
Written in 1868, perhaps earlier; published in 1899.
Song no. 3 was written for Clara Schumann's forty-ninth birthday on 13 September 1868.

MANUSCRIPTS

Canon for Four Women: *O gieb vom weichen Pfühle träumend ein halb Gehör!*

Text by Johann Wolfgang von Goethe; Levi used only the first two of five verses.
Album Ferdinand Möhring, choir conductor and music director (1816–1887), in kind memory of Hermann Levi, Munich 1874 (as former music director for Saarbrücken), Deutsche Staatsbibliothek Berlin, S 2, p. 30. It is not known whether this canon was written specifically for F. Möhring, or perhaps earlier.

Canon for Four (per tonos): *Alle Blüthen müssen vergehn*

In memory of their past conductor. Munich, March '87, Hermann Levi.
  Text by Johann Wolfgang von Goethe from *Vier Jahreszeiten*, Fall no. 12. Twelve measures written for soprano, alto, tenor, and bass. In 1994 listed in the catalog of antiquarian Hans Schneider, Tutzing, as no. 338, apparently an album page for Ernst von Possart.

LOST WORKS

These works were presumably destroyed by the composer.

Sonata for Violin and Piano

First performed on 1 May 1857 at the Leipzig Conservatory: J. Naret-Koning violin, H. Levi piano.
Source: *Neue Zeitschrift für Musik* 46, no. 19 (6 May 1857): 205. Leipzig.

Symphony in Three Movements

First performed on 24 March at the Leipzig Conservatory, conducted by Hermann Levi.
Source: *Neue Zeitschrift für Musik* 48, no. 14 (2 April 1858): 154. Leipzig.
Songs:
Das zerbrochene Ringlein (Eichendorff). First performed on 21 March 1858 at the Leipzig Conservatory. B. Nuhr soprano, H. Levi piano; sung together with the other songs Verratene Liebe and Der letzte Gruß. Source: *Neue Zeitschrift für Musik* 48, no. 14 (2 April 1858): 153. Leipzig.
Die Lotosblume (Heine?). Performed on 27 April 1860 at a subscription concert in Saarbrücken together with Der letzte Gruß and Widmung by Robert Schumann. W. Wolff soprano, H. Levi piano. Source: Printed program. Stadtarchiv Saarbrücken. The program may erroneously list Levi as the composer; it was perhaps Die Lotosblume by R. Schumann.
Songs based on texts from Adalbert von Chamisso's "Tränen," presented to Friederike Ettlinger by H. Levi on the occasion of her marriage to M. Landmann, New York. Source: A. Ettlinger, in *Biographie Jahrbuch und Nekrologe*, vol. 5, Berlin, 1903.
Serenade for a choir of women; text by Goethe from *Claudine von Villa Bella*. Source: A. Ettlinger, in *Biographie Jahrbuch und Nekrologe*, vol. 5, Berlin, 1903.
Two songs: *Keck das Barett auf das Haupt gedrückt* and *Wenn in dem Frühling die Erde erwacht*. Performed on 26 March 1861 at the Saarbrücken casino. Source: Advertisement in the newspaper *Saarbrücker Zeitung*, 25 March 1861.

Two Quartets for Male Voices: *Frühlingsfahrt* (Eichendorff?) and Volkslied

Performed on 26 March 1861 at the Saarbrücken casino. Advertisement in the newspaper *Saarbrücker Zeitung*, 25 March 1861.

Psalm 24 for Two Choirs

Performed on 22 March 1862 at the third evening of the Musical Academy in Mannheim, directed by V. Lachner.
Source: Printed program, Stadtarchiv Mannheim; also mentioned in a letter from J. Rietz to H. Levi dated 6 November 1860.

Various Pieces

For worship services at the synagogues of Giessen and Mannheim, written prior to 1860.

Source: Josef Marx in *Mitteilungsblatt des Landesverbandes der israelitischen Religionsgemeinden Hessens* 5, no. 6 (1930): 3–4. Mainz.

EDITIONS

Theodor Gouvy, *Hymne et marche triomphale*, op. 35a

Grand orchestra written for four hands at the piano, Saarbrücken 1861. Ed. S. Richault, plate no. 13652, Paris 1861.

Johannes Brahms, *Schicksalslied*, op. 54

Piano arrangement by H. Levi (not mentioned on the print), revised by Brahms. N. Simrock, Berlin, December 1871.

Johannes Brahms, *Liebeslieder Walzer*, op. 54

Arrangement for voice and piano (two hands), by H. Levi. This version by Levi has not survived; see Margit L. McCorkle, *Thematisch-Bibliographisches Werkverzeichnis* (Munich, 1984), 216–217 and Brahms, vol. 7, 141ff.

Richard Wagner, *Die Feen*

Piano arrangement by H. Levi 1881–1887, sent to Cosima Wagner on 4 March 1887; see J. Deathridge, M. Geck, and E. Voss, *RWV, Werkverzeichnis der musikalischen Werke Richard Wagners und ihrer Quellen* (Mainz, 1986), 119. Published by K. Ferd. Heckel, Mannheim, June 1888, plate no. 2216.

Heinrich Marschner, *Sangeskönig Hiarne oder das Tyrsingschwert*

Arranged by H. Levi for the stage in Munich. First performed on 7 March 1883. Score copy: Stabi no. St. th. 835.

Peter Cornelius, *Der Barbier von Bagdad*

Edited by F. Mottl and H. Levi, Munich, 1885.
Published by C. F. Kahnt, Leipzig (the piano score does not name the editors).

Cyrill Kistler, *Eulenspiegel*

Comedy in two acts by A. von Kotzebue, condensed by H. Levi to one act. Würzburg, 1889.

Published by Verlag der musikalischen Tagesfragen. Bad Kissingen. Manuscript: Stabi.

Peter Cornelius, *Der Cid*

Edited by H. Levi (name not mentioned on the piano score).
Published by J. Aibl. Munich, 1891. Manuscript: Stabi.

W. A. Mozart: Fantasy for a Mechanical Organ, KV 608

Rewritten by H. Levi for a string quartet, 1897.
Published by Breitkopf & Härtel, chamber music library no. 693, score 1516. Leipzig, 1899.

Ludwig van Beethoven, *Komm herbei Tod*

Song based on verses for Feste from Shakespeare's *Twelfth Night, or What You Want*. Arranged by Levi for one voice and piano accompaniment based on the melody by Beethoven.
Published by O. Halbreiter, plate no. 20a. Munich, 1899.
H. Levi wrote this arrangement based on the second movement of Beethoven's violin concerto op. 61 for daughters of Adolf von Hildebrand.

OPERA TEXT TRANSLATIONS

Christoph W. Gluck, *Iphigenie auf Tauris*

New translation from the French original, done together with Otto Devrient. Manuscript: Karlsruhe 1871. The version written by Levi's hand has not been found; the copy is incomplete. Library of the Badische Staatstheater, Karlsruhe.

Charles Gounod, *Der Arzt wider Willen*

Comic opera based on the text by Molière. Translated from French. Munich, 1874–1875. Manuscript: Publisher Colombier, Paris. The handwritten version has not been found.

Emmanuel Chabrier: *Gwendoline*

Translated into German by Felix Vogt, retranslated by H. Levi. Manuscript: Bayerische Staatsbibliothek. Munich, 1890.

Hector Berlioz, *Les Troyens*

Die Trojaner. I. Die Zerstörung Trojas; II. Die Trojaner in Karthago.
Retranslated by H. Levi and Emma Klingenfeld for performance in Munich in 1895.
Piano score published by Breitkopf & Härtel no. 1842. Leipzig, circa 1900.

W. A. Mozart, *Le nozze di Figaro—Figaros Hochzeit*

The translation was in part revised, in part newly edited by H. Levi. Munich, 1895–1898.
Piano arrangement published by Breitkopf & Härtel, no. 205a/1716. Leipzig, 1899/1906. Text edited by O. Erhardt, Breitkopf & Härtel's Library of Texts, no. 260. Leipzig, 1899.

W. A. Mozart, *Don Giovanni—Der bestrafte Wüstling* or *Don Juan*

Translated into German by Grandaur, revised by H. Levi. Piano score by F. Wüllner and Th. Ackermann. Munich, 1897/1910. Published as of 1924 at Breitkopf & Härtel, Leipzig, as no. 2180.
Text book: Th. Ackermann, Munich, 1896. Breitkopf & Härtel's Library of Texts no. 428. Leipzig, 1924. Re-edited and provided with an introduction by G. Kruse in collaboration with W. Zentner. Published by Reclam. Stuttgart, 1950.

W. A. Mozart: *Così fan tutte—So machen's alle*

Translated into German by H. Levi based partially on a rendition by E. Devrient and C. Niese.
Piano score published by Breitkopf & Härtel, no. 1666. Leipzig, 1898.
Text book: Bruckmann, Munich, 1887. Breitkopf & Härtel's Library of Texts no. 118. Leipzig, 1914. Re-edited and given an introduction by G. R. Kruse and W. Zentner. Published by Reclam. Stuttgart, 1950/57.

LITERARY WORKS

Henry T. Buckle, *On Women's Influence on the Progress of Knowledge*

Translated into German by H. Levi, Karlsruhe, 1867. Hand copy by Mary Levi, Leviana I, 38.

Anatole France. Two Novellas Translated by H. Levi in 1895 as *Der Prokurator von Judäa* and *Der Gaukler von Notre Dame*

The latter appeared in Munich in the journal *Jugend* on 22 February 1896, no. 8.

J. W. v. Goethe, *Gesammelte Erzählungen und Märchen*

Edited and given a foreword by H. Levi. Published by Cotta. Stuttgart, 1900.

Gedanken aus Goethes Werken, Compiled by H. Levi

Published by F. Bruckmann. Munich, 1901.
Originally compiled by Levi as a Goethe Calendar for the year 1900 and given to Cosima Wagner. After Levi's death, Levi's widow Mary had the booklet published.

Gedanken aus Schillers Werken

Manuscript from 1899/1900, Leviana II, 2.

Max Bruch's letter to Hermann Levi

This letter, discussing Johannes Brahms's *Ein Deutsches Requiem*, is dated 9 January 1867 (pages 78 and 79 in chapter 2). Clara Schumann had played parts from a preliminary piano score that Brahms had sent to her for Christmas 1866. Source: Leviana I, 53. Here is a translation:

January 9
  On the afternoon of the 7th I spent wonderful hours with Mrs. Schumann. We went through the entire *Requiem* and I must say that I am impressed. It grasps the biblical story with incomparable force and depth. The passage "Siehe, ich künde Euch ein Geheimniß an," with [its modulation from E flat major to] D flat major, is gorgeous. The whole passage (I believe in piece 2 or 3), where the orchestra develops the motif in beautiful variety, while the solo bass weaves through it with mystical melody, is wonderful. The three-quarter chorus in C minor is colossal, brilliant, enthralling, and then followed immediately by the modulation in E minor!
  The E flat major chorus "Wie lieblich" is very nice and comes at just the right time. The beginning of the C minor piece "Denn wir haben hier keine bleibende Statt" is ingenious. Its harmony and rhythm express instability well. I find the passage "Wie sollt ich mich trösten" highly unique and significant. The awareness of one's own helplessness, the desperate quest for redemption, is very moving. Most of it can be sung by a good choir; although the fugue in D above the point d'orgue is horribly difficult and the exact opposite of choral music. I find (and Mrs. Schumann

agrees) some of it too long. If I ever have a *very* good choir and a very good orchestra, then the devil can get me if I do not get this *Deutsches Requiem* (which will have been published by then) performed. The title sounds pretty strange, but it suits the work and once again the composer is right.

I'll send you *Schön Ellen* in two weeks. By the way, I would like to have Salamis back again by the 18th.

Cordial Greetings from Your M. Bruch

Bibliography

MAIN SOURCES FOR SCORES AND LETTER AUTOGRAPHS BY HERMANN LEVI

Archiv der Hessischen Hausstiftung, Fasanerie b. Fulda
Badische Landesbibliothek Karlsruhe, Handschriftenabteilung
Bayerisches Hauptstaatsarchiv München: Handschriften Abteilung Leviana, Felix Mottl Archiv, Paul Heyse Archiv
Deutsches Literaturarchiv Marbach/Neckar
Generallandesarchiv Karlsruhe
Historisches Archiv der Stadt Köln
Nationalarchiv der Richard Wagner Stiftung Bayreuth
Robert Schumann Haus Zwickau
Staatsbibliothek zu Berlin, Preußischer Kulturbesitz, Musikabteilung
Stadt- und Universitätsbibliothek Frankfurt/Main, Handschriftenabteilung: Engelbert Humperdinck Archiv
Stadtbibliothek München, Handschriftenabteilung

LITERATURE ON HERMANN LEVI

Alvin, H., and R. Prieur. *Métronomie Experimentale, Paris-Bayreuth-Munich, Étude sur les mouvements*. Paris, 1895.
Chamberlain, Houston Stewart. "Hermann Levi." In *Rasse und Persönlichkeit*, by Houston Stewart Chamberlain. Munich, 1934.
Dellin, Martin Gregor, and Dietrich Mack, eds. *Cosima Wagner: Die Tagebücher*. 2 vols. Munich/Zurich, 1980.
Devrient, Eduard. *Aus seinen Tagebüchern*. 2 vols. Weimar, 1964.

Ettlinger, Anna. "Hermann Levi." In *Biographisches Jahrbuch und Deutscher Nekrolog*. Vol. 5. Berlin, 1903.
Fellinger, Imogen. "Hermann Levi." In *Neue Deutsche Biographie*. Vol. 14. Berlin, 1985.
Gay, Peter. *Freud, Jews, and Other Germans: Masters and Victims in Modernist Culture*. New York: Oxford University Press, 1978.
Glasenapp, Carl Friedrich. *Das Leben Richard Wagners*. Vol. 6. Leipzig, 1911.
Göllerich, August. *Anton Bruckner: Ein Lebens- und Schaffensbild*. Supplemented and edited by Max Auer. Vol. 4, 1–3. Regensburg, 1936.
Haas, Frithjof. "Johannes Brahms und Hermann Levi." In *Johannes Brahms in Baden-Baden und Karlsruhe*. Catalog for an exhibition at the Landesbibliothek Karlsruhe. Karlsruhe, 1983.
Hahn, Arthur. "Hermann Levi, ein Tonkünstlerportrait." *Nord und Süd* 71, no. 212 (November 1894). Breslau.
Kalbeck, Max. *Johannes Brahms*. 4 vols. Berlin, 1921. Reprint Tutzing, 1976, vol. 2/3.
Koelle (née Murjahn), Magdalene. *Erinnerungen*. Karlsruhe, 1882.
Litzmann, Berthold. *Clara Schumann, ein Künstlerleben nach Tagebüchern und Briefen*. 3 vols. Leipzig, 1910. Vol. 3, *Clara Schumann und ihre Freunde*. Reprint Hildesheim/New York, 1971.
Mack, Dietrich, ed. *Cosima Wagner: Das Zweite Leben: Briefe und Aufzeichnungen 1883–1930*. Munich/Zurich, 1980.
Mensi-Klarbach, Alfred. *Alt-Münchner Theater-Erinnerungen*. Munich, 1924.
Ordenstein, Heinrich. *Musikgeschichte der Haupt- und Residenzstadt Karlsruhe bis zum Jahre 1914*. Karlsruhe, 1915.
Possart, Ernst von. *Hermann Levi, Erinnerungen*. Munich, 1901.
Schall, Richard. "Hermann Levi." In *Musik in Geschichte und Gegenwart*. Vol. 8. Cassel, 1960.
Schmidt, Leopold, ed. "Johannes Brahms im Briefwechsel mit H. Levi, F. Gernsheim sowie den Familien Hecht und Fellinger." In *Brahms Briefwechsel*. Berlin, 1910. Reprint Tutzing, 1974.
Schumann, Eugenie. *Erinnerungen*. Stuttgart, 1927.
Siegfried, Walter. *Aus dem Bilderbuch eines Lebens*. 3 vols. Zurich/Leipzig, 1926.
Sietz, Reinhold. *Aus Ferdinand Hillers Briefwechsel: Beiträge zu einer Biographie Ferdinand Hillers*. 7 vols. Cologne, 1958–1970.
Stern, Josef. "Hermann Levi und seine jüdische Welt." *Zeitschrift für die Geschichte der Juden*, 7, no. 1 (1970–1971).
Voss, Egon. *Die Dirigenten der Bayreuther Festspiele*. Regensburg, 1976.
Walter, Friedrich. *Briefe Vincenz Lachners an Hermann Levi*. Mannheim, 1931.
Wegener, W. A. *Muziek aan de Maas: van rietfluitje tot R. Ph. O*. Rotterdam, 1902.
Weingartner, Felix von. *Lebenserinnerungen*. 2 vols. Leipzig/Zurich, 1928.
Werner, Erich. "Jews around Richard and Cosima Wagner." *Musical Quarterly* 71, no. 2 (1985).

Index

PLACES

Aachen, 111n98, 177n7
Arau, 106n4
Alexanderbad near Wunsiedel, 97, 98, 105, 143, 144, 166, 199, 237
Altenburg, 60
Ambert, 249
Amsterdam, 33, 144, 209
Andechs, 148
Arco, 176
Augsburg, 3, 84, 119, 127, 142, 146, 178n20

Bad Cannstatt, 228, 229, 237
Bad Ischl, 80, 109n51
Bad Kissingen, 261
Bad Reichenhall, 232
Baden-Baden, 24, 35, 53, 56, 59–69, 71, 76, 87–90, 96–99, 108n31, 109n39, 111n98, 112n103, 124–25, 129, 141, 175, 244
Baden-Oos, 65
Badenweiler, 140
Bamberg, 169
Basel, 86, 99, 135
Bayreuth, vii, viii, xiii, xiv, 6, 36, 77, 93, 100, 103, 105, 115–16, 131–37, 141, 143, 146, 153, 157, 159, 160–66, 168, 170–74, 176, 178n28, 178n30, 179n34, 182n99, 183n115, 183n116, 186, 190, 193–238, 242, 248n46, 254
Berlin, vii, viii, 17, 22, 40n41, 40n49, 53, 54, 56, 77, 89, 104, 108n27, 109n51, 129, 143, 150, 156, 161, 164, 177n7, 179n46, 180n56, 182n89, 182n90, 183n112, 183n114, 191n6, 211, 214, 217, 219, 238, 249
Bernried, 124
Bingen, 27
Bournemouth, 237
Bolzano, 182n89, 238, 240
Braunfels, 177n7
Brebach, 27
Bremen, 83, 87, 95, 249n53
Brescia, 40n39
Breslau, 108n27, 137, 179n38, 247n17
Brno, 106n1
Budapest, 86, 183n116, 230

Cassel, 229, 249n59
Chicago, 209
Coburg, 183n115
Cologne, 24, 33, 35–37, 40n41, 57, 67, 86, 98, 146, 177n7, 249n59, 253, 269

Crostewitz near Leipzig, 199, 237, 247n27

Danzig, 183n115, 222
Deixlfurt, 148, 229
Dessau, 183n115
Donaueschingen, 106n4
Donnersberg, 3
Dresden, 41n49, 53, 55, 56, 80, 81, 84, 93, 99, 123, 114, 145, 183n116, 227, 249n54
Dusseldorf, 17, 63, 67, 108n33, 111n98, 249n59

Florence, xiii, 209, 219, 240, 244, 250n97
Frankfurt, 6, 10, 20, 38n4, 61, 83, 99, 107n15, 111n98, 126, 127, 163, 177n7, 180n56, 183n112, 196, 217
Freiburg, 99, 110n81, 182n90
Freystadt/Oberpfalz, 249n68
Friedrichsruh near Hamburg, 156, 213

Gaffontaine, 29, 39n28
Giessen, 1–9, 21, 33, 38n1, 56, 95, 110n84, 125, 139, 154, 170, 180n68, 194, 259
Görlitz, 177n10
Graz, 177n10, 182n87, 249n53
Greifenberg, 109n51
Griedel (Hessen), 180n68
Gries near Bolzano, 182n89, 238, 240
Gross-Tabarz (Thuringia), 179n46

Hagenau, 96
Halberstadt, 182
Halle, 183n114
Hamburg, 29, 61, 86, 95, 107n15, 137, 153, 180n75, 217, 247n17
Hamm (Westphalia), 61, 109n51
Heidelberg, 92, 110n81, 138, 182n90, 228
Helgoland, 95, 125, 139, 141, 151
Hoek van Holland, 33

Innsbruck, 176

Jena, 249n72
Jerusalem, 4, 38n5

Karlsruhe, xiii, xiv, 9, 10, 23, 24, 28, 36, 37, 43, 44, 45, 51–117, 120, 121, 124, 125, 128, 129, 139, 141, 143, 146, 148, 154, 160, 178n30, 180n75, 186, 187, 199, 200, 201, 203, 204, 206, 216–19, 222, 227, 229, 232, 237, 269
Kehl, 96
Kiel, 139, 182n90
Königsberg, 21, 107n15, 177n10, 183n115

Landshut, 225
Leipzig, 10–21, 25, 27, 28, 30, 32, 34, 37, 47, 49, 57, 70, 76, 80, 86, 98, 102, 106n4, 110n76, 111n98, 127, 130, 144, 160, 161, 177n7, 178n17, 200, 204, 207, 227, 249n53
Lenggries, 119
Lichtental, 36, 60, 64, 65, 68, 69, 87, 90, 92, 98, 141
Lübeck, 41n49
Lucerne, 92, 93, 200
Ludwigshafen, 9, 27

Madrid, 9, 27
Magdeburg, 177n10
Mainz, 3, 4, 29, 38n6, 133, 180n56
Malstatt-Burbach, 27
Mannheim, 1, 4, 5, 7–10, 21, 25–28, 30–34, 36, 38n8, 47, 55, 65, 76, 83, 84, 92, 99, 100, 106n1, 110n76, 120, 130, 134, 139, 140, 141, 143, 183n116, 186, 199, 211
Marbach, 28
Marburg, 1, 249n72
Maxau, 96
Mehlem, 177n7
Meiningen, 146
Metz, 27, 96, 249n54
Montluçon, 248n51
Moscow, 108n31, 130
Munich, vii, xiii, xiv, 7, 10, 23, 25, 36, 43, 56, 73, 75, 82, 84, 89, 92–97, 101–

Index

4, 110n76, 113–84, 186–87, 193–94, 198–244, 247n15, 247n17, 247n27, 247n29, 249n53, 249n59, 249n68, 249n72, 254

Naples, 166, 171
Narva (Estonia), 247
Neustrelitz, 112
New York, 50n5, 209
Northeim, 229
Nuremberg, 33, 40n48, 171, 180n56, 194, 233

Offenbach, 24
Osice (Czech Republic), 40n45
Osthofen, 40n48

Palermo, 171
Paris, 3, 7, 10, 12, 21–27, 29, 32, 38n5, 39n28, 47, 55, 68, 73, 81, 97, 101, 108n31, 115, 116, 131, 144, 148, 151, 181n79, 217, 218, 230, 237, 248n50, 248n51, 249n52.
Partenkirchen, 238, 240–42, 244, 249–50n72
Pont á Mousson, 96
Posen, 109n51
Prague, 2, 38n4, 40n45, 41n49, 106n1, 179n32

Rain am Lech, 177n2
Rippoldsau, 76
Rome, 38n5, 63, 151, 156
Rothenburg, 157
Rotterdam, 26, 32–37, 40n41, 40n45, 41n49, 43, 55, 61, 76, 140
Rügen, 141

Saarbrücken, 24, 26–31, 35, 37, 39n28, 40n41, 43
Salzburg, 89
Schwetzingen, 9
Sedan (Ardennes), 96
Siegburg, 183n112
Sonderhausen, 107n13
Speyer, 4, 38n6

St. Arnual, 27
St. Germain-du-Val, 248n50
St. Johann near Saarbrücken, 26, 27
St. Petersburg, 108n31
St. Veit near Vienna, 178
Stettin, 41n49
Strasbourg, 3, 95, 96
Stuttgart, 60, 73, 84, 87, 88, 93, 107n13, 108n27, 119, 180n76, 181n77, 243
Sylt, 95, 229

Tölz, 119
Trier, 27
Tutzing, 124–26, 148, 229

Überlingen/Lake Constance, 143
Ulm, 38n4

Vaduz, 178n19
Venice, 175, 176, 183n113, 193, 194
Vienna, 17, 27, 38n4, 39n17, 41n49, 55, 56, 62, 65, 73, 75, 81, 85, 86, 87, 92, 94, 95, 102, 104, 106n1, 109n59, 110n81, 111n98, 119, 120, 122, 133, 134, 137, 140, 141, 143–45, 156, 164, 177n2, 177n7, 178n30, 181n78, 203, 206, 207, 209, 210, 211, 212, 216, 222, 227, 249n54
Vilsbiburg, 177n10

Weimar, 29, 60, 80, 89, 203–5, 216, 217, 222, 232, 247n15
Westerland, 95
Wiedensahl near Hanover, 158
Wiesbaden, 34, 35, 107n15, 248n47
Wissembourg, 96
Wolfenbüttel, 95, 158
Wörishofen, 237, 253
Worms, 2–4, 24, 38n6, 40n41
Wunsiedel, 97
Würzburg, 4, 102

Ziegelhausen, 137, 139
Zofingen, 251n101
Zurich, vii, 50n8, 71, 99, 108n27, 110n81, 143, 180n56

NAMES

Abel, Ludwig, 176
Abert, Johann Joseph, 73, 84, 107, 201
Ackermann, Theodor (publisher), 262
Adam, Adolphe Charles, 23, 248n50
Aibl, Joseph (publisher), 186, 261
D'Albert, Eugen, 242
Albert, Joseph, 120
Albert, Crown Prince of Saxony, 21
Albrechtsberger, Johann Georg, 17
Allgeyer, Julius, 45, 63–65, 69, 71, 73–76, 80, 85, 86, 87, 90, 93, 94, 106, 107n22, 120, 124–26, 130, 136, 139, 140, 141, 143, 147, 167, 243
Allotria (association of artists), 156–57, 181n78, 181n79, 207, 208
Alvary, Max, 231
Alvin, H., 115
Amalie, Duchess of Bavaria, 209
Amtmann, Conrad, 124
Angermann (tavern), 164, 172
Anna, Landgravine of Hesse, 107n24, 244, 251n107
Arditi, Luigi, 75
Arnold, Youri, 107n13
Auber, Daniel François, 18, 23, 29, 88, 215, 247n13

Bach, Johann Sebastian, 6, 11, 14, 15, 20, 47, 54, 67, 73, 101, 136, 144, 169, 171, 185, 231
Bamberger, Jakob, 4
Barbier, Paul Jules, 187
Barca, Calderon de la, 93, 206
Basta, Marie, 201
Beck, Carl Heinrich (publisher), 251n111
Becker, Clara, 64, 87
Beethoven, Ludwig van, 6, 14, 17, 21, 24, 28, 29, 30, 36, 47, 55, 59, 61, 67, 69, 71, 73, 75, 76, 92, 97, 99, 103, 108n34, 115, 120–24, 130, 131, 136, 140, 142, 144–46, 148, 154, 162, 163, 167, 177n7, 179n37, 185, 194, 208, 211, 213, 218, 226, 227, 236, 240, 241, 243

Bellini, Vincenzo, 30, 67, 69, 97
Benoist, François, 248
Berlioz, Hector, xiii, 23, 25, 39n28, 47, 73, 107, 113, 115, 130, 131, 165, 178–79n30, 179n32, 185, 186, 201, 209, 218–19, 237, 238
Bernays, Jakob, 153
Bernays, Michael, 36, 125, 142, 151, 153, 160, 162, 180n75
Berrsche, Alexander, 206
Billroth, Theodor, 96, 110n8
Birch-Pfeiffer, Charlotte, 65, 108n27
Bismarck, Otto von, 95, 105, 156, 157, 166, 167, 182n90, 182n102, 213, 249n68, 249n72
Blauwaert, Ernst, 230
Blümner, Heinrich, 12
Boccherini, Luigi, 142
Bock (physician), 238
Boieldieu, François Adrien, 23, 67
Boni, Amalia, 92, 106n9
Borchers, Hanna, 216, 248n47
Böcklin, Arnold, 125, 151, 156, 249n72
Böttger, A., 47, 257
Brahms, Johannes, vii, xiii, xiv, 18, 32, 36, 40n41, 43, 44, 45, 47, 49, 50n5, 51–112, 114–16, 120, 122–50, 153–58, 163, 168–69, 174, 177n7, 178n19, 179n37, 179n38, 180n56, 185–86, 201, 206–7, 211, 213, 226, 231, 237, 243–44, 246, 250n85, 253, 254
Brand, Fritz, 165, 172
Brandes, Wilhelm, 76, 83, 84, 88, 106n9
Brandt, Marianne, 173
Braunfels, Walter, xiii
Braunhofer, Anna, 106n9
Breitkopf und Härtel (publisher), 261, 262
Brendel, Franz, 19
Bretzner, Christoph Friedrich, 187
Bronsart, Hans von, 165, 203, 227
Bruch, Max, xiv, 76–79, 109n44, 179n46, 202, 236, 263–64

Bruckmann, Friedrich (publisher), 248n47, 262, 263
Bruckner, Anton, xiii, 47, 114–16, 173, 178n30, 183n113, 200, 206–12, 223, 247–48n29, 248n45
Brucks, Otto, 218, 249n54
Brulliot, Karl, 106n9, 110n69, 160, 181n82, 182n87
Bonaparte, Napoleon, 3, 4, 6, 21, 38n5, 253
Busch, Wilhelm, xiv, 152, 155, 157, 158, 162, 167, 177, 181, 229
Bülow, Blandine von, 174
Bülow, Hans von, vii, xiii, 14, 18, 19, 39n19, 60, 82, 92, 102, 104, 107n13, 115, 120, 121, 131, 145–47, 165, 179n37, 185, 193, 195, 198, 200, 213, 220, 230, 247n15, 254, 269
Bürckel, Ludwig von, 157, 166
Bürger, Sigmund, 142

Calderon, 93, 206
Carré, Michel, 187
Carrière, Moritz, 125, 151, 154, 180n68
Chabrier, Emmanuel, 25, 115, 116, 185, 186, 201, 217–18, 249n52
Chamberlain, Houston Stewart, viii, 158, 183n114, 190, 234, 243, 245, 254
Chamisso, Adelbert von, 47, 257, 259
Cherubini, Luigi, xiii, 9, 69, 71, 76, 97, 98
Chopin, Frédéric, 108n31, 162
Clauss-Szarvady, Wilhelmine, 25, 39n28, 257
Colombier, Jean F. and M. (music publishers), 261
Colonne, Edouard, 115, 237
Cornelius, Bertha, 203, 205
Cornelius, Carl-Maria, 204
Cornelius, Peter, xiii, 17, 115, 127, 143, 178–79n30, 179n32, 185, 186, 201, 202, 203, 204, 205, 206, 232, 260, 261
Cotta (publisher), 243, 263
Creizenach, Michael, 4
Czerny, Vincenz, 96, 110n81

Dahn, Felix, 161, 180–81n76
Dante, 153, 224, 225
Danzi, Franz, 43
Daumer, Friedrich, 98
David, Ferdinand, 14, 18, 20
David, Paul, 65, 107n19
Debussy, Claude, 218, 248–49n51
Deetz, Marie, 33, 34, 40n46
Defregger, Franz von, 208
Deichmann, Councilor of Commerce, 117n7
Delacroix, Eugène, 108n7
Delibes, Léo, 173, 217, 248n50
Dessoff, Otto, 43, 92, 102, 11n98, 139, 141
Devrient, Eduard, 36, 37, 53–59, 61, 66–67, 69, 71, 73, 80, 82, 84, 88, 94, 131, 186, 200, 262
Devrient, Otto, 68, 77, 89, 97, 122, 261
Dietrich, Albert 61, 71
Dittersdorf, Carl Ditters von, 30
Donizetti, Gaetano, 29, 34, 97
Dostoyevsky, Fyodor Mikhaylovich, 200
Dressler, Lili, 216, 248n46
Drobisch, Eugen, 34
Duparc, Henri, 219
Dupont, Franz, 33
Duse, Eleonora, 235, 249n72

Eberst, Isaak Juda, 24
Eberst, Jakob, 24
Ebner, Ottilie, 104
Eckhardt, Ludwig, 107n13
Eckstein, Friedrich, 207, 249n29
Eichendorff, Joseph Freiherr von, 47, 257, 259
Ellinger, Josef, 33, 34, 40n46
Erard, Sebastian, 24
Ernst, Heinrich Wilhelm, 146
Eschenbach, Wolfram von, 94
Esser, Heinrich, 92
Ettlinger, Anna, xiii, 74, 75, 87, 94, 109n40, 148
Ettlinger, Friederike, 259
Ettlinger, Veit, 73, 110–11n84

Falkenstein, Johann Paul von, 10, 14
Fauré, Gabriel, 217, 248n51
Feidel, Rosalie, 7, 26
Feuerbach, Anselm, xiv, 63, 64, 69, 70, 86, 147, 153, 167, 243
Feuerbach, Henriette, 69, 94, 153, 174
Fiedler, Conrad, xiv, 135, 199, 207, 209, 213, 218, 226, 237–39, 247n27, 249n72
Fiedler, Mary (later Mary Levi), 136, 227, 230, 231, 238
Fischer (physician), 228
Fischer, Franz von, 165, 168, 172, 174, 183n116, 186, 193, 196, 211, 212, 219, 230, 238, 242
Flaubert, Gustave, 108n31
Flotow, Firedrich Freiherr von, 29, 67, 97
Fontane, Theodor, 150
France, Anatole, 25, 189, 191n9, 238, 263
Frank, Emanuela, 219, 249n59
Frank, Ernst, 102, 140
Franz Joseph I of Austria, 209
Freytag, Gustav, 88, 89
Fricke, Richard, 164, 172, 183n115
Friedberg, Carl, 216
Friedrich I, Grand Duke of Baden, 53, 56
Friedrich Wilhelm IV, King of Prussia, 22
Fries, Eduard de, 33
Fuchs, Anton, 173, 182n87, 199
Füller, Joseph, 98
Furtwängler, Wilhelm, 81, 109n51, 114, 116

Gade, Niels W., 14, 18, 32, 76
Garcia, Manuel, 108n31
Gautier, Judith, 170, 218
Gedon, Lorenz, 156, 158, 167, 181n78, 181n79
Gehring, Franz, 104
Geibel, Emanuel, 76, 150
Gernsheim, Friedrich, 24, 31, 37, 40n41, 47, 74, 115, 140, 206
Girard, Narcisse, 24
Gluck, Christoph Willibald, xiii, 9, 37, 55, 67, 68, 89, 97, 103, 121, 128, 132, 136, 185, 186, 212, 215, 219, 229, 261

Gobineau, Arthur, 164, 170
Goethe, Johann Wolfgang von, viii, 4, 10, 11, 23, 36, 45, 47–49, 55, 59, 73, 76, 91, 97–98, 101, 140, 150, 153, 189, 190, 215, 230, 236, 243–44, 247n19, 255, 258–59, 263
Goetz, Hermann, 115, 140, 201, 206
Goldmark, Karl, 115, 201
Gounod, Charles, 23, 81, 103, 108n31, 131, 186, 201, 261
Gouvy, Louis Théodore, 24, 29, 31, 32, 39n28, 76, 116, 260
Gozzi, Carlo, 124
Gravina, Count Biagio 174, 197
Grengg, Karl, 235
Grimm, Otto Julius, 61, 80n56
Grün, Jakob, 20
Günzburg, Simon, 38n4
Guggenheimer, Moritz, 213
Gutzkow, Karl, 53

Haberkorn, 2
Halbreiter, Otto (music publisher), 48, 258, 261
Halévy, Jaques Fromental, 34, 39n28, 69
Hals, Franz, 33
Hanfstaengl, Franz, 243
Hanslick, Eduard, 17, 170, 184n120, 227
Hasse, Max, 204
Hauptmann, Moritz, 14, 15, 76, 200
Hauser, Franz, 247n17
Hauser, Joseph, 71, 86, 106n9, 128
Hauser, Magdalena, 71, 110n69
Hausmann, Marie, 86
Haydn, Joseph, 17, 18, 24, 28, 29, 76, 90, 126, 127, 144, 146
Handel, Georg Friedrich, 18, 20, 36, 61, 101, 103, 124, 137, 139, 144, 145
Heckel, Emil, 99, 186, 260
Heine, Heinrich, 22, 47, 49, 108n31, 109n42, 254, 257, 259
Herclots, Carl Alexander, 187
Hérold, Ferdinand, 18, 23, 127
Hertz, Wilhelm, 154, 158, 180n76, 190, 242, 243

Herzogenberg, Elisabeth von, 231, 250n85
Herzogenberg, Heinrich von, 111n98, 226, 250n85
Hesse, Marie, 182n91
Hetsch, Louis, 30, 31
Heuberger, Richard, 111n98
Heyse, Paul, xiv, 94, 109n51, 119, 124–25, 127, 131, 136, 138, 142–84, 190, 208, 211, 213, 226, 241–43
Hieber, Max, 132
Hildebrand, Adolf von, xiii, xiv, 115, 226, 231, 237, 240, 242, 244, 245, 249n72, 250n97, 251n110, 261
Hildebrand, Eva, 250
Hill, Karl, 173
Hiller, Ferdinand, 14, 16, 18, 35, 57, 58, 67, 69, 75, 95, 98, 99, 101, 102
Hochberg, Bolko von, 227
Hoepfner, Friedrich, 4
Hofmann, Heinrich, 141, 179n46
Hohenemser (family), 9, 38n9
Holstein, Franz von, 14, 95, 110n76, 127, 128, 166, 178n20, 201
Homer, 153
Hoop van der, 36, 37
Hornstein, Robert von, 156, 181n77
Hummel, Johann Nepomuk, 6, 18
Humperdinck, Engelbert, xiii, xiv, 115, 116, 171, 172, 178n19, 183n112, 185, 194, 196, 199, 201, 216, 217, 226, 242
Hübsch, Heinrich, 51, 96, 110n82

Ibsen, Henrik, 201
Immermann, Carl, 47, 257
d'Indy, Vincent, 217

Jacobi, Friedrich Heinrich, 7
Jakob (priest in Andechs), 148
Jäger, Ferdinand, 166, 228
Jehuda, Gershon Ben, 4
Jencke, Carl, 34
Jensen, Adolf, 107n13
Jesus of Nazareth, 54, 157, 255
Joachim, Amalie, née Weiss, 68, 101, 103

Joachim, Joseph, 14, 18, 20, 41n49, 60, 61, 68, 71, 101, 102, 104, 107n13, 131, 139, 143, 165, 170, 180n56, 254
Johann, King of Saxony, 20
Johannes XXIII (Pope), 255
Joukowsky, Paul von, 165, 171, 175, 183n113, 193

Kahnt, Christian Friedrich (music publisher), 204, 260
Kaiser Wilhelm II, viii, 231
Kalbeck, Max, 45, 50n4, 65, 142, 146, 154, 156, 244
Kalliwoda, Wilhelm, 18, 56–60, 67, 68, 73, 76, 82, 88, 106n4, 187
Kapp-Young, 34
Karl, Grand Duke of Baden, 73
Karl Theodor, Prince of the Palatinate and Baden, 7
Karl Wilhelm, Margrave of Baden, 51
Kastel, Ephraim, 4
Kaula, Emilie, née Ettlinger, 73, 148
Kaulbach, Friedrich (Fritz) August von, 156, 209
Kaulbach, Wilhelm von, 150, 208
Keil (court councilor), 14
Keller, Gottfried, 143, 150, 189, 230
Keller, Joseph, 63
Kesch, 181n81
Kestenberg, Leo, 191n6
Kiel, Friedrich, 107n13
Kindermann, August, 121, 162, 181n82, 182n87
Kirchner, Theodor, 36, 61, 76
Kistner, Friedrich, 14
Klopstock, Friedrich Gottlieb, 11
Knebel, Karl Ludwig von, 108n39
Kneipp, Sebastian (pastor), 253
Kniese, Julius, 194–99, 226, 227
Knigge, Aldolf von, 26
Koelle-Murjahn, Magdalene, 143
Kopisch, August, 124
Kotzebue, August von, 260
Kreidel, Adolph, 88, 95, 102
Kremplsetzer, Georg, 124, 177n10
Kretschmer, Edmund, 201

Kreutzer, Conradin, 34, 67, 97
Kreutzer, Léon, 29
Kroenlein, Heinrich, 71, 82
Krupp, Friedrich Alfred, 238
Kurz Hermann, 125
Kürner, Benedikt, 110n69

Lachner, Franz, 8, 18, 43, 88, 120, 121, 122, 145, 177n2, 177n10
Lachner, Rosine, 37
Lachner, Vincenz, 8, 9, 10, 21, 25, 26, 30, 32, 35, 36, 46, 47, 51, 55, 76, 82, 83, 84, 99, 115, 120, 168, 257
Ladenburg, Hermann, 9, 38n9
Ladenburg, Seligmann, 9
Ladenburg, Wolf Hajum, 9
Langer, Hermann, 18
Lassen, Eduard, 89, 107n13
Lasso, Orlando di, 103
Lee, Georg J. V., 250n95
Lehrs, Samuel, 170
Leibniz, Gottfried Wilhelm von, 11
Lenbach, Franz von, xiv, 5, 142, 147, 149, 151, 152, 156–59, 164–67, 171, 181n77, 182n102, 213, 237, 255
Leser, Rosalie, 80
Lessing, Carl Friedrich, 53, 69, 108n35
Lessing, Gotthold Ephraim, 11, 55, 71, 153
Lessing, Ida, 67, 73, 83, 95, 98
Levi, Benedict, 1, 4–7, 38n7, 110n84, 236, 240, 195
Levi, Emma, 5, 217
Levi, Henriette, 6
Levi, Samuel Wolf, 2, 3
Levi, Wilhelm (later Wilhelm Lindeck), 5, 6, 24, 36, 141, 143, 148
Lichtenberg, Georg Christoph, 230
Lichtenstadt, Abraham Aron, 38n4
Liebig, Justus von, 5, 6, 125, 154, 180n68
Liechtenstein, Prince Rudolf of, 164
Liliencron, Rochus von, 125, 127
Lind, Jenny, 18
Liszt Franz, 18, 19, 60, 61, 80, 82, 89, 107n13, 132, 144, 154, 157, 165, 172,
174, 185, 195, 196, 198, 203, 204, 209, 222, 223, 226, 232, 247n15
Loewe, Carl, 168
Lortzing, Albert, 8, 30, 34, 38, 215, 247
Löwe, Ferdinand, 207
Ludwig I, King of Bavaria, 119, 120, 209
Ludwig II, King of Bavaria, 120, 132, 149, 150, 153, 162, 173, 174, 200, 208, 209, 224
Luitpold, Prince Regent of Bavaria, 209, 231
Luther, Martin, 234
Lübke, Wilhelm, 84

Mahler, Gustav, 43, 185, 217, 227, 230, 231, 250n83
Malibran (Garcia, Maria Felicità), 108n31
Manet, Edouard, 217
Marées, Hans von, 247n27, 250–51n97
Marmorito, Julia von, 90
Marschner, Heinrich, 18, 54, 67, 77, 82, 121, 215, 260
Marsop, Paul, 228, 229
Maszkowski, Raphael, 213
Materna, Amalia, 165, 173
Maupassant, Guy de, 108n31
Maximilian II, King of Bavaria, 119, 150
Mayer, Gottschalk, 9, 38n9
Meffert, August, 29
Méhul, Étienne Nicolas, 9, 18, 30, 73, 94, 131, 207, 229
Mendelssohn Bartholdy, Felix, 10–14, 16, 17, 20, 24, 28–30, 32, 39n17, 47, 54, 57, 59, 67, 69, 75, 76, 88, 103, 106n4, 113, 114, 137, 139, 144, 150, 169, 170, 185, 211, 254
Menter, Eugenie, 145
Menzel, Adoph von, 151
Merck, Johann Heinrich, 4
Merz, Oskar 216, 234, 248n48
Messager, André, 217, 248n15, 248–49n51
Meyer, Julius, 238
Meyerbeer, Giacomo, 18, 22–23, 34, 67, 73, 75, 100, 101, 121, 170, 201, 215
Milde, Rosa von, 39n19, 205

Moch, Emma, née Levi, 217
Moch, Gaston, 217
Moch, Henriette, 217
Molière, Jean Baptiste, 131, 261
Molique, Bernhard, 142
Mombert, Jakob, 111, 125, 143
Moscheles, Ignaz, 14, 16, 17, 110n76
Moszkowski, Moritz, 102
Mottl, Felix, xiii, 43, 111n98, 114, 127, 133, 178n30, 185, 186, 198, 199, 201, 203–6, 211, 213, 216–24, 227–29, 231–32, 234–35, 238, 269
Mozart, Wolfgang Amadeus, viii, xiii, 6, 7, 17, 24, 28, 29, 30, 34, 36, 55, 69, 77, 94, 97, 99, 120, 121, 131, 141, 143, 171, 176, 185–90, 220, 226, 236–42, 247n13, 255, 261, 262
Müller, Hippolyt, 178n14

Nachbaur, Franz, 84, 121, 162
Napoleon III, 22, 89
Naret-Koning, Johann, 20, 28, 30, 32, 49, 77, 258
Neumann, Angelo, 164, 170
Niemann, Albert, 105, 165
Niese, Carl, 262
Nietzsche, Friedrich, 99, 100, 134, 135
Nikisch, Arthur, 111n98, 114, 207
Nuhr, Bertha, 21, 259

Offenbach, Jacques, 23f.
Ordenstein, Heinrich, 111n98
Otto, Franz, 28
Öttingen, Elia, 38n4
Öttingen-Ries, Abraham, 38n4

Paganini, Niccolò, 144
Palestrina, Giovanni Pierluigi da, 18, 174
Patti, Adelina, 33
Perfall, Karl von, 93, 95, 102, 104, 122, 129, 132, 180b56, 200–203, 208, 213, 227
Peters, Carl Friedrich, 187
Pfitzner, Hans, 215, 216
Philip the Magnanimous, Landgrave of Hesse, 1

Piloty, Karl, 156
Planck, Fritz, 199
von Poetz family, 45, 70, 120
Pohl, Richard, 89, 99
Porges, Heinrich, 114, 134, 164, 170, 172, 179n32, 194, 209, 226
Possart, Ernst von, 113, 121, 128, 129, 167, 186, 187, 200, 201, 213–16, 219, 235, 237, 241–45
Praetorius, Michael, 18
Prieur, R., 115
Pringle, Carrie, 174, 194
Proch, Heinrich, 92
Pruckner, Dionys, 73
Puttkamer, Robert von, 117n12

Raberg, 29
Raff, Joachim, 73, 115, 144
Rappoldi, Eduard, 36, 41n49
Reicher-Kindermann, Hedwig, 132
Reinecke, Carl, 32, 99, 130
Reizenstein, Marie, 139–41, 147
Reutlinger, Jeremias, 73
Rheinberger, Joseph Gabriel, 49, 114, 115, 127, 128, 130, 142, 144, 145, 151, 156, 178n19, 201
Ribbeck, Emma, 174
Richault, Simon, 260
Richter, Hans, xiii, 92, 120, 121, 134, 136, 144, 165, 198, 199, 207, 211, 213, 220, 221, 222, 224, 231, 250n91
Riedel, Carl, 18
Riegl, 182n87
Riehl, Wilhelm von, 208
Ries, Ferdinand, 49
Riesser, Gabriel, 1, 6
Rieter-Biedermann (music publisher), 21, 25, 257
Rietz, Julius, 10, 14, 16–20, 35, 39n19, 47, 76, 115, 259
Rindskopf, Marianne, 24
Ritter, Alexander, 99, 202, 203, 247n15
Rocke, Leopold, 28
Rohn, Henriette, 28
Romberg, Andreas, 28

276 *Index*

Rossini, Gioacchino, 22, 28, 34, 67, 68, 97, 108n31
Rothschild, Amsel, 166
Rottenberg, Ludwig, 217
Rubinstein, Anton, 20, 36
Ruzek, Josef, 102

Saint-Saëns, Camille, 24–25, 144, 173, 248n51
Salieri, Anton, 17
Salomon, Lea, 150
Sarasate, Pablo de, 144
Sattler, Bernhard
Sauret, Emile, 146
Scaria, Emil, 165, 172, 173, 194
Schack, Adolf Friedrich von, 150, 156
Schalk, Josef, 207, 210
Schefzky, Josephine, 121, 132, 133, 140, 146, 162, 181n81, 182n87
Schieber (cellist), 132
Schiller, Friedrich von, 28, 39n32, 55, 73, 77, 101, 108n34, 153, 215, 229, 263
Schindelmeisser, Louis, 61, 197n15
Schindler, Anton, 177n7
Schirmer, Johann Ludwig, 56
Schleinitz, Alexander von, 14
Schleinitz, Marie von, 164, 165
Schlosser, Karl, 132, 133, 162
Schlosser, Max, 121, 181n82
Schlösser, Josef, 28
Schmid, 106n9
Scholz, Bernhard, 144, 180n56, 201
Schopenhauer, Arthur, 181, 229–30, 240, 244, 253–55
Schott's Söhne, B. (music publisher), 133, 217
Schroedter, Adolf, 69, 73, 108n33
Schroedter, Alwine, 73
Schröder-Devrient, Wilhelmine, 53
Schubert, Franz, 17, 36, 39n17, 67, 69, 75, 76, 98, 103, 120, 127, 148, 177n2, 178n17, 213
Schuch, Ernst von, 227
Schünemann, Georg, 188–89, 191n6
Schumann, Clara, née Wieck, 14, 18, 20, 36, 43, 44, 60, 61, 63, 65, 66, 68, 69, 71, 75, 76, 80, 87, 89, 95, 98, 101, 103, 104, 106, 107n15, 125, 129, 131, 136, 139, 141, 142, 144–46, 157, 162, 163, 237, 249n72, 258, 263
Schumann, Elise, 64
Schumann, Eugenie, 113
Schumann, Felix, 163
Schumann, Julie, 90–91
Schumann, Ludwig, 63, 75
Schumann, Robert, 14, 19, 22, 29, 39n17, 67, 73, 92, 98, 108n31, 127, 128, 142, 162, 259
Schütz, Heinrich, 18
Schwalje, Eisek, 4
Schwarz, Johanna, 45, 98
Schweninger, Ernst, 225, 249n68
Sechter, Simon, 177n2
Seeburg (city councilor), 14
Segal, Benjamin Wolf Spiro, 2
Segal, Samuel Lichtenstadt-Wedeles, 38n4
Segisser, Ferdinand, 71
Seidl, Anton, 160
Seidl, Gabriel von, 156, 193
Seifriz, Max, 60, 107n13
Seyfried, Ignaz, 55, 106n1
Shakespeare, William, 55, 59, 65, 66, 140, 167, 176, 187, 200, 241, 261
Shaw, George Bernard, 235–36, 250n95
Simrock, Franz, 104
Simrock, Karl, 124
Simrock (publisher), 75, 92, 98, 104, 126, 260
Sinzheim, David, 3
Škroup, František, 33, 40n45
Solbrig, Veit, 157, 213
Sophocles, 109n51
Spitzweg, Eugen, 248n41
Spohr, Louis, 14, 18, 30, 54, 82, 201, 206
Standhartner, Henriette, 219
Starke, 29
Stavenhagen, Bernhard, 238
Stehle, Sopie, 101, 121
Steiger, Michael, 178n14
Stein, Heinrich von, 171, 176, 183n114

Index

Stengel, Friedrich, 27
Stepan, Carl, 28
Stockhausen, Julius, 24, 84, 86, 97, 103, 111n85, 111n87, 148, 180n56
Stoecker, Adolf, viii, 161, 182n89, 241, 254
Stolzenberg, Benno, 71, 89
Storm, Theodor, 150
Strauss, Franz, 171
Strauss, Heinrich, 107n13
Strauss, Johann, 90, 237
Strauss, Joseph, 37, 43, 55, 106n1
Strauss, Ludwig, 71
Strauss, Richard, xiii, xiv, 43, 114, 160, 171, 173, 185, 206, 211, 213, 214, 216, 219, 220, 230–35, 237–38, 241–43, 247n15
Strecker, Ludwig, 133
Sweelinck, Jan P., 33

Tausig, Carl, 170, 179n32
Tchaikovsky, Peter Ilyich, xiii, 130
Tegnér, Esaias, 179n46
Telemann, Georg Philipp, 11
Terborch, Gerard, 33
Ternina, Milka, 218, 219, 249n53
Thoma, Hans, xiv, 119, 190, 243
Thoms, Anton, 130, 132, 178n14
Thooft, Willem, 33
Thuille, Ludwig, 178n19, 242
Tieck, Ludwig, 207
Tombo, August, 132
Treitschke, Heinrich von, 161, 182n90
Turgenev, Ivan, xiv, 24, 53, 88, 89, 108

Uhde, Fritz von, 209
Uhland, Ludwig, 180n76

Venzl, Josef, 132
Verdi, Giuseppe, xiii, 97, 201, 215, 227, 247n13
Verlaine, Paul, 217
Viardot, Louis, 68
Viardot-García, Pauline, 18, 24, 68, 69, 73, 84, 85, 86, 88, 96, 108n31
Vieuxtemps, Henri, 33, 39n19

Viotti, Giovanni Battista, 207
Vittoria, Tomaso Ludovico da, 18
Vogl, Heinrich, 121, 126, 127, 132, 148, 149, 160, 162, 166, 219
Vogl, Therese, 121, 133, 148, 161, 181n81, 229
Volkland, Alfred, 102
Volkmann, Robert, 49, 107n13, 115, 130

Wabel, Henriette, 71
Wagmüller, Michael, 156
Wagner, Cosima (née Liszt, divorced von Bülow), xiii, xiv, 60, 99, 100, 105, 134, 136, 153, 154, 157, 158, 161–69, 172–74, 176, 178–79n30, 181n80, 183n114, 185, 188, 189, 193, 194, 196, 198, 199, 206, 208, 220–36, 238, 240, 241, 243, 244, 245, 246, 246n10, 249n68, 253, 254, 260, 263
Wagner, Eva, 234, 244, 241
Wagner, Isolde, 60, 197, 241
Wagner, Richard, vii, xiv, 6, 9, 24, 34, 53, 55, 60, 82, 84, 99, 103, 105, 106n1, 114, 115, 120, 126, 148, 162, 165, 170, 193, 194, 200, 201, 217, 226, 234, 235, 236, 240, 246, 255, 260
Wagner, Siegfried, 165, 183n114, 229, 223, 236, 241, 242, 243
Walter, Benno, 178n14, 207
Walter, Joseph, 178n14
Warneck, Paul, 201
Weber, Carl Maria von, 24, 29, 30, 34, 59, 65, 67, 76, 80, 82, 113, 171, 213, 227, 231, 243, 247n13
Weckerlin, Mathilde, 181n81
Weingartner, Felix von, xiii, xiv, 43, 113, 114, 163, 164, 173, 206, 211, 217, 219, 222, 223, 226, 229, 242
Weissheimer, Wendelin, 34, 40n48
Weissmann, Gumpel, 4
Widmann, Joseph Viktor, 94, 125, 140
Wilhelm, Prince of Prussia (later Wilhelm II, German Emperor), viii, 97, 231
Will, Karl, 63

Winkelmann, Hermann, 173, 194
Wolf, Hugo, 216
Wolf-Ferrari, Ermanno, 178n19
Wolff, Abraham, 4
Wolff, Pius Alexander, 59
Wolff, Wilhelmine, 28
Worms, Gitel, 6, 110n84
Wüllner, Franz, 92, 93, 102, 104, 119, 121, 122, 123, 126, 127, 131, 139, 141, 142, 144, 145, 146, 156, 177n7, 178n19, 180n56, 200, 227, 262

Zahlberg, Karl, 67
Zelter, Carl Friedrich, 54, 243
Zemlinsky, Alexander von, 242
Zenger, Max, 102, 201
Zittel, Emil, 94
Zumpe, Hermann, 238

About the Author

Frithjof Haas was born in 1922 in Karlsruhe. He was trained in music at the Cologne University of Music. From 1948 to 1987 he conducted and taught at the Badisches Staatstheater in Karlsruhe. From 1987 to 1991 he lectured at the Karlsruhe University of Music. He has written three biographies of conductors (Hans von Bülow, Hermann Levi, Felix Mottl) and papers on music, particularly Brahms research.

Lightning Source UK Ltd.
Milton Keynes UK
UKHW041847020720
365946UK00001B/6